awakening spaces

awakening spaces

French Caribbean Popular Songs, Music, and Culture

Brenda F. Berrian

The University of Chicago Press   Chicago and London

BRENDA F. BERRIAN is professor of Africana Studies, English, and Women's Studies at the University of Pittsburgh. She has been a visiting professor in both Europe and Africa and is the author of *Africa, Harlem, Haiti: The Great Black Cultural Revolution* and coeditor of *Bibliography of Women Writers from the Caribbean: 1831–1986.*

The University of Chicago Press, Chicago 60637
The University of Chicago Press, Ltd., London
© 2000 by The University of Chicago
All rights reserved. Published 2000
Printed in the United States of America
10 09 08 07 06 05 04 03 02 01 00   5 4 3 2 1

ISBN (cloth): 0-226-04455-6
ISBN (paper): 0-226-04456-4

Library of Congress Cataloging-in-Publication Data

Berrian, Brenda F.
  Awakening spaces: French Caribbean popular songs, music, and culture / Brenda F. Berrian.
      p.   cm. — (Chicago studies in ethnomusicology)
  Includes bibliographical references, discography, and index.
  ISBN 0-226-04455-6 (alk. paper)—ISBN 0-226-04456-4 (pbk. : alk. paper)
    1. Popular music—Martinique—History and criticism. 2. Popular music—Guadeloupe—History and criticism. I. Title. II. Series.
ML3486.A1 B47 2000
781.64'097297'6—dc21

                                                            99-055026

♾ The paper used in this publication meets the minimum requirements of the American National Standard for Information Sciences—Permanence of Paper for Printed Library Materials, ANSI Z39.48-1992.

To the memory of my father,
Albert Harry Berrian, Sr.

To my mother,
Mary Miles Berrian

To my sister-in-spirit,
Shawna Moore-Madlangbayan

contents

Acknowledgments *ix*
Introduction *1*

/ The Safe Space: Malavoi's Nostalgic Songs of Childhood and Exile 11

2 Creole, Zouk, and Identity in Kassav's Optimistic Songs 37

3 More Than a Doudou: Women's Subversive Songs 69

4 Cultural Politics and Black Resistance as Sites of Struggle 106

5 Public Performance, Marketing Devices, and Audience Reception 146

6 The Recontextualization of Urban Music 173

7 A Deferential Space for the Drum: The Ambivalence of a Cultural Voice 206

Epilogue *233*   *Discography* *269*
Notes *239*   *List of Interviews* *273*
Bibliography *257*   *Index* *275*

A GALLERY OF PHOTOGRAPHS FOLLOWS PAGE 68

acknowledgments

The focus of this book is upon seven spaces of empowerment and identity in Guadeloupean and Martinican song lyrics from 1970 to 1996. As a teacher and critic of Caribbean literature and an outsider, I embarked on this research project in an effort to understand why popular lyrics in the French Caribbean are more accessible to the general public rather than are published literary texts. Whereas the reading and discussion of literary texts primarily occur within a formal classroom and are defined as "high culture" geared for intellectual élites, music, which crosses class lines, is played and heard everywhere: the homes, the supermarkets, the streets, the beaches, the restaurants, and the market places. Moreover, the cost of a paperback book is almost the same for a compact disc. Inheritors of an oral storytelling tradition, the French Caribbean public is more accustomed to hearing the words spoken aloud than to reading them in silence. Therefore, what I attempt is to explain how the awakening spaces of childhood and exile, gender, cultural politics, Creole language, public performance, recontextualization, and the deferential space of the drum create a mosaic which addresses the questions: Who are the contemporary French Caribbean songwriters, singers, and musicians? Who determines musical choices? What is special about French Caribbean popular music and its lyrics that captivates local and international audiences?

ALA Conferences

In March 1993, I flew to Guadeloupe in the middle of a local airport strike to present a paper for the annual African Literature Association Conference. One afternoon I found myself sitting in a hotel restaurant in the Gosier suburb of Pointe-à-Pitre, humming a popular Kassav' song that was being played through the Muzak system. My lunch companion, Keith Q. Warner, suddenly suggested that we should organize a panel on Caribbean music and lyrics for the 1994 African Literature Association (ALA) Conference that would be held in Accra, Ghana, West Africa. In a laughing manner, I declined with the explanation that I was not an ethnomusiciologist. Warner, in turn, reminded me that neither was he, but that fact had not prevented him from publishing *Kaiso! The Trinidad Calypso* (1982).

How little did I know that our conversation would evolve into a four-year research project. I presented a paper on Kassav's lyrics and performance for the 1994 ALA conference at 8:30 A.M. before a packed audience. After a lively discussion I returned to the Novotel Hotel. To my surprise, as I entered the main lobby, my ears perked up because Kassav's distinguishable zouk party music was being played over the audio system. Excited, I approached the reception desk to learn that Kassav' had performed in Accra, stayed as guests at the Novotel, and departed three days before I and the other ALA conference delegates had arrived. Obviously, fate had intervened again via Kassav's music and its favorable impact upon Ghanaian audiences.

Aux Antilles

For the 1995 spring semester the University of Pittsburgh granted me a sabbatical leave to conduct field research in Martinique and Guadeloupe on popular French Caribbean music. When I ventured into the local bookshops and record stores in downtown Fort-de-France, Martinique, to purchase sheet music, the cashiers patiently explained, to my surprise, that it was rare for the local musicians to publish either sheet music or lyrics. Also, liner notes (included with an album or compact disc) did not begin to appear until the late 1980s and then mostly if the musicians had signed with Paris-based recording companies.[1] To obtain access to albums produced during the 1970s and 1980s, I had to call upon numerous friends and make contacts with disc jockeys and a manager of a record store.

Another stumbling block was the difficulty involved in obtaining the musicians' and singers' home telephone numbers since they were on *la liste rouge* (the red list, meaning unlisted). Again, a friend came to my rescue by arranging an appointment with Christian Boutant, the regional director of Syndicat des Auteurs, Compositeurs, et Éditeurs de Musique (SACEM). After our meeting Boutant gave me permission to use his name as an intermediary, and his assistant allowed me to peruse her rolodex for specific telephone numbers.

Since French Caribbean musicians sing in Creole, I audited a Creole course under the auspices of the Groupe d'Études et de Recherches de la Créolophonie (GEREC) at the Université des Antilles et de la Guyane (Martinique). With luck, the course was team taught and coordinated by Jean Bernabé, one of the authors of *Éloge de la créolité* (1989) and Dean of the Faculty of Arts and Social Sciences. Proficient in French, I was able to grasp the broad meaning of urban-based acrolect Creole lyrics. However, the Creole spoken in the urban centers of Fort-de-France, Martinique, and Pointe-à-Pitre, Guadeloupe, differed from that of the rural areas. Consequently, a number of friends and neighbors painstakingly read my translations and made corrections after we engaged in lengthy discussions about the content of selected songs. Whenever the Creole was too difficult for me, these same friends and neighbors in Martinique and Guadeloupe provided me with French translations. Also, in some cases, several songwriters discussed and edited my translations of their songs.

Often, I thought I was playing the role of a detective because one clue or a snippet of information would lead me somewhere else. This investigation was essential when I realized that there was a paucity of publications on Martinican and Guadeloupean popular music. The few books that did exist ended with a discussion about music in either the 1950s or 1960s. Consequently, since my research was confined to the period of 1970 to 1996, I had to rely upon the journalistic writings by Gene Scaramuzzo for *The Beat* (USA) and Michel Thimon of *France-Antilles Magazine* (Martinique); the percussionist Sully Cally's *Musiques et danses Afro-Caraïbes* (1990) and *Le grand livre de musiciens créoles*, vol. 1 (1996); the musician Edouard Benoit's *Musique populaire de la Guadeloupe* (1990); and the ethnomusicologist Jocelyne Guilbault's groundbreaking study *Zouk: World Music from the West Indies* (1993).

During the months that followed, I expanded my project from its original focus on the lyrical and musical productions of Malavoi and Kassav' to the inclusion of four *angagé* singers, several jazz fusion musicians, six zouk women singers/songwriters, and a number of drummers. The two long-running bands—Kassav' and Malavoi—had been my first contact with Martinican and Guadeloupean music, for I often attended French Caribbean parties while a graduate student in Paris and during personal visits to the two islands where one heard primarily Haitian compas music. Much of my research was done at Carnival festivals, patron festivals, live concerts, nightclubs, university libraries, the Bibliothèque Schoelcher, and private home parties. While listening to the radio and watching variety and video shows on television on a daily basis, I was introduced to a wider range of popular musical styles.

〰〰〰〰〰

No book can be written without the kindness and help from a variety of people. This has definitely been a family affair, for during the course of writing this book, new friendships sprung up and old ones grew closer. Thereby, Maryvonne Charlery and Shawna Moore-Madlangbayan, two sister-friends since my graduate student days in Paris, provided me with the necessary space, time, and encouragement in Martinique over the years to embark on this research project. And my family members became converted zouk fans after listening to numerous cassettes and compact discs.

In Martinique, my thanks to Eric Andrieu of Déclic-Martinique, Andrée "Dédé" Belmat, André Bernabé, Christian Boutant of SACEM, Rose-Marie Brival Fortune, Evariste Cannenterre, Alice Lapiquonne, Sonia Marthély, Valérie and Hélène Ozier-Lafontaine, Marie-Nelly and Jean-Albert Privat, Juliette Ranguin, Eddy Renciot, Alain Sylfille, Michel Thimon, and Monique Zéline.

I will always be indebted to Jocelyn Telga, who insisted that I should devote a chapter to Eugène Mona's songs and passed along Félix Fleury's telephone numbers. The two trips to Marigot and a ride back to Fort-de-France through Sainte-Marie with stops at Mona's favorite hang-outs were extra special. There was Marie-Claude Pacquit's kind offer to translate Mona's complicated Creole songs into French. Also, Ghislaine "Gigi" Mazurin introduced me to Pôglo; José Galas gave me my first *gwo ka* videotape.

In Guadeloupe, my gratefulness is extended to Freddie Marshall, who through the intervention of his cousin Danielle Charville paved the way for me to interview Yves Honoré, Kafé, and Claude Vamur. The brothers Claude and Patrick Hoton's efforts to obtain telephone numbers and arrange interviews are appreciated, too. The Sainton family (Juliette, Jean-Pierre, and Armelle) engaged me in lively conversations about the differences between *gwo ka* and *bèlè* drums, Madame Mavounzy's songs, and introduced me to Gérard Lockel, creator of *gwo ka modèn*. Alain and Lucie Pradel arranged for me to meet the producers Patrick Borès and Henri Debs, and to see the Volt Face Band.

I especially want to thank Peter Koehler, the former Dean of the Faculty of Arts and Sciences at the University of Pittsburgh, for approving a 1995 sabbatical leave for me to begin the field research in Martinique and Guadeloupe. A 1997 Caribbean 2000 Rockefeller Residential fellowship at the University of Puerto Rico in Rio Piedras afforded me the time to complete the writing of the first draft of this book. The staff, faculty, and graduate students for Caribbean 2000, who provided comments and suggestions, were Vanessa Arce, Janette Becerra, Lowell Fiet, Annette Gueveraz, and Maria-Cristina Rodriquez.

Several people read portions of this book and offered either their comments, criticisms, or suggestions about translations and musical transcriptions: James "Buster" Alston, Jacqueline Brice-Finch, Maryvonne Charlery, Lokangaka Losambe, Gina Lucas, Shawna Moore-Madlangbayan, Emmanuel Obiechina, Françoise Pfaff, Maria Roof, Reinhard Sander, Gene Scaramuzzo, and Hanétha Vété-Congolo.

Finally, and most importantly, this book could not exist without the enthusiastic support, talent, and generosity of the Martinican and Gaudeloupean singers, musicians, and songwriters: Marijosé Alie, Frank Balustre, Jocelyne Béroard, Sully Cally, Mario Canonge, Claude, Emmanuel, and Ina Césaire, Djo Dézormo, Céline Flériag, Léa Galva, Henri Guédon, Yves Honoré, Kafé, Kali, Lewis Méliano, Jean-Claude Naimro, Pôglo, José Privat, Patrick Saint Éloi, Tanya St. Val, Jean-Paul Soime, Ralph Thamar, Suzy Trébeau, and Claude Vamur. I am especially indebted to the manuscript editor, Richard C. Allen, for his meticulous attention to details, and to the in-house editors, T. David Brent and Matthew Howard.

Although there are many, some of the special moments that still bring a smile to my face were the visits to Studio Zorrino to hear Kassav' mix songs for its 1995 *Difé* album; the private tour of Henri Guédon's art studio in northern Paris; the history lesson on French Caribbean music by Michel Thimon; the reverence shown by Kafé for his hand-crafted gwo ka; the December 1997 gathering of musicians at Simone Schwarz-Bart's private island restaurant; the discussion of Martinican politics with Marijosé Alie at her beautiful home in Diamant; and the beating of the *mendé* rhythm on a dining room table by Claude "Colo" Vamur. As they say in Creole, *Mèci* (Thank you)!

〰〰〰〰〰〰

Earlier versions of portions of this book have appeared in the following publications.

"Zouk Diva: Interview with Jocelyne Béroard." *MaComère* 2 (1999): 1–11.

"*Sé cho* (It's Hot): French Antillean Musicians and Audience Reception." In Lowell Fiet and Janette Becerra, eds., *A Gathering of Poets and Playwrights/Un convito de poetas y teatreros*. Rio Piedras: University of Puerto Rico Press, 1999.

"Eugène Mona: The Martinican Performer of *Angagé* Songs." In Lowell Fiet and Janette Becerra, eds. *Hablar, nombrar, partenecer: el juego el idioma y la identidad en la(s) cultura(s) caribena(s)*. Rio Piedras: University of Puerto Rico Press, 1998.

"*An-Ba-Chen'n La* (Chained Together): The Landscape of Kassav's Zouk." In Joseph K. Adjaye and Adrianne R. Andrews, eds. *Language, Rhythm, and Sound: Black Popular Cultures into the Twenty-First Century.* © 1997 by the University of Pittsburgh Press. Expanded and reprinted by permission of the University of Pittsburgh Press.

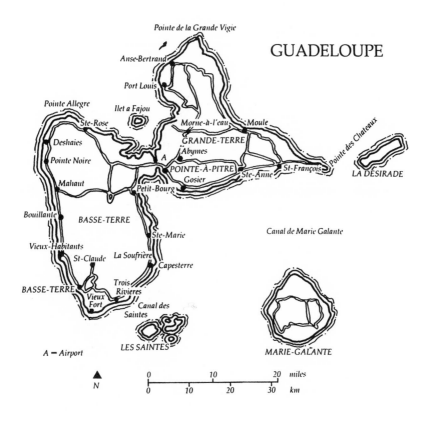

GUADELOUPE

Pointe de la Grande Vigie

Anse-Bertrand

Port Louis

Pointe Allegre

Ilet a Fajou

Ste-Rose

Morne-à-l'eau

Moule

Pointe des Chateaux

Deshaies

GRANDE-TERRE

Pointe Noire

Abymes

A

POINTE-À-PITRE

St-François

LA DÉSIRADE

Mahaut

Gosier

Ste-Anne

Petit-Bourg

Bouillante

BASSE-TERRE

Ste-Marie

Canal de Marie Galante

Vieux-Habitants

La Soufrière

St-Claude

Capesterre

BASSE-TERRE

Vieux
Fort

Trois
Rivieres

Canal des
Saintes

A = Airport

LES SAINTES

MARIE-GALANTE

▲
N

| 0 | | 10 | | 20 | miles |
| 0 | 10 | 20 | 30 | km |

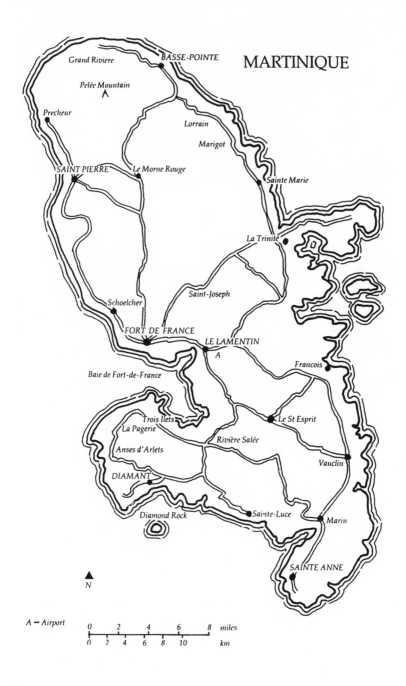

MARTINIQUE

Grand Riviere BASSE-POINTE

Pelée Mountain
∧

Precheur

Lorrain

Marigot

SAINT PIERRE Le Morne Rouge

Sainte Marie

La Trinité

Saint-Joseph

Schoelcher

FORT DE FRANCE

LE LAMENTIN
A

Baie de Fort-de-France

Francois

Trois Ilets
La Pagerie

Le St Esprit

Anses d'Arlets

Rivière Salée

Vauclin

DIAMANT

Diamond Rock

Sainte-Luce

Marin

SAINTE ANNE

▲
N

A – Airport

| 0 | 2 | 4 | 6 | 8 | miles |

| 0 | 2 | 4 | 6 | 8 | 10 | km |

introduction

The arts remain one of the most powerful, if not the most powerful, realms of cultural resistance, a space for awakening folks to critical consciousness and new vision. BELL HOOKS (1990, 39)

This book focuses on how vocalists, songwriters, and musicians from Martinique (and sometimes Guadeloupe) have treated the themes of empowerment and identity in their song lyrics from 1970 until 1996 on professional recordings that range from the biguine (featuring the clarinet and trombone) to zouk (a highly energetic party dance music with horns, drums, and technological gimmicks). This emphasis upon empowerment and identity, defined within the seven awakening spaces of childhood and exile, gender, cultural politics, Creole language, public performance, recontextualization, and the deferential space for the drum, is rooted in the fact that Martinique and Guadeloupe are overseas departments (DOMs) and régions monodépartementales of France. Because they are French citizens, the people of these two islands are free to migrate, work, and establish residency in France. Simultaneously, given that they are living in de facto colonies, they must conform to French policies that have either a positive or negative effect upon their economic, cultural, and social well being.

Just as Martinique and Guadeloupe are geographically separated from each other, so is their music. The biguine as well as jazz fusion and zouk are primarily associated with urban life, and the gwo ka and bèlè drums with that of the countryside. In Martinique and Guadeloupe, both musicians and the general public frequently say that music is primarily for dancing, and hence that "rhythm is more important than the lyrics." However, there is a long tradition of song composition, for music in the French Caribbean, like elsewhere in the African diaspora, has long been a revolutionary act. People have been creating and singing songs from the time when they arrived on these islands, forcibly transported from Africa to work on the sugarcane *habitations* (plantations). Today, people compose songs in Creole to address issues such as gender, language, and politics. But before engaging in a discussion of these issues and more in the following chapters, some background information about French Caribbean music must be provided.

History, Music, and Society

Standing behind the two island's contemporary music are three popular dance forms—the biguine, quadrille, and mazurka—and two types of drums, the *bèlè* from Martinique and *gwo ka* from Guadeloupe. The biguine, quadrille, and mazurka dominated the first half of the twentieth century in Martinican and Guadeloupean cities among the mulatto and white native elites. In the countryside, among the darker skinned agricultural workers, the bèlè and gwo ka were played and accompanied with dancing. The biguine, which began on the habitations, was the first French Caribbean dance music to make an impact upon international audiences. It has influenced Brazilian, African, and jazz music. Alexandre Stellio, the Martinican clarinetist, promoted the biguine in France during the 1920s and 1930s. In the 1960s, the popularity of the biguine and mazurka began to decline with the disappearance of the *punchs en musique* (annual live outdoor musical celebrations for each town's patron saint), *thés dansants* (afternoon tea parties), and *bals* (evening dances). These venues for the live performance of dance music were replaced by the newly constructed discothèques, where people now danced to Haitian compas, Dominican cadence-lypso, Congolese soukous, and Cuban-Latino rhythms (Guilbault et al. 1993, 21).

These four genres, in particular Haitian compas, overshadowed the locally produced musicians. If the local bands, like Perfecta and Malavoi of Martinique and the Vikings de Guadeloupe of Guadeloupe, wanted to be hired to perform at the major hotels or other venues for the amusement of tourists, *békés* (white Martinicans), *blancs-pays* (white Guadeloupeans), and the mulatto middle-class, they imitated, according to Emmanuel Césaire, the Haitian sound or incorporated the Afro-Cuban-Latino sound into their repertoire because of their own feelings for these two types of music.[1]

As a result, pride in local music ebbed drastically as Martinican and Guadeloupean musicians functioned within a creative void. This outside dominance did not end until the Paris-based studio group Kassav' exploded on the scene with zouk in the late 1970s. Kassav' and many other zouk bands enlivened an almost dormant musical culture, for the new vocalists and bands of the 1970s through 1990s began to promote an ethnic fusion, a diversity of music genres, virtuosity, and an innovating stretching of boundaries with improvisations, sophisticated synthesizer textures, jazz and funk with creative lyrics.

Beginning in 1945, a spontaneous outward migration from Martinique and Guadeloupe to France was encouraged to satisfy the labor needs of the French economy during its economic expansion after World War II. To accommodate the movement of Martinicans as well as Guadeloupeans, Bumidom (Bureau pour le Développement des Migrations des Départements d'Outre-Mer/Bureau for the Development of Migrations from the Overseas Departments)[2] was set up to check and regulate the population explosion in the French Caribbean and to distribute the emigrant laborers in France. For twenty years (1945 through 1965) a fixed quota of 5,000 emigrants (2,500 each from Martinique and Guadeloupe) under the auspices of Bumidom arrived annually in France to fill low-paying jobs primarily in the service sector (Anselin 1995, 112–14). In 1965, the number of persons emigrating under Bumidom exceeded those who left on their own initiative. By the time it ceased operation in 1981, Bumidom had secured employment for 84,572 (43.9 percent) of the 192,632 French Caribbeans living in France.

While Martinicans and Guadeloupeans were moving to France, social and economic changes were occurring in Martinique and Guadeloupe.[3] The islands' rural-based economies collapsed, with sugar exports falling from 25 percent of their export earnings in 1965 to almost zero in 1975. While sugar mills and rum distilleries were being closed down, France flooded the two islands with consumer goods and a metropolitan lifestyle. To be precise, French goods and cars arrived, and human beings departed, first the country for the cities of Martinique and Guadeloupe, and then for the cities of France. People found living in an urban center, even when underemployed or on welfare, more desirable than the alternative of trying to work a small landholding. Most of the Martinicans and Guadeloupeans relocated to the Parisian region, creating the mainly youthful foundation of a new community. However, increasing unemployment in France, compounded by an economic depression, led to the creation in 1981 of the Agence Nationale pour l'Insertion et la Promotion des Travailleurs de l'Outre-Mer (ANT, also known as DOM-TOM). The agency was set up to encourage those who had been born on the two islands to return to them. Also, the agency was to promote a Caribbean labor policy based on regional development. However, in the late 1990s, it is difficult to see how the nearly unproductive, dependent Martinican and Guadeloupean economies can absorb their returning migrants when unemployment is higher than in France.[4]

In July 1995, Martinique's population was 394,787 and that of Guadeloupe 402,815, but, as noted by Helen Hintjens, almost "a quarter of a million people from the French DOM (including their offspring) live in continental France. This includes around one third of the population of Guadeloupe and two fifths of the population of Martinique" (Hintjens 1992, 71). Presently, there is a sense of difference between the island-born French Caribbeans and those born and raised in France. The French-born, who are called *zoreils noirs* or *négropolitains* (black ears or Negropolitans), are considered to be more sophisticated and worldly but unable to speak Creole. Those born in Martinique and Guadeloupe speak French and Creole and are assumed by the négropolitains to be insulated and provincial. Although an increased mobility in both directions between the two islands and France has accelerated integration, it has not reduced inequalities.

One group of Martinicans and Guadeloupeans who emigrated to France before 1945 were the musicians. Since the 1920s, musicians who desired to be professionals moved to France in search of employment. Due to Martinique's and Guadeloupe's geographical sizes and small populations, the available hotel engagements and local balls were (and still are) not sufficient to sustain them. If musicians remained on their islands, they were obliged to work a full-time job in another sector and to perform on a part-time basis. If they chose to be professionals, they gravitated toward France, confirming Wilfred Cartey's statement: "The condition of the West Indians is rooted in ambivalence, which has driven the colonial to the capital, to the very Mecca from which his erstwhile colonial master has come" (Cartey 1991, 273). Therefore, the musicians shared in common an experience of emigration which, in turn, served as a central theme for their songs about the pleasures and agonies of exile. Furthermore, while the musicians were living and working in France, they became aware of their Caribbean identity as distinct from their Frenchness. Assimilated into French culture through its formalized educational system in the French Caribbean, the musicians were shocked to discover upon their arrival in France that the French did not consider them to be French. Instead they were viewed as being French-speaking Black, colonial subjects.

Because of the dependent status of the musicians' countries upon France, new governmental policies made in Paris affected them on a personal level.

Jean-Pierre Colin, who worked in Jack Lang's Ministry of Culture under President François Mitterrand's government, had a special responsibility for cultural development in previously neglected areas which included minority individuals and groups (Rigby 1991, 181). Colin acknowledged that modern socialism had to return to a more broadly based humanist tradition which worked for the well-being of all categories of underprivileged people. In Colin's view, the future of France lay not merely in accepting but also in actively embracing cultural diversity (Rigby 1991, 185). Since France had so evidently become a multicultural nation, it was essential for French people to transcend their fear of others and recognize the rights of their nation's former and present colonials. Also, it was most vital to accept that French culture would inevitably be transformed under the influence of all new cultural groups which were pressing for their own cultures to be granted full status.

During the early 1980s the Minister of Culture, Jack Lang, provided state support for cultural activities, especially popular music, and accepted the productions from each overseas department. To support the musicians, Lang approved the plans for the construction of cultural institutions such as the Zénith and the Georges Pompidou Centre, commonly known as the Beaubourg (Forbes 1995, 259–60). Other people instrumental in promoting diverse groups were Hervé Bourges, former CEO of Télévision Française 1 (TFI) and Radio Monte Carlo; Gilbert Castro and François Post at Celluloid; Jean-François Bizot at *Actuel*; Jean-Jacques Dufayet and Sylvie Coma at Radio France Internationale (RFI); and Rémy Kolpa-Kopoul and Philippe Conrath at the left-wing daily tabloid *Libération*. Furthermore, in 1990, the Zone Franche Association was formed to regroup professionals from the music industry in order to promote music and the circulation of musicians within the French-speaking world.

Media Exposure

On 7 August 1974, the Office de Radiodiffusion-Télévision Française (ORTF), the national radio and television service, was divided into seven independent broadcasting companies, while remaining a state monopoly. In 1982, a French government law encouraged the diversity of television channels and legalized local private radio stations. The ending of the state monopoly of radio and television broadcasting resulted in the creation of the independent 1982–86 Haute Autorité de la Communication Audiovisuelle (HA).[5] Its main functions were to look outside of France to get beyond cultural limitations (such as the import of inexpensive American television series). As a part of this new creation, the private channel TV 6 (currently known as M6, with a focus on music) was granted a license in January 1986. Another restructuring resulted in the formation of the single corporation named French Overseas Radio and Television (RFO) to handle all state-financed broadcasting in the overseas departments. Also, on 17 January 1989, the Conseil Supérieur de l'Audiovisuelle (CSA), a nine-member body which replaced the HA and the Commission Nationale de la Communication et des Libertés (CNCL),[6] mandated that forty to sixty percent of the music played over the radio airwaves and on television had to be French productions.

In 1990, as a consequence of these numerous changes, Alvina Ruprecht reported that Guadeloupe had forty-five radio stations, one semi-private station, and a state-sponsored national network chain providing radio and television transmission. Radyo Tanbou, located in a three-room apartment on the first floor of a residential apartment building in the center of Pointe-à-Pitre, Guadeloupe, and run by six unpaid volunteers, two paid reporters, and ten technicians, broadcasts in Creole thirteen hours a day. Ranked in third place, Radyo Tanbou captures 15.8 percent of the total listening audience (Ruprecht 1990, 227). There are also the French-owned Radio Caraïbes International (RCI) and Radio France Outre-mer (RFO), which have a staff of over eighty-two reporters and are located in a three-story building surrounded by metal fencing and barbed wire. Together, they reach 43 percent of the total audience and broadcast in French an average of eighteen hours a day. RFO's policy is not to broadcast in Creole because it is considered to be a regional language. On the other hand, radio announcers for Radio France Internationale (RFI) and Radio NJR lapse into Creole[7] when doing interviews or hosting a music show and join Radyo Tanbou by playing zouk, Latin American, American soul and rock, and African music (Ruprecht 1990, 228–31).

Martinique has more than twenty-five radio stations, including Radio Campus 96.7 FM from the Université des Antilles et de la Guyane directed by Eddy Renciot with student volunteers as announcers. On Radio Balisier and Sun FM listeners have the opportunity to call in their musical preferences at night. On Wednesday evenings two hours are set aside on Radio Balisier to play Haitian compas direct. Programs in Creole are heard daily, and a wide range of music from reggae to African American soul is heard on various stations.

In Paris, to accompany the large African and Caribbean populations, there are five radio stations: Media tropical on 96.6 FM; Africa numéro 1 on 107.5 FM; Radio-France Internationale (RFI) on 89 FM; 11 Latina 99 FM; and Radio Nova 101.5 FM. RFI offers modern Caribbean and African music on the nightly *Canal 1 Tropical* show hosted by Gilles Obringer.[8] Its powerful signal is transmitted from France to Africa, the French Caribbean, and French Guyana. With this proliferation of radio stations in France and the French Caribbean, songs are played at the whim and personal preferences of the disc jockeys.

In Martinique, people chose from among five television channels (RFO 1, RFO 2, ATV, TCI, and Canal Plus). Each station broadcasts one or more programs devoted either entirely or partially to music.[9] Most of the programs are located on RFO 1: three afternoon shows, *Bien glacé* (Very Cold), *Touchatou* (Dabbler in Everything), and *Nouchévou* (We Are at Your Home), and the once-a-month Friday night *Raconte-moi ta Martinique* (Tell Me about Your Martinique) documentary-style special, hosted by Gérard César, that features individual musicians. On ATV (Antilles Télévision) there is the thirty minute afternoon show *Zoukamine* (Zouk vitamin), whose name is taken from a 1994 album by Patrick Saint Éloi and whose theme music, "Colozou," is by Claude Vamur of Kassav'. On this show there is an alternation between the viewing of video clips and interviews with invited musicians.[10] Up to 1995 another ATV show, *Sa ka fèt* (How Is It Going?), hosted by Flyy, used as its theme song "Sé dam bonjou" (Good morning, ladies and gentlemen) by Jean-Philippe Marthély of Kassav'.

In Guadeloupe, television viewers have a similar choice of stations: RFO 1, RFO 2, Canal 10, Archipel, and A 1. At night they can also see Black Entertainment Network (BET) and Canal Plus on cable. Video clips are also shown between commercials. Television shows (similar to MTV and VH1) that feature only videos are found on Canal 10 and Achipel. Since 1995, the RFO variety show *Partitions* has offered a format similar to the American show *This Is Your Life* of the 1950s on which an invited musician, singer, or band is featured with friends and family members.

The Format of this Book

The stories of several singers and musicians form the foundation of *Awakening Spaces: French Caribbean Popular Songs, Music, and Culture*. These provide the basis for an exploration of seven clearly defined spaces of empowerment and identity. Over the twenty-six years from 1970 to 1996, the selected singers' and musicians' popular songs have interpreted past and current events. Chapter 1, "The Safe Place: Malavoi's Nostalgic Songs of Childhood and Exile," begins in the late 1960s with the founding of the band Malavoi. The band's name *Malavoi* is a Creole term for a special type of sugarcane. The band members share a commitment to reproduce updated versions of traditional music, particularly the mazurka and biguine. Most importantly, many of Malavoi's songs discuss childhood and exile and create a safe place out of memories of the Martinican landscape. No doubt the safe space of childhood and exile distances its composers but is a step to bring them closer to their roots.

Chapter 2, "Creole, Zouk, and Identity in Kassav's Optimistic Songs," addresses the controversial topic of the use of the Creole language in French Caribbean songs. As a band, Kassav' situates itself within an optimistic Creole zouk space that promotes the validity and importance of the hybrid nature of Creole culture, identity, and language. The band's 1984 gold record hit "Zouk-la sé sèl médiakaman nou ni" (Zouk is the only medicine we have) exploded on the international scene and made a major impact with its introduction of the party music called zouk. Since then, Kassav' has dominated the French Caribbean music scene and remained the number one zouk band. Also, because one's birth language (in this case Creole) is an integral part of the identity equation, Kassav's adamant stance to produce Creole lyrics has directly impacted the Creole-French language debate and positively elevated the status of Creole.

Chapter 3, "More Than a Doudou: Women's Subversive Love Songs," introduces a selection of Martinican and Guadeloupean women singers who have managed to overcome being silenced by male domination and a male control of language. Though these singers are still few in number, the founding of zouk in the late 1970s has been a major contribution to their arrival in the music industry. Although the pattern of a passive-aggressive woman emerged in the biguine and mazurka songs in the first half of the twentieth century, six selected zouk women songwriters have opened a subversive space to engage in an indirect power contestation to deal with male duplicity and commitment.

Chapter 4, "Cultural Politics and Black Resistance as Sites of Struggle," reveals that the French Caribbean region (with the exception of Haiti) is not famous for its *angagé* (social protest) songs. However, at the end of the 1970s, four figures emerged, Eugène Mona, Pôglo, Kali, and Djo Dézormo, to sing about socio-economic conditions and local politics. These four singers composed songs about Martinique's political status to voice their cries for justice and social action. The late Mona fused contemporary sounds with rural musical traditions. The Rastafarians, Pôglo and Kali, composed songs about the importance of knowing one's history, roots, categories of identity, and the ecological preservation of Martinique. And Dézormo's career escalated when he wrote the 1990 Carnival song, "Voici les loups" (Here come the wolves), equating the French and other European members to wolves who have come to devour the locals.

Chapter 5, "Public Performance, Marketing Devices, and Audience Reception," looks at marketing methods, dress codes, stage personae, and concert performances. French Caribbean singers and musicians do not perform in a vacuum. They move back and forth on the Caribbean and international scenes, negotiating their way in and out of the commercial exigencies of both local and French-based producers along with the expectations of their home and international audiences.

Chapter 6, "The Recontextualization of Urban Music," discusses how certain jazz fusion and zouk musicians, singers, and bands have since the 1980s grappled with the issue of crossover music. The bottom line is that the musicians and songwriters have placed themselves squarely within the notion that they are a Creole people. Taking control of their Caribbean identity as it evolves, they explore the possibility of an expansion of musical boundaries with up-to-date lyrics that reflect the changing values of the 1990s. They also take a delight in mixing Creole, English, Spanish, and French languages, rhythms, and harmonies to pioneer a cross-culturalism within recontextualization.

Chapter 7, "A Deferential Space for the Drum: The Ambivalence of a Cultural Voice," traces how percussionists struggle to shift the *bèlè* and *gwo ka* into urban venues and onto recordings of zouk and other popular musical genres. In defense of their cultural heritage, the percussionists challenge the slave legacy of devaluation and the ambivalent positioning of the drum. Through a deferential space, where experimentation occurs, the drum is reclaimed as a spiritual link to the ancestors and to a pride in being Caribbean.

With an emphasis upon the themes of empowerment and identity in popular song lyrics, Martinican and Guadeloupean songwriters clearly link performance to an emotional audience response, proving that they are repositories of cultural meaning within seven awakening spaces. As one knows, recorded music and song texts travel from one place to another, crossing geographic boundaries. Because musicians and vocalists migrate frequently to perform, they draw attention to their music and lyrics by showing how they live and view the world. Musicians and singers from the French Caribbean islands of Martinique and Guadeloupe struggle to be produced and heard, recreate themselves and their songs, and speak from an informed small physical space with a larger cultural consciousness while taking control of their Caribbean identity as it evolves.

1   the safe space

Malavoi's Nostalgic Songs of Childhood and Exile

When I think about Malavoi, four houses come to mind. During earlier visits to Martinique I had noticed a house that was in a dilapidated state, located on a convenient corner in Schoelcher at the juncture of the Collège Vincent Placoly and a street bordering on the canal. In 1994, while sightseeing with my fourteen-year old nephew on a public bus, the driver stopped to pick up some passengers. I gazed out of the bus window and noticed the house had undergone a transformation. Its walls had been painted a winter white; the old wooden shutters, a bright robin blue. Sun rays touched the house, and the blue on the shutters gleamed like the color of a vivid Caribbean sky. Who lived in it? What did it look like inside? What was its history? Why had it been abandoned for so long? A light sea breeze tickled my shoulders, and the sensation awakened a wish to knock on the front door.

The urge to see this house and to meet its owners was unexplainable. Fate intervened one sunny afternoon when I was interviewing Suzy Trébeau, a member of Kwak, who had formerly sung backup for Malavoi. I told Trébeau that I had a later interview with Jean-Paul Soime, one of Malavoi's violinists. Trébeau offered to take me since she knew where Soime lived. When Trébeau parked her car in front of "my house," I could not believe it! Chattering like an excited magpie, I extended my hand to Soime, who had seen us and opened the front gate. Upon hearing my story, an amused Soime gave me a tour of "his" home. Built on a slope, the two-storeyed house was furnished with colonial period furniture and accentuated with Japanese bonsai trees in the back garden. A lower floor, where Soime stored his instruments and albums, occasionally functioned as the rehearsal space for Malavoi. "I like old things," said Soime. "That is why my wife and I purchased this abandoned house." For me, his house was representative of the traditional music and family values that he had written about in "Kolédés" (Inseparables) for Malavoi's *An Maniman* (1994).

A month later, Shawna Moore-Madlangbayan drove me to the town of Robert to meet Emmanuel "Mano" Césaire, the former violinist and founder of Malavoi. Mano Césaire met us in the town square, and we followed him along a country, dirt road to his home on the outskirts of Robert. The three of us walked through the kitchen to enter the living room where we found Césaire's son Claude, the pianist and founder of Palaviré. Pleased that I would be able to converse with both father and son since the older Césaire was now affiliated with Palaviré, I turned my head and saw a baby grand piano that was so highly polished that I could see a clear reflection of myself. The atmosphere in the Césaire home was comfortable; the Césaires were so welcoming that it was difficult to leave at the end of the interview. We conversed like old friends who had rediscovered each other after a lengthy absence. When I recited lines from "Albé" (Albert) and "En lè mon la" (On the hill), two songs that Mano had composed in his youth for Malavoi, the Césaires expressed their genuine surprise that I, a foreigner, had cared enough to do that kind of research in preparation for an interview.

In May, Shawna and I drove south to Diamant to meet the television journalist Marijosé Alie, who had sung the popular "Caressé moins" (Caress me) for Malavoi's *Zouël* (1983). This time we rang the bell at the gate that partially hid the ochre-colored house from the eyes of passers-by. The elegant house with sliding glass doors and windows that overlooked the sea had been constructed by Alie's grandfather and renovated by her ex-husband. In contrast to her tall, laid back, tousled-hair appearance, Alie fervently expressed a deep love for the house where she had been raised. We sat on the terrace where we were serenaded by the crashing waves of the sea and the happy squeals of Alie's third and youngest daughter. Warm, loving memories of this house and its close proximity to the sea and its breezes were contained in the lyrics of "Caressé moins."

House number four was where I met José Privat. The wooden house, located in the Didier section of Fort-de-France, is a rarity because most of the wooden homes have been replaced with concrete ones in fear of fire. The house in question, restored bit-by-bit, actually belonged to Privat's brother and sister-in-law. Outside on the veranda were a dining room table as well as a detached kitchen with flowers spilling forth from pots and off the roof. A talented pianist and organist, Privat, who guards his privacy, spoke haltingly about his career and the sadness and bittersweet pleasure that engulfed him when he began to replace the very ill Paulo Rosine for Malavoi's concerts. Citing Malavoi's stringent and high standards, he was more than grateful when he was invited to be Rosine's permanent replacement. Surrounded by his brother, sister-in-law, nieces, and nephew, Privat ended the interview by posing at the piano in the living room.

Most of the Malavoi musicians have known each other since high school; four of them studied the violin with Madame Colette Franz. To me, both the name "Malavoi," which refers to a type of sugarcane, and the qualities of the band member's homes, symbolize the rooted-ness of the members of this Martinican string band and their commitment to the preservation of traditional music. Never the winner of a gold record, Malavoi, the longest running band in Martinique, is nevertheless highly respected in the French Caribbean, in France, and in other parts of the world.

~~~~~~

Migration creates the desire for home, which in turn produces the rewriting of home.
CAROLE BOYCE DAVIES (1994, 113)

It is absolutely necessary to be wandering, to be multiple, and on the outside.
MARYSE CONDÉ (Pfaff 1993, 46)

The statements by Carole Boyce Davies and Maryse Condé are complementary because they address the importance of moving beyond one's boundaries to see oneself and one's country from alternative angles. These boundaries involve a physical migration from one country to another, an internal psychological reassessment, or a combination of the two. The invention and reassessment of the concept of *négritude* attest to this. Négritude, founded by Aimé Césaire of Martinique, Léon Gontran Damas of French Guyana, and Léopold Sédar Senghor of Senegal in Paris in the 1930s, is a historical, philosophical and literary movement. Each founder takes a different position: Césaire uses the myth of Africa to affirm a new identity for enslaved or colonized Blacks in his poetry; Damas speaks of a doubled exile and of how Blacks become aware of themselves through pain and alienation; Senghor pushes forward the idea that the essence of the black race is feeling and that art and science serve humanity in its need for creativity and love.

In considering the invention of négritude, it is important to recall that its three founders were living in voluntary exile in order to pursue a higher education in the capital of the very country that had colonized their peoples. This raises a question: Would the concept of négritude have ever been articulated if the three founders had never crossed their birth boundaries, come in contact with Blacks from other nations, read African-American and surrealist French poetry, and confronted racism in France, where they were considered to be the Other rather than the Same? This question assumes that Césaire, Damas, and Senghor failed to see they had already been treated like the Other by the French colonizers on their own home turfs. Their membership in the small social and cultural élite granted them privileges that were denied to most of their countrymen. What they eventually understood, in Paris, was that they were assimilated to validate French culture at the expense of their own Caribbean and African cultures. The realization was a humiliating one. Thus, their departure from home into voluntary exile in France exposed them to another way of seeing themselves.

The Haitian writer Jacques Stéphen Alexis wrote about "Le Réalisme merveilleux" as an alternative to négritude. At the first Congress of Negro Artists and Writers held at the Sorbonne in September 1956, Alexis presented the paper "Du Réalisme merveilleux des Haïtiens" (Concerning the marvelous realism of the Haitians) during which he explained, "The nations of the same geographic zone have an internal economic and historical reality, which is neighboring, if not parallel" (Dash 1975, 44). For him, the history of colonialism and the notion of a monolithic black culture advocated by négritude writers was not sufficient, since they denied the diversity of those who were transplanted to the Caribbean region.

René Dépestre, a fellow Haitian, challenged and refuted Césaire's position of a universal black poetry and the myth of a neo-African fraternity. He insisted that "*Négritude* denies the evidence of the diversity of material conditions of social development and considers the creative sensibility of Blacks as a universal and homogenous cultural bloc" (Dash 1975, 49). Edouard Glissant, a Martinican writer, took Alexis's and Dépestre's arguments even further with his concept of *antillanité*, which embraced cultural hybridity. The younger Guadeloupean novelist Daniel Maximin linked political awareness with Caribbean cultural identity in *L'Isolé soleil* (1981). Maximin's protagonist Louis-Gabriel read Suzanne Césaire's 1942 *Tropique* essay "Malaise d'une civilisation," in which the question "What is Martinican?" was raised. After engaging in an internal interrogation, the protagonist concluded: "It is not necessary for us to look at ourselves first because it is in contradiction to our action without inferiority complexes which will make us doubt our identity. . . . Do not all Caribbean people form the same civilization?" (Maximin 1981, 193).

These writers' arguments were followed up by those of several idealistic students at the Lycée Schoelcher in Fort-de-France, Martinique, who brainstormed and decided to play several types of music that embraced the rhythms of their island and those of their neighbors, thereby aligning the students squarely with the arguments brought forth by Senghor's position on feeling, creativity, and love. Destined to call themselves "Malavoi," these young students created a liminal safe space to preserve a Caribbean continuity by blurring cultural distinctions. In bell hooks's words, Malavoi dared "to critically interrogate their locations, identities, and allegiances that inform them how to live their lives to begin the process of decolonization" (hooks 1994, 249). In their dual roles as musicians and songwriters, they provided a service to the public that strengthened compassion and deepened an insight into the psyche of the Martinican people.

This safe space is located in Malavoi's music and Creole lyrics, forming what Patricia Hill Collins calls "a site of resisting the objectification as the Other and housing a culture of resistance" (Collins 1990, 97). Instead of focusing upon the negativity of colonization and assuming that transplanted Blacks had nothing to offer, Malavoi's songs reconstruct the past by delving into memories of childhood, recalling the ambivalent feelings attending them, and also by deriving transformative powers from a union with the Martinican landscape. In response to the massive migrations during the twentieth century between the two polarities of Martinique and France, many of Malavoi's nostalgic songs are concerned with the major changes to Martinican social life. Consequently, the creation of a safe space is a means of promoting values and memories that sustain not only Malavoi but the cultures of the Americas and Africa.

Malavoi views the safe space as a buffer between Martinique and France. It is also a buffer between those who are able to take private music lessons and those with an innate musical ability. Instead of veering away from these truths, the Malavoi songwriters acknowledge them, write about them, and see this reality as a necessary stage for personal and political growth. At the same time, their songs differ from Djo Dézormo's and Eugène Mona's (see chapter 4) in that they neither dwell upon the dispossession of people nor emphasize the confusion that develops around the attempts to be liberated. Of importance is that Malavoi's songs reveal the "soul" and innate goodness of Martinicans in the belief that natural elements will make a difference in their lives. The troubling factor is that this safe space can become too comfortable and risks being too idyllic when the songwriters talk nostalgically about childhood and exile.

Of course, another way of looking at this safe space is to see it as the location for creative expression that grants Malavoi the power to confront dislocation. This is the space where Malavoi speaks openly about the introverted effects of childhood and exile without fear of censorship by the music critics and the general public. Thus, at the very center of this safe space is the performance factor and the public's perception and reception of Malavoi. Another factor is that certain Malavoi members come from the urban mulatto élite, which automatically gives them certain privileges.

Accustomed to seeing local bands that are largely composed of mulattos, the Martinican public do not consider the membership of Malavoi to be un-usual. After all, they represent a segment of the overall population that has access to expensive imported musical instruments, private music lessons, and the means to travel to France. Therefore, the purpose of this chapter is to discuss how some of the Malavoi songwriters, in a privileged position, nostalgically depict childhood and exile while moving in and out of the geographies of Martinique and France.

Malavoi and its Beginnings

Dubbed the string orchestra from Martinique because of its violins, Malavoi was founded in the late 1960s by Emmanuel "Mano" Césaire. He grew up in the lively neighborhood of Terres-Sainville in Fort-de-France, known for its numerous barber and beauty shops where barbers and hairdressers sang and played the guitar, banjo, or mandolin. With three of his friends (Christian de Négri, Marcel Rémion, and Jean Paul Soime), Césaire attended Lycée Schoelcher and studied the violin with Colette Frantz. By 1968, Césaire first founded a group called the Merry Lads, which played in the rotunda at Lycée Schoelcher, with students dancing on the first and second floors. Eventually, the young musicians started performing for noontime get-togethers, at after-dinner dances, and in the town of Robert. Increasingly popular, the Merry Lads changed their name to Malavoi when they started recording 45 rpm singles. With Pierre Jabert and Julien Constance as singers, Malavoi recorded songs like "Albé" (Albert) and "En lè mon la" (On the hill). Eventually, the group received an invitation from Marc Pulvar, who was then the Assistant Mayor of Rivière Pilote, to play for a dance in Rivière Pilote. Excited but nervous, the group refused but finally accepted the important engagement. From then on, more requests were made for them to play, and the band grew in membership.

Malavoi has undergone three stages of growth. The musicians first played violins, piano, guitar, bass, and percussion, and the group was mainly known as a salsa band (Chénard 1982). During 1975, the band's make-up changed with the introduction of two trumpet players to replace two of the violinists. In addition, Serge Lossen played the bamboo flute; Paulo Rosine the piano; Dédé Saint Prix the congas and other percussion instruments; and Jean Marc Albicy replaced Marcel Rémion on the bass. Malavoi played at many dances, continued to make records, and made constant appearances at the Lido club. During the second stage Césaire left and de Négri became the sole violinist. Plagued with constant replacements of musicians and weary of working seasonally with the same repertoire of songs, Malavoi played for what they thought would be the last time at a 1978 dance in Lamentin. However, after several discussions in 1981, Césaire and Paul "Paulo" Rosine reconsidered launching Malavoi for the third time.

One of Malavoi's strengths is that it is composed of musicians who continue to perfect their craft.[1] Another strength is that under the late Rosine's leadership Malavoi received even more exposure by playing six nights a week, with a condensed version of the band, at a piano bar in Fort-de-France in the 1980s. The full band performs irregularly because its musicians and soloists hold full-time jobs which require each musician to work out a deal with his employer for release time to travel with the band off the island. In spite of these restrictions, Malavoi has recorded thirty-two albums.

In the beginning, Rosine had the idea of a group with ten violins, but Malavoi returned to its original composition with four violins, piano, guitar, bass, drum, and percussion, adding a soloist and backup singers. Rehearsing every week at the Ciné Théâtre, in the center of Fort-de-France, Malavoi developed a repertoire that moved toward the nostalgic, concentrating on the European Antillean biguine, mazurka, and waltz (known as the *grand bal* music). In 1983, the director[2] of the Centre Martiniquais d'Action Culturelle (CMAC) invited Malavoi to be the first Martinican group to participate in the Caribbean festival of Cartagena in Colombia. After that performance, the Martinican band received a flood of invitations, including those from France, Switzerland, Japan, the United States, Germany, Holland, Belgium, and the Caribbean.

Malavoi's recognizable style had been identified with a blending of Brazilian samba, Haitian compas, Jamaican reggae, African Cuban music, Santo Dominican merengue, European quadrille and waltz, and the French Caribbean biguine. Therefore, in 1986, when the album *La Filo* (Philosophy) was released by George Debs Productions containing the zouk song "Ababa,"[3] Malavoi's faithful fans were outraged and some quit supporting the band. These fans had classified Malavoi as a traditional band and were accustomed to a particular kind of music from them. They viewed the band's performance of zouk as a sellout. Nevertheless, their anger was tempered later when they heard the biguine and a samba beat of "La Case à Lucie" (Lucie's place), penned by Rosine:

Lé ou lévé
Zié ou pôkô rouvé
Ou dou boutt
En ti chimen an
Ka veillé la pote la

Ou za bisoin décollé
Épi ronm épi labsinte
En bèl coutt mabi déyé ï
Lè ï ronzè
Ou minm koté la
Ti manmaille
Ki sòti lékòl
Ka fè djindjin épi ou
Pa ni ayen yo pa fè

Pou tiré ou en fond trou a
Mé sa pa sèvi ayen
Mwin min'nin ou bod lan mé
Ou di mwin ka fè cho
Mwen min'nin ou la kanpagn
Ou di mwin ka fè frèt
Lè mwin mandé ou ki sa
Ou sé lé mwin fè ba ou
ou répon'n mwin kon sa
"Min'nin mwin kay Lucie
Souplé."

∿∿∿∿∿∿∿

(Just got up.
Eyes half-closed.
Camped across the road,
you lie in wait for the door.
You already would like "to be lit up"
from the rum and the absinthe.
A doubled shot of *mabi*.
Eleven o'clock
and you haven't budged.
Coming out of school
are children,
crossing to boo you.

We tried everything
to get you out of this difficulty,
but nothing has been effective.

At sea
there's mist.
In the countryside
there are shivers.
Where can we take you?
"Take me for a drink at Lucie's Place.")[4]

The Martinican crooner, Ralph Thamar, recorded "La Case à Lucie" with
Malavoi in October 1986 in Studio Davout with Jocelyne Béroard and Edith
Lefel in the chorus. Because the song was well received, it was re-released in
1987 on an album bearing its name: *La Case à Lucie*.

The popularity of "La Case à Lucie" is rooted in the custom of drinking
rum. Rosine's lyrics are a reminder of the Martinican psychiatrist Frantz
Fanon's metaphor in *Peau noire, masques blancs* (1952) of the divided, com-
partmentalized space to capture the colonial situation. Playing with Creole
and the sounds of a piano and violins, Rosine offers a song that is placed
between Martinique and Brazil. A superficial listening to the song's lyrics
reveals a casual recollection about how much a Martinican man enjoys
drinking rum, absinthe, and *mabi*. Entering a favorite hang-out, Lucie's
Place, to have a drink with his buddies is perhaps the man's only pleasure in
life. The warmth of companionship and the smoky club atmosphere duplicate the home he has been seeking. A close listening to the song reveals that,
although it is not noon, the man's eyes are already puffy and half-closed.
Someone tries to offer him help, but it is rebuffed; therefore, the song's casual message changes into a cautionary warning about social drinking that
borders on alcoholism. Teetering on this divided space is the man's selfhood
that is integrated and confined to Lucie's Place. With a glass in his hand
topped off with rum, the man hides in a short-term safe space, engulfed in
alcoholic fumes, to escape from the repugnant outside reality, mirroring the
dependent and passive stupor in which Martinicans find themselves in relation to France.

Remembering the Past

The cousins Ina and Mano Césaire have collaborated on several songs,
"Sport national" (National sport), "Apré la pli" (After the rain), and "Exil"
(Exile), for Malavoi; she is the lyricist, and he, the composer. Their songs,
steeped in the sounds, images, and richness of the Creole heritage, suggest
that Martinique is a microcosm of the entire Caribbean region. Each song
portrays an environment wherein they speak of familial values, such as

patience, endurance, love, stability, and some fun. Ina Césaire describes her collaboration with her cousin to be a sharing of the same childhood with a difference of two or three years in age. They have some of the same memories and spent their vacations together at their paternal grandmother's home in Morne Rouge.[5]

The Césaire cousins are so close that there is often no need for them to talk when they are busy composing a song. They both had fun writing "Sport national," for the favorite sport of Martinique is *milans* (gossiping):

> Palè
> Babiyè
> Kankanè
> Dépalè
> Dòktè
> Shikanè
> Sé kon sa nou yé!

~~~~~~~~~~

> (The monopolizers
> The chatterers
> The malicious gossipers
> The mumblers
> The know-it-alls
> The playful squabblers
> We are like this!)[6]

Special names are assigned to all kinds of gossipers, ranging from the palè, babiyè, kankanè, dépalè, and dòktè to the shikanè. Each type of gossiper takes on a life of its own. Living on an island totally surrounded by water can be claustrophobic, causing people to be unusually curious about each other. Everyday life becomes a ritual; therefore, a neighbor's change of pattern or behavior gives rise to gossip which can have a malicious edge. As described in "Sport national," gossip relieves the tension and enlivens an otherwise boring day:

> Sé an spôr nasional
> tout moun inmin di moun mal
> Adan péyi nou yan

Kankan sé frè a milan
Palé pou di ki sa?

~~~~~~~~~~~

(It's a national sport.
Everybody likes to be the next to say something bad.
In our country
isn't the malicious gossip king?)

Whereas the Césaire cousins poke fun at the gossipers in "Sport national," the memory of their grandmother's land in Morne Rouge is the reason for composing "Apré la pli." Their love of the countryside is associated with the fresh smell of the earth after a rainfall: "Mé la pli tonbé / anlè razié / Sé kon si Bon-Dié / ka fè jé" (The rain falls / on the herbs / It's like God / amusing himself).[7] Next, the cousins recollect their childhoods as carefree children, playing among the hills:

Lè man té piti,
Man té inmin tand la pli.
Man né an môn-la
Ki la ba-a
Lòt koté, solèy
ka lévé.

~~~~~~~~~~~

(When I was a child,
I liked the sound of rain.
I am from the hill
which is there.
From the other side
the sun rises.)

The song goes on to say that the various moods, color tones, and shades of a day after either a heavy rainfall or a light shower in the middle of the day collaborate to inspire the child's freedom of movement. There is also the noonday heat with its lassitude or harsh glare from the direct overhead sun. An early sundown brings a respite from the harsh sun and offers a promise of an evening of cooler moments with a swift, jet-black night full of twinkling silver stars.

Ina Césaire once said: "I preferred to be with my grandmother, my cousins, near my roots. I always felt like an emigrant in France, and I lived like a foreigner. I liked certain aspects about the country, but it was not my country."[8] Obviously, Césaire's sensitivity toward and love for her country were not suppressed by her exile. The autobiographically tinged songs "Apré la pli" and "Exil" appeal to the listener's sensory stimulation with references not only to the smells of the earth but to the commingling of freshly watered flowers and grass. Thus, while engaging the listener in an intense sensory journey, Césaire recalls a Martinican landscape that promises a new beginning and a cyclical regeneration where fantasy and reality fuse.

Elements of the landscape capture Ina Césaire's imagination, shape her destiny, and allow her to repudiate the cold French environment. While living on an island lush with greenery, Césaire noted how commonplace plants, fruits, and flowers were. After her move to France she encountered a different landscape from the one she valued in Martinique. Exile in France is a necessary condition for her, her cousin Mano, and other Malavoi singers and musicians, because, as noted by Max Dorsinville, it offers "that sense of distance necessary for the emergence of the artistic, cultural, and psychic authenticity of being in the world" (Dorsinville 1976, 69). As a consequence, Césaire's songs and writings are infused with an over-repetition of comments on her island landscape and its seasonal rhythms.

Ina Césaire moved to France with her parents, Suzanne and Aimé Césaire, and five siblings in the early 1950s. The family lived in an H.L.M. (low-income housing, similar to the American projects) on the outskirts of Paris in Petit Clamart (Schwarz-Bart 1989a, 76). During these years Césaire developed very ambivalent feelings about France. Her mother Suzanne's storytelling soothed her; she was exposed to Michel Leiris's ethnological publications about his trips to Africa and her father's négritude poems. Influenced by Leiris, Césaire studied ethnology and received a diploma in Peul (an African language spoken by the Peul, or Fulani, in Guinea, Senegal, Mali, and elsewhere) and African civilizations at age twenty. Later, she completed a doctoral thesis on Peul nomadic aesthetics (Schwarz-Bart 1989a, 77). Finally, after more than twenty years in France, Césaire returned to Martinique to collect and publish folktales, to write plays and a novel, and to direct the Martinican Office of Patrimony.

Like her father in his early poems in *Cahier d'un retour au pays natal* (1939) and *Soleil cou coupé* (1948), Césaire recovers her personal voice by channeling it towards a synthesis with nature. Whereas Aimé Césaire vegetalizes and animalizes the sea, sky, and stone in his disguised love for the earth (Sartre 1969, xxxiv), Ina Césaire describes a quiet, languid landscape. For her, the sea symbolizes the flow from the past, embracing the present and emptying into the future. The sea also symbolizes a dream-like movement in time and space from the hidden beginnings of childhood to the enlightened future of the adult. Also, unlike Aimé Césaire, who wrote poems about the anguish, disfranchisement, and uprootedness of the Black man in Martinique, Ina Césaire envisions a rejuvenating landscape that provides her with security and a sense of belonging.

As a trained ethnologist, Ina Césaire recognizes the value of the Creole language and its *contes* (folk tales). She does not believe in a fetishistic past but plainly speaks about exile in all of its disguises: loneliness, homesickness, and love for the abandoned island home. Overcome by an intense desire to return to her island home, Césaire writes songs that refute Michel de Certeau's proposal that "the function of the city is to produce a universal and anonymous subject" (de Certeau 1988, 94). Wanting to reclaim Martinique, while living in France, Césaire refamiliarizes herself with the local plants and tropical climate of her childhood. Her preference is the rural community, not the urban one, because it is the physical foundation of Martinique's economic base and the recognition of the Self rather than the anonymous subject.

From an older generation, her father Aimé Césaire wrote poems about himself and his African ancestors who were uprooted. Because of this uprootedness he called upon a nature from which he derived his strength. In an interview Césaire stated: "I am in fact obsessed by vegetation, by the flower, by the root. There is nothing gratuitous in that, it is linked with my situation, that of a black man exiled from his native soil. It is a psychological phenomenon from which I have never freed myself and which I feel to the point of nausea" (cited in Sieger 1981, 66). Interestingly enough, his daughter Ina and nephew Mano both inherited his innate love for nature. The cousins' birth land was not fraught with brutality, for they were from a later generation where the physical and mental despair of their people had been submerged under the glamour of Sheraton-style resort hotels, superhighways, well-stocked stores, and beautiful ranch-style houses. In addition, they grew up in middle-class households where they were shielded from the poverty of the masses.

Emile Snyder observed that Aimé Césaire restructured a poetic destruction of the universe, and his poetry abounded with a "convulsive sky," "exploded stars," "splitting craters," "braziers of flames" and "primal debris" (Snyder 1976, 40). On the opposite end, Ina and Mano Césaire constructed

a lyrical universe wherein love and affection for Martinique were expressed
and embedded in the earth. At the same time, they were fully aware of the
French colonizers' intrusion and efforts to destroy their culture, and they
therefore used Martinique as an archetype to redefine themselves. By remembering home the Césaires engaged in a French Creole journey to counteract
the feelings of exile within and outside of their own country, continually
constructing a safe space.

While listening to her cousin's music late at night, Ina Césaire writes lyrics
to match the rhythm and melody, describing Mano's music as being "olfac-
tive, a music that always thinks in odors and smells good."[9] Thus, a vivid
description of a singing bird and odors after a rainfall in the Césaire cousins'
songs written for Malavoi evokes the Martinican landscape. To accomplish
this, Ina and Mano Césaire drench themselves in the bright colors of Martinique as they remember the dynamic tropical landscape where semantic and
ideological transformations occur.

The pianist and arranger of Malavoi, Paulo Rosine, joined the Césaire
cousins in their reconstruction of intimate portraits of Martinicans by sharing their passion for plants. He liked puttering around his garden, rubbing
his hands in the fertile soil, and breathing in the fresh scent of daybreak.
The opening line "Mi jou a ka ouvè / rozé a rozé en flê" (Daybreak is here /
Water the flowers)[10] from Rosine's "Jou ouvè" (Daybreak) provides a description of an ordinary day that begins with a rising sun. The watering of
the flowers is a cleansing of the songwriter's thoughts that brings clarity to
his life. The cyclical quality of planting flowers and working with his hands
to produce beauty both transform and provide a clue to Rosine's inner vision. Tilling the soil allows the solitary and very private pianist, composer,
and songwriter the time to think and reposition himself within the Malavoi
collective.

"Jou ouvè,"[11] a lyrical celebration of the dawning of a new day with its
daily transformations and rituals, is associated with the delight of being alive
and well with reawakened sensations, sounds, rituals, and commitments.
Even the sound of a rooster's crowing is soothing to the ears. People from
afar and those who are in town hear the 6:00 A.M. Angelus, look at their
watches, and get up to attend mass. Daybreak is the time to give respect to
the home and to put a body into action. The night creatures disappear to be
replaced by the overpowering smell of the *ti baum* in the garden.[12] Since "Jou
ouvè" is a visceral identification of Rosine with his island, Malavoi played it
at his funeral on 2 February 1993 to accompany him on his journey. Scenes
from the televised coverage of the service at the Cathedral of Fort-de-France

show an enormous crowd of mourners, which included dignitaries like the mayor, Aimé Césaire, singing along with Malavoi during the funeral procession.

While singing for Wabaps, Les Gentlemen, Malavoi, Marius Cultier, and Fal Frett, Ralph Thamar developed an interest in pursuing a full-time career in France. In a 1995 interview he remarked: "I wanted to live from music because it did not look good for me to participate in so many bands. I never needed to return [to Malavoi]. I left for Paris in 1987 and embarked on a solid career."[13] Going on tour with Malavoi around the Caribbean and abroad piqued Thamar's interest in pursuing a full-time career. His supervisor told him that he had to make a choice between banking or singing. Out of kindness, he gave Thamar a two-and-a half year sabbatical, allowing him the possibility to resume his position at the bank if he did not succeed with his singing career.

From 1969 to 1986, Thamar was Malavoi's off-and-on soloist. At the tender age of fourteen, he sang for the first time in public with Malavoi in 1966, and then became the group's soloist in 1969. In 1973, the eighteen-year-old Thamar lost interest in school, withdrew, and began to work at odd jobs so that he could sing. However, his mother intervened and found him a job because she thought it was important for him to have a fixed income. Juggling a full-time job at a bank with singing stints with a number of musicians and bands, Thamar gradually cultivated a smooth voice suited to various singing styles. When Malavoi disbanded around 1978, he alternated between playing the trumpet and singing part-time as a guest soloist for several bands. Then, in 1980, Rosine got in touch to tell him about the revived Malavoi, and Thamar's second stint as Malavoi's soloist lasted for almost eight years.

In 1987, in preparation for his first solo album *Exil*, Thamar made a request to Mano Césaire: Would he please write the first song? But Thamar did not want just any song. He asked Césaire to put a little of his heart into the composition and give something of himself. Replying in the affirmative, Césaire promised to share a part of himself. He got in touch with his cousin Ina, and together they composed the beautiful "Exil" in French:

J'ai si longtemps rêvé de ce pays lointain
Que j'ai reinventé ses bruits et ses parfums
Les rythmes d'aujourd'hui mêlés aux sons d'hier
Scandent ma nostalgie, rechauffent mon hiver
Parfois île volcan et parfois île fleur

J'en connais des beautés
J'en connais des douleurs
Des contes oubliés naissent du souvenir
Entre les pleurs, on se prend à rire
Nous avons marché sur tous les continents
Cela fait longtemps que nous voyageons
Nous avons erré souvent
Mais aujourd'hui nous sommes arrivés
Aujourd'hui nous traversons l'eau une dernière fois
Car nous connaissons déjà tous les pays
Une vieille chanson dit: "Nous ne sommes pas gens d'ailleurs,
Nous sommes gens d'ici."

Fumées d'herbe odorante et de lampe à pétrole
La mèmoire parfois chante en langue créole
Enfant de l'à-peu-près, je poursuis en rêvant
Une voix qui d'hier parle enfin au présent
Et la voix douce-amère, la voix de l'orphelin
Redit les mots, les mots qui ont faim.

~~~~~~~~~~~

(I have dreamed for a long time about my country.
So far away
that I reinvented its noises and perfumes.
Today's rhythms mixed with yesterday's sounds
stress my nostalgia, reheat my winter.
Sometimes the volcanic island and sometimes the flower island.
I know about some of its beauty.
I know about some of its sadness.
Forgotten folk tales born from memory.
One laughs between tears.
We trotted across all the continents.
We've traveled for a long time.
We have often roamed,
but today we have arrived.
Today we shall cross the ocean one last time,
because we already know all the countries.
An old song says: "We are not people from elsewhere.
We are people from here."

Smoke from sweet-smelling herb and the kerosene lamp.
Sometimes memory sings in the Creole language.
A child nearby, I dream of a voice which
from yesterday finally speaks in the present.
And the bittersweet, orphan's voice
repeats the words which are intense.)[14]

The opening lines in the first stanza refer to the variegated beauty, sadness, and rhythms of Martinique. The memories provide a liminal scope during which they are exorcized, thus transforming the past and validating its importance in the making of the self. By writing in the refrain, "Nous ne sommes pas des gens d'ailleurs / Nous sommes des gens d'ici" (We are not people from elsewhere / We are people from here), the Césaire cousins negate assimilation through a cultural reconstruction. They also demystify the colonial reality, assert the specificity of Caribbean heritage, and end up with a personalized historical journey into the interior of a safe space through a child's voice in the final lines.

Marijosé Alie, the first woman singer and songwriter to sing lead for Malavoi, recalls similar memories. Speaking about "Caressé moins," which first appeared as the opening song on *Zouël* (1983), she explains: "I wrote it because it reflected my state of mind during that moment. I was missing tenderness and affection. The song came directly out of my feelings at that particular time in history."[15] Upon listening to the texture of Alie's voice, a wistfulness is detected underneath a sexy quality of smokiness that wraps around the listener:

Solèy la ka couché
Lalin la ka lévé
Cocotié ka bougé
Caressé moins

～～～～～～～

(The sun is setting.
The moon is rising.
The coconut tree is moving.
Caress me.)[16]

As the song proceeds, Alie seldom uses words longer than three syllables. Her style is simple, with uncomplicated stanzas, while she shifts from one image to another, building her case for a warm, welcoming Martinique. The sensuous command "Caressé moins" is inserted at the end of each of the song's stanzas, composed of four jagged utterances to reinforce Alie's need to escape a terrible bout of homesickness and a lengthy cold winter in Dijon, France, in order to feel the tactile warmth and sunshine against her skin.

Malavoi begins "Caressé moins" with an overture of violins and a piano solo, emphasizing a very nostalgic, lonely woman's need to sing about her beloved Martinique. Living in France and being confined to an apartment slowly erodes Alie's confidence in herself. The apartment intensifies her desire to reenter the safe space of a tightly knit, familial community in contrast to an unknown closed one among strangers. A voluntary exile, she was in France to obtain material advantages, but the experience offers no spiritual solace. To regain her sense of self, Alie uses her Creole language not only to compose "Caressé moins" but to cushion her aloneness and loneliness. In fact, Alie's discomfort and struggle against a self-imposed oppression duplicate the sentiments expressed by the Guadeloupean writer Gisèle Pineau: "I did not live an Antillean childhood in the tropics. I knew the city, its alignments of gray buildings, the cold winters of France, the snow, the wool coats, and the undeniable feeling of being excluded" (Pineau 1995, 289). Cut off from home, Alie turns to her memories to sustain her by providing familiarity and a certainty of experiences. As a result, her vocal delivery of "Caressé moins," accompanied by a romantic melody that simulates the sound of a blowing wind, culminates in a liberating moment.

On the other end of the spectrum is "Mwen menm bout" (I'm worn out, at the end of my rope) by the violinist Jean Paul Soime. In this cleverly written song, food metaphors are utilized to express a dissatisfaction with the socio-political state of affairs in Martinique:

> Zòt tout sa ki kanni
> Kon lédjim dékouché
> Tout an lannuit dan bouyon si
> Zòt tout lè kò bwarenn
> lè briskan, lè krazé

>

> (All of you who are vegetating
> like roots marinating

all night long in a bitter broth.
All of you whose sterile body
has lost its bearings.)[17]

Grasping the relationship between the political and the personal, Soime continues with the metaphorical statement: "An nou sisé sos-la / Annou bwè lagout-la / Mwen menm bout" (Sop up the sauce / Down to the last drop / As for me, I am worn out, at the end of my rope) to challenge the status quo and the apathy that categorizes his people's responses to French colonial dominance. Food imagery is used to refer to sterility and a change of life. The implication is that malaise and exhaustion are symptomatic not only of a woman's body going though menopause or a man's middle-age crisis but of the oppressed Martinique. To be specific, Soime's food imagery is not simply about eating but an ideological statement of Martinicans' acceptance of being consumed by France.

In contrast, age and youthful innocence are ritualized in connection with the African continuum of spiritual generational continuity as sketched by Soime in "Kolédés" (Inseparables), a song about the formation of friendship between a boy and a girl who play together, argue, and make up:

Nou enmen kon ti moun ka enmen
Dan solèy
Dan mitan shimen
Ka shamayé toujou
Fè nou trapé shagren lanmou
Pou dé bo séré dan razyé
Fè ròl pèdi konou kon zybié
Nou enmenn kon ti moun sa enmen
Dan lanmé
Déchiré rad nou
Nou séré lougarou
Mété lavi nou an danjé
Pou dé bo séré dan razyé

Ti moun sé kolédé
Toulou man pé kèy sa oubliyé'w
Toulou man sé enmen'w toujou
Le nou peche djôkô
Fè yo tjuit kotakot brilé

Kon dé bo séré dan razyé
Ti moun sé kolédé.

~~~~~~~~~~

(We loved each other like children do
in the sun.
In the middle of the road
we argued non-stop.
We invented love pains
to obtain two kisses exchanged in the tall grass.
We were lost birds.
We loved each other like children do
in the sea.
We tore up our old clothes,
and we hid ourselves from the werewolves.
We put our lives in danger
to obtain two kisses exchanged in the tall grass.

As children, we resembled the *kolédés*.
Toulou, I won't forget you.
Toulou, I will know to love you always.
When we used to fish for some *dyôkôs*,
we fried them together
like two kisses exchanged in the tall grass.
As children, we were like *kolédés*.)[18]

Assuming that there are no limits, the sea and the sun excite the children
who play figuratively in the safe space between reality and the spiritual or,
better still, the idyllic present and the turbulent future. The free-flowing sea
and its crashing waves symbolize a peace that is empty of tension. The two
friends grill dyôkôs (tiny fish too small to be cooked separately) and exchange furtive kisses in the tall grasses. While grilling the dyôkôs, the fish
automatically stick to one another, a metaphor for the cooperation of both
sexes needed to reconceptualize the present and future direction of Martinique.

According to Soime, "The song is an image of two children who like each
other and are inseparable like the fish. It is a question of love between two
children, a childhood love with its risk and the desire not to go too far. It is
also the violence of some childhood love affairs when they playfully josh

each other while catching the fish."[19] This nostalgic longing for childhood projects a cultural and historical reconstruction of the Self. As Renato Rosaldo notes, "Nostalgia is a particularly appropriate emotion to invoke in attempting to establish one's innocence and at the same time talk about what one has destroyed" (Rosaldo 1985, 108). Since Martinique and Martinicans, in their various moods, are ever changing, the social history of childhood visually associated with the comfort and longing for ethnic food and childhood kisses formulates a safe space. Also, the recollection of ethnic food confirms Derek Walcott's statement: "You build according to the topography of where you live. You are what you eat, and so on" (Walcott 1977, 12). Hence, a return to childhood is a look inward to exile oneself from outside forces that negate rather than nourish a positive concept of the Self.

Shifting from the Safe Space

An uneasiness about living in France has been expressed in both Alie's and Ina Césaire's songs. When Césaire picked up her pen to compose songs, she was living in Martinique while Alie was in France. Although both hold French passports, their skin color separated and marked them as foreigners. Rather than accept an adaptation to France, they recreated their community of birth abroad to negate isolation and nostalgia. Their writing of "Exil" and "Caressé moins" resurrected their culture and reconnected the umbilical cord to their birth mother (Martinique) while they were living with their stepmother (France). Through the medium of their song lyrics they retrieved their Martinican identity to dispel the notion of not belonging. Finally, rather than dwell on the fragmentation of the Caribbean cultural identity, Alie and Césaire focused on home.

In July 1996, Déclic released Malavoi's *Shè Shé* (Searching), an album which is based upon an idea suggested by Ina Césaire about Simeline and Marie, two elder Martinican women in their seventies who lived in a neighborhood called Quartier Destiné, located on a hilltop not far from an unidentified town. Simeline, sitting in her rocking chair, dreams about her youth, marriage, and children. Her most frequent reverie is a search for answers to explain why family members migrated, promised to return, but rarely did. Structured like a lyrical novel that begins with a dream and ends with a return to the site of the original dream, the title song "Shè Shé" asks questions such as the following: "Ki sa mwen wè" (What have I seen?), "Ki sa mwen shèshé" (What have I retained?), and "Ki sa mwen kité" (What have I forsaken?).[20] The answers are found in the dedication of *Shè Shé:*

A tous nos amis de rêverie
Nos frères venus d'ailleurs
Mères et soeurs, cousins d'Amérique
Bâtisseurs d'irréel, buveurs de l'éternité
Citoyens d'une nouvelle alliance
Nous que la mer tient séparés
Mais que la terre en tournant rapproche de notre île de paroles
Nous vous saluons, invités à la table du continent des langues
Que les mots, les notes, les mélodies et les rythmes nous unissent.

~~~~~~~~~~

(To all our daydreaming friends.
Our brothers who come from elsewhere.
Mothers, sisters, and cousins from the Americas.
Builders of the unreal drinkers of eternity.
Citizens of a new alliance.
We whom the earth by turning draws closer
to our island of words.
We greet you, guests at the table of the continent of languages.
May the words, the notes, the melodies. and the rhythms unite us.)

To bring some clarity to the exile issue, Rosine previously said: "We have come to realize that we need to identify our culture before we can make political progress. During the seventies there was the political struggle for independence. Today, we fight differently, we fight culturally."[21] With Malavoi's music, Rosine was adamant about two co-existing aspects. He described the first as "an inscribed regional aspect in the rhythms and in the manner of expressing how one feels." And for him, the second was "universal in terms of technique and the interpretation of music with a violin."

The creation of a safe space of childhood and exile via music and thoughtful lyrics exposes how the Malavoi songwriters searched for a self-definition by returning to the root of their band's name. Fully apprized of Martinique's sugarcane history, Rosine adapted the lyrics of a traditional song called "Malavoi" and changed its musical arrangement; this revised version became the band's signature song.

A particularly rare variety of sugarcane, *malavoi* was a means of survival and nourishment to slaves during the era of slavery. In addition, the plant's

unusually rich sugar content yielded high returns in its processed state to the
béké owners of the sugar and rum factories. However, the Black canecutters
who worked under miserable conditions did not benefit economically:

O voi sé o voi Malavoi é sé Matinik
Kel joli plan bagay la
Lè blan poté la Matinik Gwadloup
Koko péi sé an bagay nou tout' ewmé
Kan' Malavoi sé an bagay ka wanôté
Way lè blan poté voyé
Poté vini la Matinik Gwadloup

Man ka bwé wonm man ka limin
Man ka jwé sébi
Man libétin man toumanti pasé péson
Way lè blan poté voyé
Poté vini la Matinik Gwadloup

Mansé Léoni
Malavoi pa diksioné
Malavoi peni pikan

〰〰〰〰〰〰

(This sugarcane called malavoi truly symbolizes Martinique.
What a wonderful plant the whites brought
to Martinique and Guadeloupe.
The coconut is a fruit we all love,
but malavoi sugarcane is a plant that yields high returns.
Oh! The colonists had it brought here.
Had it brought to Martinique and Guadeloupe.

I drink my rum, I smoke and
I play dice.
I'm a free man, a man more tormented than others.
Oh! The whites brought the plant here
to Martinique and Guadeloupe.

Listen Miss Léonie.
Malavoi sugarcane doesn't have a thousand leaves.
Malavoi sugarcane isn't prickly.)[22]

The literal translation of the Creole term *diksioné* is dictionary, but in relation to the song, it translates into "doesn't have a thousand leaves," rendering
the interpretation of "no complications." The speaker's sarcastic tone and
references to leaves and thorns imply that all is not well with the canecutters.
Yet in the first refrain the canecutters declare: "Man libétin man toumanti
pasé péson" (I am a free man, a more tortured man than others). This indicates that the speaker supports the song's first lines, which state that "O voi
sé o voi Malavoi é sé Matinik / Kel joli plan bagay la / Lè blan poté la Matinik
Gwadloup" (This sugar cane called *Malavoi* truly symbolizes Martinique /
What a wonderful plant / the whites brought to Martinique and Guadeloupe). This stance, of course, is in opposition to Joseph Zobel's *La Rue
cases-nègres* (1950) and Simone Schwarz-Bart's *Pluie et vent sur Télumée
Miracle* (1972), where the canefields are hot and prickly and represent the
oppressive past. The band Malavoi sees this variety of sugarcane in a different light, reinventing it as a musical rhetoric of protest and utilizing it in a
more subtle way to deal with colonial domination.

This reinvention of the past and a symbolic return to a safe place are
not exclusive to French Caribbean musicians. For example, the South African writer, Njabulo Ndebele, writes likewise about the intimacy of home in
connection with his twenty years of exile (Ndebele 1996, 28). For Ndebele,
home is the entire country associated with long memories and a concept of
belonging to a historic process. Upon his return he sees a South Africa
that had previously been denied, a home where the enrichment of an ethical
consciousness in the public domain can be reconstituted through social insight.

In a similar vein, the Malavoi songwriters not only reach back to the history of Martinique's sugarcane but also recall and blend different rhythms,
dispersing seeds across the African diaspora which collide and create a synthesis, a new social insight. For instance, in Soime's "Mizik Mat'nik" (Martinican dimension) the West African country of Guinea represents their ancestral homeland:

Lè nou sôti Guiné
Rasin nou pas rashé
Gren-la dan san nou
Y ka mashé

Nou ni fôs la
Tou lè jou fòk li parèt

~~~~~~~~~~

(Torn we were from Guinea
though our roots weren't torn away.
It's our seed that's opened countless trails.
Forging our force.
The one we draw on every day.)[23]

Theirs is not so much a search for their African origin (like Ndebele and the négritude writers); it is an effort to rebridge the gap with the spiritual continent of Africa. Although the song articulates an interest in Guinea, it is based on hearsay and oral tales rather than on actual concrete knowledge. As a consequence, the Martinican home, fixed in the history of the malavoi sugarcane, fills their immediate emotional needs. Whereas the sea, which has always been in movement and a conduit for the Middle Passage, carries their *gren* (seed) back to their ancestral home of Guinea.

By choosing childhood and exile, two "in between" safe spaces, and reintegrating themselves into a familiar milieu, the Malavoi songwriters are afforded a search for origins fixated in the nostalgic past. The danger resides not in resisting the reality of exile but in remaining rooted in nostalgia and disorientation. Like exile itself, the songs are both escapist and adaptive with stress-free and sentimental music. For example, Rosine's description of Martinican people in the 1988 "Gens moins" (My people) is honest: "Yo santimantal / Lanmou yo pasioné" (They are sentimental / Love impassions them).[24] He simultaneously refers to the generosity and compassion that some of his people display towards others and notes how they draw on a variety of cultural influences. As a matter of fact, Rosine has said:

We are very special people. We have been impacted by French culture, but we live far from France in a Caribbean milieu populated by the English, the Spanish, etc. We hear Latin American music. . . . We also have our own music. We consider the diverse elements; they are a part of us. We live in this universe. (Erwan 1987, 21)

Exile causes an awakening through feelings of restlessness and unease, a questioning of personal and national identities, a probing into the past, and an interrogation of the future. Exile is also a way to look critically at oneself and one's nation from afar. It provides a means and a venue for a new vision of the country left behind. Exile causes one to alter his or her perspective and is crucial in defining place. Consequently, Malavoi transfers memory into its songs to capture the soul and spirit of Martinique and its people before being overcome by socio-political ambivalence. By reexamining their childhoods and past customs, the songwriters utilize nostalgia to keep them creative enough to reclaim the Martinican landscape as a redemptive feature.

Without question, Malavoi, like Martinique, spans the two worlds of the Caribbean and France. The fact that Malavoi's band members move between the two locations attests to this. The recycling of the past is the first strategy for forging a national consciousness. To look critically at oneself and one's country is not easy, but the two safe spaces of childhood and exile enable one to begin the first step toward an interrogation of the future. Yves-Marie Séraline and Michel Traoré's one-hour film, *Viva Malavoi* (Long live Malavoi), which premiered on RFO Martinique on 1 January 1984, both pays tribute to Malavoi and allows the band's music to speak for itself.

Since Rosine's death in 1993, the Martinican population has been wondering about Malavoi's future. Without a doubt, Rosine's death leaves a great void, but the remaining members are determined to continue the legacy of producing music rooted in the Caribbean experience. Thus, Malavoi's nostalgic, nomadic musicians and songwriters emphasize cultural affirmation, value an idyllic childhood, and express a longing for the maternal warmth and sensual embrace of Martinique. Although they privilege childhood and exile, they are gradually fashioning a Martinique where one questions French departmentalization and regionalism. The Barbadian novelist George Lamming once remarked, "to be in exile is to be alive" (Lamming 1960, 24), opening a passageway into both a very vital space and a transitional phase which will lead into others that are even more expressive and self-affirming for French Caribbean musicians and songwriters.

2 creole, zouk, and identity in kassav's optimistic songs

The high point of the Kassav' mania was in the 1980s. It was impossible to escape hearing one or more of Kassav's songs on the radio airwaves or even in the streets of the main cities of Martinique and Guadeloupe. In fact, my first contact with Kassav' and its zouk music occurred in March 1988 when I traveled to Guadeloupe. While walking along the hot, steamy concrete sidewalks near the waterfront in downtown Pointe-à-Pitre, the melodies and lyrics of "Mwen malad-aw" (I'm sick with love of it) and "Syé bwa" (Saw the wood) were heard over and over. Having lived in Zaire, a country located in Central Africa and the birth place of soukous, I assumed the band playing the two songs had to be Zairean. Subsequently, I accosted several people about the two songs I kept hearing.

"Who is that singer with that odd voice?"

"It's Jacob Desvarieux of Kassav', a Guadeloupean who grew up in Senegal."

"Is the band Zairean or Guadeloupean?"

"Neither one. It is a zouk band composed of Guadeloupean, Martinican, African, and French métro musicians."

Guadeloupeans were playing Kassav' records in their homes, and posters advertising Kassav's *Vini pou* (1987) were on display in the record stores. Curious, I grabbed several of Kassav's albums along with band members' Jocelyne Béroard's *Siwo* (1985) and Jean-Philippe Marthély and Patrick Saint Éloi's *Ou pa ka sav* (1985). I asked a record salesman in one of the stores for permission to listen to my selections. Determined to make a sale, the salesman bombarded me with stories about Kassav'. Not having to be nudged, I purchased *Vini pou,* which was to be the first of my growing collection of Kassav's productions.

In 1994, I met with Sonia Marthély (Jean-Philippe's wife); she advised me to get in touch with Béroard (Kassav's only woman soloist), which I proceeded to do with a letter. One February morning I heard the phone ringing on the second floor where I was staying. I had just gone downstairs and opened the front door to catch a public bus. Regardless, I only hesitated for a split second before running back upstairs to answer the phone. To my surprise, it was Béroard telephoning from Paris to say that she had received my letter and was planning a trip to Martinique.

To give Béroard time to be with her family, I waited two days to call her after her presumed arrival in Martinique. Her father answered the phone and told me that his daughter had fallen ill and canceled her trip. Crestfallen, I called Béroard at her home in Paris and asked if she would be rescheduling her visit. Her response was that Kassav' was working under a time constraint to complete the mixing and dubbing of the upcoming *Difé* album. However, would it be possible for me to come to Paris? My answer, of course, was a loud "Yes."

In May 1995, I flew to Paris to spend a week with friends and to interview Kassav' at Studio Zorrino. For two days my body throbbed from the heavy bass on "Difé, soupapé" (Too much pressure). In between the dubbing sessions, I interviewed three members of Kassav'. All four of us were nervous. To my shame, I spoke with Béroard for two hours unaware that the tape recorder had not been turned on. Béroard had noticed the tape was not turning, but she was too embarrassed to tell me. Luckily, she was amenable to redoing the interview the next day.

That same day I spoke to Jean-Claude Naimro who plays the keyboard, composes, and arranges many songs for Kassav'. Naimro talked about his first solo album *En balaté* (1985) and his three songs: "Ou chanjé" (You've changed), "Pèd filaou" (You have lost your destiny), and "An mouvman" (In movement). Later that same day, when I interviewed Patrick Saint Éloi, I found him to be the opposite of Béroard and Naimro. His body language indicated that he was not thrilled about giving an interview. In the beginning his answers were monosyllabic. Frustrated, I told him that I was tongue-tied and nervous. Stunned by my admissions, Saint Éloi (who is actually a very shy and introverted person off stage) replied that he was just as nervous because he had never been interviewed by an American professor. After this revelation, the interview went smoothly, especially when I questioned Saint Éloi about the symbolism of light, rain, and dreams.

Ironically, I did not get to meet Claude Vamur, the Kassav' trap drummer, until another trip to Guadeloupe six months later. Vamur was in Guadeloupe with Kassav' to promote the *Difé* album. Just before a sold-out concert was to begin, Kassav' discovered that the microphones had been stolen. After heated exchanges and a three-hour search for more microphones, Kassav', to its discomfort, had to face a very angry crowd in the Baie Mahault stadium and perform with one microphone. Yet, as soon as Jacob Desvarieux struck the first chord on his guitar, the unruly, boisterous crowd settled down. Then a woman yelled out, "Vas-y, Jacob.

Amuses-nous bien! (Play it, Jacob. Entertain us well), a signal for the audience to dance and sing for the rest of Kassav's three-hour concert.

The next week I kept my appointment with Freddie Marshall at the Centre Culturel des Arts. Marshall had been one of Kassav's first promoters in the late 1970s. In his company was Vamur, who agreed to meet with me on another day to discuss his two solo albums *(Lévé mwen* and *Héritage pou . . .)* and work with Kassav'. A man of his word, Vamur and I did meet two days later, and we discussed, among many topics, the blending of the gwo ka mendé rhythm into zouk. To emphasize his point, he hummed and played the mendé rhythm on the dining room table.

~~~~~~

Creole is the main medium of communication in the Caribbean. We speak Creole. We need Creole. We cannot function without Creole. MERLE HODGE (1990, 204)

Within the political context of the French overseas departments, Martinicans and Guadeloupeans take opposing sides about the status and importance of French and Creole. Whereas Martinicans have been ambivalent about the use of Creole outside an informal setting, Guadeloupeans advocate Creole as a political banner. After centuries of being forbidden from speaking Creole in school, in other formal sectors, and in some "respectable" homes, French Caribbean people are now proud to speak Creole partially due to the impact of Kassav's zouk music for the last eighteen years, an interest that goes beyond local boundaries. For instance, after a 1990 visit to Martinique, Jean-Pierre Jardel, a French sociologist from the Université de Nice, commented on the changed status of Creole even in Paris:

When I was in Martinique, Creole did not officially exist. People spoke it only among friends, in their homes, etc. A movement began and drew in others in the 1970s. Then in 1976 I left Martinique for four years and had the biggest surprise to hear Creole spoken at Orly [Airport] to announce the departure of planes destined for Martinique and Guadeloupe.[1]

No doubt about it, the use of Creole has been surrounded in controversy for much of the twentieth century. The arguments have centered upon its viability as a language and its usefulness in international circles. The controversy and arguments are tied into the ambivalence of, and silent acceptance by, French Caribbeans regarding their position as colonized subjects, since

primacy has traditionally been accorded to the French language. An insidi-
ous way of subjugating and colonizing the Caribbean subjects was to wipe
out their indigenous language(s) and to invalidate the Creole language they
created during forced enslavement. Without a voice or valid language, the
colonized Caribbeans posed no threat to the French colonizers and their policy that French was the true language.

During the mid-1970s, the linguist Jean Bernabé and his team of teachers
at the Université des Antilles et de la Guyane in Martinique formed the
Groupe d'Etudes et de Recherches de la Créolophonie (GEREC) which,
through its journal publications *Espace créole* and *Mofwaz,* built up an interest in the study of Creole.[2] The GEREC group debated, but never resolved, two issues about Creole within its publications: (1) the creation of
an orthographical system to transcribe Creole into written form and (2)
the relationship between acrolect and basilect Creoles in connection with the
emergence of other interlectal forms.[3] Fully aware of these debates, the
newly formed musical group Kassav' chose, just like its predecessors, to
write in acrolect Creole, which closely resembled spoken French.

Situated between a rich oral tradition and a growing scribal one, the
founders of Kassav' set forth to create an optimistic Creole space and simultaneously brought the intellectual debates to a closure in its music. Initially,
a Guadeloupean group from the late 1970s until the early 1980s, its originators—Pierre-Edouard Décimus, George Décimus, and Jacob Desvarieux—
were compelled to adopt a Creole term heard throughout the French Caribbean for its group and a Martinican Creole word for its music. Their decision to mix the two Creoles stunned the radicals and autonomists but fell
clearly in line with the Guadeloupean Dany Bébel-Gisler's belief that Creole
was a language of resistance and the "umbilical cord binding Guadeloupeans to Africa, to others, and to ourselves" (Bébel-Gisler 1989, 23). By
pushing forward the open-endedness of Creole identity, language and music
for creative exchanges, the newly formed Kassav' positioned itself squarely
as an advocate for Creole, because orality functions as a counter discourse
to assimilation, regionalism, and departmentalization. Kassav's Creole lyrics
were situated in an optimistic space that was midway between French and
basilect Creole, and its music allowed the group to decipher its own reality,
bringing attention to events that were usually not visible.

Knowing that there have been battles over Creole and French, Kassav'
deliberately takes the position that Creole is the more important of the two.
Kassav's songwriters promote Creole by looking at its poetic beauty, rich
imagery, and rhythmic wordings within the fluid rhythm of a line. To capture
a larger international audience in the 1980s, Pierre-Edouard Décimus delib-

erated on how to make Creole as appealing as possible. He began to replace certain Creole sounds with others more easily assimilated by foreign ears. Having studied how to write Creole, Décimus was aware that "certain sounds in Creole could *heurter [les] oreilles* (offend the ears). He opted for a modified Creole that privileged the vowels i, a, è and o for a harmony that would express his *métissage culturel* (Western, African and Indian cultural mixing) leading to the formation of zouk music" (Ampigny 1992, 60).

Highly opinionated about Creole, Patrick Saint Éloi, one of the Kassav's soloists and songwriters, said: "It is imperative when one writes songs to follow the evolution of Creole expressions which are invented all the time. There is always a new word and it's necessary to be on the site to know it."[4] As for Décimus, he proclaimed, "We [Kassav'] do not compose in French for political reasons. I think in Creole when I compose my compositions and transcribe them in Creole on paper. I am not at ease with French and we [Kassav'] want to be known in Creole" (cited in Laurencine 1985, 18). The concept of "being known in Creole" is utilized in the natural rhythm and in the inflection of meaningful lyrics. Two examples are found in Jean-Philippe Marthély's "Ou pa ka sav" (You don't know) from *Ou pa ka sav* (1985) and "Ki non a manmanw" (What is your mother's name?) from *Gorée* (1986). In the first, Marthély conjugates the verb *savoir* (to know): "An pa ka sav / Ou pé ké sav / An pa jen sav" (I do not know / You will not know / I never know), and he repeats the ending of a phrase by producing subtle shifts to illustrate the versatility of Creole with the vowels "a" and "e." In the second, "Ki non a manmanw," Desvarieux, Saint Éloi, and Marthély insert the Guadeloupean "Ka ou fè?" (How are you?) and Martinican "Sa ou fè?" (How are you?) Creole greetings. This mixture of Guadeloupean and Martinican Creole within songs actually creates a new grammar for Kassav's compositions.

The popularity of zouk music, with its insistence upon Creole lyrics, is viewed as a social and political phenomenon. Max Jeanne states: "Cultural practices will take over as political acts and help to form a national consciousness" (cited in Ruprecht 1990, 121). To support Jeanne's statement, Kassav' and other zouk singers legitimize and elevate the status of Creole. Through their stage presence and concerts, zouk performers encourage a collective voice that creates a feeling of confidence and credibility. This stance appeals to the youth searching for a national identity. By establishing such an ideological space and pointing to Creole roots and identity, Kassav' and other groups—Taxikréol, Kwak, and Dissonance—empower their Guadeloupean and Martinican audiences to affirm an indigenous Caribbean cultural identity. Jean Bernabé, Patrick Chamoiseau, and Rafaël Confiant speak of Creoleness as an internal process of freedom and a new self-consciousness that enable the individual to envision his own depths: "That is to say: a freedom. And, trying in vain to use it, we perceived that there could be no internal vision without a prior acceptance of self. One could even say that the internal vision is the direct result of this acceptance" (Bernabé, Chamoiseau, and Confiant 1989, 29). Without question, Kassav's internal vision is derived from a positive acceptance of self. This self-acceptance is reinforced in its insistence upon creating Creole lyrics.

Kassav's Discovery of Zouk

Kassav' is a French Caribbean group that has had a major impact on the Caribbean and world music industries. Having sold over a million records worldwide, Kassav' has created much interest in its sophisticated, complex, heavily layered disco-like music called zouk. It is a band that networks and listens carefully to other sounds across diverse landscapes. Kassav's curiosity about harmony and search for new sounds also result in a physical and psychological movement beyond a departmentalized landscape—a movement that shows that a shared cultural landscape does not depend on a specific fixed site.

Most often, Kassav's singers/composers write about social harmony, emancipation, cultural consciousness, hope, and respect between women and men. Ironically, these themes are the opposite of what is actually taking place in Guadeloupe and Martinique, where youth unemployment is extremely high and people are still migrating to France. There are constant strikes which affect the operation of the airports, hospitals, banks, and post offices. A steady influx of illegal migrants arrives from Dominica, St. Lucia, and Haiti. The sudden arrival of European Union (E.U.) nationals, such as the Portuguese, Spanish, and Italians, is seen as a potential threat to the locals. Already, in public and private construction sites, many local masons and carpenters are being replaced by E.U. nationals. Also, the divorce rate and family violence are rising rather than declining. Yet, the most frequently heard music on the radio and television in the region is the lively, jumped-up zouk. The reason is defined by guitarist Jacob Desvarieux: "It is a language; it is a permanent festival. It indicates a mind-set rooted in joy, communication, and happiness" (cited in Plougastal 1986).

By teasing its audience with double-coded messages in tunes steeped with Caribbean landscape images, Kassav' manages to reveal the opposing sides of happiness and despair by firmly placing itself both inside and outside of the Caribbean. Through zouk music and lyrics, the multiracial band expresses a yearning and a hope for a return to social harmony with nature in connection with an identity that transcends confined, false, colonial boundaries. Kassav' also struggles with the domination of local and multinational record companies to establish its own creative landscape. Therefore, this chapter will explore how Kassav' creates an optimistic space with its zouk messages about identity centered in the Creole language.

The Creole name *kassav,* according to Kassav's only woman soloist, Jocelyne Béroard, "refers to a crushed cassava mixed with coconut and sugar to make a cake. . . . There is a kind of poison in it. You've got to know how to extract this poison before you eat it. . . . So because they had to extract what was poisoning Martinican and Guadeloupean music, they called it Kassav'."[5]

In the mid-1970s Pierre-Edouard Décimus, a sound technician and bass player for the Vikings de Guadeloupe for over ten years, became restless and wanted to create a new sound to counteract the Haitian influence. He enlisted his younger brother George (another bass player), and they released their first album, unavailable today, *Caso et Vikings de Guadeloupe Exploration* (1978). After leaving their producers, Freddie Marshall of Guadeloupe and Jacky Nayaradou of 3A Productions in Martinique, Décimus moved to Paris to start anew. In his efforts, he needed help from someone who could play Caribbean and other types of music, as well as be familiar with studio work. He found this person in the much-sought-after guitarist, Jacob Desvarieux, who had previously worked with him and Guy Jacquet (guitarist for the Vikings de Guadeloupe). Décimus, his brother, and Desvarieux added a horn section and modified the sound after listening to certain American groups—Kool and the Gang, Blood, Sweat, and Tears, and Earth, Wind, and Fire. This search for a new sound became an obsession, causing Décimus to utter the following:

> It's true that I conceived the idea. But without Jacob Desvarieux (to whom I pay homage on my next record) and my brother Georges Décimus, Kassav', without a doubt, would not have had the success it has had. . . . I had been Kassav's founder, bass player, and manager. I have done all I could possibly do within the group. . . . The music speaks directly to people's hearts. (Cited in Ampigny 1992, 60–61)

In Paris, in the late 1970s, the frustrated but determined Décimus continued his search to end the preference for Haitian music over the Guadeloupean and Martinican local music scene. Finally, in 1978, the three musicians launched a successful musical career that would break the dependence of Guadeloupe and Martinique on Haitian pop styles and have commercial appeal beyond the French Caribbean. First, after much sound experimentation and a close listening to other Caribbean music, as well as to South American, African, and African American music, the trio released Christmas and carnival records under the name *Soukoué Kô Ou* (Shake your body), utilizing the Guadeloupean *gwo ka* (or *ka*). Second, after enlisting Freddie Marshall's support as a musician, producer, and radio personality, the trio released *Love and Ka Dance* (1979) and *Lagué moin* (1980) under the name Kassav' and named their music "zouk." This new sound, according to Gene Scaramuzzo, was a marriage of "traditional Antillean musical elements with outside influences, all treated to the state-of-the-art Paris studio technology with which Desvarieux is so adept" (Scaramuzzo 1994, 30).

The choice of the term *zouk* and of the name *Kassav'* was strategic. *Zouk*, a Martinican Creole word, refers to a party at which the greatest freedom of expression is permitted. Since French Caribbean music is associated with singing and dancing, the hot, loud, and intense tempo of zouk encourages its listeners to jump-up in the streets, especially during Carnival time. Bearing this in mind, the formation of bands in Guadeloupe and Martinique previously had followed nationalistic lines. The Décimus brothers and Desvarieux, on the other hand, carefully selected singers and musicians over a five year period (1979–83) based upon their qualifications rather than a French nationality.[6]

Kassav' songs deal with love and hope while revealing a need to free themselves from the imperialistic chains of the music and recording industry. Careful attention to Kassav's *An-ba-chen'n la* (1985) reveals tracks about how zouk puts a person in such a frenzy that she/he is sick with love of it ("Mwen malad'aw"); how a man sees a female *matador* and falls to his knees ("Filé zètwal");[7] and how a woman wakes up to a bad day and derives comfort from her music ("Mové jou"). Each song introduces its listener to a different fusion of musical styles. As each song unfolds, it draws the listener into a world of West African highlife, Congolese soukous, African American blues and jazz, or Haitian compas. However, the heavy bass is always there with horns, a snazzy keyboard, a mixture of drum rhythms, and a hard rock guitar. In zouk, rhythms are built on top of each other, making it the most frequently heard music on the radio and television in the French Caribbean region and causing Edouard Glissant to observe that "the contemporary artist is engaged in becoming the spokesperson of the collective consciousness of the people, recalling lived history and inspiring future action" (Glissant 1989, 236).

Colonialism, imperialism, and transregional migration have devastated the Caribbean region economically and left its populations struggling for survival. Fully aware of the ongoing struggle to weather the effects of colonization, Patrick Saint Éloi, one of Kassav's soloists, synthesized a concentrated use of images to compose the title song, "An-ba-chen'n la" (Weighed down by the chains). This song recalls a landscape that carries a turbulent and violent history:

> Byen souvan nou ka pati lwen
> Lwen di péyi nou
> Pou nou pòté mizik
> An nou alé
> I ja lè pou lè mond savé
> Kè léz Antiy ka ègzisté
> Kè sé lanmou ki ka koumandé nou
> Asi pon an
> Nou si solèy
> Adan tchè nou
> Nou ni tanbou
> Farin manniok, épi koko, épi shalè
> I ja lè pou lè mond savé
> kè léz Antiy ka ègzisté
> Kè sé lanmou ki ka koumandé nou
> A nou piti tou piti

> Ni on sèl solèy
> Ni on line
> É ni on sèl Kassav'
> Osi kon sé le di
> Van la van la ja ka tounen
> Zouk la pwen on lòt direksyon
> Pou èksplozé
> Pou inondé lè mond antié

> Nèg la téja konèt nèg la
> Manyè dansé bòd lanmè la
> Tou sa pou yo té pé maré yo
> Anba chen on bato-w
> Démaré! anba chen'n la maré
> Anba chen on bato-w

Ni dé sièk
Bato la rentré,
Ni sa ki janmen rivé
Eskè lèspri an nou maré
Toujou anba chen on bato
Démaré!

Sé la bato la ladjé mwen
Bon djé mèsi mwen byen kontan
Si zòt vlé mwen ké di sa
Pouki sa mwen pé ké janmen pati
Pouki
Di nou pouki
Sé la kè mwen apwan lavi
Sé la kè mwen konèt lanmou
A si on pyé fwomagè non
An é non an mwen téja maké

Anba chen-la maré
Anba chen on bato-w demaré
Anba chen la bato
Sé la listwa menné nou
Jòdi la sa ké vini

~~~~~~~~~~~~

(Quite often we travel
very far from our home
to make our music known elsewhere.
It's about time for the world to know
that the Caribbean is a part of it,
and that we breathe love from it.
On the bridge we have the sun, and
in our heart, the drum
as well as manioc, coconut,
and heat.
It's about time for the world to know
that the Caribbean is a part of it
and that we breathe love from it.
Too small, too little

There's only one sun
and one moon.
There is also only one Kassav'.
The wind turned,
and zouk arrived
to explode and inundate
the entire world.

The Black man already knows
his Black brother led him
to dance along the river
so that they can be prisoners
chained in the boat.

Two centuries ago
the boat arrived.
Many did not finish the journey.
Are our spirits still chained
to the bottom of that boat?
Unchain yourself.

It is here where we disembark.
My God, how pleased I am.
If you want, I will tell you
why I will never leave from here.
Why?
Tell us why?
It's here where I learned about life
It's here where I encountered love.
Under the *fromager*
our names were already written.
Chained.
We were chained in the bottom of the boat.)[8]

Saint Éloi additionally evokes a landscape of chained bodies, facing horror, punishment and death during the Middle Passage. He brings to the surface that people far from home should hear Kassav's music. Then, with confidence, he offers the hopeful solution that zouk will seduce and captivate the entire world. Saint Éloi predicts a continuity through the musical medium of zouk that crosses the landscape between the colony and its colonizer and the internal landscape within the Caribbean islands and the African diaspora. Paying homage to the supernatural world, the singer also refers to the burial of the slaves' name underneath the *fromager* (a sandbox tree associated with obeah and known as the hiding place for zombies).

Kassav's tour to Senegal in West Africa provided Saint Éloi, the talented musician, singer, and songwriter, with the venue and subject material for "An-ba-chen'n la." One of the most memorable excursions for him was the visit to the museum on Gorée Island, where slaves had been held in abominable conditions for exportation to the New World. Saint Éloi saw the cramped rooms, the rusty chains, and "the window of no return." This museum had a direct impact on his music after he listened to the rhythms of Senegalese drums. According to Saint Éloi, the visit to Gorée Island caused him to have haunting dreams about slavery upon his return to France.[9] He could not enjoy a peaceful sleep until he wrote "An-ba-chen'n la." By actively writing and singing the song, Saint Éloi threw off the shackled chains (haunted dreams) and underwent a rebirth. Therefore, for Saint Éloi, zouk negates the colonial acculturation that prioritizes French cultural elements, proving that *delving within* rather than outside one's own African ancestry and French Caribbean landscape provides the answer for the future.

Harmony and Hope

Zouk is primarily a dance music, and its rhythm is more important to its French Caribbean listener than the lyrics. Consequently, people are quick to say that Kassav's songs are nonsensical and "lightweight." As soon as one pays attention to Kassav's compositions, it is obvious that great care is allocated to the wording. The songs' themes range from nostalgic references and a longing for one's island landscape to social commentary, male/female relationships, and harmony and hope. In 1983, Desvarieux's song "Banzawa"[10] on the album *Banzawa* with George Debs Productions was popular, but it was George Décimus' hit "Zouk-la sé sèl médikaman nou ni" (Zouk is the only medicine we have) on *Yélélé* (G. Debs 1984) which boosted the band to international stardom (see chapter 5).

Kassav's abandonment of the "mother" islands for France brings forth a strong form of nostalgia for the very landscape it left. The self-exiled Décimus, Naimro, and Saint Éloi are alienated and suffer from the cold French weather and people. Yet the three performers recapture and reinstate their islands' traditions in alternating open, oblique, or subtle ways. In Pierre-Edouard Décimus's "Wonderful," found on *Kassav' #3* (1980), a woman and man's intimate communion with the island landscape lives in their blood. Every time Décimus has the chance, he returns to Guadeloupe. The tune "Wonderful" expresses his exact emotions:

Lè mwen débaké
En tè kon, on boug fou
Paskè mwen touvé péyi la wonderful

~~~~~~~~~~~~~~

(When I landed,
I was like a fool
because I found the country to be wonderful.)[11]

Clearly, Décimus neither finds France to be beautiful nor wonderful. He continues with "Senti jan sé moun la yé / Sé moun la yé / Yo ka limé difé / Lè yo ka dansé / Gadé jan sé moun la yé / Jan moun la yé" (Feel the people's energy / the way they are / Feel their heat / when they dance / Just look at way they are / the way they are).[12] For Décimus, Guadeloupe is a place where people openly express their feelings and dance with abandon. He becomes spontaneous in this familiar landscape imbued with bright colors that stimulate his psyche.

Jean-Claude Naimro's first recorded romantic ballad "Korosol" (Soursop) from *Yélélé* recalls his love for Martinique with its exotic fruit, the *korosol*. He explains he deliberately chose korosol because it is indigenous to the Caribbean while pineapples, coconuts, and mangoes are found also in Asia and Africa.[13] Korosol is a bumpy, thin-skinned delicate fruit with a unique, sour flavor that, when sweetened, is appropriate for a homemade sherbet or a delicious drink. Equating his nostalgia for Martinique with korosol is like contrasting the cement walkways, skyscrapers, hectic pace, and anonymity of France with the lush greenery, sandy beaches, and slower rhythm of the Caribbean. In short, korosol is his solace after he has resided in France:

> "Korosol" is a title that speaks about the return to one's country because Antilleans who are in Paris suffer from nostalgia. I wanted to translate the people's emotions who live in France and can no longer return to the French Antilles. It is why I get angry with God so that I can return home where it is hot.[14]

In 1992, Kassav' starred in Euzhan Palcy's film *Siméon,* which relates the tale of a French Caribbean man who desires to be known as a guitarist, composer, and creator of a music that would be popular worldwide. "Mwen alé" (My departure) and "Mwen viré" (My return) are two of the songs written by Béroard for the movie and that appear on *Tekit izi* (1992). In "Mwen alé," Siméon, the main character in the film, recites the mixed feelings that he encounters upon leaving his island for France. His departure is linked to those who have already left before him. The mothers who remain behind cannot be forgotten, for they cry out at night for their children's safe return. Upon Siméon's departure his daughter's parting statement of encouragement, "Ou pé alé / Trasé chimin-w / Woulé é é" (You can leave / Follow your path / Go there),[15] echoes that of the mothers. Siméon's response is "Mwen la ka tchembé / Pas a pa lòt bò / An té ké vlé mò / A pa lòt bò / An té ké lé mò" (I am holding on / because I do not want to die / far from my country / It isn't over here / where I want to die).[16]

Later, in "Mwen viré," Béroard sings of Siméon's desire to leave behind the greyness of Paris in order to feel some sun on his skin because, like a tree, he cannot grow if his roots are cut off. Stable tree roots promise growth and recovery associated with courage. As a result, Siméon recalls his island's familiar geography to offset the insecurity of living abroad and to avoid experiencing a cultural discontinuity. Also, it is music that sustains Siméon, brings him fame, and enables him to return to his island home in triumph. What Siméon has in his heart is expressed in his fingertips on the guitar. The drums make him vibrate; the island rhythms flow and surround him.

The Soloists' Love Songs

Enhancing his career with several solo albums, Saint Éloi, called *chanteur de charme* (singer of charm) and *kréyòl lover* (Creole lover), attributes his career boom to "West Indies" from his *Misik-cé lan mou* (1982). Composer of double-coded, poetic songs of hypnotic imagery, he invents a vital, sensuous, and vibrant Caribbean. Also, under the guise of delivering a song about the Caribbean, Saint Éloi's lyrics duplicate copulation: "Lè mwen santi an ti lodè vanille / Mwen sav sé-w / ki ka vini doudou" (Whenever I smell vanilla / I know that it's you, darling / who is coming).[17] Associating the smell of vanilla with sweet things, soft textures, and sensual pleasures, Saint Éloi proceeds with "Mè doudou ou tèlman dous apré lanmou" (But darling you are so sweet after making love) and ends with "An dékolaj' ankò / pou nou sa monté, monté, monté" (Another trip together / so that we can get higher), intimating that the love act will be repeated more than once. The couple vibrates to the sensual quality of the Caribbean landscape, is entangled and interconnected with the landscape, and moves toward a mutual burst of life.

This fusion of man, woman, and landscape reveals Saint Éloi's passion for a land, symbolizing a receptive woman's body. His vision of the Caribbean, and in particular Guadeloupe, is caught between sensation and memory, for "Ti zouézo ka shèshé flè pou butiné" (Birds are looking for flowers to gather nectar). The ascending melodic phrase of "West Indies" accentuates Saint Éloi's voice as he pronounces "an dékolaj' ankò" (another trip together) to set the stage where passions are enacted.

The romantic relationships, explored in Saint Éloi's lyrical texts as well as those by Jean-Philippe Marthély, establish a new rapport between women and men. Instead of projecting a macho image to support the rumor that there are three women for each man in the French Caribbean, the two song-writers equate love with vulnerability, doubt, fear, and respect for women. With great emotion and much tenderness, Marthély, a second tenor, sings about a man's deep love for his wife in the beautiful ballad "Bèl kréati" (Beautiful creature) from *Touloulou* (1984).[18]

Épi ti mélodi ta la, sé sèl manyè
Mwen ké fè-w wouè, ou ké konprann ou ké sézi
Bon djé sa mwen ka fè, si ou pa la

〰〰〰〰〰〰

(This song is my only way of making you see,
understand and grasp.
God knows I'm lost without you.)[19]

So dependent on his wife's support, Marthély, without hesitation, also sings "Mwen ka tatoné mwen avègle / Sé tròp pou mwen / San ou doudou pa ni jou pa ni lannuit" (I grope along like a blind person / I need support / Without you, my love, there's neither day nor night). In retrospect, Marthély does not think that he would be as successful as he is if his wife had not helped him to build up his self-esteem in the tough world of entertainment.

Switching from this slow, tender, and very personal ballad, Marthély moans, groans, shouts, and scats on the sexy "Sé pa djen-djen" (It's not a joke) from *An-ba-chen-n la*. Again, the message is about a loving relationship between a man and a woman, but this time Marthély extends it to encompass a fusion of the spiritual and the physical:

Sé pa sèlman kò dan kò
Sé tèt la ki pli enpòrtan

Gadé ki jan i ka ba nou bon la fòs
Pou nou pé wouè douvan nou
Ko nou ka dékolé tchè
Nou toujou ansamn menm'
Menm' lè nou lwen yo ka bat menm' jan

~~~~~~~~~

(It's not only our bodies together that count.
The way we treat each other is more important.
Look how we're getting stronger
to think clearly about the future.
Our bodies rise with our hearts together.
Even when we are apart,
our hearts beat to the same rhythm.)[20]

The Creole expression *djen-djen* (making fun of everything) implies foolishness and childish behavior. Reinforced by the chorus with a heavy bass, Marthély places a great importance on the absence of *djen-djen*. He begs the woman to *gadé* (look at) him so that they can *réfléchi* (reflect together) as a couple. The verb *réfléchir* (to reflect) is repeated twice with an emphasis on the first syllable. Then Marthély adds "*réfleksyon* (let's reflect), acknowledging that both parties are actively engaged in their relationship. To assure the woman that he loves her, he coaxes her with "Wouvé zyé / lévé tèt / pa kité douvan prann-w" (Open your eyes / Lift up your head / Think ahead).[21] If she looks directly at him, she will surely know that their love is planted in a firm ground.

Saint Éloi reveals that men feel, hurt, and betray as do women. For example, on his fourth solo album, *Zoukamine* (1994), he relates the tale of an older man who loves a younger woman in "Ki jan ké fè" (What am I going to do?).[22] Reversing the stereotypical male power role within a relationship, Saint Éloi introduces a man who loves a younger woman who has left him. He tries to persuade her to return, because "Tou sa ki senp / toujou pli bèl / Nou té ja konprann sa / Pou enmé pani laj" (Simple things / are always more beautiful / We had understood this / Love does not care about age).[23] Saint Éloi's lyrics, writes Jocelyne Guilbault, "are considered by many Antilleans of both sexes to be a true revolution in the song-text traditions of their countries" (Guilbault et al. 1993, 158). This baring of Saint Éloi's soul about a man's vulnerability when he loves establishes a pattern and inspires other French Caribbean men and women to compose such lyrics.

Saint Éloi's metaphors of a wounded bird who cannot fly, a hat blown in the wind, and a cloud on his life are combined to describe the disappointment and hurt that creep into a relationship in "Pa douté" (Don't doubt). To explain his choice of metaphors, Saint Éloi says:

> The image of the wounded bird is weak, but it is also a bird that can leave. There are two connotations and I frequently return to them. When one counts on someone, it is with the expectation of being appreciated. Sometimes external elements disrupt this joy because there are jealous people so one must be on guard. If the couple wants to get together again, the man only asks for one solution, which is for the woman not to doubt him and his love.[24]

The man is both wounded and bewildered when the woman that he loves is incapable of accepting the fact that he has never been unfaithful to her. Refusing to give up, he affirms that "Mwen pa janmen menti ba ou" (I never cheated on you) and asks the open-ended question: "Poutchi ou ka douté di mwen" (Why do you doubt me?).[25] Hence, he, the wounded bird, does not evade flight but has a confrontation with the object of his love. Though the rain cloud obscures the woman's vision, it can bring, at the same time, light and trust.

Working with Béroard gave Saint Éloi and other male members of Kassav' a certain amount of sensitivity toward women. On a RFO television show in Guadeloupe, Saint Éloi stated: "As a composer you must pay close attention to your surroundings and details, be observant and aware of the illusions."[26] What attracted Saint Éloi to women were their eyes. For "Si cé oui" (If it's yes) from *Bizouk* (Zouk kiss), a woman was told that "Sé en dé zyé-w ka mwen ké konprann sa" (It's through your two eyes that I will understand). To make sure that his point was well taken, the sentence, "Ou sé an mòso a mwen ki dous é ki sa fè mal" (You are a part of me that is soft and hurts), had to be repeated four times. For the duet "Silans" (Silence) on *Difé* (1995), Saint Éloi alternated between Creole and French with the guest singer Della Miles. His and Miles's voices blended together as one as they narrated the story of lovers who engaged in a silent communication with their eyes. Saint Éloi categorically announced in Creole, "Silans-la ka palé an zyé-w" (Silence speaks through your eyes); Miles responded in French, "Et tes yeux qui disent toujours je t'aime / Je t'aime, en silence" (And your eyes which still say I love you / I love you silently).[27] The two engaged in a call-and-response and harmonized well along with the chorus. The silence, in question, needed to be broken so that the man could sing about his unfailing love despite the woman's downcast eyes. He cautioned his beloved to remember to "Sonjé byen sa nou té di / Si nwasè tonbé asi nou / On limyè kè nou té séré toujou la pou lanmou" (Remember what we said / should a sad fate befall us / A hidden light within us / will always be there for love). Sounding like a film score with thirty-five violins, "Silans," the last song on *Difé* (Heat), with Saint Éloi's bilingual creative lyrics, was appreciated after the intensity of the other eleven songs.

In "Ou chanjé" (You have changed) from *Tekit izi* (Take it easy), Naimro relates how distance and mistrust can creep into a relationship when the husband is unfaithful.

> Mwen ka dan lavi sa ka konté
> Séki ou rivé viv on armoni
> Sa pa fasil mwen té konprann
> Nou té ja dépasé
> Sa lé zòt' pa ka rivé kontwolé
> Mé aktyalman mwen konstaté ou chanjé
> Palé-w di sa pa menm branché
> Poutchi mwen menm mwen sé an nonm osi

> Mwen té pé mò pou mwen pé sa gadé-w
> Pourtan fout ou chanjé
> Ou toujou ka révé ni de jou-w ka sòti
> Mwen kabyen risanti ki ou prèsé pati
> Mé, fout ou chanjé
> Mannyè palé-w chanjé
> Ni de nouvo silans épi nouvel absans
> Pa djè retéw paysans
> Ou byen chanjé, chanjé
> Ou di mwen bonswè san menm jété an zyé
> Ou ni mal tèt
> Ou pa lè mwen palé
> Mwen douvan-w ka fè sanblan
> Mé mwen ja konprann
> Zyé mwen ka wouè zimaj mé tèt mwen ka pansé
> Ki janmen di mwen-w chanjé
> Palé-w di sa ou ja troublé
> Poutchi mwen menm sé nonm osi

Mwen té voudré twouvé an moun
Pou di ki sa pa vré
Ou byen chanjé

Dousè zyé-w chanjé osi
Mwen ja ka diviné
Ki tchè-w an balans
Soufrans mwen koumansé
Si ou chanjé, chanjé
Pétèt mwen menm osi chanjé
Dé lè mwen tou jenné
Difè-w dé ti karès
Lè ou sòti lan mès
Ou byen chanjé
Sonmèy ou ajité
Lavi mwen chalviré, préokipé

∿∿∿∿∿∿∿

(I think that what counts in life
is to be able to live in harmony.
It is far from easy.
I believe that
we have surpassed
what others have had a hard time controlling.
But now, I've noticed you have changed.
I have tried to talk to you about it.
Tell me why you avoid a conversation.

I am only a man who would give
his life to keep you.
How you have changed.
You are always dreaming.
Some days when you are going out
you are in a hurry.
How you have changed.
Even the way you speak has changed.
There are new silences, new absences,
and you are hardly ever patient.
How you have changed.

You told me "Good night"
without even looking at me.
You have a headache.
You don't even want to hear me speak.
I am too near to you to pretend,
but I already understood.
My eyes saw the picture, but in my head,
even your friends say you've changed.
When I spoke to you about it,
that troubled you.
Why?
I would like to find someone
who tells me that it isn't true.
You have really changed.

You no longer have a softness in your look,
and I suppose your heart is in balance.
So, my suffering is beginning if you change.
Perhaps I have changed, too.
I am feeling ill at ease
about caressing you
when you return from mass.
How you have changed.
Your sleep is troubled.
My life is pained; I am worried.)[28]

Accustomed to having his way, the husband is astounded when he notes how his wife indicates her disapproval. The clues are small exchanges in conversation with the husband, tinged with pauses and evasive answers. The wife's voice tone changes followed by a physical withdrawal from her husband upon her return home from a Catholic mass. Terms of endearment are replaced with the person's given name. The husband's betrayal causes the loss of harmony in his marriage. In addition, a return to the old familiar ways with his wife is not possible.

Enunciating each word with pathos, Naimro expresses the man's regret that he caused his wife's change of attitude. The movement from *ou* (you) to *lavi mwen* (my life) in the final line demonstrates the strain under which the couple lives. Nevertheless, since Creole lyrics have both a literal and figurative meaning, a further reading of this song assumes that the wife is involved in an extramarital affair. Two clues are when she avoids looking directly at her husband and claims to have a headache. A third is when she refuses to discuss why or if she has changed. Given these three clues, one understands the husband's uneasiness and unhappiness when his physical gestures toward his wife are rebuked. According to Naimro, "A song on this topic was badly needed to demonstrate that there are some Caribbean men who regret the harm they inflicted on the woman in their lives."[29] Obviously, Naimro is correct in his assessment because this song garnered for him the 1993 Prix SACEM-Martinique as composer of the year.

Another version about how change creeps into a relationship is found on Béroard's solo album *Milans* (1992). Singing with precision and a suppressed passion, Béroard delivers a haunting but jazzy tune in her rendition of "An lè" (Take me higher). The opening lines are about a woman who regrets that she is frequently alone. Only the lingering scent of her man's cologne lets her know that he has been home. In spite of this, the woman does not despair, for she believes they can recapture the romance that once took her to the seventh heaven. She asks her lover, "Es ou sé lè mennen mwen / nou ké alé / an lè ya" (Would you lead me / so we could go / even higher?),[30] accompanied by an expressive chorus that strengthens Béroard's verses as they unfold and end in a communal experience.

Hope and Collectivity

Undauntedly, Kassav' focuses on the individual, the couple, and the collective group. The singers and composers do not deny that love may hurt. Usually, they end their songs with the wish for reconciliation. Coming from a tropical climate, the group anchors its songs in a specific space and landscape. Images of the sun, the ocean, the wind, the boat, and the rainbow are metaphors for life patterns. The sea is a symbol of affinity where one sits and meditates. The boat is a means for bringing food (fish) or pleasure. As for the sun, Caribbean people either bask or suffer under its rays. Sometimes the sun can be quite brutal, burn up the crops, and dry up the water reservoirs. At other times, it energizes people, lifts up their spirits, and causes much happiness.

For *Lagué moin* (Let me go), Pierre-Edouard Décimus wrote "Solèy" (Sun) which did not win the fans' attention until Béroard sang another version on *Vini pou* (1987). This new rendition of "Solèy" found Kassav' exper-

imenting with the verbs *chofé* (heat and reheat) and *kléré* (light up), under-
scoring Kassav's message of hope:

> Solèy ki ka kléré
> És' ou ké pé chofé ké a moun ka soufé
> Ké a moun ka pléré
> Lè yo pèd on zanmi
> Solèy ki ka chofé
> És' ou ké pé kléré kè a moun ki mové
> Ké a moun ki pa janmen enmé dan lavi

~~~~~~~~~~

> (Sun, you who shed light.
> Could you heat up the hearts of those who suffer?
> The hearts of those who cry
> when they lose a friend?
> Sun, you who warm us.
> Could you shed light on
> the hearts of those who are evil?
> And the hearts of those who have never loved in life?)[31]

The nouns or the infinitives for hope, light, and heat recur frequently in "Solèy" to stress Kassav's optimism that the current inertia and despair that permeates the French Caribbean psyche will change. If the sun succeeded in
making unhappy people happy and healing those who mourn, one ought to
believe that life moves forward into an energetic space. Whenever a song
begins with a bleak outlook, Béroard insists that it should end on a note of
hope: "Yes, we have got to have hope. Lots of people, who don't understand
our songs, catch just a little chord or word in French or Creole. Then they
say, 'It's music to be happy. Music of the sun. Music to dance.'"[32]

Kassav' members work hard at their craft. Always rehearsing, changing,
and evolving, they are not afraid to delve into feelings. Again, in Saint Éloi's
"Zoukamine" (Zouk vitamin), the title song from *Zoukamine,* we hear a
message of hope, warmth, and tender commitment:

> Ni on tan pou ri
> On tan pou réfléchi

An ka poposé on térapi
Pou pé agi

~~~~~~~~~~~~

(There's a time for laughter
and a time for reflection.
I propose a therapy
in order to take action.)[33]

Saint Éloi's lyrics are specific, offering a zouk vitamin for peace in the world with a percussive, spicy, Brazilian-tinged melody. In fact, the 1994 "Zouk-amine" is both a response to the 1984 "Zouk-la sé sèl médikaman nou ni" and to Saint Éloi's disappointment in the escalating violence in Guadeloupe:

> "Zoukamine" developed from a personal interest to which I attest. When I began to write this song in Guadeloupe, there were some violent incidents. People can be very evil. So I proposed a therapy in this music to think of other things.[34]

The song is positive, continuing with the vision of *bizouk* and now *zouk-amine*. In "Zouk-la sé sèl médikaman nou ni" Desvarieux declares he is sick with love for zouk. Now, Saint Éloi offers a prescription to cure societal ills, stating: "A zoukamine is not dangerous for love. Savor it with moderation."[35] The ever-present sentimental yearning to rediscover the Caribbean home landscape, a pristine environment that abounds with natural beauty and social harmony, offers an escape from the ambivalence of living in France and a continual search for a new, unfettered identity through the medium of zouk.

Since the Kassav' members are based in Paris, *Difé*, released in 1995, introduces tunes with up-to-date studio technology that are hummable and danceable, as well as accessible and thoughtful lyrics about racial prejudice, homelessness, and drug addiction. For example, Naimro's "Trop filo" (Enough philosophy) returns to the message that he imparted in "Pèd filaou" (You have lost your destiny) on his 1985 solo album *En balatè* (Buried) about who his friends are when he is feeling low. Co-written with Roland Brival, a Martinican actor, singer, and writer, Naimro asserts that a person needs to exude self-confidence and believe in what he thinks rather than rely on others who will not help him up if he stumbles. On the other hand, Mar-thély's meditative "Jijman hatif" (Snap judgments, or prejudices), backed up with hard underlying rhythms and exuberant singing, is a plea for social and racial tolerance of differences. Marthély recalls how the French colonial educational system brainwashed him into believing that he was part of a condemned, inferior race. His retort, located in the third verse, is the following:

Lè ou pa konnèt
Pa fè labalèt
Ou ké prann-y an tèt
Lavi moun sé pa la fèt
Jijman hatif, sé jijman hatif (× 2)

∿∿∿∿∿∿∿∿

(When you don't know,
don't spread bad news.
It'll only come back to you.
Don't play with people's lives.
Snap judgments are nothing but snap judgments.)[36]

The line structure for "Jijman hatif" resembles an inverted pyramid. The final line of verse three is highlighted in bold print in support of Marthély's annoyance and impatience with people who quickly judge and sentence total strangers out of ignorance. The final verse, "Kouto sèl ki sav / sé kouto tou sèl ki sav / Pa fè labalèt / ou kè prann-y an tèt" (When you don't know / What's inside another / Don't misjudge him / It will come back to you), reinforced with a hard rock and inventive instrumental section, inflicts pain upon the listener in the creation of a sharp ending to jerk him into a sudden awareness. The full Creole expression is "Kouto sèl ki sav' sa ki an tchè jiroman" (Only the knife knows what's in the heart of a pumpkin), meaning "No one knows the pain of another." Also, the reference to a knife draws attention to the expression that "It cuts like a knife," which refers to the intensity of the emotional pain that is felt upon being unfairly treated.

Kassav' has been very concerned about what is happening to today's troubled youth, who constitute a large percentage of the runaways, drug addicts, and the homeless. During the past decade drug problems and teenage prostitution have been rising at an alarming rate in Martinique, Guadeloupe, and France. After much discussion Kassav' chose the term *difé* as an album title and included it as part of the titled song "Difé, soupapé" (Too much pressure). With very eclectic music composed by Marthély and Philippe Joseph and lyrics by Béroard, a vision of a smoke-filled street with flashing red

lights, honking horns, and voices that soared above the harsh rhythm has
been summoned up.

Di fé, soupapé
Difé, soupa soupapé
Di fé soupapé
E é é

An lo dézòd an lo makakri
Dépi yonn douvan, fèy désann
Zafè kò mèl ki pran plon
A fòs domi adan "sakésifi"
A fòs fè sanblan
Lèspwa désann
An lè do malédisyon

Di fé soupapé . . . E é é (× 5)

Ti manmay ka brilé a lannuit
Pèd an la fimen
Yo sé lè kwè
Mé douvan yo an pangal
Pou yo i za ta, é bagay la tchuit
Lavi yo anchyen
Asi la tè lèspwa ni gal
Ki moun' ki ké sa ba yo lanvi goumé
Mété rèv yo pli woué pa ladjé
Di mwen ki moun' si sé pa woué mwen
Pou limyè yo kléré dèmen maten
Di fé soupapé . . . E é é
Pou di fé pa limé, an nou vwéyé dlo a monté
woywo wowo

An nou vwéyé dlo a monté woy
Wouzé-w, Wouze-w
Fò wouzé yo, woy woy woy wouzé yo
Bay an ti lanman
Vwéyé, vwéyé dlo!
Difé, mé zòt shèché sa zòt touvé,

Difé, di fé, di fé
Pou difé pa limé an nou vwéyé dlo a monté

~~~~~~~~~~

(*Too much pressure*
Open the relief valve.

We're lost in confusion and hypocrisy.
Aiming to put down the one who reaches the top.
No matter who gets fired.
By macerating and doing things halfway,
hope goes astray
and we say it's our curse.

Too much pressure.
Open the relief valve.
Children are burning in the dark.
Becoming drug addicts.
Aimless in this future in ashes.
They think it's too late.
Cards are spread out on the table.
What have we done with their future?

From now on earth, hope has got scabies.
Who will give them the will to fight?
To add ambition to their dreams and never give up?
Tell me who can it be apart from you and me
so their light can shine tomorrow?

Too much pressure.
Open the relief valve.

If you want to avoid an explosion.
Open the relief valve.

Open it now.
Give them a hand.
Give them love.
Get hope back to them.

Hard times. We've got what we've been playing for.
Too much pressure. Open the relief valve!!)[37]

Searching for a way to help these young people, Kassav' asked who can help the youth to reassess their priorities. While Kassav' expected the youth to feel better about themselves, the band did not think the youth should bear the entire burden of their disappointments. So, they asked adults to reach out and redirect those who took or might have contemplated the wrong path. If not, a lack of love without a helping hand could increase the youth's chances of becoming more self-destructive.

The urgency of this matter was stressed by Kassav' by placing several stanzas in bold print. Kassav' espouses a doctrine of social responsibility. However, the Creole lyrics are hidden beneath a complex web of metonymy, making it difficult for an Outsider to unravel their meaning. The text is also compounded with two points of view. The youth express their confusion; the narrator implores the adults to fulfill their parental responsibilities. The hard, driving beat of the bass dictates the erratic movements of the youth as they walk the streets. Desvarieux's heavy metal guitar documents the youth's fears. Béroard repeats "Difé, soupapé" (Too much pressure) more than ten times to put people on alert. The call-and-response pattern between Béroard and the chorus cries out the song's two messages: Open the relief valve before the youth explode, and give them something to hope for.

Trans-Atlantic Connections

In 1982, Kassav' moved out of the studio for its first live concert in Guadeloupe, the country of its three founders. Soon thereafter, Kassav' evolved into the prime musical force whose appeal spanned the entire French Caribbean region due to its interdependent communication with other musical forms encoded in its live performances. By 1986, the group reached superstar status in the French Caribbean, Paris, and throughout French-speaking Africa. There were frequent grueling ten-month tours in Europe, Asia, Africa, and the Caribbean. The band released one or two albums per year, reaching nearly twenty-eight by 1987. In addition, Kassav's records were illegally pirated and dubbed, especially in French-speaking Africa and the Caribbean. These activities made the group the most widely heard popular entertainers in French-speaking Africa[38] and the Caribbean.

To express thanks for its fans' support and a pride in its Caribbean heritage (which provided the foundation for its music), Kassav' returned to Guadeloupe to perform a free concert on 23 February 1986 and to receive a gold record. Before an enthusiastic audience of 50,000 (more than fifteen percent of Guadeloupe's population) Kassav' played its hit, "Zouk-la sé sèl médikaman nou ni."[39] Coming from a region where the sale of 3,000 to 5,000 copies of a single album was a major success, Kassav' made history by being the first French Caribbean band to sell enough records to win a gold record (France's Disque d'or).[40] With a sale of more than 200,000 worldwide, "Zouk-la sé sèl médikaman nou ni" was one of the biggest hit songs ever recorded by a French Caribbean band.

The song, listed on the local hit chart for six months in 1985, consists of two phrases, one for the refrain and the second for the verse. The song lasts for six minutes and twenty-four seconds. Desvarieux's gravel voice enters on the first verse, commenting on how hard life is and asking the question: "Ki jan zot fè pou pé sa kenbé?" (How do you manage to keep in shape?).[41] Décimus's voice is then amplified in response to Desvarieux's question, "Zouk-la sé sèl médikaman nou ni" (Zouk is the only medicine we have), to which a chorus replies, "Sa kon sa" (That's how it is). Desvarieux then requests, "Ba mwen plan la mwen pé sa konprann / Ba mwen plan la poko sézi / Si janmen an jou mwen tonbé malad'" (Give me the secret for it so that I can learn / Give me the secret for I have not understood / so I'll know for the day I get sick).

Although Béroard insisted "Zouk-la sé sèl médikaman nou ni" did not embrace a distinct political ideology,[42] the song stimulated a lively public political debate in the French Caribbean. In the 1980s, the Nationalist party interpreted the slogan "zouk was 'the only solution'" to be a political attack on the state of local affairs. Zouk supporters, like the linguist Jean Bernabé, saw zouk "as a practice integrating fundamental elements of the Creole *convivalité*. . . . Such therapy, moreover, would fit in with the belief that the salvation of our countries must first go through a cultural revolution, a decolonization of minds" (Bernabé 1986, 15–16).

In this respect, zouk symbolizes a liberating influence that forges a trans-Atlantic link among dominated Blacks in colonial and post-colonial societies in the Caribbean, Africa, and Europe. To resist assimilation into metropolitan French culture, most Kassav' members mingle with other immigrant musicians, family, and friends. By so doing, they also create unique cultural boundaries. As a result, a steady reinforcement of their own identity, zouk, and Creole, along with an infusion of different musical rhythms, sustains the band's global appeal.

Kassav's records enjoy phenomenal sales in Europe. As a place for the exchange of population and cultural commodities, the imperial capital, Paris, is an important site where African diasporan colonial peoples play a vital role in the global economy and culture. Fully aware of this role, Kassav' recognizes that it has African diasporan, Asian, and European audiences. The sold-out concerts at the Zénith, a prestigious concert hall in Paris, in 1985, 1986, 1987, 1989, 1991, 1993 and 1996, have anchored the group in the limelight. In 1986, the French press conducted numerous interviews which, among other things, generated an audience of more than 300,000 at the *Fête de la musique* in the outskirts of Paris on 21 June. This continuous positive response has reinforced Kassav's initial goals: to create a new sound, to succeed financially, to provide Caribbean people with personal and national pride, and to make the French Caribbean culture, Creole language, land, and values more widely known.

Capital Domination and Marketing

For over nine years Kassav' has been struggling to enter the American market. The group first came to the United States in 1988 and played two nights before a Caribbean audience at the Club Ritz in New York.[43] Kassav's last tour was with the 1994 Africa Fête held in major American cities such as New York, Washington, D.C., and Miami. The initial decision to enter the United States market occurred with the signing with CBS (now Sony)[44] after eight consecutive sold-out nights at the Zénith in Paris in 1987. The November 1987 contract with CBS led to the release of the album *Majestik Zouk* in 1989, which garnered two gold records for "Doméyis" and "Raché tchè" (Heartbreak)—two songs derived from traditional music co-written by Wilfred Fontaine and Marthély, with music by Naimro.

Ironically, through the CBS/Sony contract guaranteed a constant production of Creole lyrics, there were fewer releases. The production of only one album every two years led to wild speculations: the band had broken up, had reached its peak, was no longer popular, or its special sound had died a quick death. In the French Caribbean a band was not considered to be popular if it did not issue a new album at least once a year. Always concerned about its Caribbean audience, Kassav' circumvented the CBS/Sony restrictions by issuing some albums under the names of individual members. Each Kassav' vocalist was recruited by other artists to be a guest singer for such projects as the 1992 Malavoi's *Matébis* (Cutting School) and Shades of Black's *Wonderful;* the 1993 Mario Canonge's *Trait d'union* (Connecting Link); the 1994 Tabou Combo's *Unity.* According to Gene Scaramuzzo, because the group found these limitations "anathema," upon reconsideration Sony "turned the band over to their Tristar label, a subsidiary whose main goal was the United States promotion of Sony artists who were successful outside the States" (Scaramuzzo 1994, 53).

In the Caribbean, Kassav' has had to contend with disc jockeys and béké and Lebanese sponsors who decide which song on an album is the best one to be featured. Because of the rapid turnover of hits, the local radio stations do not keep an archive and basically play only the most current hits. There is no time slot set aside once a week where the "oldies but goodies" are played on a specific radio station. Fearing saturation, Eric Andrieu of Déclic-Martinique suggests the alternative "to keep the group in the limelight by encouraging the local disc jockey to promote another tune from the already popular album."[45]

French Caribbean musicians want to be successful in their home islands as well as on the international market. The decision to move to Paris is viewed from two perspectives: on the one hand, musicians become dependent on the marketing whims of a multinational recording company; on the other hand, the French venue provides the platform and stimulus for further exposure and experimentation. It is a catch-22 position. The French metropolis imposes conditions that ignore a musician's cultural uniqueness and socio-economic needs. French recording companies only release new albums during the Christmas and summer holidays, whereas in the Caribbean there are three major seasons: Christmas, Carnival, and summer. Repeatedly, individual musicians or bands request a staggered release and an aggressive promotion of new albums to coincide with these three periods. Many négropolitains return to the Caribbean in February to celebrate Carnival and to spend money on records to take back to their homes in exile. The musicians and bands, based in France, wish to capitalize on this available income, but their requests for seasonal releases have so far been in vain.

Although there is no infrastructure for mass distribution of music in Martinique and Guadeloupe, there are local record producers.[46] These producers provide the initial funds for the making of records, but the singers and musicians do not earn any royalties until they have repaid the fees for the sound engineer, the rental of the studio, the production of the CD in France, the equipment rental, and the distribution and marketing of the album. For example, after "Pa bisouin palé" (No need to talk) sold over 129,000 and "Siwo" (A good man) 150,000 copies, Béroard received only enough royalties to pay rent on her Paris apartment for four months (Kpatindé 1989, 32). This accounting problem with Georges Debs Productions of Martinique, along with others, is one of the reasons Kassav' left and signed with CBS in 1987.

The power relations entailed in the CBS/Sony contract and the constraints that Kassav' suffered are clear examples of the commodification and domination of cultural productions—in this case, zouk, by capital and industry. Today, with the CBS/Sony contract, Kassav' receives a monthly salary as a corporation, but the band did not have a signed contract with George Debs Production from 1984 to 1987. During this time period Kassav' recorded twelve albums and received other awards such as the Maracas d'or and the RCI Trophée beside France's Disque d'or and the Prix SACEM-Martinique. Very naively, the band thought that a verbal promise was sufficient.

As performers, the members of Kassav' promote a professional and cultural consciousness by demonstrating a solidarity with their compatriots in the French Caribbean and by reaffirming their Caribbean identity. Since Creole is primarily an oral language, Kassav's live performances become verbal readings of the lyrical texts. Consistently, Kassav' celebrates trans-Atlantic landscapes which provide creativity, nourishment, and life.

In 1987, Kassav' organized an annual talent contest called the *Le Rêve Antillais* (The Antillean dream), first in Guadeloupe and later in Martinique, to promote new talented amateurs with the promise of producing a record with the winner. Unfortunately, there were problems with the local sponsors and misconceptions so that *Le Rêve Antillais* was eventually canceled. Another Kassav' effort that was initiated by Jacob Desvarieux but quickly spiraled out of control was the zouk extravaganza called the *Grand Méchant Zouk* (Big bad zouk). Two shows were coordinated by Desvarieux in 1988 and 1990 with other well-known singers and musicians in Guadeloupe, Martinique, French Guyana, and Paris. However, due to greedy promoters and some unpleasant incidents during the second *Grand Méchant Zouk* show, Desvarieux and the rest of Kassav' withdrew their support. Finally, in an attempt to discuss the zouk phenomenon in a formal setting, Kassav' helped to organize a symposium on zouk sponsored by the Conseil Général de la Guadeloupe on 25 August 1988. The topics ranged from the possibility of using zouk music to boost the Guadeloupean economy to the development of internal structures to export music. Guilbault's analysis of the conference was that traditionalists and separatists expressed concern about the use of music as a unit of production and exchange. An often heard question was, "Can zouk be treated as 'goods and services' and still promote cultural specificity and autonomy and reflect local social and political goals?" (Guilbault et al. 1993, 31). Kassav's answer was that Caribbean music was constantly changing; therefore, its music was a mixture of many musical genres that were evolving.

Kassav's slick, sophisticated, layered sound evokes feelings by touching the inner core and memories of both its musicians and audiences. Kassav's mixture of Martinican and Guadeloupean Creoles forces a new language into existence. The speed and cry of "Zouk-la sé sèl médikaman nou ni" and the offering of a zoukamine create a new discourse for its listeners to rediscover the specificities of French Caribbean culture, history, and language through a celebratory union between body and music. Marie-Line Ampigny notes that Kassav' "encourages the blossoming of talent, the emergence of sponsors and producers, increases the sale of records and cassettes, and guarantees nightclubs' profits" (Ampigny 1987). Kassav's Creole lyrics are constantly being reformed by combining elements drawn from other regions. Through Creole and its zouk music Kassav' pushes the open-endedness of creative exchange with other cultures. Finally, with its multiracial group of musicians, Kassav' proudly demonstrates in its optimistic Creole lyrics that zouk overcomes political barriers and encompasses social and cultural ties that are not yet possible in France's overseas departments.

1. Jean-Paul Soime, former violinist for Malvoi and founder of Matébis. (PHOTO: PHILIPPE BOURGADE, 1990)

2. José Privat, pianist for Malavoi, in his brother's living room in Didier. (PHOTO: BRENDA F. BERRIAN, 1995)

3. Jacob Desvarieux *(left)*, Jocelyne Béroard *(center)*, Patrick Saint-Éloi *(right)*, Jean-Philippe Marthély *(top)*, and Jean-Claude Naimro *(bottom)*, of Kassav'. (COVER PHOTO FROM THE COMPACT DISC *Difé*, COLUMBIA 480697-2)

4. Promotional picture of Kassav' for *Difé*, that was also used for its twentieth anniversary concert at Paris-Bercy, 12 June 1999. (PHOTO: MICHEL BOCANDÉ, 1995)

5. Patrick Saint-Éloi as an adult and as a young boy. (COVER PHOTO FROM THE COMPACT DISC *Zoukamine*, SONODISC 7283)

6. Posters in downtown Fort-de-France advertising Tanya St. Val's *Mi* tour. (PHOTO: BRENDA F. BERRIAN, 1995)

7. Eugène Mona *(far left)* in concert. (COVER PHOTO FROM THE COMPACT DISC *Témoignage Live,* HIBISCUS 512404-2)

8. Pôglo in his Dillon home. (PHOTO: BRENDA F. BERRIAN, 1995)

9. Kali and his banjo. (COVER PHOTO FROM THE COMPACT DISC *Roots*, HIBISCUS 512404-2)

10. Djo Dézormo ponders his next lyrics. (COVER PHOTO FROM THE CASSETTE TAPE *Kritik*, DL 12005)

11. *(Clockwise from left):* Christiane Obydol, Dominique Zorobabel, and Jane Fostin, of Zouk Machine. (COVER PHOTO FROM THE COMPACT DISC *Clin d'oeil,* BMG 74321164582)

12. The pianist Mario Canonge shares his range of Caribbean music. (COVER PHOTO FROM CASSETTE TAPE *Arômes Caraïbes,* KANN 08756)

13. *(Clockwise from left):* Richard Marie-Claire, Hervé Laval, Franck Donatien, Danièle René-Corail, Janick Voyer, Gilles Voyer, and Max Télèphe, of Taxikréol, at Lamentin Airport. (COVER PHOTO FROM THE COMPACT DISC *Siwo Fuel,* TK 695-01)

14. Claude and Emmanuel "Mano" Césaire of Palaviré in their home in Robert. (PHOTO: BRENDA F. BERRIAN, 1995)

15. Henri Guédon in his art studio in northern Paris. (PHOTO: BRENDA F. BERRIAN, 1995)

3 *more than a doudou*

Women's Subversive Love Songs

In the 1990s, I have become a little jaded from reading novels by French Caribbean women writers that duplicate the pattern of a suicidal *doudou,* or a severely depressed woman protagonist who has been betrayed by the man in her life. Therefore, when I listened to Jocelyne Béroard's "Siwo" (A good man), "Pa bisouin palé" (No need to talk), and "Mové jou" (A bad day), zouk songs that deviate from this pattern, I searched for more information about the history of women lyricists and singers. Digging for facts, I heard about the Martinican singers Léona Gabriel and Lucie Granel. Information was forthcoming about Gabriel with a copy of her book *Ça C'est Martinique* (1968), but I was unable to locate copies of Granel's recordings.

By chance, I happened upon Elena Surena's essay about the image of women in French Caribbean music, which included a lengthy discussion of Gabriel's songs. What I uncovered was that the number of women who composed their own songs in Martinique and Guadeloupe was minimal. As an extension of the popularity of videos and zouk since the 1980s, the desire to be a singer has risen among women between the ages of eighteen and thirty. Driven by high unemployment, young, naive women look toward a singing career. They see it as an instant step to stardom and public recognition and have thereby flooded the market with a lot of mediocre songs.

While wading through these songs, which were mainly flops, I noticed that they were primarily composed by men. Fortunately, there were some gems composed by women that described an autonomous, independent woman. To situate this chapter into a historical context, I decided to discuss Gabriel and six zouk women composers who disclosed taboo subjects while recreating a French Caribbean woman who was more than a doudou. My interest in the term *doudou* originated when I heard it used in most of the biguine and zouk love songs in which it meant only "darling" or "[my] love." Some male composers corrupted this term, making the doudou a pushover or an appendage for the man in her life. With the emergence of Gabriel and other women composers, the original meaning of doudou has been restored.

〰〰〰〰〰〰〰

The fun part was arranging the interviews. Léa Galva and Suzy Trébeau of Kwak were kind enough to come to my place since I was dependent upon public transportation. Trébeau spoke about her admiration for Béroard and determination to be a singer. She especially liked the video that was made of her song "Histoire d'amour" (Love story), found on Kwak's *A dé, vlopé* (1994). The map of Africa was used as a backdrop in the video to illustrate that women across the African diaspora have similar love stories to relate.

Galva was very candid about her decision to leave Kwak at the height of her career over a salary dispute. She also expressed her gratefulness to the Guadeloupean singer-dancer, Joëlle Ursull. While a dancer in the latter's shows, Galva gained hands-on experience about the world of show business. Thus, in March 1995, when the interview took place, she was looking forward to the future and confident that her career would soar. In her case, Galva succeeded as a solo singer and as a hostess of an afternoon television show.

The most unusual location for an interview took place in May 1995 in the women's public bathroom in the Grand Carbet in Martinique with Tanya St. Val before her concert. Pressed for time and disturbed that she had not been informed of my scheduled interview with her by the local manager, she nonetheless consented to talk to me about some of her most popular songs. St. Val reminded me that she was a very sensitive person, felt things deeply, and poured so much of herself into her zouk love songs. Her fascination with African American blues and soul music led to the creation of her *Soul Zouk* (1991) with the arranger Willy E. Salzédo, for which she sang "I Miss You" in English. The interview came to an abrupt end when St. Val's French male manager, Dominique Roussier, charged into the women's bathroom, asking her to join the band on stage for a sound check. To say the least, the interruption was quite humorous.

〰〰〰〰〰〰〰

Since 1995, I have stayed in contact with Béroard. She is passionate about the misfortunes that befall African and French Caribbean low-income children based in Paris. For Christmas 1997, she organized a toy Kwanzaa for over one hundred children, asking many of the Paris-based Caribbean singers to sing and perform for free. In spite of her encounters with subtle and overt racism on French television shows and in concert halls, Béroard acknowledges that she owes her career, in large part, to her fans. As a consequence, she takes the time to hug them, to pose for pictures, and to share a joke. The most frequently heard sound is her spontaneous laughter. This laughter is needed to break the tension because, in spite of the glamour, Béroard and other women singers and composers endure their share of ups-and-downs in the difficult world of the French-based and Caribbean music industry.

~~~~~~

To be a woman and Antillean is a destiny difficult to decipher. MARYSE CONDÉ[1]

The fact that women sing and compose songs is, in the context of Caribbean societies, an act of transgression and defiance. Their presence in the chorus or as soloists in contemporary music gives a new dimension to the music world. French Caribbean women are struggling to overcome gender stereotypes, inequality, and a lack of real social autonomy on both public and personal levels. As songstresses and songwriters, standing in the limelight of a stage in a concert hall or a nightclub, they have to cope with the gaze of male lust and women's envy that magnifies them into the objects and fantasized images of a male-dominated society. Visible performers, they are obligated to project a stage image such that their songs become an extension of their personae. However, they must be careful to avoid being used solely as marketing gimmicks. In spite of these constraints, the women recognize that the production of commercial music continues to rest, among other things, upon public performance which brings forth entrenched values that favor men who control the industry. The economic benefits and the environments in which musical performers work challenge a woman's morality.

Before the mid-twentieth century, Martinican and Guadeloupean men and women, in general, assumed that only "street women" or women from the lower class would consider being professional singers in a predominantly male-run industry. A woman who traveled and performed at various concert halls or clubs in the company of male musicians was not viewed as respectable. The slur of prostitution and societal conventions about appropriate moral behavior for women ensured the man's place in the competitive market of the commercial music industry. Therefore, when the Martinican Léona Gabriel announced to her family her decision to sing professionally in the 1920s, the news was received with a stunned silence followed by misgivings.

A product of the local bourgeoisie, Gabriel knew that she and other Martinican women were being raised to be wives and mothers as sanctioned by the Catholic church. Consequently, the central theme of her songs, still popular in the 1990s, was romance—with its courtship patterns, happiness, marriages, disappointments, and break-ups. In addition, Gabriel affected and adopted a singing style that originated when mulatto mistresses entertained their French lovers with Creole songs. This method consisted of singing gallicized Creole with a French intonation. Instead of singing in a natural voice, a nasal tone was affected to duplicate a more pronounced French accent. In fear of being identified with the lower class whose Creole was said to be more authentic, Gabriel adopted this singing style by not breathing from her diaphragm and prolonging the final notes. Since then, this affectation became so popular and acceptable that contemporary women singers were judged critically when they punched out a song in the fashion of an African American jazz or gospel singer.

Another technique adopted by Gabriel was the writing of Creole, a very expressive language, in an oblique manner. This creative Creole formed the basis for a self-invention as stated by Aimé Césaire in his search for *le mot* (the word). Caribbean writers were in a constant search for a hybrid language that was without a fixed system of orthography. Its double meanings or secret code and the graphic nature of its images were necessary linguistic inventions to maintain discourse among the slaves. Edouard Glissant attributed this technique of Creole writing to a conspiracy that concealed itself by public and open expression. He explained:

There has been much comment on the use of antiphrasis in Martinican speech. It appears that the Martinican is afraid of expression that is positive and semiotically straightforward. . . . We use ornate expressions and circumlocutions (a diversionary tactic) in order to better demonstrate our real powerlessness. (Glissant 1989, 124–25.)

Glissant's comment about language being diversionist is applicable to those singers and novelists who portray passive and exploited women who succumb to social and sexual oppression that mirrors the continued economic and political exploitation of the French Caribbean. What he forgets is that the use of antiphrasis in Martinican speech grew out of the slaves' oppositional stance against the slave masters. Since the slave master spoke Creole, the slave resorted to speaking in parables to evade being understood. This evasive stance is not necessarily one of powerlessness but a subversive step for contestation.

Two more viewpoints about Creole are offered by George Lipsitz and

Merle Hodge. Like Glissant, neither Lipsitz nor Hodge separate the Creole language from cultural identity. They see the ability to write in an elusive Creole to be a liberating, powerful force. In his comments about this force, Lipsitz says: "A part of the meaning of any Creole song lies in creative word-play, designed to both disguise and gradually disclose the meaning, to nurture an oppositional vocabulary incapable of control by outside authorities" (Lipsitz 1994, 105). Hodge reports that Creole survived because it expresses the Caribbean personality, for, "ninety-nine percent of Caribbean people, for 99 percent of their waking hours, communicate in a Creole language that is a fusion of West African syntax and the modified vocabulary of one or another European tongue" (Hodge 1990, 204). This historical development of the Creole language and appropriation of Creole are steps toward cultural nationalism and a fusion of the fragmented oppressed self (see chapter 2). This also explains why some of Gabriel's songs and those of the six women to be discussed in this chapter contain two meanings: one literal and the other figurative.

Such songs are similar in theme to a novel like Myriam Warner-Vieyra's *Juletane* (1982) wherein the heroine goes mad and wills herself to die when her Muslim husband marries a third wife. The heroine's self-destructive behavior confirms that the French Caribbean woman evades an issue and only attempts to liberate herself. The emotionally victimized woman is a reflection of sacrifice and powerlessness, and she embraces a passive stance. Historically and politically, the French Caribbean woman is colonized as an objectified body and is sexually subordinate to the male. In spite of this, several contemporary women songwriters are taking steps to change this perception of the French Caribbean woman. Exhibiting a strength of character and a high motivation combined with creativity, six zouk singers—Jocelyne Béroard, Léa Galva, Edith Lefel, Tanya St. Val, Suzy Trébeau, and Joëlle Ursull—have moved out as singers within male-dominated bands to gain independent public acclaim as soloists. They are indebted to Gabriel's trail-blazing presence in the commercial world of music during the 1920s through 1960s, which helped to break down some of the stereotypical barriers erected to limit the opportunities for women.

In terms of socio-economic arrangements defined by race, class, and gender, Condé interprets the French Caribbean woman's condition as a maker of history and an agent of culture. She concludes that "Feminine discourse is neither optimistic nor victorious. It is loaded with anguish, frustration and revolt. . . . Throughout the world, the woman's voice is rarely triumphant. The feminine condition is everywhere characterized by exploitation and dependency" (Condé 1979, 113). Whether creative writers or songwriters,

French Caribbean women are caught in a struggle between visibility and invisibility. And the majority of songs authored by them support Condé's position that the French Caribbean woman's dependency negatively affects intimate relationships between women and men.

This discussion centers on how French Caribbean women are undergoing a change from a passive stance to a more active one. Coming from an oral culture where people listen to the radio and watch television in place of reading, the women are well aware that their songs are seen and heard as extensions of themselves. In the Caribbean community there is a tendency not to differentiate between the persona as performer and the singer's personality. Wanting to be liked by their Caribbean public and to sell their packaged product, several songwriters carefully write songs in Creole to redirect themselves away from male domination, reclaiming their slave forebears' resistance to oppression. On the literal level, the songs conform to the status quo level, but, on a figurative level, they are challenging. Through the creation of the subversive gender space, the women construct, challenge, and carve out a place wherein they indirectly contest male power in their love songs that address duplicity or commitment.

Léona Gabriel, the Mentor

A native of Rivière-Pilote, Martinique, Gabriel spent part of her childhood in French Guyana and Panama. Upon reaching adulthood, she desired to be a singer, composer, and radio announcer. Yet, none of these careers was considered an acceptable choice for a well-bred, middle-class woman during the first half of the twentieth century. The assumption was that a woman should care about an education, a marriage, and the raising of a family. However, Gabriel moved to France, where she got the chance to pursue her singing career as the featured singer (under the name Mlle Estrella) for Alexandre Stellio's orchestra.[2] After several years in Paris and two marriages,[3] Gabriel returned to Martinique to host a weekly radio show *Ça! C'est Martinique* for Radio Martinique during the 1940s through 1960s. Every Saturday she sang one of her own songs and recited a historical literary piece about the Martinican landscape to the accompaniment of either the trombonist Archange Saint-Hilaire's orchestra or sometimes the clarinet player Hurard Coppet.

Unable to divorce herself from inherited bourgeois values, Gabriel reveals in her songs the prejudices of her class in her use of three common descriptive nouns to categorize women: the *pacotille* (cheap goods), the *léchèl poul* (hen beneath a ladder), and the *doudou* (darling or my love).[4] A *pacotille* is a woman of loose morals who does not hesitate to prostitute herself. *Léchèl poul* belongs to that category of poor rural women who migrate to town with muddy bare feet in order to work as servants and to improve their status. Finally, *doudou* is a familiar term given to a woman with affection and attachment. It is not to be confused with the term *doudouisme* (sweetness), referring to an idealistic view of life in the French Caribbean as well as a term that has degenerated into a negative connotation of an easy woman.

To stay within societal conventions, Gabriel's "Jennès bò kanal" (Youth from the canal) delicately alludes to sexual behavior by hiding behind food metaphors. Food and its preparation function as symbols of nourishment and a woman's sexuality when the *pacotilles* or young *kaprès* (*câpresses*, women of mixed Indian and Black heritage) with black eyes and straight hair are described as "difé lenfè a sou la tè" (hellfire on earth, a euphemism for a prostitute) and "popòts fòls" (crazy dolls) who are like "En ti piman dan blaff" (a hot pepper in a lemon-based fish stew).[5] Not easily fooled, men meet these women for brief, passionate, sexual interludes. Their payment for these brief encounters gives them economic power.

Class distinctions in songs of this period are embedded in gender struggles. "Léchèl poul," a traditional song that has been attributed to Gabriel, recounts the story of a young woman who is determined to move up the social ladder. Born in a rural area, the woman moves to town to work as a servant. Because of her dire finances, she walks to town rather than arriving by public or private transport, thereby placing her status below the bourgeoisie. Nonetheless, once she takes up residence in town, she begins to behave like a lady:

Léchèl poul sòti Morne vèr
Dé pyé i plen labou
I en ni plasé kay lè Alpha
Fanm la posé i en matadò (× 2)

~~~~~~~~~~~

(Echelle poule left the village of Morne Vert
with two muddy feet.
As soon as she got a job as a servant with the Alphas
she started behaving like a *matador*.)[6]

The léchèl poul changes her social standing to that of a *matador*.[7] Under the guise of a matador, she commands respect; nobody dictates her social position. Not at all naive, she assumes a new identity despite the resistance of those in another social class who object to her entry into their enclosed world.

Since music provides a medium by which a composer defines the range of attitudes and expectations that characterize a certain time period, Gabriel wrote about women who suffer, regain hope, and move beyond being the easy doudou.[8] Most of her love songs are couched in subtle wordplay, as seen with "difé lenfè." Powerlessness is transposed to an alternative position of autonomy and control. Tackling the traditional seduction and betrayal syndrome in "A si paré" (As it seems to me), Gabriel introduces an unnamed woman who loses her beauty and sexual innocence to a *gwo misyé* (an important man) who leaves her for a *kannay* (cheap good-for-nothing woman). Hurt and angry, the woman lashes out as follows:

Ah! alé misyé, sa ou fè a pa ké pòté ou bonheu,
Alé ingrat, ti manmay la mwen ké swagné y ba-w
Alé méshan loyé kaz là, mwen ké payé y ba-w
Mwen sé kréyòl, mwen ni kouraj, mwen ké wouè ou isi
A Fort-de-France

〜〜〜〜〜〜

(Go away! What you have done will not bring you any luck.
Go away, you ungrateful man, I will take care of the child for you.
Go away, you bad man, I will pay the house rent for you.
I am a Creole; I am strong; I will see you down-and-out in the streets of
    Fort-de-France.)[9]

The doudou's fantasy about romance and marriage is not met. When the sexual act renders her pregnant, the father of the child deserts both offspring and lover. The transition from an innocent to an experienced woman leaves the betrayed mother in a vulnerable state. The indirect coded message is that the male seducer is fickle due to his preference for the wicked Other Woman. Nevertheless, what gives the doudou courage is her pride. Though the man tries to destroy her, she has the courage to overcome her tragic situation. Because she insults the man who abdicates his paternal and financial obligations, he is reduced to a vacuous person with no substance. Through her verbal onslaught she becomes the oppressor, and he, the potential victim. She diminishes the effect of the man's abandonment by treating him with scorn and pity, foreseeing the day when he will be down-and-out in the streets of Fort-de-France while she makes something of her life. "I am a Creole; I am strong" carries the message that, come what may, she will fend for herself and stand on her own two feet. His leaving will not undermine but strengthen her determination to succeed. Hence, this doudou's outburst and growth negates Clarisse Zimra's assessment of her being nothing more than "a pet animal whose affections do not run deep and who can, therefore, be discarded since she's expected to recover just as casually" (Zimra 1990, 146).

Gabriel fashions another doudou who seizes her own representation in "Linfidèl ou lanmou Lily" (The unfaithful or Lily love). In this narration, a reversal of social roles occurs. Lily, a woman who declines to submit to patriarchy, leaves her male lover. A critical issue is that Lily's abandonment affects his stature among his male friends. The unhappy lover highly regarded Lily because of her mulatto caste. When he describes her as someone with brown skin, black eyes, and coral lips, he paints an exotic object rather than an autonomous woman:

> Lanmou Lily sé lavi, mwen tchè
> Mwen enmé fi-ya, é si joli
> Kon Lily ka pasé dan lari
> Jenn kon vyé ka kouri déyè li
> Mé Lili mété-y a trompé mwen
> Mwen ka vini fou, mwen ka pèd la rézon
> Mé mwen palé Lily, mwen kité mwen

~~~~~~~~~~~~~

> (Loving Lily is my life. My good buddy,
> I love this girl; she is so pretty.
> When Lily walks down the street,
> the young and the old run after her.
> But Lily is unfaithful.
> I am going crazy; I am losing my wits,
> but I don't want Lily to leave me.)[10]

The suitor can tolerate Lily's waywardness, but he refuses to accept her departure. Thus, all transgressions will be forgiven because he places so much importance upon her physical attractiveness. Being seen in Lily's company enhances his self-esteem, and he defines his self-worth through her. Consequently, Lily can use her physical beauty as an instrument of power to reverse the role that is accorded to men, making the suitor subservient to her will.

These themes from Gabriel's biguine songs set the pattern for the women singers of zouk love. In the early 1980s, the band Kassav', founders of zouk music (see chapter 2), hired the Martinican Jocelyne Béroard as a full-time soloist. She started singing her own zouk love compositions as well as those by other Kassav' members. Also, to the delight of other aspiring women composers, Béroard followed in Gabriel's footsteps in her choice of subject matter with up-to-date references. Next came women of a younger generation among whom were Léa Galva, Edith Lefel, Tanya St. Val, and Suzy Trébeau. These women's lyrical songs broke the silence enshrouding taboo topics such as incest, domestic abuse, rape, suicide, and broken friendships. To accomplish their aim, they wrote in a Creole that allowed metaphoric interpretations.

Frustrated Hopes and Duplicities

French Caribbean societal attitudes regarding men and women are both conservative and contradictory. The Caribbean myth is that the female child is taught self-sufficiency. She matures into a Caribbean woman who is strong and able to handle anything. The child is also told that it is very desirable to have a dominant male partner. The contradictory message is that the woman is "her own woman," but once she enters a marriage or a live-in relationship, she must take on the childbearing, childraising, and housekeeping duties that place her in a subordinate position to the man. While he roams outside of the home, she is primarily confined to domesticity.

The male child is not raised with the same survival skills as the female. He tends to be very spoiled and to rely upon his mother or other women members in the family household. Later, his heavy dependence on female relatives is carried over into a relationship with an inferior, adult woman partner. Yet, the French Caribbean male internalizes the ideology of male dominance, creating another paradox. He subconsciously resents his dependence on a woman. This resentment turns into a hostility directed toward his wife and/or a need to establish another relationship or a series of relationships with other women. Because of her own socialization, the woman not only is hurt and insecure but also thinks that she is somehow responsible for her mate's irresponsible behavior.

Béroard sings skillfully about a man's irresponsible behavior during a stormy love affair in "Mové jou" (A bad day).[11] Using the first-person singular *mwen* to personalize her song, she forces the direct involvement of either all or some of the listener's five senses— sight, touch, smell, taste, and sound. Subtle references to music, spilled coffee, a last cigarette, and a thumb tack reveal a woman who confronts her wayward boyfriend who returns unrepentant and upsets her further. Not content for her to have the final word, he takes her last cigarette, sparking the woman's anger:

Mwen di zòt mwen faché
Mwen lévé faché
Roye, mwen kòlè
Pas jòdi mwen faché,
Mwen ké kouché faché

~~~~~~~~~~~

(I am telling you that I am angry.
I woke up angry.
I am very uptight.
Yes, today I am angry.
I will go to bed angry.)[12]

Obviously, the woman loses faith in this man after he tests the limits of her endurance. Her anxiety level and disappointment have increased as her self-worth declines along with her stoicism in the face of his nonchalant behavior. Signs of her disappointment in him are already given with the spilled coffee and her stepping on a thumb tack. With each incident the hurt is sharp and a warning of more pain to come. Although aware of his woman's distress, the neglectful boyfriend does not respond to the unspoken and indirect message that she still loves him when she allows him to take her last cigarette. As the saying goes, the brain knows what is right, but the heart does not. To emphasize the woman's displeasure, Béroard stretches out the length of *faché* (angry); she holds the note to emphasize a sweeping need for change. At the same time, she invites the listener to sway and respond to the echoing of her voice, supported by the chorus in the foreground. Her voice rises to a higher pitch with an emphasis on the first syllable of the conjugated verb *fâcher* (to be angry) each time that she uses it. Béroard explains this technique: "If I sing about love and tenderness, I am going to find the right feeling. I have no other reason to look for the beauty of expression while cheating because I will not be credible. If you say 'Mwen faché,' it's necessary to feel it" (Pulvar 1990b, 39).

This attention to strong emotions in her lyrics and delivery was also duplicated by another Martinican younger singer, Léa Galva. While a child, Galva avidly watched televised musical variety shows. She studied classical and modern jazz dance and debuted at SERMAC in 1982 with Suzy Maniri. In 1985, she got her first chance to sing in the chorus for Tony Chasseur in a piano bar in Fort-de-France. Their meeting and collaboration resulted in a one-time recording session of "Oublye ma vi" (Forget my life) with the band J. M. Harmony. When she moved to Paris to continue her study of classical dance, Galva successfully auditioned for Joëlle Ursull, a Guadeloupean singer. During her eighteen months with Ursull's show, Galva observed the ins-and-outs of show business. Upon her return to Martinique in February 1992, Galva sang as Suzy Trébeau's replacement in the chorus for Malavoi. This stint led to a fruitful meeting with an old friend, Jean-Luc Guanel, who told her about the new singing group Kwak.

When she became a new member of Kwak, Galva was asked to bring an original composition for the group's first album. Remembering a song she had left in a desk drawer, Galva arrived with "Kontinué" (Continue): "At this time I did not know how to write music. I knew how to listen to it. I knew how to sing it. However, I recorded a melody on my little walkman with the text and gave it to Philippe Joseph. It was he who arranged the score." [13] The irony was that Galva wrote "Kontinué" out of a combination of heartbreak and a determination to overcome the pain caused by a husband who had abandoned her for a younger woman while they lived in France. Out of anguish, loneliness, and anger, the devastated Galva sat down and wrote the award-winning autobiographical song:

Pa ni lontan ke nou konnèt
Mé lavi séparé nou
Sonjé lòtjou nou té ansanm
Zié'w té pozé anlè kò mwen
Jou dèsten nou vini kwazé
Byen lwouen di mwen l'anvi enmé
Ou shangé tout koulè lavi
É lanmou mwen vin' déklanshé
Tou sa nou té imajiné
Mwen ka pansé, ké oublyé
Shagren lévé, mwen ka pléré
Solèy koushé an lè tchè mwen

Refrain
Kontinué alé

Kontinué enmé-w
Sé wou tchè mwen lé
Sé wou mwen enmé
Jòdi mwen sav, adan lavi
Ké tout bagay sé pou an tan
Shéshe lèspwa pou sa tchenbé
Mé san ou ayen pa ka konté
Lanmou mwen
Pli gran de jou an jou
Viré bo mwen
Pa janmen kité
Pèsonn gashé santiman nou

~~~~~~~~~~~~~

(We met not so long ago,
but life separated us.
Do you remember that we were together not so long ago?
You had looked at me,
and our destinies met.
I had no intention of loving anyone,
but you entirely changed my life,
and my love grew for you.
I think that all that we had planned
will have to be forgotten.
Sadness came, and now I am crying.
The sun has gone out of my heart.

Refrain
I keep going.
I continue to love you,
for my heart longs for you.
It's you that I love.
I know now that nothing in
life lasts.
I am grasping for some hope to keep me going,
but nothing counts without you.
My love
grows day after day.
Come back to me.

Let's not allow
someone to destroy our love.)[14]

"Kontinué" revealed that, although Galva and her husband had been married only for a short time, someone still managed to separate them. She admitted in a personal interview, "I lost everything. My husband had not been tender with me. I found myself all alone in Paris."[15] Not willing to terminate the marriage despite his confessed betrayal, she makes two proposals: "Viré bo mwen" (Come back to me) and "Pa jamen kité / Pèsonn gashé santiman nou" (Let's not allow / someone to destroy our love). Ignoring both, her husband was unable to find contentment within a monogamous relationship. Eventually, his spiritual restlessness and sexual promiscuity resulted in a divorce, leaving Galva to suture her ruptured heart that used to overflow with love.

Grappling with her husband's betrayal allows Galva to forgive him and to concentrate on healing. The challenge is for her to move beyond past hurt to contemplate a future happiness. As she works through an understanding and acceptance of her husband's subterfuge, she undergoes a self-restoration which is discussed in her second hit "Mennen mwen" (Lead me). In this chronicle of her healing process, lonesomeness resounds in the song's slow beat as the spurned wife appeals to her estranged husband: "Ou rivé avoué sa ou ka risanti / É tchè mwen ka konnié ka kouvè tambou a" (You have arrived to confess what you feel for me / And my heart resonates over the beat of the drum).[16] With a pounding heartbeat Galva absorbs the blows of her husband's words. Upon reflection she reassesses her options, recovers her pride, and renews her belief in love: "É menm si ou pé pa dèmen / Oublye lè pasé / Avansé / lanmou ka gidé nou" (And even if tomorrow / you cannot forget the past / Let's move on / Love will guide us).[17] Falling in love is a risk, but Galva so values herself that she is prepared to seek a new commitment. She indirectly indicates her readiness and capacity to love anew in her title choices of "Mennen mwen" and "Kontinué."[18]

As already noted in Gabriel's "A si paré" and Galva's two songs, there is a continued interest in love triangles. Joëlle Ursull also treats this theme but with a different twist. "Joujou" (Plaything), located on Ursull's third solo album *Comme dans un film* (Like in a film), is concerned with the betrayal of friendship because of competition over a man. Doubly hurt, a woman suffers when her best friend steals her boyfriend, an act which, in turn, ends their long-term friendship. A code of honor is broken because it is understood that a woman friend is not to be involved with her best friend's boyfriend or husband. The wounded woman internalizes the double betrayal, and Ursull's comments, written at the beginning of the song, are poignant: "There is no greater disgrace than the betrayal of friendship. . . . Friendship is a gift. . . . I had given it to you on a silver plate."[19] To be a rejected person is a painful experience, but to be betrayed by your closest friend is devastating. The damaging message is that a temporary romantic relationship with a man might very well be more valued than long-term friendship between women. A woman's friend is thus potentially disposable, but a male partner is indispensable. In spite of this, "Joujou" closes with the retort: "Mé jòdi gadé byen / Sé on nouvèl fanm ki la douvan vou / An pa on joujou" (Today I am fine / A new woman stands in front of you / Not a plaything).[20]

Trained as a professional dancer, Ursull won fourth place in the 1979 Miss France beauty competition, which resulted in a modeling career for Nina Ricci. Her desire to be a singer caused her to drop modeling and to accept Guy Houllier's and Yves Honoré's invitation to be a member of Zouk Machine, the first all-woman trio singing group in Guadeloupe. Ursull sang on Zouk Machine's first album in 1986 and performed with the group for its first Zénith concert in 1987 (see chapter 5). When another popular singer asked to join Zouk Machine, Ursull was replaced without her consent.[21] The fierce competition that surrounded Ursull's membership in and expulsion from Zouk Machine could have been another reason for the writing of "Joujou." After a heated exchange with the promoters, Ursull reestablished herself as a soloist with the release of three albums: the zouk love *Miyel* (1988),[22] the crossover *Black French* (1990), and the diversified *Comme dans un film* (1993). Also, in 1990, the leftover bitterness from being ejected from Zouk Machine disappeared when she was invited to be the first French Caribbean singer to represent France at the Eurovision musical competition.[23] Lucky for Ursull, she triumphed over major disappointments to become more successful.

Some women enter into a slumber or numb state when life fails to reward them. Preoccupied with this numb state or depression, the Martinican Edith Lefel composed the March 1995 hit "Somnifère (Paroles des femmes)" [Sleeping pill, women's words] on *Jeux de dames* (Women's games). The women mentioned in this song are homeless, drug addicts, or victims of domestic abuse. These women ache to be desired. An enormous amount of courage and will power are required for them to fight against the effects of the *somnifère* (sleeping pill). To arouse these women out of their slumber, Lefel's voice projects with clarity: "Mwen té ké préféré pati / Savé kò / Ki ka rèv kon, inosan" (I would prefer to leave / and to know myself / who dreams like an innocent person).[24] Most importantly, the women need to remove themselves from abusive relationships and to find men to whom they could say: "Respecté fanm, konsidiré sété maman" (Respect a woman like your own mother). Imagining herself a storyteller, Lefel gives voice to her concerns about women who define themselves by the misfortunes of their gender. She comments, "I write about everything that touches, moves, or delights me. The voice is like a loving hand to amuse oneself, to communicate and to reflect together" (Ampigny 1992–93, 26).

Born in Cayenne, French Guyana of Martinican parentage, Lefel has spent most of her life living in France, where she started as a backup singer for groups like Malavoi, Kassav', and Ethnikolor. Called *la petite sirène de la chanson antillaise* (the Antillean song's little siren), she got her first major exposure to the public when in 1985 she recorded the popular "Iche Manman" (Mama's child) with Jean-Luc Alger and Dominique Gengoul for Lazair. This was followed by her first solo album, *La klè* (1988), for which she received the 1988 RCI Trophée for the track "SOS mémé" (Grandmama SOS) as best woman interpreter. After the success of this song, Lefel continued to rise in popularity with *Mèci* (1992), a gem of an album with such songs as "Rupture" and "Marie." In addition, her liaison with the Martinican music impresario Ronald Rubinel has afforded them the opportunity to function as a team; she, the singer and songwriter, and he, the composer.

One of their team efforts is Lefel's *Mèci* (Thank you), which contains the track "Marie," whose video clip was shown on the American VH1 network television channel. For this original track, Lefel poignantly relays the tale of Marie, "an bèl nègrès" (a beautiful Black woman), who is dying:

> Adan koin an chanm lopital
> An nonm asiz la ka pléré
> Y ka tchenbé lanmen Marie
> Pa ka rivé palé
> Y ka sonjé y pa ni si lontan
> Sété an bèl nègrès tèlman djé
> Yo té toujou ka plézanté

~~~~~~~~~~~

> (In a hospital room
> a man, who is seated, is crying
> while holding Marie's hand.
> Unable to speak.
> He recalls how not too long ago

she was such a cheerful, beautiful Black woman.
They were always teasing each other.)[25]

Through the use of indirect style, Lefel constructs Marie, a character who is more than the woman-wife-mother syndrome. From indirect speech to Marie's reported but unspoken thoughts, Lefel mediates between the internal and external sides of Marie's consciousness. The stress of juggling her husband's and later her children's incessant demands is overwhelming. Thus, Marie's passive protest is manifested by depression and a total physical exhaustion. When she is hospitalized, her bewildered husband reports in the refrain that "Marie tro fadtigé / ka mandé libéréi / Souffrance-li ké fini" (Marie is too tired / She asks to be liberated / So that her suffering will be over).

By giving voice to the husband's thoughts, Lefel gives us an insight into his view that the marriage is perfect although he spends his time building his career. The husband assumes no responsibility for maintaining the home and raising the children. To his surprise, he comes home to find a neglected wife having a physical and nervous breakdown, reminding one of Velma Pollard's comment: "If you love, you become a wife. If you are a wife, your concerns take on a pecking order."[26] The wife Marie is not the Virgin Mary, the ultimate in purity and womanhood. The wife achieves a freedom from her husband's oppression only in death. Her decision to die is the ultimate appropriation of power, for she controls how long she wants to live. Marie's death becomes the mirror through which her grief-stricken husband recognizes his victimization of her. This reflection of himself is acknowledged through Marie and a choral reminder that they are together for life, followed by Marie's last words as voiced by Lefel, who likes to build upon the call-and-response pattern of "ki an lè la tè / ki an gran syèl-la / Jòdi nou pli fò / Paskè nou pli ho" (Whether it be on earth / or in heaven / We are stronger today / because we are together on a higher level). Thus, Marie's death raises the possible reconstruction of the husband's self.

Without question, another interpretation of "Marie" is that Lefel paints the archetypal pitiful female who "works herself to the bone" to satisfy a self-absorbed husband. Marie lives through her husband and sees herself through his eyes as an appendage. Not seeing anything positive about herself in his eyes, which further validates her unworthiness, she virtually wills herself to die in order to receive her husband's love. Therefore, Marie's decision to die is a final act of subordination. Her last words speak about an inevitable meeting with her husband in the afterlife, implying love is eternal. As a consequence, her husband's gesture of expiation is thereby undermined by her death.

The subversive naming of "Mové jou," "Joujou," "Somnifère," and "Marie," ingrained in the fragments of the women's lyrical narrations, provides a message: There are many layers and complexities to a woman's life. The songwriters address the multidimensional aspect of women through their songs of protest. Each of their songs proves French Caribbean women resist confrontation and adhere to cultural expectations. Nevertheless, their elusive use of language to render more than one interpretation of a song is enough to contradict Elizabeth Wilson's remarks that French Caribbean women's fiction reveals "a pattern of rejection, resistance, and attempted liberation, followed by failure and deeper alienation because of aborted attempts at revolt" (Wilson 1990, 45). It is through subterfuge, the twists and turns of their protest songs, that the women songwriters find ways to replace the passive aggressive and neurotic image of themselves.

The women songwriters dare not be too transparent with their messages because they want to maintain public adulation. Rather than focus upon confrontation, they offer opinions about the importance of the collective unit. They hide behind their Creole so that they will not be offensive. The use of metaphorical language and symbolism requires listeners to sort out the songs' meanings. For instance, Suzy Trébeau,[27] who also sings for Kwak, writes about the silence that enshrouds a rape in "San mandé" (Without asking) and about an unrequited love in "Zone intérdite" (No Entry) from *A dé, vlopé* (To hug each other). Utilizing the Creole technique of double entendre with a word such as *chouboulé* (upside down, to describe a victim's state of mind), only the well-tuned listener will grasp that "San mandé" recounts the story of a rape. It may very well be that the song deals with an incestuous rape, a sordid reality for many young French Caribbean women who until recently dared not to reveal that the perpetrators often were their own fathers or stepfathers.

Singing with sadness, Trébeau describes the turning of night into day. The night protects the rapist and conceals his identity when he breaks in his victim's home. When daylight arrives, the rapist walks the city streets without fear, convinced that the victim will be too ashamed to denounce him to the authorities, let alone to her mother. Trébeau asks the following four questions:

Poutchi yo ka détwi la vi-w?
Es fòt nou si sa ka rivé?

Poutchi yo ka détwi la vi-w?
Poutchi yo ka malmennen nou?

~~~~~~~~~~~

(Why do they destroy your life?
Is it our fault if it happens?
Why can they destroy your life?
Why do they mistreat us?)[28]

Close attention to sound effects is necessary, for, at the end of the song, foot-steps are heard along with the opening of a door. Its closure is in the absence of human voices.

Sa sé lavi lè tou sa ki pou.
Défann-ou ka akizé-w ka
Ou ka retrouvé kò-w dan lá pen.
Lanmou détwi.

~~~~~~~~~~~

(That's how life is.
When those who are supposed to defend you, accuse you.
You find yourself in pain.
Love is destroyed.)

The victim's faith in human beings (and, in particular, man) is shaken. The physical scars will heal, but the psychological ones might not. To be able to trust another man is almost an impossibility. Silence permeates as the victim covers up the rape for fear of public censorship. The woman's fear of a society that places blame only on the raped victim allows the rapist to walk away free. Her choices are limited and severely determined, for rape is often treated as a fabrication and suggests the complicity of the woman. The foot-steps in the corridor with the opening and closing of doors are all part of the continued nightmare of the nightly violation with which the victim lives. There is no post-rape narrative that traces the victim's survival strategies.

Trébeau's decision to voice the unspeakable and to describe the interior life of the victim duplicates the African American novelist Toni Morrison's determination "to rip the veil drawn over proceedings too terrible to relate" and "to find and expose a truth about the interior life of people" (Morrison

1987, 34). The rapist must be held accountable for his brutal crime. Since "San mandé" is about a woman who represses the rape, Trébeau's singing about it opens up a public discourse wherein a mediation between resurrecting the rape and seeking reparation for the raped victim can begin.

Raised in a household where one brother is a percussionist and the other is a drummer, Trébeau used to sing along with the songs she heard on the radio. In 1988, one of her brothers, who played for Guy Vadeleux, told her that a singer was needed in the chorus for José Versol. This brief opportunity resulted in an invitation to sing backup for Eric Virgal at Studio Hibiscus, followed by other gigs with Simon Jurad, Jacky Alpha, and Malavoi. For five years she sang in the chorus for Malavoi and learned how to breathe properly as she performed. Simultaneously, she became a member of the first Taxikréol, which quickly folded and resurfaced without her, but with new members, in 1994. Finally, she was approached about joining the group Kwak.

Full of enthusiasm and grateful for being able to do what she enjoys the most, Trébeau divulges a carefully guarded secret with "Zone intérdite." The song is about a woman who unwittingly falls in love with her boss. The barrier is that he is committed to another (veiled reference to being a married man). A strength of character and a reminder not to engage in an extramarital affair prevent the woman and man, in question, from crossing the barrier. There is a mutual attraction, but they refuse to succumb to their emotions. Neither one dares to articulate her/his feelings for the other because "Dé ti pawol pé chanjé lavi" (Two little words can change a life).[29] During a personal interview Trébeau made the following comment:

> "Zone intérdite" is really my baby. It is a forbidden and autobiographical story. Actually, I told what happened to me. It's so personal. It's a message about my life. I composed it for myself, and it has sold well. Many women have been moved emotionally; therefore, I do not regret it.[30]

With the French Caribbean woman's denunciation of man's cruelty in a male-dominated society, songs like "Mové jou," "San mandé," and "Kontinué" discuss lack of fulfillment, romantic abandonment, and the intense hope for a meaningful relationship with a man. The woman who opens herself to love and happiness is betrayed and constantly hurt. She is a picture of sexual vulnerability. Consequently, the majority of French Caribbean women's songs abound with what bell hooks calls "a litany of loss, abandonment, and broken promises: desire is a wound" (hooks 1990, 194). The wound springs from extreme anguish and pain. The wound also opens up the subversive gender space in contestation. Stitching up the wound and verbalizing the pain will heal the interior schisms. To circumvent a society that believes that women are to submit to men, the women songwriters devise techniques by which it appears on the surface that they are powerless. Their songs provide a subtext of opposition by breaking the silence on rape, abandonment, and domestic abuse.

Shared Commitment

Despite the duplicities and frustrations that occur between men and women, women songwriters have not given up hope. Consequently, a second theme in their love songs is a shared commitment with a man. The women are fully aware that the French Caribbean man tries to avoid speaking openly about his emotional sentiments for a woman he loves. To voice his feelings is an expression of weakness and a diminishment of a macho image. In a stereotypical relationship, the man takes the initiative while the woman presents a softness. The Guadeloupean Tanya St. Val warns men that women who project a soft but cool image have a good reason because of their past relationships. In "Fanm mou" (Soft women) from *Mi* (1994), St. Val cautions men, "Pa oubliyé / fanm kè zòt ja enmé / ou fékanté / menm blésé" (Don't you forget / all those women whom you've loved / you've been with / and hurt).[31] She also advises them not to forget, "Fanm ki byen dous / fanm ki cool" (Women who are so gentle / Women who are cool).

Although the dominant image is of someone with a soft exterior (as the title of the song indicates), St. Val admits there is an underlying toughness that enables a woman to cope when she experiences the ups and downs of a love affair. Consequently, she talks about a woman's integrity and gives men the following advice:

> Wè sé nonm la . . .
> Fanm ki fanm, fanm ki janti
> Fanm béni fanm pa ni pri
> Fanm ou flè fanm dégoudi

~~~~~~~~~~

> (Yes, men,
> a woman who is a woman is kind.
> Women who are blessed have no price.
> Rejected women and resourceful women.)

In spite of the song's simplicity, St. Val's final message in "Fanm mou" specifies that only some women are capable of managing their affairs. The adjec-
tive *mous* bears the connotation of being indecisive and lackluster. In an
interview with the singer, St. Val insists that "Fanm mous" represents "a
sentimental woman who was discreet, liked to suffer but disliked scan-
dals." [32] Also, identifying herself as a sentimental woman, St. Val asks: "Does
a woman give herself so much trouble to know about love because she insists
that she should have someone?" [33]

St. Val presents a similar observation in "Lanmou kréyòl" (Creole love)
from *Zouk A Gogo* (1984), commenting: "It is a poetic song. A painting. A
star shooting across the sky. A possibility that we surely love in the tropics. . . . Living in Paris I had the urge to speak about love in Creole" (Chénard 1994, 14–15). Utilizing natural elements—the stars, the moon, the *fi-
lao* (a pine tree)—"Lanmou kréyòl" opens with a description of a star in the
sky that casts a spell over lovers and, in particular, the woman: "On zétwal
an syèl la ka anvouté mwen / Lalin la ja kléré menm lèspri an mwen" (A
star in the sky is casting a spell over me. / Even my mind is already lit by
the moon). [34]

St. Val's fresh, uplifting singing style exhibits the vulnerability needed to
touch an audience and the spunk to deliver a song with good timing. During
her performance she explains the man's love might not be forthcoming. In
spite of this, his lukewarm response only encourages the woman to be more
persistent, to glow under her lover's gaze, and to become the initiator. In the
song's refrain, St. Val states:

Dé twa tibo kréyòl ki ké ba-w bon fòs . . . mmm
Lè-w ké tini shagren an ké kajolé-w
Lè-w ké vlé tandrès an ké ba-w karès
Lè-w ké tini émosyon an ké ba-w sansasyon
Pou-w pé toujou santi-w ranpli dafèksyon

~~~~~~~~~~~~

(One, two, or three Creole kisses will give you
the strength you need.
When you feel sad, I'll console you.
When you need tenderness, I'll caress you.
When you are emotionally drained, I'll stir up your senses
so that you always feel truly loved.)

Hence, the woman gives her lover priority over herself; her love for him unleashes a fantasy that they will be together.

By anticipating and catering to his needs, the woman naively thinks that love will strike him. Determined to wear down the man's resistance, the woman takes the risk, stakes her claim, caters to her object of affection, and tries to force him to love her. The adjectives *éfèrvésan* (effervescent) and *fòsforésan* (phosphorescent), from the last stanza, are used to illuminate the woman's determination to get the target of her love to agree to a romantic relationship:

Vini gouté an lanmou Kréyòl
Pou lanmou on nou pé éfèrvésan
An kè an mwen
Pou ménaj an nou pé fòsforésan

(Come taste this Creole love
to keep our love effervescent
in my heart, and
to make our coupling phosphorescent.)

She is convinced that love will bubble up into an ecstatic emotion between them. Afterwards the intensity of their love will be even more convincing because it glows in the dark.

The initial perception is that the woman is in control in "Lanmou kréyòl." Since she is the one who actively pursues the man, she is convinced that her lavish attention and affection are worthwhile. During her efforts to possess the man, she makes it increasingly difficult for him to resist. She is the active giver while the man is the passive recipient in spite of her determination. After all, the final decision about the fate of a permanent union still rests in the man's hands, making her the subordinate and him the dominant. The warning is that this woman should be on the alert because all of her pampering might not endear her to the man of her desire. To be frank, the man might be incapable of loving her in the way that she wants.

"Lanmou kréyòl" was an example of St. Val's wish to sing the blues. Performing since age nine, when she sang for her father Tino St. Val's band in Guadeloupe, St. Val's interest in a musical career began with exposure via her father. Over a period of several years she sang in the chorus, backing up many male bands such as Expérience 7 at the Henri Debs studio in Pointe-à-Pitre. Through this apprenticeship she developed a strong voice well-suited for rich, bluesy phrasing as noted on most of the tracks for *Soul zouk* (1992). In a 1994 interview St. Val mentioned that the album opened up more doors for her. "With *Soul zouk,* I wanted to open up more horizons for myself. I am produced by Phonogram, I am a part of what one calls a 'major' multinational company" (Thimon 1994d, 34). Later on, she proclaimed: "I have put a little blues in the music that I make and adore. I have always liked the blues and jazz, but I am a Guadeloupean, an Antillean, and I have the colors of my country to defend" (Alcide 1994, 53). To defend her stance on African American soul, blues, and jazz, St. Val finally admitted that her dream was "to mix the rhythms and colors of *zouk* to the sounds of African American idols."[35]

St. Val was not alone in her love for African American blues. The Martinican singer and composer Jocelyne Béroard established her career singing the blues in French piano bars. In Paris, during the early 1970s, Béroard asked her brother Michel, who dabbled in music for a while in Paris, to put her in contact with some musicians. He agreed, and, at age twenty, she began to sing backup for various Caribbean and African male bands. For instance, she sang for the pianist Roland Louis and the percussionist Henri Guédon, and she traveled to Réunion to sing with the African Cabo Verde Show.[36] Béroard also performed jazz songs so well that people mistakenly thought she was an African American. Like her idols—Billie Holiday, Carmen McRae, and Sarah Vaughan—she brought out every nuance in a song; she was an independent, self-directed entertainer whose strength rested on discipline.

Always searching for new sounds and more innovative ways of singing, Béroard even spent some months in Jamaica, singing backup for Lee "Scratch" Perry. Her way of communicating was simple, but she exuded a very relaxed manner while conveying her readings of love ballads. Not knowing it at the time, a turning point in her career occurred when she sang in the chorus on Kassav's second album *Lagué moin* in 1980. Four years later, she joined the group full time, helping to inspire a new generation of women singers and songwriters. Fully aware that she was carefully watched by people inside and outside of the music industry, Béroard cultivated, with great care, a very dignified and gracious public image.

In "Dous'" (Sweet), with its strong focus on a couple's passion and enduring love, Béroard sings a duet with Jean-Claude Naimro on Kassav's 1995 *Difé* (Heat). Highlighted with a Stevie Wonder harmonica solo and a raggamuffin (mixture of zouk and reggae) beat, "Dous" is about a man who cannot imagine spending his last day on earth without the woman he loves: "Si sété dènyé jou ki rété nou / Sé épi ou tou sèl mwen sé lé karéséy / Dousiné tan an ki la pou nou" (If we had no more than a day to live / It's only with you I would want to share it / I would savor the time which remains for us). A burning passion, which will not be extinguished, consumes both him and his wife. The husband cherishes his wife and believes in the sanctity of their love. Likewise, living securely with someone who expresses his deep love for her makes the woman feel valued; therefore, she exhibits a very gentle, soft, sweet side. With their nurturing love, the couple raise their children to be independent, loving beings.

Béroard's 1985 "Pa bisouin palé" (No need to talk) could be regarded possibly as an early affirmation to this image of the sweet French Caribbean woman. For over eight weeks the song stayed on the Top 50 chart:

Choir:
Frison, frison, frison, frison

Béroard:
Fénmen lapòt la-a
Oswé ya man pé ké ladjé-w
Oublyé déwo la pani pèsonn'
Limen bouji-ya
É vini la pou ou kouté
Tou sa tchè mwen lé di-w
Dépi jou a ou gadé mwen
Pa bizwen palé
Pa bizwen palé
Pa bizwen, di mwen
Sé solèy ka lévé lè maten
Pa bizwen palé
Pa bizwen palé
Menm si sé nonm sèlman
Ki ni dwa di
An . . . vini pa pati

Choir:
Van lévé
Lan mé pé
Pou ou kouté

Chanson ta la
I dan tchè mwen
Dépi lontan-an
Ay doudou, vini pran frison an

Béroard:
Sé sa tchè mwen lé di-w
Chak fwa ou gadé mwen

Choir:
Ay doudou, vini pran frison an

Béroard:
Sa tchè mwen ka chanté
Lè-w ka souri ban mwen

Choir:
Vini pran-y, vini pran-y

Béroard:
Lè-w ka palé ban mwen

Choir:
Vini pran-y, vini pran-y

Béroard:
Ou sav' sé ba-w tou sèl

Choir:
Vini pran-y, vini pran-y
Tchè mwen ka frisonné

Saint Éloi:
Sa ki rivé-w la
Mwen po ko jan vwè-w kon sa
Dépi yonn dé jou
Ou ka palé dè lanmou
Si sé paskè
Ni an moun ka fè-w vibré
Palé ba mwen franchman
An po ko jan vwè-w kon sa

Choir:
Lésé lanmou a palé
Sa-y ka mandé
Sé trop'
Lésé lanmou a palé

Marthély:
Pa bizwen palé
Pa bizwen alé pli lwen
Kon lanmou sé la
Pa bizwen palé
Annou fenmén zyé
É rété adan menm tenmpo-a

~~~~~~~~~~~

(*Choir:*
Shivers and shivers and shivers and shivers.

Béroard:
Close the door.
Tonight I won't let you go.
Forget about the outside; nobody exists but us.
Dim the light,
and listen
to what my heart has to tell you.
No need to talk.
No need to talk.
I already know
that the sun rises in the morning.
No need to talk
Even if it's generally men
who have the right to say:
Come closer and stay.

Choir:
The wind started to blow,
and the sea got calm
in order for you to hear
this simple song which is yours.

It has been lingering in my heart
for so long.
Oh Baby, feel me shivering.

Béroard:
This is what my heart sings
when you smile at me.

Choir:
Oh, Baby, feel me shivering.

Béroard:
This is what my heart sings
when you smile at me.

Choir:
Come for it. Come for it.

Béroard:
When you talk to me . . .

Choir:
Come for it. Come for it.

Béroard:
My heart shivers
just for you.

Choir:
Come for it. Come for it.
No, my heart trembles for you.

Saint Éloi:
What's the matter with you?
You've never been like this before.
For several days now
you've been talking about love.
Is it because
someone else makes your heart tremble?

Tell me frankly.
I never saw you like this before.

Choir:
Let love speak.
Don't ask for too much.
Let love speak.

Marthély:
No need to talk.
No need to go anywhere else.
When love is here,
there's no need to talk.
Let's close our eyes,
and stay with the same rhythm.)[37]

Reminiscent of the African American Teddy Pendergrass's popular songs, "Turn Off the Lights" (1978) and "Close the Door" (1979),[38] Béroard opened her song with the softly spoken command "Fénmen lapòt la-a" (Close the door), rather than giving an order like Pendergrass. Unlike Pendergrass, who sang about making love, Béroard shut out external distractions to enable her and her man to talk freely about their feelings and the direction of their relationship. Suspicious, the man questioned her preoccupation with the subject of love. He thought she was going to leave him. To soothe him, she kindly reaffirmed her strong love for him with the chorus encouraging him to remain and listen.

A power game between man and woman is played out in Béroard's "Pa bisouin palé" and Teddy Pendergrass's "Close the Door" and "Turn Off the Lights." In Pendergrass's songs, the man wants a submissive woman. To prepare the woman for seduction, he teaches her how to close the door, light a candle, and take a bath. Young American audiences are moved by the sensuousness of the music and the lyrics. However, some American adults are dismayed that Pendergrass gives away the secrets to teenagers rather than let them discover the beauty of seduction and adult sexuality.

In contrast, Béroard's opening command "Fénmen lapòt la-a" from "Pa bisouin palé," is interpreted "As partners, let us share this experience and talk about the state of our relationship." In response, Saint Éloi, who sings the part of the immature lover, is not comfortable with the request. He knows that he gives her physical satisfaction. For him, sex is the equivalent of romantic love, and he assumes that there is no problem. If she wants to talk about their relationship, the only plausible reason is that she must have another lover. On the other hand, the mature lover, whose part is sung by Marthély, realizes that he must satisfy his woman intellectually and physically. If he succeeds, then their relationship can grow out of a sharing of mutual concerns. The closed door and candlelight symbolize the innermost region of the composer's mind (Béroard's intent in writing "Pa bisouin palé").

The closed-off room with a lit candle as a cocoon is a reconfiguration of strength and a preparation for the outside world. The closed room is Béroard's privileged, protective space to make either a crucial single or joint decision. In addition, it is also a temporary kumbla space before reentering the public arena. What is interesting about "Pa bisouin palé" is that, with the exception of the woman's initial, gentle request, it is the second male singer who actually advises the first man to listen to the woman. In her decision to use a male intermediary to voice her opinions Béroard defers to patriarchy. Since this technique makes the song safe because it conforms to cultural expectations, Béroard uses the collective voice to tell her story. Not only is her voice heard but those of Marthély, Saint Éloi, and the chorus, proving that men and women must be able to converse to solve their problems. Thus, Béroard emphasizes a communal voice, not an individual one. No voice has more priority or authority than the other; the four voices enrich the final message.

The woman's attempt to be independent in "Pa bisouin palé" is a departure from the status quo. Called the queen and diva of zouk, Béroard's intent is to show the woman's uneasiness with the inequality that slowly creeps into a relationship. The woman wants to avoid guessing what her man actually thinks about her. She has a powerful need for open communication and wants her questions to be answered truthfully. The closing of the door, according to Béroard, is a way for the woman to find herself in an intimate space to tell her man that she is going to be the one who talks.[39] Yet, instead of the woman singer voicing all of these concerns, the second male singer does. Consequently, the song demonstrates the woman's dependence on the approval of others and acceptance of societal norms that favor male wisdom. It also proclaims that Béroard, a realist, understands her Caribbean public and knows how far to go with her lyrics.

For Béroard, there must be clouds if one cherishes the rainbow of hope. Her quest for this metaphorical rainbow and sunshine within the confines of a relationship continues in "Ké sa lévé" (I will be able to rebound). Here, the closed door halts further pain because "Lanmou a ja bout" (Love reached its end),[40] and the affair or marriage is over. The final parting releases enough adrenaline in the woman to overcome the pain and disappointment. With clear diction enforced by a snazzy keyboard and a plaintive singing style, Béroard says:

An ké sa lévé
Mem si mwen pou manjé labou
Lévé lévé lévé lévé
Désann an fen fon lenbé a
An ké sa lévé
An ké sa lévé
Touvé fòs-la y séré
Lévé lévé lévé lévé
Mal fanm pa ka tonbé lontan lontan

~~~~~~~~~~~~~~

(I will be able to rebound
even if I fall lower than the earth.
I will be able to rebound
even if I drown in the pit of my despair.
I will be able to find the strength
where it's hidden.
I will; I will be able to rebound;
real women don't stay down for long.)[41]

The uplifting and repetitive *lévé* ("get up," but in this song "rebound"), mentioned four times in lines two and four, reinforces the woman's optimism that she will learn how to live without her lover or estranged husband. Also, the repetition of *lévé*, combined with an increasing rapidity that builds up into a resounding crescendo, serves to reinforce the woman's determination.

Well aware that the Creole term *siwo* is used by men to describe a kind, mollescent woman, Béroard appropriates it to characterize a good man (or even a sugar daddy) in her song entitled "Siwo":

Mwen di'w siwo ba mwen
An nomn' dous' kon siwo
Mare'y épi ralè'y vini
Mè pa mennen ba mwen

Yonn' pou tewbolizé tchè mwen
Siwo

〜〜〜〜〜〜〜〜

(I say, give me a good man
as sweet as honey.
Catch him. Grab him for me.
But don't bring me a man
who will play with my heart.
A good man.)[42]

This strategy of reversal and the double-layering playfulness lead to a belief in change. Directed specifically at women, Béroard preaches a lesson on how to negotiate. The hard driving heavy-on-the-bass rhythm on "Siwo" is perfect for promoting the message: I want a good man who will treat me right. Furthermore, in a candid interview, Béroard makes the following remarks:

> I'm not trying to take the place of a man. I am a woman. Also, I am not saying I am a man's equal. We [women] are different. . . . We're different, but we complement them. Nevertheless, I love teasing men because they are really macho most of the time from Caribbean countries. These songs make women feel comfortable when they hear them because that's the way they would love to act, to love or to speak. But they know they can't do that because their men won't accept them.[43]

Therefore, the subversive space of gender in popular music functions as a medium of debate to articulate concerns that make men uncomfortable. The subversive space also defines the range of expectations women have for their relationships with men.

The Shift Away from Indirect Contestation

Having a woman as a role model provides an incentive and inspires successive women to stretch the social and spatial boundaries. In several interviews Béroard mentions Gabriel as a role model. The much younger singer, Trébeau, cites Béroard as her inspiration. In an interview Trébeau recounts her first sight of Béroard at the May 1982 Caribbean Feminist Song Festival.[44] She relates how Béroard, accustomed to singing in French piano bars, followed a hot Carnival jump-up song by the Guadeloupean Lewis Meliano (see chapter 5) with two salsa numbers and encountered a negative reaction from the audience:

> I always liked Jocelyne Béroard. She always fascinated me even when I did not know her. . . . Although she was badly insulted by the audience at the *concours,* she told us: "You do not know me now, but I am sure that one day I will return and you will call me 'Madame Jocelyne Béroard.'" And now she is Madame Béroard. Thanks to her, I told myself you can do what you want, too.[45]

When asked about her recollection of this event, the modest Béroard responded that the flow of energy between her and the musicians on stage brought tears to her eyes when she sang Henri Salvador's "Je suis en paix avec le monde" (I am at peace with the world), made famous by Malavoi. The audience taught her a lesson: she should have known what kind of music was appropriate for the festival.[46] The unspoken thought was that she had lived in France too long and lost touch, but the Salvador song saved her. Of course, at the time, Béroard did not know Trébeau, but she was flattered to learn how her actions and brief speech had affected someone so young.

These women singers-songwriters were grateful to Gabriel, and others like Lola Martin and Jenny Alpha of Martinique and Manuela Pioche and Moune de Rivel of Guadeloupe, for paving the way.[47] These older women's professional conduct provided the example for Béroard's refusal to buckle under male control when she clashed with Jacob Desvarieux, the guitarist and now informal leader of Kassav'. After their disagreement Béroard did not perform again with Kassav' until Desvarieux called her to discuss her joining the band full time. In a 1986 interview, Béroard discussed her thoughts about the conflict:

> I am very spontaneous. I have always defended myself against a man. But when Jacob returned to see me, all was arranged. With men, it isn't always evident. Often with our Antillean men they ask an enormous amount from a woman. It is necessary for her to be their mother or sister. Since "Mové jou" I am a full-time singer. Since "Pa bisouin palé" my image has changed. People pay attention to me. I would like to record an album that is a little aggressive, in the genre of the Pointer Sisters, something energetic to dance, to laugh, and to destroy this genre of doudou. There are very few women singers in the French Antilles and even less women who move away from the stereotypical image. I would like to break this cliché. (Conrath 1986)

Galva also fought *doudouisme*. In October 1994, she raised eyebrows when she quit the Martinican group Kwak because she was tired of being underpaid by Jean-Michel Mauriello, Kwak's manager and the producer of Studio Hibiscus. Her complaint was that Kwak was not receiving its proper share of record and concert royalties. Mauriello became defensive and accused Galva of being unreasonable. Despite Mauriello's denials Galva did not back down. Rumors spread that Galva had put her career in jeopardy. However, this was not the case because she accepted the offer to host the RFO Channel 1 afternoon television show *Clairière* (Clearing). Afterwards Galva continued to sing in night clubs, and, in late November 1995, she started hosting *Touchatou* (Dabbler in everything),[48] another afternoon four-day-a-week RFO 1 television variety show, and released her first solo album *Galvinisée,* produced by Rubicolor in 1996.[49]

In 1994, the Martinican public's reaction to Galva's reason for leaving Kwak was mixed. Some called her a greedy status seeker because she was courageous enough to expose how naive young recording artists, who are eager for fame, are exploited by recording contracts that put them at a financial disadvantage. Others, like the local musicians, applauded her in private and called her to lend their support. In spite of the controversy, Galva represented Kwak at the March 1995 Prix SACEM awards ceremony. Kwak, in turn, auditioned several soloists to replace Galva and chose Axell Hill, who was heard on their 1995 *Le Ga' mèci* (Thank you guys).

An often quoted proverb in French Caribbean folklore is "Une femme déchue tombe comme une châtaigne / Un homme déçu tombe comme un fruit à pain trop mûr" (A hurt woman falls like a chestnut, a hurt man like an overripe breadfruit).[50] This proverb celebrates the strength and determination of Caribbean women. The leaves and fruit from the chestnut and breadfruit trees are similar. However, the breadfruit splatters when it falls on the ground, whereas the chestnut, protected by a hard shell, does not break easily.

Fully aware of this popular proverb, Béroard penned a loosely written but clever version of it called "Fanm chatenn'"(Chestnut woman). The surprise is that she writes from a male point-of-view, with Jean-Philippe Marthély as the singer. In the first stanza, general questions are raised: On whom can a woman count? Where has the man gone? In stanza two, Marthély shifts a register, advising the woman not to cry even if she and the children are hurt by a husband/father who strays afar. In the third and fifth stanzas, his advice to the abandoned woman is, "Pa blanmé tout sé nonm la" (Don't blame all the men).[51] If the woman's ex-husband chooses to father children who live in another household, Marthély cautions not to be aligned with such a man: "Ou sav mwen menm sé nonm osi / Ni dé jou nou ka pri" (You know that I'm just a man / We can get lost in our games sometimes). Most importantly, the man equates the woman's survival skills to that of a chestnut: "Chatennn tonbé / ka ripousé, umm sa vré" (Hmmm it's true that a chestnut falls / then sprouts).

Accompanied with a snappy, fast musical beat and strong backup singing, Marthély brings the song to its conclusion with the insistence that a woman's life does not end with her man's departure. If her husband's departure results in her being the sole provider, all she needs to do is to draw upon her inner resources, reevaluating herself and rediscovering her identity as an independent woman. Lonely but not loveless, her children, friends, and other family friends comfort her. After all of this, she will be more careful in her choice of a mate.

The open-ended final question, "Es ou pa ka di nou pé rivé chanjé sa?" (Should we be able change that?), sung as a refrain three times, is weighed down with hope and optimism, confirming the woman has not given up on men. The next man who enters her life will be different, because she, like a *soucouyan* (a conjurer who changes into an animal) sheds the old skin and puts on a new one. In the future she will play a more active role in making sure that her voice and opinions are heard. Verbalizing pain is a prelude to ending it; therefore, the Creole proverb comparing a woman to a chestnut is a testimony to her durability.

The previous use of the term *matador* by Gabriel in "Léchèl poul" to mock a pretentious woman has undergone a revision over the past years. Its new meaning refers to an independent woman; Ursull employs it within this context in "Amazòne" from *Black French*:

Mandé mwen tou sa ou lé
Pa mandé mwen bésé tèt mwen
Amazòne man élivé
E sé byen amazòne an ké rété

〰〰〰〰〰

(Ask me anything,
but to bow my head.
I was brought up like an Amazon,
and an Amazon I will remain.)[52]

The diminutive Ursull grows in stature when she proudly compares herself and other women to the famous warlike Amazon women of Greek mythology and warrior women of Benin, West Africa. According to the myth, Amazon women were famous for their prowess and leadership skills; therefore, Ursull's wish is to emulate them. After she declares in the refrain that she intends to remain an Amazon woman, Ursull reassesses French Caribbean history and remembers how women toiled to build up their civilization. To reciprocate, Ursull owes a debt to her women ancestors and is committed to hard work for the benefit of society. Her advice to women is as follows:

Bati lavi-w anlè zafè-w
Mè pa bat lavi-w anlè on moun
Amazòne an travay-ou
Amazòne an lari ya

~~~~~~~~~~~

(Base your life on something that is yours,
but do not base your life on a person.
Be like an Amazon in what you do.
Be an Amazon in the street.)[53]

While building up her career Ursull traveled to many places, where she met those who tried to hinder her. Eventually, with a fierce pride in the Amazon woman in the last stanza, Ursull coined the motto: "Ou ké pézé kò mwen / mé lèspri mwen pa ka pézé" (You may break my body / but not my spirit). To prove her belief in the motto, Ursull posed for the *Black French* cover dressed in red with her head tilted upwards. This position, along with her playing of the gwo ka, spoke louder than words. In a subversive fashion, the *Black French* cover forcefully announced that Ursull, the Amazon woman in red, was passionate, alive, and independent.

With this optimistic strong faith in a woman's spirit and a belief in romantic relationships, Béroard's "Fanm chatenn" sums up most of the messages explored in the selected songs of Gabriel, Galva, Lefel, St. Val, Trébeau, and Ursull that have been under discussion. Two important messages are that the French Caribbean woman knows how to rebound from disappointments; she will not lose faith in being involved in a committed relationship. The woman craves to be loved but wants faith, trust, and mutual self-respect for herself and her man. To love involves courage and a self-confidence in herself and her partner. The search for romantic love and the selection of a faithful partner coincide with a woman's self-esteem. Despite the rising divorce rate, marital separations, and love triangles, the woman continues to believe in the myth that love is forever. Carrying the symbolic chestnut shell on her shoulders, the French Caribbean woman displays both a resilience and a determination. Music and lyrics exercise power and recreate new social meanings and experiences. With persistence, a woman songwriter challenges the dominance of men in the entertainment field. The pacotilles, léchèls pouls, and doudous of Gabriel's songs are slowly being replaced by the independent fanm-matadors and amazònes with their subtle and not-so-subtle messages about rewriting the subject of love and romance. Each day the French Caribbean woman contends with the dualistic messages: (1) she is independent but oppressed and (2) she is equal but not the same. In response, "Pa bisouin palé," which means "no need to talk," implies listen to what I (the woman) have to say before you (the man) engage in a conversation of mutual satisfaction with me.

4 cultural politics and black resistance as sites of struggle

Parlez-vous de la musique de Mona? Savez-vous que les textes de Mona sont difficiles? (Are you speaking about Mona's music? Do you know how difficult Mona's texts are?) These questions and others about Eugène Mona were asked repeatedly by strangers and acquaintances in Martinique once they learned about my research project. Their concern about my not being able to decipher Mona's lyrics was valid, for I had to ask for help. It was not easy to understand Mona's idiosyncratic Creole on the vinyl albums that I had borrowed. Fortunately, Marie-Claude Pacquit and later Hanétha Vété-Congolo offered to transcribe several of Mona's songs.

Called a mystic, Mona, who died in 1991, had made quite an impression upon his fans. People's voices lowered to almost a whisper when they spoke about the singer. In either wonderment or with quavering voices, they talked about his overpowering personality and the spell that Mona would cast upon them during his live concerts. One woman placed her hand over her heart and started weeping when she told me how she had learned of Mona's untimely death. She had just attended what was to be Mona's last concert at the Grand Carbet Concert Hall days before his death.

Wanting to learn more about Mona from someone who had known him very well, I made the first of two appointments to meet Félix Fleury at his restaurant, Le Ghetto, in Marigot, a town along the north coast. Fleury had been one of Mona's closest friends as well as the manager of Mona's band. During the drive to Marigot, I remembered that this was the town where Mona had lived and derived the inspiration to compose most of his songs. A simple place with *bakouas* (traditional hats) displayed along the wall and a large picture of Mona before the bar, Le Ghetto was the place Mona went most Friday afternoons to converse and to share *un pot* (a drink) or two with friends and some of his band members. By coincidence, my two visits also took place on Friday afternoons. To arrive on time for the second interview, I had to flag down a taxi since the car I had been in had broken down while its driver tried in vain to negotiate a very steep hill.

While serving drinks at the bar and passing along customers' orders to the kitchen help, Fleury would talk to me about his working relationship and friendship with Mona. During an especially busy period, I ordered a late lunch and tried to visualize Mona. Also, caught up in hearing about Mona's career, I suddenly realized that dusk had fallen, and I had missed the last bus to return to Fort-de-France. Fleury told me not to despair, for he would ask one of the men at the bar to take me home. Not sure that the chosen man was sober enough to drive safely, I asked Fleury if the appointed driver was drunk. A bemused Fleury assured me that this was not the case.

The thirty-minute drive back to Fort-de-France turned out to be an impromptu two-hour tour with detours to places that Mona had frequented. First, the driver took me to meet his family, who lived next door to a banana plantation. "Look," he said. "Meet an American who has come to write about Mona." Second, the driver showed me where Mona had taken the photo for his first album *Boi brilé* (1976). This friendly and informative man also pointed to the area where Mona had suffered his fatal stroke. Touched by this man's kindness and desire to talk about Mona, who had been his personal friend, I, the humble interviewer, thanked him profusely. So enthralled, I worked for days on end on the Mona section of this chapter while listening to his songs for inspiration.

〜〜〜〜〜〜〜〜〜

One morning Ghislaine "Gigi" Mazurin called to ask if I would be free that afternoon to meet someone. The surprise was a trip to a private home in Dillon (a southern suburb of Fort-de-France) where I met the Rastafarian singer/poet/painter Pôglo. Upon entering Pôglo's home, which was full of paintings, flowers, and bright colors, I intuitively felt I was in a place where people were very happy. After an exchange of greetings, the three of us began to talk about Pôglo's paintings and his preference for the colors yellow, blue, and red. When he approached a bookcase, Pôglo picked up and handed me his 1989 album *Pa molli* and a hard copy of the song lyrics. After reading a copy of his song "Lèspwa" (Hope), I understood Pôglo's color preferences. He saw the primary colors as a reflection of the state of affairs in Martinique. After we had conversed for over an hour, I finally asked Pôglo the question I had wanted to

raise since my arrival: What about the presence of Rastafarians in Martinique and his decision to join the movement?

~~~~~~~~~~~~~~

My introduction to Kali was via his song "Ile à vendre" (Island for sale). Intrigued, I purchased
the four-track compact disc and listened carefully to the satirical lyrics while on a short visit
to Martinique. Two years later, after I had searched for a video about Martinique to show my
Caribbean literature class, a colleague brought to my attention a Caribbean audiotape series
narrated by the Jamaican cultural studies critic, Stuart Brown. Interestingly enough, Kali's
"Ile à vendre" was on the sound track for the video. Next, during a 1993 trip to Martinique,
banners were up in downtown Fort-de-France, announcing Kali's upcoming concert. And, as
an extra treat, a friend took me to Déclic Martinique to meet Kali's manager, Eric Andrieu,
who agreed to pass on questions that I had prepared for Kali. A couple of weeks later, Andrieu
mailed me Kali's written responses along with a poster and a copy of Kali's *Lésé la té tounen*.

Disappointedly, the timing was never right for me to interview Kali in person. Either he had
just left Martinique to go back to France or I was in the States or somewhere else. Finally,
during a visit to Guadeloupe in December 1996, I turned on the television set to find out that
Kali had performed the night before. Again, so I thought, I had missed seeing Kali—this time
by a day. However, purely by chance, I caught the same plane to Martinique with Kali the next
day. It was while waiting in the baggage area of the Lamentin airport that I finally got my
chance to talk to him.

~~~~~~~~~~~~~~

During a Christmas visit to Pittsburgh, the music journalist Gene Scaramuzzo advised me to
meet and talk to Djo Dézormo about his *angagé* songs. At the same time, Maryvonne Charl-
erly, a friend in Martinique, sent me a fax with Dézormo's work and home phone numbers in
Rivière-Pilote. One afternoon I placed an overseas call and talked to Dézormo's wife, who told
me at what time I could reach her husband at the radio station where he worked. Following
his wife's advice, I called and spoke to Dézormo for about thirty minutes. During our conversation he told me the history of "Voici les loups" (Here come the wolves) and "Moyeloup
2809F90" (Moye the wolf 2809F90).

During Carnival 1995, I happened to be in Martinique for the festivities even though Martinicans had been suffering through a bank strike. Nonetheless, not wanting to cancel Carnival,
the shows, parades, and private parties took place, but the morale was low. Notwithstanding,
Dézormo's 1991 hit, "Voici les loups," resurfaced as a reminder of its warning about the
arrival of more metropolitan French people and other E.U. members who might take away the
scarce jobs from Martinicans. Therefore, the January-March 1995 bank strike was a legacy

of colonialism because the French-born businessmen and béké management were earning more money with extra perks than the locally born Martinicans.

~~~~~~

It's necessary to call upon the imagery of all that is in our head, consciously or subconsciously, which determines our goodwill and our modes of being in the world. PATRICK CHAMOISEAU (1993, 4)

It is the culture which he inherits that gives a man his human dignity as well as his material prosperity. It teaches him his mental and moral values and makes him feel it worthwhile to work and fight for liberty. JOMO KENYATTA (1938, 317)

Apart from Haiti, which has it own tumultuous political history, the French Caribbean has not been known for its *angagé* (socio-political) songs.[1] Its most common theme, explored in chapter 2 and a section of chapter 3, is heterosexual love. The speculation about why socio-political issues are not dominant themes in music has been directly tied to the political structure of Guadeloupe and Martinique as departments of France. As noted in the Introduction, before the late 1940s, the two islands were agriculturally self-sufficient. Earnings from the export of fruits and rum exceeded the cost of French imports, and basic food needs were met. Unfortunately, around 1968, sugarcane prices plummeted due to hurricanes, high wages, urban migration, and production costs, requiring the two islands to take out overdrawn bank drafts from France. Most of all, since the islands became subject to E.U. (European Union) regulations for fruit and vegetables, the territories' agricultural production declined while there was a boom in housing and road construction. However, these improvement in living standards were somewhat artificial, because the building of houses and roads did not in itself directly bring in money from outside the islands for new jobs. Instead, the population became more dependent upon welfare subsidies. Also, in the mid-1990s, the two islands were unable to fulfill the E.U. quota allocated to them for bananas because of stiff competition from French West Africa and even stiffer competition from the Dole and Chiquita plantations in Central America. Thus, by becoming a part of France, initially as départements d'outre-mer (overseas departments) in 1946 and later as decentralized régions mono-départementales (mono-departmental regions) in 1982, Martinique and Guadeloupe have traded "some autonomy and power over decision making for material and political security" (Hintjens 1995, 71).

Certainly, the two independent English-speaking neighbors, Dominica and St. Lucia, look upon Martinique and Guadeloupe with envy because of their veneer of prosperity. On the other hand, these same neighbors also cast pitiful glances at these French islands because their traditional agricultural economy has been sacrificed and exchanged for metropolitan, as opposed to indigenous, signs of wealth: expensive cars and imported French food along with more modern and substantial health and educational systems. A negative consequence is that these political and economic dependencies spill over into the cultural space.

While collecting songs representative of the nineteenth-century era of Saint-Pierre (the former Martinican capital destroyed by the 1902 eruption of the Mount Pélée volcano), Victor Coridun (1990, 36–37) was able to find some that dealt with social issues. Two were Carnival songs: "Défans ka vini fòl" (The defense is becoming stupid) and "Montangn é vèr" (The mountain is green). The former satirized the prejudices and faults of the colonial aristocracy; the latter praised Victor Schoelcher, the nineteenth-century French abolitionist credited for being the agent to grant freedom to the slaves in France's colonial territories on 27 April 1848.

In the twentieth century, song lyrics also reflect the island society. In 1940, some unidentified French Caribbean soldiers composed "Nèg ni mové mannyè" (The black man has bad manners),[2] a song that created an uproar among the more conservative element of Guadeloupean society. The soldiers wrote the song while they were stationed in North Africa, waiting impatiently for their repatriation after being demobilized. Although the satirical song is misunderstood by some Guadeloupeans who accused the guitarist Gérard La Viny (who later recorded the song) of devaluing the Black man, "Nèg ni mové mannyè" nevertheless enjoyed an enormous success in Africa and the Caribbean. Its double-entendre language about three social classes and racial categories in their masculine forms strikes a nerve. Objections are uttered as soon as people hear the lines, "Béké ka bo madanm yo / Milat ka karessé yo / Nèg la ka fouté-i baton" (The béké kisses his wife; the mulatto caresses his [wife]; and the Black man uses his stick),[3] a verse reinforcing the negative stereotype about the Black man's sexuality. The second verse fares a little better as it addresses the availability of instrumental choices among the three racial groups: "Béké ka jwé violon / Mulat ka jwé piano / Nèg ka bat gwo tanbou" (The béké plays the violin; the mulatto plays the piano; and the Black beats the big drum).

Probably, La Viny's intent in recording the song was to amuse and to encourage Blacks and mulattos to reassess their apathy and willingness to sell themselves for so little. Straddling the disjunction between truth and stereotype, La Viny pointed out false, and somewhat real, perceptions depending upon the listener's location and the historical moment. The underlying historical assumptions about the three instruments and owners were as follows: Due to his privileged position of owning most of the Caribbean land, the béké had the financial advantage and money to play the violin, associated with classical European music. The mulatto, who aspired to be like a Frenchman, had less leisure time but earned enough white-collar money to purchase a piano, which was associated with bourgeois taste. The Black, who was primarily found among the rural and urban working class, earned less money. If he were a manual laborer, he carved out his own drum and beat on it.

From 1940 to 1943, Constant Sorin was governor of Guadeloupe under the direct authority of Admiral Robert, commander-in-chief of the French forces in the western Atlantic, who had lived in Martinique. When France was defeated by the Germans, Admiral Robert swore allegiance to Maréchal Pétain, who headed the Vichy regime in France, and formulated a plan to protect Martinique and Guadeloupe from a possible British-American occupation. The plan was so successful that the two islands were totally isolated from the rest of the world, and Sorin imposed a police state in Guadeloupe. All the locally elected officials were removed and replaced by appointed mayors and city officers. Sorin levied a tax on all merchandise and kept a close eye on the black market. Guadeloupeans suffered under Sorin's regime; many succumbed from malnutrition. During their scrounging for food, cooking oil, and soap, a resourcefulness and interest in the ways things had been done in the past resurfaced. An example was the method of making soap by pressing coconut oil. Hence, out of suffering, Guadeloupeans were proud of their ability to be creative and more reliant on their innate skills.

Dany Bébel-Gisler's 1985 biographical novel, *Léonora: l'histoire enfouie de la Guadeloupe* (Leonora: the buried story of Guadeloupe), vividly described this difficult period and mentions two popular songs that captured the Guadeloupeans' sentiments. One of them referred to the pervasive hunger and the introduction of food rationing: "Gouvènè kondanné nou manjé / éspagéti a gran fèy, pandan nou / ka mégri gouvèné la ka ri" (The Governor made us eat / plain spaghetti / While we thinned / the governor grinned) (Bébel-Gisler 1994, 92). Sorin the man and his policies were hated by the Guadeloupeans. A property tax was imposed, and the youth were carefully monitored. When Sorin left Guadeloupe after De Gaulle's Free French troops overpowered the Vichy soldiers, Guadeloupeans rejoiced and sang "Viv Dégôl viv Lézalyé / Soren tonbé pou léternité" (Long live De Gaulle, long live the Allies / Sorin has fallen, never to rise) (Bébel-Gisler 1994, 93–94).

To tell Martinique's story, there are Raphaël Confiant's 1985 first novel in French, *Le Nègre et l'Amiral* (The black man and the admiral) and Patrick Chamoiseau's 1986 *Chronique des sept misères* (Chronicle of seven miseries). Like the Guadeloupeans, Martinicans suffered from malnutrition and a shortage of medicine during World War II. Among the many scenes from *Le Nègre et l'Amiral* are the youth who attempt to flee the island, the black market, and the army's raids on the poor for scarce food. When De Gaulle's troops land on Martinican soil, he is viewed as a twentieth-century Schoelcher who returns to liberate people from bondage.[4] In *Chroniques des sept misères* Chamoiseau provides a recitation of how Martinicans and Martinique are transformed into being more self-sufficient through the three years of Vichy domination.

After the end of World War II, the poet Aimé Césaire, known for his prewar book-length négritude poem *Cahier d'un pays natal* (1939), was voted in as both the mayor of Fort-de-France and the Deputy of Martinique in the French National Assembly in 1945. He was continually reelected to his two posts until his retirement from the National Assembly in 1993. Poet, playwright, and essayist, Césaire expounded an anti-assimilationist position, promoted the study of blackness, and joined the French Communist Party. In 1956, Césaire resigned from the Communist party, accusing it of racism, and reversed his positions regarding the promotion of assimilation and departmental status within France. As founder of the Parti Progressiste Martiniquais (PPM) in 1958, he campaigned to require the French permeation of education and language on the island to the exclusion of other external or internal elements. Thus, Césaire and his party's lobbying fell in line with France's political *mission civilisatrice* (civilizing mission) to remake "primitive" Martinicans into good French citizens by extending to them the French language, culture, civilization, and economic system while simultaneously rejecting African values and promoting a racial distinction between mulattos and Blacks. To continue this schism among the colonized people of its African and Caribbean territories, France chose Martinicans and Guadeloupeans to occupy civil service positions of authority in African countries. Far from identifying themselves with the independence movements in French Africa, these assimilated Martinicans and Guadeloupeans prided themselves in retaining their status as French citizens.

What ought to be pointed out was the PPM delivered both the decisive and affirmative votes in the referendum to keep Martinique a department, and Césaire openly embraced General De Gaulle during his brief visit in Martinique in 1964. However, by the 1990s, after thirty years of service, Césaire was tired and no longer an effective politician. In fact, the ultra-left considered Césaire to be a bourgeois Uncle Tom, a sell-out, and someone who clung to French sovereignty. Credence was lent to this position when Césaire delivered his emotional 29 May 1981 speech, declaring a moratorium on discussions of the island-department's political status when François Mitterrand and the French Socialist party won the 1981 presidential elections. In fear of a total separation from France, Césaire and members of the PPM voted for Mitterrand, although 72 percent of Martinican voters rejected the French Socialist Party's regional decentralization program. This voting pattern meant, according to Richard D. E. Burton, "that since the formation of the PPM in 1958, the party's policy of autonomy or *autogestion* within a French framework stood a serious chance of being implemented and voted in by the metropolitan French not the Martinicans."[5]

Very concerned about the state of affairs in Martinique with its outward gaze upon France, two Martinican composers, Fernand Donatien and Jolème Nayaradou, penned songs that were considered to be of a controversial nature. "La Consommation" (Consumption),[6] one of Donatien's three prizewinning Carnival songs, complained about the bleak state of affairs: factories closed, the market for island-grown fruit and vegetables in decline, and much of the population subsisting on social welfare checks. Yet, a French supermarket chain, Prisunic, thrived with imported goods. In his song "Les Faux mulâtres" (False mulattos),[7] Nayaradou blamed the mulatto élite for the island economy and the preference of French goods and lifestyles. With much disdain, he criticized the well-dressed mulattos who attended the same schools, only spoke French, and drove late-model cars. They maintained this style of living by borrowing money which they did not (and could not) repay. The label of "false mulattos" had been assigned because the lenders had a difficult time getting the mulatto borrowers to reimburse them.

Neither Donatien nor Nayaradou used pseudonyms, a common practice among their calypsonian counterparts in other islands. However, four Martinican singers in the 1970's—Mona, Kali, Pôglo, and Dézormo—did choose professional names. This chapter is about the struggles of these four singers and songwriters to carve out a cultural political space in which to expose the paradoxical socio-political and economic problems that have either hampered or aided the emancipation of their countrymen and women.

Mona: The Barefoot Performer

Whenever a Martinican talks about Eugène Mona,[8] she or he almost never forgets to mention that he sang with bare feet. Having inherited the French snobbery for proper dress, Martinicans have been unable to conceive of a singer performing without shoes. A spiritual man of the land and the hills, Mona did not want to break contact with the land from whence he came. His performance was a gift from God; therefore, he kept a link between himself and his ancestors, whose spirits surrounded him in the air and on the ground. When Martine, the daughter of Mona's best friend Vava Dovin, asked him why he never wore shoes, Mona's response was: "It is not with my feet that I sing. Even you, Martine, when you wear high heeled shoes, you must feel good about yourself. Standing ready to sing is the same for Eugène, his toes will give him the energy to dance" (Mandibèlè 1992c, 18).

Born Venus Eugène Nilècame in Vauclin along the northern Atlantic Ocean coast of Martinique on 13 July 1943, he changed his name to Eugène Mona at age twenty. Nobody knew exactly why he chose this name. The speculation was that the key was provided in the liner lines on the 1976 *Boi brilé*, where he stated: "Monanationale [*Eugène=bien né* (well born)]." The well-born Mona conceived of himself as an extension of others and the cosmic universe. He was convinced that he was born to be a messenger. At various times during his career, his actions and decisions were misunderstood by the Martinican public. Vulnerable, but determined not to wallow in self-pity, Mona responded with "Tan pis pour moi" (Too bad for me):

An ké vini fou fou
An ké vini fou
Manm sé pa pou lè fanm
Kon an dèvyen fou
an son fou de tout
Et moi, après tout, je me resemble
à un fou
Moi, tan pis pour moi

~~~~~~~~~~

(I'm going to go crazy.
I'm going to go crazy,
but not for women.
When you go crazy,
you don't care about anything.
And, after all, I look like
a fool.
That's too bad for me.)[9]

The label "crazy" carried many connotations. The performer Mona was judged to be "crazy" because he rebelled against the traditional manners of the performer. He appeared barefoot, shed his shirt on stage, and sang lyrics packed with abstract (sometimes senseless) symbolism. "Crazy" also connoted the dependent child status that Martinique had with its maternal mother France. Mona exhorted his followers to snub French values that were adopted and practiced by the Martinican élite. A proud Black man from the *mornes* (hills), Mona also conducted himself with an "I don't care" attitude.

In attempting to strike a balance between his private life and public personality, Mona addressed himself in the third person singular. Whenever he granted an interview, he called himself "Eugène Mona" because, on stage, Mona represented the Martinican. However, he utilized the first person singular with his family and close friends, for they were on equal footing. Speaking in the third person further supported his critics' contention that he was "crazy." In response to such negative criticism, two musicians, Moune de Rivel and Edmond Mondésir, defended Mona's behavior. According to Rivel, Mona was like an organism within an organism. She arrived at this conclusion because Mona referred to himself as a "living cell for whom music is a serious thing which requires constant and daily work on physical, psychic and spiritual levels" (de Rivel 1982). Taking it a step further, Mondésir said: "Mona is a symbolic representation of the Martinican people's soul" (Mondésir 1992, 42).

Raised in a humble household shared with a brother and sister, Mona was apprenticed to Emile Dispagne, from whom he learned to work in wood and become an accomplished carpenter. The end result was that his work as a carpenter led him to carve his chosen musical instrument, the flute, after he began his second career as singer and musician. In 1963, at age twenty, he seriously ventured into music, becoming a member of a mini-orchestra in the little nightclub Chez Nana in Fort-de-France until 1964. But his artistic career, as a professional musician, really began four years later in 1968, when he performed with the M. F. Renard folk group in the *concours* (contest) of popular songs at the patron saint festivals. Also, as soon as Mona moved his residency to Marigot along the north Atlantic Coast of Martinique, he became interested in playing the flute. Due to his love for wood and his first profession as a carpenter, he deliberately chose to play a bamboo flute (called *flajolé* or *toutoun-banbou* in Creole).

Max Cilla, a fellow flutist, was approached by Mona about flute lessons. During their first sessions Cilla noticed immediately that Mona was a naturally gifted player who only needed to learn formal techniques for playing the flute. Usually, Cilla noted it was the other way around for musicians:

"There are several stages in the musical progression. You begin by interpretation then there is the stage where one becomes the creator. Even with some knowledge of the flute as an instrument, Mona was already a creator" (Mandibèlè 1992a, 26). With delight, Cilla proceeded to teach Mona various methods on how to improve his technique.

From 1976 to 1986, Mona produced six albums with Jacob "Jacky" Nayaradou for 3A Productions in Fort-de-France (Nayaradou 1992, 39). He released his first album, *Boi brilé,* in 1976, inspired by the blues of Louis Armstrong. As the title indicated, Mona drew upon his almost worshipful communion with the earth, the countryside, and the smell of burning wood. Through the adoption of African American blues in the title track "Bois brillé" (Burnt wood), he struggled with sadness while singing about the pain and wonder of being born a Black man:

Lé mwen lévé lématen
Mwen ka pran bout kòd la
Mwen ka maré ren mwen
Pou mwen ay fè tren mwen
É gadé zannimo mwen
Lè-w sizè mwen fini
Mwen ka pran gran wou-a
Mwen ka lévé zyé mwen
Pou mwen mandé kouraj
"A la divinité" O-O
Poi y pé pa mwen
An mannyè pou mwen pa sa
Santi lanmizè mwen, santi lanmizè mwen
Bondyé fè mwen pou sa
Y ba mwen an bwa brilé
Y ba mwen an pil san
É man byen rézistan
Dapré-y
Man pa bèl
Y pa bèl

Konprann mwen.
Nou pa fèt pou "le luxe"
Pa menm pou "le calice"
Nou pi dwatèt admi
Dapré sa mwen ka wè O-O

É mwen ka tann, é sa listwa kité ba nou,
"Dans les archives," "dans les archives"
Non nou sé "Bwa Brilé"

Tjé nou pa diféran
Bondyé fè nou pou sa
Y ka ba nou lénon blan
Otis té "Bwa Brilé"
Y té ni an non blan
Armstrong té "Bwa Brilé"
Y té ni an non blan.
Luther King té "Bwa Brilé"
Y té ni an non blan.

〰〰〰〰〰〰

(When I get up in the morning,
I wrap the cord,
attach it around the waist,
attend to my chores, and
go tend to the animals.
At 6:00 P.M. I finish my day.
I take the main route, and
I raise my eyes to the sky
to ask for courage
from the Divine One
so that he grants me
a way to overcome my misery.

The Lord made me for that.
He made me burnt wood
He gave me blood in quality.
He made me resistant.
In his opinion,
I am not handsome.
He is not handsome.

Understand me.
We are neither made for the luxuries
nor for the communion-cup.

We haven't got the right to be admitted
to what I see. Oh, Oh.
I hear and wait for what history bequeaths us
"in the archives," "in the archives."
We are burnt wood.
Our heart is not somewhat different.
God made us for that.
He gave us white names.
Otis was burnt wood.
He had a white name.
Armstrong was burnt wood.
He had a white name.
Luther King was burnt wood.
He had a white name.)[10]

This blues song encompasses the psychological state of a Black man who is exploited, dominated, and dispossessed. It also reveals the conditions under which the Black poor farmer lives in rural Martinique, getting up in the morning to till land he does not own. This daily ritual is well captured when Mona sings: "Lé mwen lévé lématen / Mwen ka pran bout kòd la / Mwen ka maré ren mwen" (I get up in the morning / I attach the rope around my trousers).[11] Wrapping the rope around a peasant man's waist is representational of the man's determination to face another day with an erect posture. As the song continues, Mona also reflects upon the drudgery and misery when he questions the divine about his lot in life. Translated literally, "Bois brillé" means "burnt wood," but it is used here as a metaphor for Black skin. Interested in the history of Black people as well as their music, particularly Negro spirituals and Louis Armstrong's music, Mona decides that "Man must feel good about himself." He pushes forward this position by insisting that the Black man had a historical place before slavery and after colonialism and the construction of archives.

To whom did these white names belong? They were all assigned to African American men: Otis Redding, a singer; Louis Armstrong, a trumpet player; and Martin Luther King, a Baptist minister. These three deceased men had talents and messages that influenced people like Mona across cultural lines. Cutting across divisions and the low status assigned to Blacks in Martinique, Mona's "Bois brillé" elevates the color "black" from the category of subordination and victimization to one of assertion and resistance.[12]

On the second album Mona attacks the social posturing of the mulatto élite, based in urban centers, who see themselves as Frenchmen. Taking a nationalistic stance he emphasizes the cultural revival of dignity and identity that remain (almost intact) in the mornes. Here, in the mornes of Marigot and Sainte-Marie, a communal history is periodically revived through *bèlè* drum and song gatherings and the warrior *ladja* dances.[13] Instead of snubbing poor rural Blacks for speaking Creolized French, living in a small *kaz* (hut), and having a "Black" skin, mulattos should not think of themselves as light-skinned French people but as a distinct people and move away from the divisiveness of ethnic separatism. Therefore, his songs "Lakay Adan" (Adam's house) and "Ti bouchon" (The penis) provide a political platform for Mona to espouse rural and sexual values that need to be transferred to urban dwellers who stray too far from their ethnic origins.

On the third album, where the popular "Doudou Menard" (Darling Menard) was introduced, Mona reveals his thoughts about women, listing feminine qualities like tenderness, affection, and comfort. The novelist Patrick Chamoiseau notes that he listened to "Doudou Menard" almost every day while he was writing his second novel, *Solibo magnifique* (Magnificent Solibo) in 1988 (Chamoiseau 1992, 60). Highly inspired, he passes on the song's title to his female protagonist (changing the spelling to *Doudou-Ménar*). Chamoiseau duplicates the oral production of the song within the narrative of the novel, sprinkling Creole puns, exclamations, expressions, and metaphors. Without discussing his novel with Mona, the two men parallel each other in duplicating orality into their compositions: the underlining of humor with pessimism, the supernatural with Christianity, and confusion with depression. Mona, the *porte-parole* (the speaker), is transformed into the storyteller Solibo from Chamoiseau's novel for the promotion of the Martinican *mémoire vraie* (true memory).

A self-taught person who had difficulty reading and writing, Mona tries to cram too many ideas in one song. "Agoulou sé lan mò" (Greed is death) is an example of this tendency. In a strong voice, Mona discusses the life cycle: Man is born to die. Therefore, the structure of "Agoulou sé lan mò" resembles a religious testament, opening with: "L'hymne national de la mort / Pas mwen pa sav si lè mò ni lè sonjé ya ja pasé pa le shimen di lavi / Mé mwen épi-w nou sav nou kay pasé pa le shimen de lan mò" (This is the national hymn of the dead / Because I don't know if the dead know they're alive / but I know that you and I are following death's path).[14] Midway through the song, rhetorical questions are asked about the personification of death:

Poutchi ou kryé y volè?
Sa iza volè ta-w?

Poutchi ou kryé y volè?
Bon djé pa lè-w lé ou mò.
Pasé nou ka pasé, pasé an tè-a.

〰〰〰〰〰〰〰

(Why do you call him a thief?
Did he steal anything from you?
Why do you call him a thief?
God will not want you when you're dead.
We're just in passage on this earth.)

Wondering why so much fear surrounds death, Mona then inserts the folk saying, "Mi an ti fraz ki ka fè-w médité / Sé pa an sel séson bef-la bizwen la tchè / Mouch la ka pitché fò / É i pa ni séson / Avan lè-a rivé an nou dansé bèlè" (Here is a little sentence that will make you meditate / Because bees sting hard / and they haven't got a season for that / Before the time [death] comes / let's dance the bèlè) to reinforce the reality that death cannot be avoided. This is not to say that whenever one of his friends died that Mona did not grieve. For instance, the militant Emile Laporte's death inspired Mona to write "Agoulou cé lan mò."

On his fourth album, simply entitled *Eugène Mona*, Mona was adventurous enough to change the tone and key of the flute for all of his songs. In his sensitivity to external phenomena and local politics, Mona varied his songs to locate an unbiased reflection of himself, his personality, and his ability as a performer. First, since he totally identified with nature, he was disturbed that French construction companies cut down trees to pave the way for concrete buildings. Second, after the deaths of his band drummer Ernest "Vava" Dovin and the bèlè drummer Emmanuel "Ti Emile" Casérus, Mona wrote "Tambou séryé" (Serious drum), which can be considered a tribute to them by looking at what can be produced from the merger of nature and man's natural talent. As far as Mona was concerned, music does not exist for itself but as a companion to natural impulses. Emotion dictates the rhythm; the voice by its sounds translates the message. Consequently, Mona's lyrics function as an associate to music which reflected life's moments.

Vava Dovin,[15] one of Mona's closest friends and a percussionist, served another function in Mona's band, that of Mona's private counselor. He provided Mona with the strength and rigorous energy to rehearse and rework his musical compositions. Vava and another friend, Pierre-Louis Michalon, spent numerous hours talking about a range of topics with Mona. Understandably, Vava's death left behind an inconsolable Mona who found it to be virtually impossible to perform. "The loss of Vava," according to Cilla, "was a mutilation for Mona" (Mandibèlè 1992a, 28). For Mona, who believed that death was transcendent into a new life, Vava's death precipitated a *traversée de désert* (dry period of early retirement). During his struggle to make a fifth album, released around 1984, Mona turned away from the traditional drum to look at African American jazz because of its origin in pain. He imitated the spontaneous improvisations of jazz forms and remixed them with traditional folk music. With this newly created music, Mona penetrated the French market where avid jazz followers were intrigued with his mixture of traditional music and jazz. The French did not understand the lyrics, but the experimental music touched something within them. Articles that appeared in the French press were very favorable. For instance, *Le Monde* carried the caption "Un magicien: deux soirées magnifiques, une star authentique" (A magician: two magnificent evenings, an authentic star); *Libération* ran another flattering caption: "Une étoile du Monde Noir est née" (A star from the Black world is born). The irony, however, was that this album addresses Mona's disillusionment with local politics and with the politicians who were in favor with the French.

After the appearance of this fifth album Mona began to suffer again from bouts of depression. He paid several visits to Sainte-Marie to see Père Elie for religious counseling. In the course of his search for mental and spiritual peace, Mona went to Jamaica, where he met Rastafarians for the first time and listened to reggae music. There, he was drawn to Bob Marley's music and lyrics about Jah, brotherhood, and defiance of all forms of oppression. However, Bob Marley's untimely death on the heels of Vava's plunged him into a deeper depression which Mona found more and more difficult to shake off. Upon his return to Martinique Mona recorded his sixth album. On the cover, he wore a white turban with the picture of the Lion of Judah and other Rastafarian emblems in the background, basing the theme upon "Il faut que l'homme soit bien avec lui-même" (Man must reconcile with himself).

Called a mystic, a very caring person, and a deeply religious man, Mona was subjected to mood swings from extreme joy to depression. The theme of spiritual discovery (already discussed in "Agoulou cé lan mò") assumed a central place in his repertory, revealing a preoccupation with faith and enlightenment. The symbolism of the tree as a repository of life was replaced with the belief that the devil lurked among its leaves. Retreating to the foyer de la Trinité at Brin d'Amour, Mona composed "Sové Jesus Christ" (Save Jesus Christ), during which he asked the Lord's pardon. Still unable to shake off his depression, Mona finally succumbed to it and entered a self-imposed retirement from 1986–90. Immediately, wild rumors circulated that Mona was experimenting with drugs or had had a nervous breakdown. But Félix Fleury, the band's manager, explained that the singer underwent a religious experience akin to the suffering of many devout Christians.[16]

Portions of his creativity had been repressed in his struggle to satisfy the music industry that invested money in him and wanted a profitable return. Mona strove to be a Martinican singer on his own terms; this struggle led to his psychic dislocation. He, a Martinican, was a mixed product of several cultures, with the African culture (for him) being the most important. Having been in the public spotlight for over twenty years, Mona's body and spirit were weary from grief and health problems. Therefore, his self-imposed *traversée de désert* was necessary; Mona had arrived at the crossroads between sanity and madness. To fuse his fragmented parts of the self, he had to rest and call upon Père Elie, family, and friends to touch him with their healthy hands and to serve him as mediating figures. During his four years of retirement, Mona passed his time traveling and singing for church choirs.

Finally, in 1990, Jean-Michel and Marilène Mauriello of Studio Hibiscus joined the list of concerned people who persuaded Mona to come out of hibernation. Not only had the time come for the singer to pass on the "wise" words, but also Mona's salvation rested in the creativity of music. Following the Mauriello's advice, Mona assembled his former musicians to rehearse old and new numbers, producing *Blanc mangé*.[17] This seventh and last album took six months to record because it underwent two periods of production: first, a live performance and second, recordings in the studio (Mandibèlè 1992b, 38). Sadly, Mona died before its release by Studio Hibiscus in 1991.

Although the chosen songs for *Blanc mangé* were recorded in 1991, Mona actually wrote them in 1984, 1985 and 1986. "Face a Face" (Face to face), located on this posthumous album, is the reflection of a man who looked hard at society and evaluated it while he was in hibernation. There are many double meanings in the lyrics; the song is not easy to sing or play. At first, Mona wanted to give "Pokoyson avan tou" (Precaution above all) as the album's title and the main song instead of "Face a Face." After contemplation, he decided to leave as his title song a mystical image about moving in the direction of a white light to guide him into an unavoidable peaceful future. Thus, his choice of "Blanc mangé" left people perplexed. They could not decide if Mona was discussing a coconut dessert or was being intentionally vague about a religious or social message. Without being superstitious, Madame Mauriello asked: "Was this song a premonition?"

Regardless, Mona liked to throw out challenges, as noted in "Face a Face,"[18] an intense ballad in which he discovered that a person cannot run away from destiny. Man or woman has to face life squarely, feel good about him/herself, and accept his/her weaknesses and strengths. However, each person must know his/her ethnic history. Using the format of a Baptist preacher who repeated the same phrase to command attention and to reinforce a specific idea, Mona chose "O-O mwen ka di-w sa" (O O I am telling you about it) as an introduction. He also tagged on the Creole proverb "Sa ki sav sav / Sa ki pa sav pa sav" (Those who know, know / Those who don't know, don't know) at the end of almost every line.[19] The repetition of this phrase stressed the seriousness of the song's message.

In retrospect, "Face a Face" was Mona's last will and testament, a song tinged with some bitterness and a quiet desperation. The self that emerges from the transforming experience chooses to "pass on" his story to other generations who have to face their own destiny. By altering and inverting "Sa ki sav sav / Sa ki pa sav pa sav," Mona voices his disgust with the superficial general attitude of Martinican society. He had been disappointed when he made an appeal to the *Corps musical* (the musicians' union) for funding to form a large band and was turned down. Rather than dwell on this disappointment, he sustains an optimistic viewpoint in the second verse of "Face a Face":

Fòk koupé an fouté
Asèpté gwo difé
Gwo mòdan ni an tan
Pou y ka shanté lavi
Gwo mòdan ni an tan O wi
Pou y fini èspwaté

〰〰〰〰〰〰

(Turn off the furnace
to accept the sacrifice of a big fire.
Today the Boss man
enjoys life.
Tomorrow he will be compelled
to end [his] exploitation [of others].)

For *Blanc mangé*, Mona also composed "Lizo," dedicated to Claude Lise, president of the Conseil Général (who saw Mona in Saint-Pierre eight days before his death). Mona argues with the politician about his political career and tries to put him on guard against his shifty entourage: "Pasajé ka domi pa ka lèv / Félix, mandé pasan ou-a / Pasajé, fodra ou lévé" (The passenger is sleeping but doesn't wake up / Félix, ask for your passage / Passenger, you must get up).[20] Lise has to be warned to protect himself. Mona cautions, "Lizo, Lizo, Lizo, antouré épi javelo" (Lizo, Lizo, Lizo, you are surrounded by javelins). Not content with a warning, Mona makes the following suggestion: "Lité, lité, lité, pa mété bouch-ou adan / dépéché-w, waye" (Fight, fight, fight / Watch your mouth / Hurry up). In effect, Mona suggests to Lise that, if he is not a keen observer and careful in his dealings in politics and with politicians, poor decisions will come back to haunt him.

Very angry about the influx of drugs and its negative impact upon the largely youthful and impressionable Martinican population, Mona composed "Maître Chacha" (Mister Chacha).[21] All of a sudden, the world has gone awry; all past values no longer are pertinent. Now, *diables* and *criminels* (devils and criminals) prey upon, manipulate, and destroy the weak (Martinicans). At the same time, the Martinican small-time drug traffickers and drug addicts are denounced for placing themselves in such a vulnerable and self-destructive state: "Ka pitché tchou ou / Ka pitché tchou" (They sting your ass / They sting your ass). Mona angrily notes "5000 hommes à ma gauche / 5000 hommes à ma droite" (5,000 men to my left and 5,000 men to my right) as a reference to the combined annual average of 5,000 Martinicans and Guadeloupeans who migrated to France each year from 1945 to 1975. Furthermore, the "5,000 to the left" can be in reference to the number of victims; the "5,000 to the right," to those who initiate a battle against drugs.

In spite of the warning about the destructiveness of drugs in "Maître Chacha," Mona issues a second alarm with "Pa touché lou-a" (Don't touch the wolf) on *Blanc mangé*. Using *lou* (the wolf) as a symbolic term for drugs such as crack, cocaine, and heroin, Mona explains that the *gwo misyé* (big men) and *gwo sèvèl* (big brains) are those who market drugs. However, the little people, who ingest the drugs, either run to their deaths or are usually arrested and imprisoned. On the other hand, the big men, who are lawyers, Mafiosi, tomcats, and stuffed shirts, have enough money to hide behind the wall of respectability and money. To offset such destructive behavior and the profiting from the drug trade, Mona's solution is to replace the white drug with locally produced nutritious products such as manioc and *toloman* (arrow root): "Toloman fou nou manjé / Pa kouté sé misyé / Farine an pou nou manjé" (We must eat toloman / Don't listen to these men / We must eat [manioc] jelly). If these young drug addicts do not heed Mona's advice, they will pay the consequence: "Pa touché, pa touché lou-a / I ké dévoré-ou / Pa touché, pa touché lou-a / I ké déchiré-w" (Don't touch it, don't touch the wolf / It's going to consume you / Don't touch it, don't touch the wolf / It's going to destroy you). To avoid choosing an external opiate, Mona implores the Martinicans to look within themselves for salvation.

Obviously, Mona's messages were not sufficient enough to stop the influx of drugs into Martinique. Nevertheless, his overpowering personality, dancing, and movements on stage during live performances electrified his audiences. Endowed with special powers, Mona's songs cast a spell upon his audience. In her effort to understand Mona's stage presence, Maryvonne Charlery described her attendance at a Mona concert in central Fort-de-France in the Parc Floral before cement paths were laid down in the 1970s.[22] A graduate student on leave from a French university for the summer vacation, Charlery described Mona's arrival on stage. Simply dressed in white, he used a rough timbre of voice to sing and danced the *ladja* in his bare feet. She found his performance to be unusual and mesmerizing. When the dust encircled her and flew into her face, Charlery suddenly became a captive to Mona's voice. Without being fully aware of it, Charlery felt that time had stopped for a brief moment, and afterwards remarked on how unusual and mesmerizing was Mona's performance.

Père Elie also was not immune to Mona's charisma and special aura. Whenever he saw Mona, he noticed that the singer carried himself like a sorcerer or a priest (Elie and Maxme 1992, 29). Whenever Père Elie saw Mona in person, or on the stage, he thought that Mona's movements and gestures indicated that the singer was a sorcerer or shaman. Once he understood that fact, then what Mona was saying in his songs fell into place and started to make sense. Also, Mona's posturing explains why the musician Lucky Longlade called Mona a *rasin* (root). In addition, Fleury remarked that "Mona deliberately wrote vague rambling texts. It was his revenge on the Martinican public who gave him a late acknowledgment or no acknowledgment at all."[23] Mona, too, had to be able to deal with the studio, producer, and public to gain recognition and acceptance for his music and lyrics. It was an ongoing battle, since, rather than popular biguine or zouk songs, he primarily wrote traditional songs that did not bring in a large profit for the producer.

Although Mona's stage personality, voice, lyrics, and music lighted a fire, the flames did not radiate out far enough. Larger than life, Mona believed man had an internal potential that was a manifestation of God. Interestingly enough, the clairvoyant Mona had already begun preparing for an early death at the young age of forty-eight. Having complained of pains in his leg (two days before his death), he slept on the floor and told Fleury he was going to be part of the earth soon. Fleury did not find this to be unusual.[24] Sometimes Mona was called "De Gaulle,"[25] and he compared himself to the classical composer Mozart who died in 1791 at the age of thirty-five. As predicted, two hundred years later, in 1991, Mona passed on into the world of the ancestors. He died from a cerebral hemorrhage on the evening of 28 September 1991, after he had carried a pregnant woman on the verge of giving birth to the safety of an ambulance.

The social hierarchy in the music industry did not provide Mona with stability and with contacts to other musical groups. His ambivalence to the social order and his own ambiguous position revealed an inner confusion. Mona wanted to be acknowledged. Yet, he wanted to remain apart with his insistence upon dancing the ladja on stage. He was well aware of the pretentiousness of the fragmented social order. Born poor, Mona was unable on a regular basis to attend school to which light-skinned kids from middle-class families had access. He spoke about the snobbishness and segregated reality. Consequently, Mona was separated from other bands by his perception of class and his poor education. Singing about the Black man's struggles, Mona attempted to alleviate some of his pain. His expression of pain was a means of bringing an end to it or, at least, attenuating it. Also, through performance, Mona conceived of a Black consciousness as an open, culturally negotiable space which is always in the making.

According to Pierre-Louis Michalon, a life-long friend of Mona's, "Eugène Mona's lyrics all have a double sense that many Creole speakers do not understand, refuse to understand, and will never understand. They are timeless and sometimes troubled" (Mandibèlè 1992a, 27). Mona expressed the humanity of Martinican people in face of economic and racial upheavals in a changing country, shifting from a departmentalized state to a regional one. For him and Michalon, the place of mediation was under the *manguier* (mango tree) where nature was law, and the word was a changing and living force. For hours, the two friends imagined, created, invented, and composed.

The Rastafarians: Pôglo and Kali

Rastafarianism came to Martinique in the latter part of the twentieth century. Unlike the Rastafarian originators in Jamaica, the Rastafarians in Martinique did not espouse an ideology associated with a specific political personality or movement. Instead, Rastafarianism owed its initial inspiration to the Black British band, Third World, who gave a live concert in Fort-de-France in 1978, and to the popularity of Bob Marley's reggae music. Nevertheless, the Rastafarian faith took root and slowly gained ground in the low income areas outside of Fort-de-France. What attracted the young people who joined were the dreadlocks, the dietary constraints, the reggae music, and the policy decrying Martinique's moral decay.

By the mid-1980s, the Rastafarians were a small but strong community and had developed a politically conscious movement against departmental-ization. Their overall perception of the French style of government was that Caribbeans were being made into French clones and being discouraged from forming ties to Africa. After Third World's concert more than ten reggae bands, among which were Zion Train, Black Star Liner, 6th Continent, and Pawòl, were formed and in operation. Even an eight-year-old, Prince Aziz Varasse, made a record. In addition, reggae was frequently heard on the radio with programs like "Steppin' Out" with Ras Dou, and "Reggae Relax" with General Isho and Prince Fumance, on RBR (Radio Banlieu Relax), 96.2 FM (Smith 1988, 23).

Pawòl, led by the Rastafarian poet Pôglo, was a departure from the tradi-tional band in that it added theatrical skits. During its 1988 concert at Grand Carbet in Fort-de-France, the band had a theatrical set constructed to depict Babylon on one side with painted cardboard skyscrapers and Zion on the other side with a Lion of Judah flag and mountains. Accompanied by a woman acrobatic dancer to underscore the songs' lyrics, Pôglo sang and moved with Pawòl's nine-piece band who played upbeat Jamaican style rhythms mixed with zouk and folk music (Smith 1988, 23). During this unique concert, Pôglo's solo numbers, performed between the dancing and theatrical skits, were executed with very dramatic body gestures and vocal ranges.

Pôglo, whose Ethiopian name means a drop of water, was the pseudonym for Eric Lugiery, who searched for a Caribbean sound by using the popular Martinican Creole expression "Pa moli!" (Don't give up the fight). Since childhood Pôglo liked to sing, daydream, and draw on pieces of paper. Soon he began to write poems even on the tax forms that he filled out on his job. In the mid-1970s he wrote a poem "Identité" (Identity) and, by coincidence, the sun shined through the window and its rays fell directly on the paper on which he was writing. Pôglo took this to be a sign to quit his job, which involved travel in western Europe, and to explore his musical interests (Dan-iel 1989, 14). While in London in 1979, he was initiated into the Rastafarian philosophy by two elderly gentlemen.

Through his exposure to the Rastafarian philosophy, Pôglo was drawn to a cultural force derived from the African continent. He adhered to the Rastafarian requirements concerning dietary restrictions, the growth of dreadlocks, and the condemnation of misery around the world. Next, he took a pilgrimage to Senegal, Mali, and the Gambia in 1980 where he met griots, played the kora and balafon, and received the Ethiopian name "Pôglo" because he conducted himself in a very discreet manner (Daniel 1989, 14). A week after his return to Martinique Pôglo formed Pawòl with fourteen of his musician-friends.

With the introduction of a very different style, Pôglo, called the "hard poet," raised people's consciousness about the struggle of Black people who live in misery throughout the Third World. His first concerts with Pawòl were quite simple; he recited poetry only to the accompaniment of drums. After several jaunts around various poor communities of Fort-de-France, Pôglo realized humbly that he was drawing his creativity from the misery of others. Calling himself an *ouvrier du verbe* (a verb worker), Pôglo got up every morning at 4:00 A.M., went to the countryside, and practiced his voice in the woods in order not to bother anybody. As soon as he felt that his voice was in shape, he called some friends (one of whom was Kali) in Paris to say he was arriving to make a record in a recording studio. After one day and a half the 45 rpm demo of "Pa moli" was done, but the sound mixing was not completed until seven months later. In 1988, this song was re-released on the album *Pa molli*,[26] which contained the other songs under discussion.

The single "Pa moli" created a commotion because most people by now were accustomed to listening to zouk music. However, "Pa moli" was a mixture of reggae with some biguine, rock, and zouk. In addition, people were not accustomed to listening to Pôglo's unique singing style with its curious vibrato. What was of interest, however, was Pôglo's technique of increasing sales of his record. He decided to set up a radio-cassette player on the sidewalks of Dillon (a southern suburb of Fort-de-France) and to perform free by playback. Considered to be a wise man and respected by young and old alike in Dillon because he mediated conflicts in the neighborhood, Pôglo's strategy caused people to purchase his record.

Pôglo's other passion beside music and poetry is painting. His songs are therefore constructed like a tableau where he pays keen attention to colors, movements, and birds. He tries to merge as one with his lyrics.[27] The popular "Pa moli" is basically a message of encouragement when he cautions: "Sé pa tou sa-w rwé an gan lan / Fòk anni mété-w ka jigé / Pas sa-w la ka jijé / Mi-w pé twouvé anba kouch-w" (Don't be in such a rush / to judge the other / because one day you might find yourself making the same mistake).[28] His primary use of the Rastafarian colors of green, red, and yellow comes into fruition when he defines the song "Lèspwa" (Hope):

Ver' Koulé lèspwa
Jôn richess lavi
Rouj sang pou lavi
Blé an fon syèl la
Dé twa ti gout' lèspwa
Tonbé asou laté
La pli rouzé ti grenn'
Pou dèmen poté lèspwa
Limié poté lavi
Krévé o léténeb
Solèy chofé laté
Rasin lévé lavi
Arkansiel kléré
Alians Jah Jah an syel
La pli bondié tombé
Rouzé lèspwa lavi

Limié kléré syèl la
La jwa za ka dansé
Van lavi souflé
Lanmou za ka chanté
Chanton pou la viktwa
Dousé anlé violans
Chanton pou la viktwa
Lanmou anlé ladié

Bra lévé dan syèl
San jis an bout dwet
Dé pié-w asou laté
Chouton ô liniorans
Limié kléré syèl la
La jwa za ka dansé
Van lavi souflé
Lanmou za ka shanté

〰〰〰〰〰〰

(Green, color of hope
Yellow, life's riches

Red is life's blood.
Blue, the sky's background.
Two, three small drops of hope
have fallen upon the earth.
Rain moistened the little grains so that
tomorrow can bring hope.

Light, bearer of life,
split the darkness.
The sun heats the earth, and
the roots of life rise up.
The rainbow illuminates.
It's the alliance of Jah Jah in the sky.
God's rain falls to water life's hope.

The light clears up the sky.
Joy is put to dance.
Life's wind begins to blow,
and love already sings.
Let's sing for the victory
of kindness over violence.
Let's sing for the victory
of love over war.

Arms raised toward the sky.
Full of life.
Two feet on earth.
Let's wipe out ignorance
in order to light up the sky.
Joy dances.
The wind of life breathes,
and love already sings.)[29]

A merger of Pôglo's religious beliefs and sensitivity about poverty is found in "Sasévwé" (That's true). Having embarked on trips to Europe and Africa, he is conscious of how small Martinique is in relation to the rest of the world. However, in spite of its size, Martinique is a country with "Tèlman tèlman gwo pwoblèm" (So many big problems). As a consequence, Pôglo's advice is to believe in Jah (God): "Sèl chèf mwen sav ki dan syèl la / Sèl chèf mwen sav sé Jah Jah" (I know one Master who is in the sky / The only Master

I know is Jah Jah).[30] A Rastafarian, he could await with dignity the Judgment Day, when the last shall be first and the first shall be last. Also, living in Babylon (the French department of Martinique and the temporal captivity of the spirit), Pôglo's only escape is in the rural countryside to communicate with birds who fly away at will:

> One day, I wrote a song in the country. The blackbirds around me prevented me from concentrating. They entered into my sound. My song could not be made. Then I made the song with the birds. I did not want that. They came all by themselves.[31]

A wearer of many hats—dreamer, poet, painter, husband, and father—Pôglo's artistic career creates a watercolor of various sensations connected to a stream of national consciousness. As for the birds, they are agents of transformation.

A fellow Rastafarian friend is Jean-Marc "Kali" Monnerville,[32] who was born on 21 February 1959, in Fort-de-France, into a family of musicians. His father, Ivon Monnerville, is a musician; his mother Liliane Ransay a writer; his maternal uncle, Max Ransay a vocalist and musician, and his brother Paul Ives "Pim" Monnerville a drummer. Pim and Jean-Marc were raised with a reverence and respect for the bèlè drum. They also spent a lot of time in Saint-Pierre, home of the biguine, but their parents moved the family back to Fort-de-France to send them to a better choice of schools (Cally 1996, 118).

In 1974, the fifteen-year-old Kali left Martinique to study music in France, where he met other French Caribbean and African musicians. At age sixteen, Kali launched a group called Gaoulé (of which Jean-Claude Naimro, now Kassav's keyboard player, was a member), issuing the album *Gaoulé* (1975) with a mixture of funk, biguine, Haitian compas, and reggae. Kali chose the title *Gaoulé* (Thimon 1989, 20), for it is the name of a massacre of slaves who revolted in the eighteenth century in the southern part of Martinique. Brief stints with other groups followed, finally leading him to the reggae band Marfata and a contract with the Hilaire Hartoc Band at the Hotel Latitude in Carbet. Around 1979, when the Hilaire Hartoc Band dissolved, Kali assembled four musicians (David Montanez on drums, Vasco Noverazz on keyboard, Joseph Patiron on bass, and José Jean-Marie on guitar) to form 6th Continent (May 1995, 8). The contract at the Hotel Latitude permitted the new band to have a stable income. While at the hotel Kali met Rémy Bellenchombre, ex-leader of La Guerilla, who was to become a collaborator on Kali's future songs and also the leader and partial financier of 6th Continent.

Kali and 6th Continent built up a reputation with the playing of light zouk music mixed with Jamaican-style reggae. An important date for 6th Continent was 22 May 1979, when it held its first big concert at Grand Carbet Concert Hall in the Parc Floral for the Rastafarian community and all other Martinicans. This led to an invitation to record their first album in Guadeloupe, but the record's pressing and distribution were delayed for two years. Finally, in 1981, its track "Reggae Dom-Tom" became the group's first hit. On 21 June 1983, in Paris, the band replaced the internationally acclaimed Nigerian musician Fela Ransome Kuti and performed before an audience of 50,000 people at the Fête de la musique at the Place de la Concorde (May 1995, 9). When the group signed with CBS, the company team asked them to shave off their beards and to change the direction of their music with *caisses claires* (clear registers). Some of the musicians complied, but Kali refused and the band disbanded in 1986.

After the dissolution of 6th Continent, Kali endured two tough years in France in his efforts to survive as a full-time musician. He and the percussionist Charly Labinsky tried different formulas: private soirées, clubs, animations, and schools. They even did studio work to earn 800 Francs a session. Calling this his "survival" period, Kali also hung around Jacob Desvarieux and Jean-Claude Naimro of Kassav' in the studio. He made drums to sell, and his parents helped him out financially. Next, he played the *chouval bwa* with Pakatak; he toured and recorded "Carrément News" (Straight talk) with Pier Rosier of Gazoline until he branched off to begin his own solo career. Finally, tired of life as a migrant and two years of piece work, Kali returned to Martinique in 1987 to gain some inspiration through forming his own band.

Having grown up in a household where Alexandre Stellio's 78 vinyl records were played constantly, Kali decided to return to the mazurka, waltz, and biguine in a search for authentic roots for his first solo album. Already an accomplished drummer and guitarist, the restless Kali kept looking for a new direction in his music. His search ended when Rémy Bellenchombre gave him the precious gift of an old family heirloom, a Norman banjo (formerly owned by Bellenchombre's father). Liking a challenge, Kali switched to playing the banjo because it had been a popular traditional instrument in the Martinican past. Therefore, the banjo permitted him to return to more traditional music although it was not an easy instrument to play because its strings broke too often.

A gifted composer and multi-instrumentalist, Kali put his talents to good use in his first solo effort. Appropriately called *Racines* (Roots), this pot-pourri of musical styles and topics was released in 1988, featuring fresh bi-guine remixes of songs by Léona Gabriel, Alexandre Stellio, Loulou Boisla-ville, and Eugène Mona. Kali liked to create new lyrics and to recreate old ones. Through this constant process of reinterpreting the old lyrics, he moved beyond imposed constraints. However, it was Kali's banjo playing that held the place of honor, and the title song "Racines," based on a bolero, stood out. Over a period of two weeks Kali and his newly formed, nine-member band played three live sessions at the Coco Loco nightclub near Fort-de-France's pier to test the audiences' reception of the banjo in prepara-tion for the album. "Racines" and the pianist Vasco Noverazz's "La fete St. Pié" (Saint-Pierre's Festival) were the only original songs written for the al-bum. Finally, Kali's satisfaction with the album increased because it was played in Germany, Japan, Holland, and the United States. By 1989, 30,000 copies of *Racines* were purchased, among which 20,000 were sold in Ja-pan.[33] In July 1989, Kali was awarded the Maracas d'or and two Prix SA-CEM awards for *Racines,* and he toured Canada and the United States with his uncle, Max Ransay.

Indebted to Mona, Kali finished *Racines* 2 in 1990 and opened it with a reprisal of Mona's "Poté bambou"(Carry the bamboo), followed by *mus-ique de bals* (ballroom music) of the 1920s and '30s. The music for "Monté larivyé" (Go up the river), a personal song, was composed when the then seventeen-year-old Kali sought some form of inspiration on a march up the river in Saint-Pierre. This song of his youth reached the limelight when Kali decided to compose the lyrics with Bellenchombre and to sing it for the 1992 Eurovision competition.

Completely surprised and taken off-guard, Kali was selected to be the third Caribbean, but the first Rastafarian, to represent France at the 37th Eurovision competition, held in Sweden. This invitation proved that the Mit-terrand socialist government was serious with its promotion of regional dif-ferences in the artistic and political arenas. Kali's determination to perform the Creole biguine "Monté larivyé," with the concession of singing a French phrase that was repeated three times "Entre les roches et les racines / Un jour tu verras la source de la rivière" (Between the rocks and the roots / you will see the river's source one day),[34] was done with serious deliberation. As usual, and not deviating from his position to promote the revised traditional music, Kali searched in vain to compose a "très roots" (very roots oriented) song with a modified mixture of French and Creole.

Not very disappointed, Kali came in eighth place among twenty-three en-tries. After all, "Monté larivyé" was heard by over 350 million television viewers and translated into twenty-seven languages. Kali was grateful for the attention and publicity. In addition to other musical awards,[35] another feather in Kali's cap was an invitation to perform at the second Konda Lota Festival (an association that defends peace and love) at the Hitomi Memorial Hall in Tokyo, Japan in 1991.[36] When Kali strummed the first note on his banjo, the audience of 3,000 Japanese reacted with an immediate enthusiasm, having already been warmed up to Malavoi and Kassav' who preceded him in earlier concerts.

Lésé la tè tounen (1993), the fifth album, is a departure from *Racines 1 et 2, Live au New Morning,* and *Roots.* Here Kali looks for a more international sound that crosses many geographical boundaries. He tackles autobiographical topics such as an emigrant's arrival in and difficult adjustment to France in "Pran patché-w" (Pack up your bag) and the Rastafarian code in "Hey, Rasta." Kali likes being different, so *Lésé la tè tounen* (Let the world turn) makes a big turn when a reversed migration away from France is advocated. In "Pran patché-w," again co-written with Bellenchombre, Kali urges the islander/migrants to "Pran patché-w / Épi viré bò kay manman-w / Pran patché-w / Sé la la vi-a bon" (Pack up your bag / And go back home / Pack up your bag / That's where life is good).[37] Martinique might not be perfect, but family awaits him and it is home. Not one to veer away from negativity, Kali adds, "Menn si lavi lòt bò pa fè di-w an milioné / Anba kokotyé ou ké pé sipòté lanmizé" (Even if life abroad hasn't made you a millionaire / Misery is easier to deal with under the coconut trees).

"Blan enmen Nèg" (The white man likes the black man), which is the next song, is an excellent companion piece on the subject of migration. France is a place of failed dreams and lost hopes. "Lé mwen rivé / A té Paris / Sa mwen wé sé ki / Mwen pa té ké / Pé respiré" (When I arrived / on Parisian soil / I immediately saw / that I would not be able / to breathe).[38] Always a cynic, Kali also observes:

Blan enmen koulè nèg la
Blan enmen tann misik nèg la
Mé i pa enmen Nèg la
Viv adan menm lari-a

(The white man likes the color black.
The white man likes to listen to black music.

but he doesn't like the Black man
to live on the same street with him.)

The narrative tells how the Caribbean migrant is not seen as a threat if he
remains in the cultural space of a musician. Once the migrant encroaches
upon the metropolitan French space in the métro (subway), he is seen as both
a threat and an intrusive presence for the French public and police:

Je n'aurais jamais cru qu'ils étaient comme ça
Polis toujou ka rété mwen
Ou vérifié papié mwen
Ils ont déclaré
Égalité, Fraternité, é

∿∿∿∿∿∿∿∿

(I never believed they were like this.
The police are always stopping me
to verify my papers.
They declared:
Equality, Brotherhood, etc.)

No Caribbean migrant should stay where his French passport fails to protect
him from police harassment; his skin color isolates him from the metropolitan community. To avoid this isolation, marginalization, and the hypocritical
motto "Liberté, Égalité, Fraternité," Kali suggests that the Caribbean man
should return to the island where he *does* belong. Exasperated, the narrator
wonders why he left his country to come to France to suffer from police
harassment. Obviously, having a French passport is not sufficient if one is a
Black man.

Affectionately called "the banjo man," Kali reevaluates Martinican culture, and he is praised for constructing an archeological image of it through
his music with up-to-date changes. In addition, he believes that an album of
twelve songs should be heard for at least two years before the next recording
is done.[39] Kali's re-doing of biguine classics (integrated with reggae) supports
Paulin Hountondji's reasoning that it is better to know the traditions as they
are, beyond any mythology and distortion, in order to meet the challenges
and problems of today (Hountondji 1983, 142–43). An admirer of Bob

Marley, Kali makes a distinction between English and French Creole reggae music; his opinion is that the drum in English-speaking reggae is mystical but that it is warlike in French Creole reggae.[40]

Martinicans are becoming more conscious of the need to preserve their natural landscape, particularly after the active campaigning and demonstrating of the outspoken Association pour la Sauvergarde du Patrimoine Martiniquais (ASSAUPAMAR), which since its founding in 1981 has been the sole association to have worked towards safeguarding the Martinican landscape. This local association opposes the destruction of Martinique's natural beauty and her archeological and historical sites, and it takes a firm stand against any further upsetting of an already fragile ecological balance in what remains of the country's mangroves and forests by money-hungry developers, urban planners, and highway builders. The movement also defends those who are in danger of losing their land and homes to developers' projects. The Green Movement, backed by the local magazine *Antilla,* publishes its own magazine *Koubari* and regularly broadcasts on private and public radio stations. Staunch opponents of *bétonisation,*[41] or the spread of shopping centers, supermarkets, chaotic housing developments and other concrete edifices, the association's members (as well as a great many nonmembers) do not want their country to be turned into another St. Martin, Nassau, Puerto Rico, the American Virgin Islands, or a Miami beach hotel strip.

An ecologist himself, Kali stirs up the issue of the cement-building invasion to have befallen Martinique in the last ten years. His and Bellenchombre's satire about the state of affairs in Martinique is expressed in the 1991 "Île à vendre" (Island for sale), in which the revolutionary left (labeling them civil servants) is ridiculed with the comment that even Martinican snakes are anaesthetized. Indulging in thoughts that most people keep to themselves, Kali draws attention to how detrimental this development has been to the green spaces rather than to the oft-touted "progress" that bétonisation is made out to be. The carved-out cultural political space situates Martinique in the false image of prosperity which is touted as a positive place for tourists. Having a tourist guide calling his passengers on board to show off the island, Kali sings in French. "Nous passons devant le volcan Pelé / N'ayez pas peur les éruptions sont controlées" (We are passing before the Mont Pélée volcano / Don't be afraid the eruptions are controlled).[42] Engaging in what Leah Hewitt calls "a sarcastic interplay between culture and geopolitics" (Hewitt 1995, 248.), Kali parodies the languages of the politicians and tour agents by slipping in and out of Creole, French, and English. The title of the song conveys the message: There is an island for sale. In case the message is misunderstood, the *Ile à vendre* CD cover depicts a little Martinique, assaulted by skyscrapers and squeezed in by concrete walls.

The Emblematic Singer

The five-day, pre-Lenten Carnival in Martinique is preceded by several weeks of Carnival celebrations, the elections of kings and queens in the different towns, zouk parties, *vidés* (jump-up processions of Carnival parades), and sponsored dances by social organizations. These take place in the French Caribbean every weekend of January and February until *Samedi gras* (Shrove Saturday). Every year a theme based on a major political, economic, or other predominant issue of the year before is chosen for Vaval, the name given to the Carnival king, whose funeral pyre is built and effigy is set afire on the night of Ash Wednesday. On other islands which hold the event, Carnival officially closes on Shrove Tuesday (*Mardi gras*). This is not the case in Martinique, Guadeloupe, and French Guyana.

Samedi gras, the first day of Carnival, opens with school children's parades and floats. Carnival gathers momentum on *Dimanche gras* (Shrove Sunday) with the first of many vidés. Through the streets of every town, the day begins with the *pyjama vidés* and continues into the afternoon with groups of Mako-Zombies, cane cutters, market vendors, transvestites, Carolines, and *nèg gwo siwo* (thick black molasses, sometimes called Kongos) parading through downtown. The Mako-Zombies are dressed in costumes that resemble spirits, and the straw and chiffon disguise of a Caroline represents a woman who is bent over from carrying her husband's weight. The *nèg gwo siwo* are men who cover their bodies with a glistening, sticky mixture of molasses and soot. They are the solemn and fierce visual reminders of the people's African forefathers and their enslavement. Slicked down with molasses and soot, they have no difficulty whatsoever in opening a pathway through the revelers during the parade.

Lundi gras (Shrove Monday) is the day of burlesque marriages with the wildest and most outrageous assortment of couples possible. There are men parading as brides, some made up to be several months pregnant, but invariably wearing wedding veils and bridal gowns. Women parade as men, some dressed as grooms with their transvestite brides on their arms. One is likely to see a tall, obese woman with a male dwarf and mock marriages being performed on street corners. Others dancing down the streets to loud, blasting music may be dressed as caricatures of the opposite sex. Shrove Monday is said to be propitious for the fecundity of new unions. One should perhaps inspect the November birth registers. Sometimes calm but always hilarious, Shrove Monday is a day of no inhibition, a day when social taboos are abandoned.

Mardi gras (Shrove Tuesday) marks the appearance of the red devils who wear hideous masks with huge teeth, horns, protruding eyes, and black and red costumes covered with little mirrors to chase away the evil spirits. Children and grown-ups alike don skin-tight red-devil costumes and brandish evil-looking tridents. The color red is seen everywhere to represent the *diablesses* (women sorcerers) who surge by the thousands into the streets. Red also symbolizes life and passion, and the excited populace charge like running bulls. And though the streets clear at nightfall, revelry continues inside at private parties, clubs, and dance halls.

On *Mercredi des Cendres* (Ash Wednesday) everyone fills the streets dressed in black and white as Martinicans, Guadeloupeans, and the Guyanese commence the final, most high-pitched day of the Carnival celebrations. Although white and black are often thought to be the colors of mourning, on this day they represent the full moon (white) and the new moon (black), reminders of the arduous sugarcane harvesting that is to follow Carnival. Thousands come to join in the vidé that forms Vaval's street-upon-street funeral procession. In Martinique, it is a dusky 7:00 P.M. when the final cortege brings Vaval to his funeral pyre and his effigy burns at the Baie des Flamands in Fort-de-France, close to Fort St. Louis, while people cry out: "Vaval pas kité nou!" (Vaval, don't leave us) (Renault 1993, 64). Red flames and sparks rise in the night, sputtering as Vaval turns to ashes, bewitching onlookers as they watch the conflagration. The spirit of Carnival lingers on until four or five in the morning at zouk parties and banquet balls. Only at dawn is Carnival over, and it will be celebrated again the following year.

Carnival cannot be celebrated without its own vidé music, singing, and dancing in the streets. Organized song contests take place in the communes, and some of the winners are promised a recording contract. Since Carnival is an exuberant event, human behavior can be quite raucous. People dance to the "tam-tam" (drum) rhythms and sing songs that range from condemning French and local politicians to sexually lewd ones about body parts. This festivity and air of permissiveness provide the cultural political space and time for Djo Dézormo to release his albums.

Undoubtedly, Dézormo's "Voici les loups" on *Voici les loups* was a smash hit for Carnival 1990 because it touched upon some serious political and economic issues. Coming from the southern commune of Rivière-Pilote, the home territory for the Mouvement Indépendantiste Martiniquais (MIM), Dézormo happened to be one of the party's active members. In view of the reputation of his party affiliation, it was natural for Dézormo to compose the 1990 "Voici les loups."

> Nou ké organizé
> Gwadloup, Matinik, Guyan
> An sanblé mizikal
> Pou lè gran méshan lou
> Vidé ka pwopozé
> Gwadloup, Matinik, Guyan
> An gran vidé vaval
> Kont le gran méshan lou
> Pa oublyé manmay
> Janvier 93
> Kay débatché kay nou
> Yan kalité vyé bèt
> Pa oublyé manmay
> Janvier 93
> Kay débatché kay nou
> Lè gran méshan lou
>
> *Refrain*
> Hou hou, voici lé lou
> Lè lou ki lé èstentché nou
> Kay ni fè, kay ni fè
> Erèz dibonnè nou ni le dépité
> Kat dépité fransé, fransé matinitché
> Atos, Portos, Aramis, Dartagnan
> Hou hou voici lé lou . . .
> Erèz dibonnè, nou ni lé de konsèy
> Konsèy jénéral, konsèy réjional
> Trop konséyè pa bon
> Lé konséyè pa lé péyè

~~~~~~~~~~~

(We are going to organize
in Guadeloupe, Martinique, and French Guyana
a concert
in honor of the big bad wolf.
They are offering in

Guadeloupe, Martinique and French Guyana
a huge Carnival parade
against the big bad wolf.
Don't forget guys
that in January '93
they will disembark in our countries.
A beast never seen before.
Don't forget, guys,
that in January '93
they will disembark in our countries.
The big bad wolf.

Refrain
Ho, ho, here comes the wolf.
This wolf that seeks to eliminate us.
Much suffering is to come, much suffering is to come.
Just think. We have our deputies.
Four French deputies, French from Martinique
Athos, Portos, Aramis, d'Artagnan
Ho, ho, here comes the wolf.
Just think. We have our two councils.
The General Council, the Regional Council,
but too many councillors is not a good thing.
The councillors always get way with it.)[43]

The singer supported his party's advocacy of major changes, rejecting departmental status and any Marxist analysis for the struggle for liberation. Like the MIM, Dézormo appeared to thrive on difficulties and controversies.

Dézormo articulated in "Voici les loups" what many Martinicans agonized over (in silence) about the upcoming European Union. For the fourth time in his musical career Dézormo hit upon a theme and tapped into his people's preoccupation. By token of the free trade agreement, it was common knowledge that as of 1993 an E.U. European could settle, set up a business, work, or buy land in Martinique. Coming on the heels of the 1992 week-long, locally televised mock jury trial of Christopher Columbus, the year supposed to commemorate his coming to the Americas, the result of the E.U. phenomenon registered in people's minds as surely as the gavel of the mock jury's verdict pronouncing Columbus as guilty on all counts. (The mock jury was composed of actual Martinican lawyers and court magistrates.)

Dézormo's "Voici les loups" could not but be an instant success.[44] An initial 1,000 copies were pressed, but the demand by record store owners, disc jockeys, and the public required another pressing of the record. Dézormo's explanation of "Voici les loups" was that lethargic Martinicans had to be awakened from their slumber (Kali was to repeat the same theme in the 1991 "Ile à vendre"). Dézormo said, "I write for myself first and then for my people, for their dignity, and finally I write for others" (Pulvar 1990a, 11).

Dézormo's use of humor to disguise statements of social criticism spilled over into a reinterpretation of "Little Red Riding Hood" with a Martinican Creole twist (Mandibèlè 1990, 12). When Riding Hood asked the wolf: "Why have you got big feet like that? Why have you got big teeth like that?" The wolf answered: "To kick your ass and to devour you." The sheep, newly introduced into the song, delivered the retort "Kay ni fè." The straight French translation is "Nous avons le fer" (We have the iron), meaning "We are in misery," but the Creole word fè signifies "misery" and also a man's penis. Without question, Europe is a big wolf with 340 million people, in contrast to the sheep, little Martinique, with 397,000.

Dézormo's satirical vision of Europe is that of big wolves that travel in a pack. To avoid being eaten up, he gives thanks that the four French deputies, Athos, Portos, Aramis, and D'Artagnan, are in the French Assembly to protect the Martinicans like the swashbuckling three musketeers and aristocrat d'Artagnan from Alexandre Dumas's *Three Musketeers*. The imitative *bèèè* sounds of bleating sheep, who refused to integrate into the European Union in January 1993, and the howling of wolves are heard on the record as well as the command *mach* (march) directed at the wolves to leave Martinique. He concludes by advising the children not to forget January 1993. With *bèèè* followed by *mach*, Dézormo gives back some dignity to the Martinicans.

After the Carnival furor dissipated over "Voici les loups," Dézormo's warning about carnivorous wolves became personal when he received a royalty check for the meager sum of 2,809 francs 90 (about $582).[45] Highly insulted, Dézormo publicly attacked Jean-Michel Mauriello (the Italian producer of Studio Hibiscus who was involved in a 1994 dispute with Léa Galva of Kwak) in the song "Moyeloup 2809F90" (Moye the Wolf 2809F90). Not very original ("Moyeloup" is a play on Mauriello's name), the songwriter flatly stated in French:

Moyeloup, tu n'es pas un loup.
Tu n'es plus qu'un loup.

Tu n'es pas un loup.
Tu es agoulou.

~~~~~~~~~~~

(Moyeloup, you are not a wolf.
Moyeloup, you are more than a wolf.
Moyeloup, you are not a wolf.
Moyeloup, you are greedy.)[46]

Like most French Caribbean musicians and singers eager to have a record, Dézormo probably did not read the fine print on his contract or negotiate it through an entertainment lawyer to protect his interests. On the other hand, this episode was a further demonstration of how Dézormo (the colonized) was dependent upon Mauriello (the colonial master) for the symbolic food (record royalties). Although the weaker of the two, and almost devoured by the wolf, Dézormo struck back with the self-produced "Moyeloup 2809F90," a song heard on most radio stations and in the bars.

Dézormo, whose birth name is Joseph Gros-Désormeaux, likes to take on thorny social issues with sharp-edged comments as they explode around him. For instance, from the late 1960s until the early 1980s, Martinique and Guadeloupe were marked by a violence that was provoked by many student and union strikes. In Guadeloupe, bombings, shootings, and kidnapings became an integral part of the political scene in spite of the general population's condemnation of this violence.[47] Unemployed youths stormed the streets of Pointe-à-Pitre and Basse-Terre at the time of a building strike, and a number of teachers, doctors, and journalists were accused of and arrested for undermining state security. In the streets of Fort-de-France, the local police attempted to maintain some kind of order by constructing barricades, throwing tear gas, and arresting students. They also called upon the French gendarmes.

By all means, Dézormo could not let it go unnoticed that there had been cooperation between Martinican police and French gendarmes to stop the demonstrators. Knowing how important these events would be in the new Martinican-authored history texts, Dézormo composed "Blé pal blé fonsé" (Pale blue, dark blue) as early as 1975, castigating the police involvement in another violent phase of Martinique's history.[48] This bold judgment coming out of a song that was hummed in bars, played on private record players, and censored by the government, resulted in Dézormo's arrest.

As a member of the MIM, Dézormo opposes French national elections and any campaign visits by French candidates.[49] He also supported the high school students who organized a march in the streets of Fort-de-France on 22 May 1976, to push for the passing of a bill for an annual paid holiday in recognition of the abolition of slavery. From the students' perspective, the French Revolution and the fall of the Bastille had no direct bearing on their culture. Yet Bastille Day on 14 July was (and still is) a national holiday in the French Caribbean.

Expending much political energy on what some thought was historical trivia, members of the left joined in the students' campaign to change the official date of the 1848 emancipation from 27 April (date of the proclamation of abolition of slavery in Paris) to 22 May (date of the slave uprising preceding the arrival of the abolition decree in Martinique). Using song to record historical events, Dézormo's interpretation of the campaign and the student demonstrations resulted in "Sé lè 22 mé" (It's 22 May). Unfortunately, this time the socio-political content of the song in connection with the uprisings was censored by government officials who unexpectedly barred "Sé lè 22 mé" on the government radio station RFO (Radio France Outre-Mer). What the students and the left pushed for was a rewriting of Martinican history to emphasize the role of slave rebellions in the struggle for liberation and to deemphasize the patronizing Schoelcher image. Quoting "Pli bèl dat: 22 mé, sé pa 14 jiyé" (The most beautiful date is 22 May, not 14 July) from "Sé lè 22 mé," the persistent demonstrators managed to have 22 May officially marked as an annual, paid holiday for the first time on 22 May 1984. Imbued with nationalism and the desire for independence rather than an autonomous state, Dézormo's leitmotif was his defense of people and his country.

Musicians like Dézormo turn to the cultural political space of Carnival because it displaces diverse, social forces. Carnival provides an imagined space to play out desires and political positions. It is a meeting place of persons of different social classes. The impossible is made the possible with the pairing of life and death, laughter and tears, and the grotesque with the beautiful. After twenty-one years in the music industry during which some of his songs were censored, Dézormo's uncensored voice can now be heard on any radio station. As a full-time employee of Radio Lévé Doubout Martinique (RLDM), a radio station owned by the MIM, he has the opportunity to talk about how the cultural and political climate has changed in Martinique in the last ten years.[50]

At the end of the 1990s, no increase in the number of jobs can keep up with population growth. Even tourism in comparison with the English-speaking Caribbean is negligible. Industrial production is very limited, and the agricultural economy is still in decline. From 1968 to 1998, ten of the eleven sugarcane factories closed down in Martinique, and the yearly export of one million tons of processed sugar dropped to 80,000, followed by a decrease of 89,000 tons of unprocessed sugar to 8,000 (Conan 1999, 88). As a result, Martinique is even more economically dependent upon mainland France. As for employment, within the French system of decentralization, "geographical origin is not regarded as a strong basis for a claim to employment in a particular area" (Hintjens 1992, 71). While Martinicans and Guadeloupeans continue to migrate to France in search of employment, mainland French civil servants come to the islands with an added salary incentive of 40 percent. Angry about this subsidy, Martinicans and Guadeloupeans organize strikes for wage increases almost on a monthly basis.

Creating a Renewed National Consciousness

History and cultural politics in Martinique have changed from the old tension and rivalry among the békés, mulattos, and Blacks to the new relationships among békés, Blacks, and the metropolitan French.[51] When the Socialist party with François Mitterrand as the presidential candidate won the 1981 election, the Martinican left changed its attitude toward the békés. Césaire's PPM, a nationalist-autonomist party whose allegiance shifted toward the French Socialists in the 1980s, formulated a plan for the island's development and initiated a meeting with various béké owners of industries and firms. Since the official policy of the French government sanctioned regionalism and decentralization, Martinicans had to come to terms with their own specificity and identity, moving beyond the traditional social and political hierarchy based on skin color.

Since 1981, French socialism has been espousing "the right to difference" and the flourishing of local cultures. The songs of these four singers and songwriters—Mona, Pôglo, Kali, and Dézormo—push forward historical referentiality. They bear witness to the way Martinicans have survived colonialism, been partially responsible for their condition, and initiated some attempts to counteract their dubious state. The slight transformations have been located in the space of cultural politics created by Mona with his outcries against drug infiltration, government corruption, and the desperate plight of poor Blacks; Pôglo's statements about the growth of misery and poverty; Kali's cynical observations about bétonisation and racial tensions; and Dézormo's warnings about being consumed by a greedy Europe.

Without discussing it among themselves, the four singers are trying to reinvent a national consciousness separate from négritude. Admittedly, the frustration of trying to envision a coherent Martinique, compounded with the deaths of his friends, destabilized Mona. By choice, Mona withdrew into a cultural political place—*traversée de désert*—to negotiate his grief and disappointments. He chose solitude to develop new attitudes toward his music. The two nature lovers, Pôglo and Kali, joined the Rastafarian religious sect to protest the evils of Babylon (France). As for Dézormo, who has been given the title of *chanteur emblématique de la cause martiniquaise* (emblematic singer of the Martinican cause),[52] he battled with the French administration over satirical songs.

Pôglo's songs allow the mind to wander away from the opacity and camouflage of Martinican politics. The study of Rastafarian philosophy functioned as a guide book for him and Kali in their recognition of social divisions constructed since slavery and the continuous impact of French socio-political and economic structures. Joining forces with Mona and Dézormo, the Rastafarian singers created a space out of disorder and difference, and all four composed nationalistically oriented lyrics about economic hardship, ethnic divisions, and migration.

A cultural political space appears to be the only place where there is some action. The singers are alert to what is happening to their country. They are conscious of the need to preserve their island's natural landscape, language, and agricultural products against homogenization. Their music is based on traditional sounds, rhythms, and instruments. The singers blend together disparate musical materials and make them into something uniquely Martinican, using Creole as a language of resistance. Rather than opt for *le même* (the Same), they are open to *le divers* (the Diverse) linked to cross-cultural exchanges. Within the space of cultural politics, the songwriters/musicians move in and out among other cultures.

Mona, Pôglo, Kali, and Dézormo shifted toward a permanent fusion of their fragmented parts through the linguistic spatial use of Creole and the space of cultural politics. Through these carved-out spaces they challenged French regionalism and the Martinican politicians who were in support of it. With deliberation, Mona did not aim for an easy clarity in his songs, whereas Pôglo, Kali, and Dézormo alternated French and Creole in their lyrics while simultaneously incorporating Creole proverbs and metaphors to establish a distance between them (the insiders) and the French recording industry (the outsiders). The four singers' lyrics shattered the silence about political affairs and eventually gathered together the social forces of which they were a part to repair the damage that had been wrecked by oppression. Hence, the four songwriters sought to recreate a national consciousness through the lyrical space of cultural politics as a site of struggle.

5 public performance, marketing devices, and audience reception

From 1976 until the present, my attendance at a variety of concerts in Carnival villages, concert halls, a cultural center, nightclubs, and patron festivals (even a paillote) have afforded me an opportunity to observe audience responses and exchanges with musicians and bands. In February 1995, Mario Canonge and Ralph Thamar gave a jazz fusion concert at CMAC to honor the late Marius Cultier and to promote their newly released *Hommage à Marius Cultier*. The audience's silence did not surprise me, because the music journalist and historian Michel Thimon had already prepared me with a description of Cultier's music as a sit-down, intellectual exercise. The audience politely applauded when it was deemed to be appropriate and basically remained silent until Thamar slid into "Gadé mas pasé," a mélange of recognizable hit songs that included "Fonds Larion" (which he had recorded with Akoustik Zouk). Upon hearing these familiar songs linked with Carnival, the audience became more participatory with whistling, cheers, and spontaneous hand clapping.

In December 1995, Mano Césaire invited me to the Manikou Night Club in Lamentin, the second largest town in Martinique, to see Palaviré. As usual, the band did not come on stage until midnight, when it proceeded to play nonstop for almost ninety minutes. A surprised guest was Pipo Gertrude, the young singer who replaced Thamar as soloist for Malavoi. Pipo and his brother, Jean-Claude Gertrude, a singer for Palaviré, teased each other on stage, interacted with members of the audience, and engaged in a call-and-response on songs made famous on *Plézi* (Palaviré's first CD). The crowd danced and shouted back and forth in Creole to Pipo and Jean-Claude. In return, the Gertrude brothers and other Palaviré members responded with improvisations and featured individual solos to showcase their skills. At one point, I wondered if the floor and balcony were going to collapse from the number of people who had managed to squeeze into the overcrowded space.

In contrast, to cut expenses, some nightclubs like Queen's in Schoelcher play zouk and American music at the highest decibel and invite singers to lip sync their songs to programmed music called playback. One evening Jean-Philippe "Pipo" Marthély of Kassav' came to perform at the appointed hour of midnight. Dressed in jeans, a jean jacket, and heavy-looking Timberland boots, Marthély, who was on the island to pay his wife and children a private visit, stood in the center of the dance floor with a microphone in his hand and mouthed the words to some of his prerecorded songs, while several couples danced directly in front of him. When he finished, the crowd surged forward and surrounded him. From where I was standing, I thought he had managed to give the crowd the slip. However, short in stature, Marthély simply could not be seen. It was as if the eager fans had obliterated him. Finally, he emerged from the middle of the crowd, walked around the dance floor, and greeted his admirers in a rapid fire mixture of Creole and French while simultaneously shaking their hands.

The Tanya St. Val concert held at the Grand Carbet in May 1995 was a little unusual. Although the weather was suffocatingly hot inside and outside of the concert hall, St. Val's stage attire was a mixture of the Caribbean and France. She wore an ankle length, sleeveless, cotton dress with knee high, black leather boots with chunky heels reminiscent of the Super Fly days. Her singing was strong, but she did not win the contest between a sound system and a band that alternated between distorting and drowning out her voice. Trying to be a good sport, she managed to complete her repertoire in spite of the sound handicap and ill-prepared band. When the concert came to an end, St. Val gave a short speech about safe sex and threw condoms into the orchestra area. At first, the Martinican audience was too stunned to reach for the condoms. After St. Val explained that the distribution of condoms at concerts in France was fashionable, individual members stood up and caught the prophylactics. Why the change of attitude? St. Val had dropped the name "France," the mère-patrie of Martinique.

In December 1996, Freddie Marshall organized a series of concerts in downtown Pointe-à-Pitre with an eclectic group of singers and musicians across the Caribbean. In preparation, a luncheon-by-invitation for the entertainers was held at a restaurant on a private island with the mayor of Pointe-à-Pitre. The hostess and owner of the restaurant was Simone Schwarz-Bart, a novelist and playwright. Since I had taught two of her novels, I was doubly pleased to meet her, the musicians, and singers. While I was mingling with the guests, Marshall asked the entertainers to give a sample of what they would be performing over the weekend. Among the entertainers were the Martinican singers Dalila Daniel and Franck Balustre, with whom I shared a table. The impromptu concert was a *clin d'oeil* (wink) at the enormous amount of talent that the Guadeloupeans would be able to see.

My attendance at these public and private performances was fun, but nothing has matched the excitement of Carnival. Creative writers and ethnomusicologists have written about Carnival, but their descriptions do not completely capture the excitement of being there, and neither will my own. I witnessed Carnival crowd dynamics firsthand by "running down the streets." The motion of the crowd maintained my balance, lifted me off of my feet, and pushed me along. Made-up like a butterfly and dressed in red for *Mardi gras* (Shrove Tuesday), I sang and danced behind the Plastic Système Band, linking my arms with friends. The vidé (parade), peppered with broken-down cars, verbal play, songs laden with sexual innuendos, outlandish customs, and drinking, was quite a spectacle, reinforced by nightly concerts by entertainers based on the islands and the négropolitains who came from France.

〜〜〜

People who are curious search for sounds; they seek out harmony and melody because they are curious. Your curiosity can be limited by your environment, or you expand it to take in things from outside: a bigger curiosity for a bigger world.
MANU DIBANGO (cited in Evans 1991, 7)

It is rare to find printed song texts included with a French Caribbean compact disc because of the expense and the fact that the culture is largely oral. What is noticeable is the amount of attention that is paid to music rather than to the lyrics. When inquiring as to why this is so, the most common response during many interviews with producers, musicians, and singers is: "Music is more important than the lyrics." If it is the case that lyrics have no importance, I queried why are they written, and why does the public join in to sing portions of songs during live concerts? A shrug of the shoulders is not an uncommon response.[1]

The musicologist Simon Frith provides an answer with his argument that, unlike written poetry, music is an integral part of lyrics, for people always hum or sing the lyrics to a tune. To continue this argument, Frith adds: "The theory of lyrical realism means asserting a direct relationship between a lyric and the social or emotional condition it describes and represents. One should look at the way life is critically focused on and imaginatively transferred" (Frith 1989, 82). Obviously, a song is a performance; its lyrics are spoken aloud and heard in the singer's accent. The lyrics, in combination with the sound of the voice, suggest what a singer really means. "Lyrics," as Langdon-Winner once put it, "can set words and the world spinning in a perpetual dance" (cited in Frith 1989, 91).

The comment "Music is for dancing" is another often heard response, for the singing of Creole lyrics and the sharing of its expressive communication with music and dance are the main purposes of a French Caribbean live concert. As noted by the singer Ralph Thamar, "Creole is a very imaginative language. A Creole word carries many images according to the tone in which it is pronounced, its place in a sentence, and its multiplicity of images in a single word" (cited in Erwan 1987, 20). Obviously, the singing of Creole lyrics is the means for singers and bands to earn some money and to develop faithful followers during live concerts.

Generally, near the beginning of a live concert, the performers quickly establish a rapport with the audience. They will sing either a haunting ballad or a recognizable fast number to pull the audience inside the performance. The soloist sings at the top of the note or a little behind to capture the audience's attention. As soon as the soloist reaches the top note and proceeds to improvise a bit, the audience shares the soloist's and musicians' performance space. The opening number is then followed by a series of songs from a newly released album mixed in with well-known past hits. The next step is to slow down the tempo and insert one or two very emotional romantic ballads, during which the soloist or soloists pull out the stops. To bring the concert to its end, the audience is teased and whipped into a frenzy with a potpourri of four or more hits in a fast sequential order, leaving the audience gasping and begging for more.

This fluctuation of moods and tones during a live performance is needed. To add another level of excitement, soloists and musicians interact among themselves on stage. It appears as if they are engaged in a contest about who is the best singer or musician. During a well-staged concert, the leader introduces the singers and musicians, who take turns to give a solo act. If they are astute performers, they instinctively know they must immediately grab the audience's interest, keep it guessing, and shock it with lights, a raised stage, or another gimmick into screaming and yelling to close out the show. The aim is to have the audience leave with the knowledge that it shares rhythms and songs with the band through the vibration of the floor on which they stand, sit, or dance.

Without a doubt, all entertainers ought to pay attention to the desires of their audiences, which is an important element if they want to succeed. Also, knowing how to negotiate different public performance spaces comes from close observations of gestures, comments, and appropriate clothing for each environment. What is acceptable in one place is not necessarily the same for another location. At present, in an American setting, a distance exists between the audience and the performers at a live concert, because American fans find it difficult to separate reality from fantasy or reality from hyper-reality. Often, when American fans reach out for the entertainers to tear off the latter's clothing, the more aggressive ones almost strangle their idols. To avoid this, bodyguards and police construct artificial barriers to enforce the distinction between reality and fantasy. These borders also keep the overzealous audience away from the objects of desire, allowing the musicians to remain in charge of their concerts.

Most often, the opposite exists in the French Caribbean. With the exception of a stadium or Carnival village, entertainers are not usually separated from their audience during a live concert. Frequently, individuals jump onto the stage and dance in front of the musicians and singers, making themselves spectacles of their own show. This spontaneous demonstration of affection and the appreciation for the musicians' skillful playing are reinforced when the musicians speak directly to the audience, asking it to clap, to sing along, or to make other movements to increase the tension and suspense of the show. The audience, therefore, is an active one. If not, the musicians are very concerned because, after the creation of a public performance for ninety minutes or more, the musicians want the audience to be keyed up enough to buy a record or two the next day.

The Public Persona: Its Preparation, Packaging, and Pretense

In the French Caribbean, a few sometimes take the stage persona to be the real person. In such instances, people jump to conclusions about entertainers' images. This was certainly the case when Lewis Mélanio (née Méliano John-Lewis) of Trois-Rivières, Guadeloupe, burst on the Guadeloupean musical scene in the early 1970s. First of all, she does not fit the stereotypical image. Rather than being a size six, light-skinned woman, the large-framed Mélanio is dark skinned and big boned. Second of all, rather than wearing a long hair weave, Mélanio sports an African braided hairstyle sitting high on her head like a tower with beads to give her extra height.

Initially, men in the industry did not know how to handle or promote Mélanio. Faced with their distress, Mélanio took charge of her career with the help of the RFO Guadeloupe television personality Jean-Pierre Sturm. Despite the jeers and slights made by people in the music industry, she managed to be the first dark-skinned woman to perform a solo act at the Cultural Arts Center in Pointe-à-Pitre. Not only did people backstage take affront at her skin pigmentation and weight, but they cruelly attempted to drug her, to turn off her microphone, to raise the volume of the music to drown out her voice, and unsuccessfully to smear her as a loose woman.[2] Mélanio's response to this negative behavior was the song "Négresse," sung in Lingala (a language spoken in the former Zaire) rather than in Creole. It is found on

her *Lewis Mélanio et les Skah Shah d'Haïti #1 Plus*. In a highly pitched affected voice, she sang how proud she was to be a Black woman. And during
an interview, she explained her artistic philosophy: "An artist is not just anyone. She's someone who reflects; sees what others do not see; and seeks different ways of expressions."[3]

The notion of feminine beauty can be an oppressive concept for some
Black women in a European context. One cannot forget that Martinique
and Guadeloupe are overseas regions of France; therefore, their citizens are
bombarded with visual images of very thin, white French women with blue
eyes and long blond hair. These images of European women as the standard
of beauty and the desire to look like them are pervasive. In an effort to be a
part of this stereotypical image, some career-driven Black women performers
remake themselves into imitative white women, trussed up with wigs or
streaked hair. As a consequence, even within the French Caribbean performance industry, a dislike for dark-skinned women (like Lewis Méliano) is articulated.

This positioning of French Caribbean women singers is quite ambivalent:
the singers take pride in their Blackness but also desire to look European if
doing so will sell CDs. To this end they wear hair weaves, false eyelashes,
colored contact lenses, acrylic nails, and long dangling heavy-looking costume earrings. Tight, low-cut dresses also add to the allure. Women entertainers are taught how to sell songs, engage audiences, and perfect their stage
presentations. Unfortunately, some women are willing participants in their
own exploitation because they want to see themselves on television and in
the magazines during their quest for stardom.

Photographic images exist within a complex state of cultural signification—a state created in part through the input of co-writers, co-producers,
studio musicians, video directors, technicians, and marketing specialists.
Photography can be used as a form of propaganda in an effort to promote
sexuality. Hence, the cover of a compact disc and the message in the photograph, in other words, its packaging, do not usually correspond to the music
and lyrics. Sex appeal is exploited and used as a promotional tool to sell
more records through the medium of photographs and videos. An often-seen
picture of the Guadeloupean trio Zouk Machine, promoted by the French
airline company AOM for the group's album *Clin d'oeil* (1994), depicts the
three women, Jane Fostin, Christiane Obydol, and Dominique Zorobabel,
with tousled hair weaves and youthful slender bodies wrapped in black satin
sheets. The impression is that they function as fantasized images, for they
look like three vixens stereotypically clad in black. Zouk Machine thus plays
into what Susan McClary calls "cultural conversations about gender, power,

and pleasure" (McClary 1991, 150–51) by presenting an image of themselves as sexual commodities.

Contrary to the women, most of the male performers seem to have some
amount of control over their projected image. Mario Canonge dresses like
the next-door neighbor in jeans and T-shirts; Ralph Thamar is usually well-
groomed and impeccably dressed without affectations; Pipo Gertrude
dresses like a young man in jeans; Dédé Saint-Prix wears large yellow or red
glasses and brightly colored Bermuda shorts with African dashiki tops. In
addition, Jean-Michel Rotin wishes to project either the image of the slinky,
cool, detached Michael Jackson or of the hip-hop coolster. Male band performers dress casually but, when they perform, they are well-attired whether
they are in shirt and tie (like Malavoi) or jeans and T-shirts (like Kassav').

The fact that men are more in control contrasts greatly with the women.
Intense pressure is levied upon the women performers. Anxious to succeed,
they succumb to what male agents and promoters propose. But today, the
world is topsy turvy, for some European women are pumping their lips and
butts with silicon to look like the Black British model Naomi Campbell,
while some Black women undergo liposuction to have thinner hips and butts
and starve themselves to look like the anorexic Kate Moss. The two groups
of women are running after prescriptive images—two expressions of the do-
minating aesthetics at the end of the twentieth century. The question is, Who
is going to project a new natural image?

The Sexy Mama and Sassy Trio

In Martinique and Guadeloupe it is a common sight to glimpse women at-
tired in bare-backed, tight-fitting dresses. However, their mode of dress is the
opposite of what the public deems appropriate content in songs written by
women. Patriarchal social values restrict women's self-expression regarding
sexual desire in their literary publications and recorded lyrics. Consequently,
explicit sexual lyrics written and sung by young, urbanized women are generally frowned upon and considered to be in poor taste. In addition, E. Anthony Hurley (1997, 58) writes about the rarity of explicit expressions of
frank sensuality in women-authored poetry. Hurley does, however, cite an
exception: Annick Collineau de Montaguère's "Toi, l'amour" (You, love)
from her 1989 collection *Nostalgie,* in which she frankly says: "Caresse-moi
encore / De tes baisers j'ai faim / Promène-les sur mon corps!" (Caress me
some more / I am hungry for your kisses / Run them over my body!).

Other exceptions are found in the traditional bèlè and gwo ka songs in
the countryside, and in the freedom women acquire once they reach senior-

citizenship status. One such person was Madame Lise Mavounzy. A former queen for one of the annual *Fête des Cuisinières* (Festival of women cooks) held every August in Pointe-à-Pitre,[4] she launched a singing career in her eighties. Hence, Madame Mavounzy's erotic songs are acceptable because she enjoys the elder status that allows her to sing whatever she wants. In her odd, raspy voice, Madame Mavounzy sings songs on *A la recherche du temps des biguines* (recorded in about 1959) about married women who engage in affairs ("Téléphonez la femme au galop"); a woman who sleeps with three different men ("Lucifé, Belzébithe, Macmahon"); a pregnant woman who is indifferent to her pregnancy ("Roulé la bodé"); and a woman who enjoys sexual encounters ("An ké ba'w sa"). The last one, "An ké ba'w sa" (I'll give you some), is the most suggestive of the four. With unblushing candor, Madame Mavounzy inserts sentences, couched in sexual innuendos, to describe four lovemaking positions such as: "An ké ba-w sa / A la zizipanpan / An ké ba-w sa / A la mandé poban" (I'll give you some / to tire you out / I'll give you some / to beg for more).[5] Visible images of sexual prowess come to mind along with allusions to the way a woman stands with her legs apart, leans over to pick up the charcoal, and thrusts forward her breasts to entice a male customer to buy "something." The woman is a willing partner and quite inventive; she takes great pleasure in her body and in what she can offer.

Lyrical sexual innuendos outside of the carnivalesque frame were permissible when the elder Madame Mavounzy sang them. After all, she looked like anybody's grandmother: a tall, robust, grey haired, spectacle-wearing woman. In other words, Madame Mavounzy represented safety, because she supposedly had passed her prime. However, the Guadeloupean public was not prepared, and thereby quite stunned, when the young twenty-year old trio of Zouk Machine proceeded to do likewise in the emerging zouk arena. Here were young women barely out of their teenage years who, according to the Guadeloupean male public, were bursting with sexuality and posing a threat to weak-kneed men. The assumption was that these young women knew how to "give them some."

In the early 1980s, the Expérience 7 team of Yves Honoré and Guy Houllier decided to package songs and to trade in on young women's sexual allure. They initiated discussions with Freddie Marshall, a Guadeloupean producer, about the formation of an all-woman band, and they called upon the Guadeloupean woman guitarist Maritz Picord. However, in spite of numerous rehearsals, the formula did not work. Next, the Expérience 7 musicians-composers conceived of a singing trio of women, and they approached Christiane Obydol, Joëlle Ursull, and Dominique Zorobabel. This first formation of Zouk Machine began with singing engagements at the *bals* (balls) and town festivals. While Zouk Machine was slowly building up a reputation and attracting fans, the women traveled to Paris where they sang acapella at the Club de la maison des Antilles at the Place de la Nation.

In 1986, the three singers caught the eye of Jocelyn Christophe, a young director of Tympan Productions. Christophe was searching for new talent to promote, and he pitched to Zouk Machine and its managers the idea of giving a concert at the Zénith concert hall in Paris. To prepare, Zouk Machine released its first album bearing the same title and song as their name: *Zouk Machine: Back Ground Expérience 7* (1986). In the song "Zouk Machine" the trio decide who will be in charge of a relationship:

Jòdi jou tou sa shanjé
Sé mwen ki ka méné
Kon sa ki fatigé

〜〜〜〜〜〜〜

(Today everything is going to change.
It is I who is going to decide
who will be tired.)[6]

Taking control, the trio boldly sings in stanza five: "Mété-w pou nou alé, do love me / do love me yeah / Sé tan mwen" (Prepare yourself so that we can make love, make love / It's my time).[7] Their frank declarations and aggression certainly appeal to a large and youthful audience, because Zouk Machine pronounces what the young Guadeloupean women want to hear and say themselves.

Regardless, *Zouk Machine: Back Ground Expérience 7,* which had been produced by Henri Debs Productions, sold only 2,000 copies. However, after Zouk Machine did a series of guest spots on Guadeloupean radio stations, magazine interviews, and a television video along with eleven appearances on television in less than fifteen days, the sales reached 50,000 copies. And not surprisingly, Zouk Machine won its first gold record, for eventually more than 300,000 albums were sold (O'Franc 1994, 21). Terribly excited, but against Christophe's advice, Christiane Obydol's mother insisted that Zouk Machine should give a concert in Burkina Faso, West Africa, at President Thomas Sankara's invitation for FESPACO (Pan-African Film Festival). The local arrangements were so badly organized that twenty days before the scheduled Zénith show Ursull threatened to quit. Since there was not enough time to find a replacement to learn the songs, Ursull was issued a separate contract as an incentive to stay on. The coveted concert at the Zénith took place on a rainy day in April 1986 before an audience of 3,500. Unfortunately, the sound system was poorly hooked up, and Zouk Machine did not sing well. After this disappointment, Ursull finally left, under debatable circumstances, to be replaced by Jane Fostin. This second formation of Zouk Machine moved to Paris and signed with BMG/Ariola and the Album management team.

Most of the time, the trio does not control the language for most of its songs. Shown off like trophies or exotic objects, Zouk Machine sing an abundance of sexy zouk songs jointly written by the Expérience 7 team. Honoré and Houllier work well together: Houllier on lyrics; Honoré on music. They bring to a song their distinctive vocal arrangements. Life's illusions and contradictions are at the heart of the songs.[8] Although the women characters in the Houllier/Honoré-authored songs often complain, the final message is usually "We [women] will wait for you regardless of how much you [men] disappoint us."

As usual, there are exceptions, for a change of departure occurs in "Maldòn" (Bad deal), which stayed number one on the hit charts for nine weeks:

Obydol:
Ka sa yé Misyé Bobo
Fò pa-w konprann Bibi sé on kouyòn
Si tout lé mwen o founo
Fò-w antann vou on jou kè ni maldòn
Netwayé, baléyé, astiké
Kaz la toujou penpan
Ba-w manjé ba-w lanmou
É pou vou an ka fèy an shantan

Zorobabel:
Ka sa yé Misyé Bobo
Pa mandé Bibi rété kon madòn
Menm si an fè on ti solo
Ou sav kè sé toujou vou ka kontròl
Byen dè fwa an té vlé
Enprowvisé é fè ou ti boujé
An kaz la ka rété
Ka santi mwen kon si an prizonyé

Chorus:
Aaaah pa mélé mwen kon sa
Ké ni maldòn han han
Pa fè mwen-y, pa fè mwen-y
Wo Oh si-w vlé kè pou boujé
Sa kontinyé bon fil
Pou mwen pé boujé

Fostin:
Ka sa yé Misyé Bobo
Hum! Bibi enmé mizik ki "chèbran"
Lazè, K7, "Video"
Ka méné méné lwen pou on ti moman
Nétwayé, baléyé, astiké
Kaz la toujou penpan
Ba-w manjé, ba-w lanmou
É pou vou an ka fèy an shantan

〰〰〰〰〰〰〰

(*Obydol:*
What do you think this is Mr. Bobo?
Don't think that Bibi is stupid.
If I'm cooking all the time,
just wait, you'll have a revolt on your hands!
Cleaning, sweeping, dusting.
The house is always spotless.
Feed you, love you,
and I do all this while singing.

Zorobabel:
What do you think this is Mr. Bobo?
Don't ask Bibi to stay here like a dummy.
Even if I sing solo,
you know that you're the one in control!
There are times I would like to improvise,
and go out on a whim,
but in the house I stay
and I feel like I am a prisoner!

Chorus:
Hey, don't do me like that.
You'll get a bad deal.
Hum, don't try me, don't try me, don't.
If you want us to stay together,
you'd better loosen the leash.

Fostin:
What do you think this is Mr. Bobo?
Bibi knows her music,
CD, tape, video cassette.
Sweep me away for a little while
Cleaning, sweeping, dusting.
The house is always spotless.
Feed you, love you,
and I'd do all this while singing.)[9]

"Maldòn," Zouk Machine's second most popular song, is about Bibi, a seemingly conventional wife, who sweeps, dusts, and cleans the house until it is spotless. Nonetheless, she is no longer content to remain in an unnoticed housekeeper's role. Feeling pressured, Bibi feels she has become a prisoner in her own house. This enclosure leads Bibi to question Bobo's credentials as a husband. As a result, Bibi's intensity of mixed feelings (wanting to feed him and to have her fun) and search for self-fulfillment are articulated separately by Obydol, Zorobabel, and the then newcomer Jane Fostin. In the first refrain Obydol warns Bobo not to think that Bibi is stupid. Zorobabel follows up this line of thought in the second refrain with "Pa mandé Bibi rété kon madòn'" (Don't ask Bibi to stay here like a dummy). In the third refrain, Fostin reminds Bobo that she wants to be rewarded for all that she has done as a good wife.

The very popular "Maldòn" is a cry for recognition of women's rights among the teenage and middle-class audiences. The song focuses on an expression, "Pa fè mwen" (Don't try me), that female teenagers commonly use whenever young boys are rude to them. The vocal range allows Fostin's voice to soar up, and Zorobabel and Obydol to add nuances. Each singer uses a microphone, and each part is clearly sung. When their voices blend as in a chorus, not one voice drowns out the others. Aimed at a wide audience, Houllier's and Honoré's "Maldòn" and other Zouk Machine songs are deceptively simple. Both "Maldòn" and "Zouk Machine" are very danceable with compelling grooves and great energy, and they radiate the message: "We're not going to let you men walk over us."

Kassav's Reactions to Audience Demands

Kassav' is the first French Caribbean band to run like a well-oiled machine with its flashy shows: lights, smoke machine, confetti, outlandish costumes, and dancers. All of these props are used for their shows at the Zénith in Paris, but due to the enormous transportation expense, the band travels abroad without all of its paraphernalia. Because of this decision, Guadeloupean and Martinican fans, who have seen Kassav's shows in Paris, wrongly criticize the band for not caring enough for Caribbean people. The next criticism launched against Kassav' is their failure to begin a concert on time. In fairness, this is not unique for Kassav'; the rule of thumb in the French Caribbean is to perform late. The notion of time differs culturally. Caribbean time is slower than that in time-conscious Europe and the United States. Lowell Fiet calls this distinction a "functional specificity"[10] because artists want to be accepted by their own public and by those elsewhere.

Not wanting to slight its local audiences, when Kassav' planned its November–December 1995 *Difé* (Heat) tour of the Caribbean, enough financial backing was found to pay for the cost of more than one hundred and fifty kilos of material for lights and fifty kilos of sound by Sylvain Dégras and Tec Pro Scène (M.A. 1995, 8). The effort paid off for, 60,000 *Difé* compact discs were sold within fifteen days of its release. Changes in the band's repertoire had to be made to fit the locations of concerts. To stay in touch with a younger audience, Kassav's opening acts for its November 1995 *Difé* concert in Martinique were VIP (the raggamuffin group Véritables Icones Publiques) and the young zouk group Kwak.

In concert, the Kassav' performers exude self-confidence. Handsome and energetic, Jean-Philippe Marthély, Jean-Claude Naimro, and Patrick Saint Éloi play the roles of sentimental lovers as they croon into the microphone, singing romantic double entendre songs. Jocelyne Béroard, dressed in the latest Paris fashion, brings "class" and a woman's perspective on romantic relationships. Having a spontaneous relationship with its fans, Kassav's audiences feel as if they know each of the band members personally. For example, on the 1993 *Kassav' Live au Zénith sé nou menm'* (Kassav' live at the Zenith that's us), the audience gives automatic call-and-response answers to questions raised in the songs. The audience sings along with the chorus, breaking into spontaneous clapping to increase the band's quick tempo. While playing "An mouvman" (In movement), Naimro warns the audience

that "Ce morceau est très dangereux" (This piece is very dangerous). To entice the public, he repeats the sentence stressing the first syllable of "morceau"; the public happily sings the last line of the song. Also, when it is Saint
Éloi's turn to sing "Bay chabon" (High energy), he alerts the audience that
Kassav' is about "communication." The album's title says it all: *nou* (we)
include a total fusion with Kassav' and its audience.

On *Kassav' Live au Zénith sé nou menm'* and other albums, it is apparent
that Saint Éloi uses his voice as a functional instrument: a body, a person,
and a character. The result is that the listener, in his fanciful dreams, hears
the pop singer being personally persuasive. It is the performing rather than
the composing voice that is taken to be the key to Saint Éloi's character. The
listener assumes it is someone's life heard in the singer's choice of Creole
lyrics. As a consequence, Saint Éloi's setting of words to music becomes the
preferred reading, particularly during a live performance where the listener's
immediate pleasure of identification is involved.

Saint Éloi's distinct vocal style, which is widely imitated in Guadeloupe,
is the space where he expresses a vulnerability. He accomplishes this by shifting from a major to a minor key. He also utilizes a controlled yet distinguishable melisma with a slight vibrato with a carefully placed air intake between
the notes along with a specific timbre in his voice.[11] Also, as in most of his
songs, Saint Éloi manages in "Ki jan ké fè" from *Zoukamine* (1994) to shift
back and forth between feelings of need and hope:

Sé flè la fané adan kaz la
Limyè paka rantré ankò
Jou la sa nou té palé pli fò
Sa paté janmen rivé nou
Yonn é lòt nou fè sa nou té pé
Pou nou pa viv kon égaré
Eskè sé pas ou pli jenn ki mwen
Kè nou pa ni dwa enmé
Ay, ki jan ké fè

Sé prézans-aw ki ka mèt
On gran jwa adan vi en mwen
Ki jan ké fè
Sé absans-aw ki ka mèt an gran tou
Adan vi an mwouen
Le-w vlé sové an lov enposib
Fòk ou sèten kè tchè ya-w lib

Si-w tripé si sa mwen ka di-w la
Ou ké vwouè nou ja enmen
Ki jan ké fè

Se absans-aw ki ka mèt an gran tou
Adan vi an mwen
Ki jan ké fè
Sé prézans-aw ki ka mèt
An gran jwoua adan vi an mwen
Viens bébé viens
Ki jan ké fè
Ki jan pou mwen fè, di mwen
Si nou té aprann aprésyé
Apwan aprésyé
Tou sa ki senp ki bèl
Enmé-w jan ou yé
Enmé mwen jan an yé osi
Nou té ké swiv menm shimen la
Édé la dèstiné pou nou pa pèd ayen

Ki jan an pé fè, ki jan
Ki jan pou mwen fè di mwen
Tou sa ki senp
Toujou pli bèl
Nou té ja konprann sa
Pou enmé pani laj
É sé sa lavantaj osi
Ou pé pa fè ayen
Kont sa si sé la dèstiné

Alò ki jan pou fè
Ki kan pou fè
Ki jan an pé fè, ki jan
Ki jan pou mwen fè di mwen

ᗯᗯᗯᗯᗯᗯ

(The flowers are faded in the house.
No light filters in.
On this very day we had shouted at each other.

This had never happened before.
We tried our best
not to live like lost souls.
Is it because you are younger than I am
that we haven't got the right to love each other?
Oh! What am I going to do?
It's your presence
that fills my life with great happiness.
What am I going to do?

It's your absence that leaves a gap
in my life.
When you want to rescue an impossible love,
you have to make sure that your heart is free.
If you ponder on what I am telling you,
you'll realize we love each other.
What am I going to do?
It's your absence that leaves a wide gap
in my life.
What am I going to do? What am I going to do?
It's your presence that fills
my life with great happiness.
Come darling, come.
What am I going to do?
Tell me what to do. Tell me.

If only we had learned to enjoy
nice, simple things.
If I had loved you the way you are;
if you had also loved me the way I am;
we would have followed the same track
and helped our destiny to avoid losing
something.

What can I do? What can I do?
Tell me what to do. Tell me.
Simple things
are always more beautiful.
We had already understood this.
Love does not care about age.

Also, the advantage is
you cannot do anything
to stop it if it's your destiny.

What to do?
What to do?
What can I do? What can I do?
Tell me what to do. Tell me.)[12]

"Ki jan ké fè" opens with an acoustic guitar and synthesizer. The first movement's steady beat is soft, followed by a second movement of violin strings
mixed with the synthesizers. A live brass section is on top with a twelve bar
introduction to simulate a languid feeling. Saint Éloi enters, using the upper
register in a falsetto style. The chorus responds later with a downward vocal
movement while Saint Éloi shifts into his natural voice. As Saint Éloi sings
about an older man who pleads for his former lover to return, the timbre of
his voice expresses the man's quiet despair. The older man frantically
searches for a way to resolve the argument that drove him and his young
lover apart. To express the man's refusal to accept the relationship might be
permanently over, Saint Éloi repeats the polite question: "Ki jan ké fè? (What
am I going to do?) more than once. This happens to be grammatically incor-
rect; it should be "ki jan an ké fè." In an effort to make Creole sound pleasing
to the ear, Saint Éloi drops the subject pronoun *an* (I) and lengthens the pro-
nunciation of *jan* to *jaan*. By doing this, one actually hears the subject pronoun while Saint Éloi makes the explicit meaning of the Creole lyrics co-
exist with the resonance of his voice. Thus, changes in the instrumentation
and the shifting of accents on specific words with voice-overs create the desired romantic mood with a sad undertone.

   Though ethereal like Marthély, Saint Éloi, a balladeer, possesses a strong,
easy listening voice. Saint Éloi's voice and lyrics are mesmerizing, two qualities that stand in conjunction with his melodies and stage presence. In addition, male power is evoked in his songs about emotional relationships. He
dares to be transparent about his needs and feelings, owning up to dependency, insecurity, and vulnerability and openly speaking about the ways in
which men project the image of an ideal lover. The yearning, lush ballads of
Saint Éloi, along with other zouk love songs penned by Marthély and
Naimro, reveal that French Caribbean men, who are considered to be very
macho, are willing participants in the thrill of the chase and the wonder of
first love, but they are unwilling victims of the pain of loss.

   By communicating wholly through rhythm and Creole zouk melodies,

Saint Éloi and other Kassav' members manage to cross many linguistic boundaries and to tap into the inner vitality of people of all ages. Having attended many Kassav' concerts, Manu Dibango notes that "Kassav's show is polished and professional. The pace and delivery are quick and sharp, with arrangements that emphasize collective effort rather than individual virtuosity" (cited in Evans 1991, 114). Jacob Desvarieux's raspy delivery, an occasional openness with bent notes, provides a contrast to Saint Éloi's slick delivery. Marthély, who is gifted with an unusually rich tenor voice, exudes versatility, changing his voice for each song and circumstance.

The reward for Béroard is in the sounds that she creates and the pleasures she brings to the audiences. For example, Chénard describes Béroard's voice as being "tainted with a bitter blue" (Chénard 1986a); it is an authentic cry, conveying an immense sensitivity. While traveling among the Caribbean islands with his trombone, the American Henry Shukman overheard Béroard's voice on the radio. His opinion of her voice is that it is "the finest . . . in the French Caribbean, clear and soft and pure like a choirboy's but rasping too when she wants it to be" (Shukman 1992, 103). And Béroard's description about her delight in writing lyrics for Kassav' supports the bond between female creativity and the body itself: "My biggest drama is the text. I like the rapid and jerky rhythm of words which can be enchanting like in 'Siwo.' When I am asked to remove, to suppress or simply to shorten a song, I become sick. Four minutes are just too short" (Th. Dz. 1995a, 41).

Malavoi's Reactions to Criticism

Malavoi and Kassav' have been the two longest-running bands in the last decades of the twentieth century. In their music, they have stretched the boundaries, always looking for something else to do and keeping up-to-date with the current happenings in the music world. Yet, in spite of its reputation, Malavoi, like Kassav', has dealt with its share of criticism. In 1987, the young journalist Jean-Marc Paty accused Malavoi of not giving a sufficiently aggressive sound and enough punch to the violin. The violinist Jean-Paul Soime's response to Paty was, "Our manner of being punchy is not like everybody's. We manage the softness and the irony in our riffs, sustaining the voice or the soloist. The richness of our music is in the syncopation not the regularity" (quoted in Paty 1987). Mano Césaire, Malavoi's founder and a violinist, also added, "Our music was syncopated well before the Saint-Pierre catastrophe."[13]

Obviously, there is a generational gap. Today, the middle-aged Malavoi musicians are playing an older dance music for younger audiences who do not know the dances. Some of their young critics (like Paty in 1987) want them to play louder and faster (more "aggressively," as if aggressive is good), whereas their middle-aged and older audiences want to hear the sound to which they are accustomed. On more recent recordings, the Malavoi musicians have attempted to please both audiences. One hears them playing the melody on the violins more softly and then more loudly. For example, on stage the Malavoi violinists display a Martinican flavor. In contrast to classical violinists who are more formal in delivering their performance, the Malavoi violinists dip, bounce, and dance while playing their instruments. As René Ménil describes it: "The violins intervene not as a decoration but as an integral part of the musical development, adding more complicated nuances to the opening theme at a higher level" (Ménil 1987, 27).

On stage, the Malavoi violinists display their individuality. Deemed to be some of the most conservative musicians, violinists traditionally play classical music such as Beethoven, Chopin, and Dvorak. However, the Malavoi violinists stray from the classical to play popular Caribbean music. Their playing of electronic violins allows them to function more in the style of electric guitar players, moving from the background into the foreground. To add some diversity, each violinist possesses a differently colored violin: Soime, red; de Négri, white; Césaire, brown; and Porry, blue. This touch of originality endears the violinists not only to foreign audiences, but to Caribbean ones as well (especially when they dance in unison with the music while playing their colorful instruments).

The band's originality and ability to adjust to different venues are important, too. Whenever Malavoi's agent negotiates a foreign contract, several changes occur. First, the band performs for more diverse audiences in musical festivals, private parties, night clubs, and larger theaters. Second, the songs become more standardized and shorter with less improvisation. To give an example, in France, Malavoi sets the tone to invoke tradition because Caribbean immigrants are in attendance. For more than two hours both those who have recently arrived and those who have been in France for years sing along and dance to familiar music, enlarging and recreating their islands in France.

Working within a band with its numerous rehearsals requires an enormous amount of listening, juggling, and compromising.[14] This musical circle of exchange among Rosine and the band members is the basis for bringing them closer together. In addition, over the years, Malavoi performers have had a close relationship with their local French Caribbean audiences. Such a level of comfort causes the audiences to call the musicians by their first names and to converse about them as if they are personal friends. Also, posters, autographed photographs, and magazines, featuring intimate interviews with Rosine and other individual performers, elevate the band's popularity.

Beginning in the late 1980s, to reach a wider audience, Malavoi like other French Caribbean bands agreed to videotape individual songs. One of them, "Titin bèl" (Beautiful Titine) from *An Maniman* (Just so), was filmed in 1994, depicting a German woman tourist on holiday in Martinique who explored all the island's glories: the fish market, the beach, downtown Fort-de-France, and beautiful Martinican women. Although music exists as it is performed, the "Titin bèl" video has absolutely nothing to do with the actual lyrics, which are as follows:

Asou bò gran mashé
Jwenn an kaprès trésé
Tifi-a té bèl
Boush mwen koulé myèl
Sans mwen rizé
Mwen menm ki byen fringan
lèskanp mwen za filé
Dan an sèl balan
Mwen ladjé vyolon
Koumansé shanté

Refrain
A Titin ou bèl an maniman
Fout que "la belle est belle"
An maniman
La bèl é joli
An maniman
Y ni an mal aryè
An maniman
La bèl é joli
An maniman
Y ni an fant dan douvan
An maniman

Titine:
Ou abo sa palé
Ou abo sa shanté

Sé pa sa mwen lé
Mizik ou-w byen bèl
Alò fè mwen dansé

Violinist:
Mandolin akordé
Sé an lèt ti shanté
Ki zòt tout konnèt
Mashin san navèt
Ansanm nou shanté

~~~~~~~~~~~

(*Violinist:*
Near the big market
I met a young, well-coiffed *câpresse.*
She was so beautiful
that my mouth turned into honey,
and my entire body trembled.
I, who am dapper
and very neat,
grabbed my violin
in one quick movement
to sing.

Refrain
Ah, Titine, you're so beautiful.
How "beautiful is beautiful."
Just so.
The beautiful is pretty.
Just so.
And not bad from behind.
Just so.
The beautiful is pretty.
Just so.
Not bad in the front.
Just so.

Titine:
Your mouth is wide-opened.

You know how to sing well,
but that doesn't interest me.
The music is wonderful.
Make me dance.

Violinist:
The mandolin, once strung,
plays a little song
that we all know.
What an instrument!
Let's sing together.)[15]

Adapted from a folk tune with the revised lyrics by Soime and a new musical arrangement by Nicol Bernard, the "Titin bèl" song narrative is actually about a male violinist who meets the beautiful, plaited-hair, half Indian-Black *(kaprès)* Titine, who turns his mouth to honey. He is so enthralled with Titine that he picks up his violin to play and sing about her great beauty, her elegance, and the gap between her two front teeth. To his joy, Titine likes his music, teases him, and dances to the lyrics he makes up on the spot in her honor.

Although videos are important in the promotion of cultural imagery, it is misleading to assume that they are authentic representations. What comes into play with Malavoi's *Titin bèl* video is the director's privilege. In other words, the video director asserts his right to interpret the song as he sees fit. Under pressure to film a video within the budget and to sell a marketable product, the director and producer most likely had to release the *Titin bèl* video during the high winter season of tourism (rather than the summer season preferred by the musicians, when Martinicans in France return) to inspire tourists to buy as soon as they saw it on television. This probable decision reminds one of Philip Auslander's comment: "By being recorded and mediatized, performance becomes an accumulative value, a commodity" (Auslander 1996, 198). Thus, tourists rather than Martinicans were deemed to be the more important of the two (local and foreign) audiences. To compete in the international market of world music, Malavoi realized that compromises had to be made. The pitfall is that the tourists who do not know Creole might think the mediatized representation of *Titin bèl* is an accurate dramatization of the lyrics.

Regardless, videos, called promotional pictures, are tied in with the marketing of compact discs and have increased Malavoi's sales.

The Local Music Industry and Statistics

Traditionally, Martinican and Guadeloupean musicians and singers are low on the ladder of social respect. If they come from middle-class families, they have some formal schooling in music. For example, Emmanuel "Mano" Césaire, Jean-Paul Soime, and Christian de Négri of Malavoi all attended the same school to study the violin. Marijosé Alie and Jocelyne Béroard studied classical piano: the former was taught by her grandmother and the latter by her schoolteacher mother. Tanya St. Val and her compatriots Pierre-Edouard and George Décimus grew up in musical households because their fathers played in local bands around Guadeloupe. Most singers receive their professional training on the job and pay their dues for several years by singing backup and playing as session musicians in the recording studios.

Speaking about recording studios, until the mid-1980s the business aspect of the biguine and zouk musics in Guadeloupe and Martinique had been dominated by two brothers of Syrian origin—Henri and George Debs. Their record companies, Henri Debs Productions and GD Productions, were the biggest labels and wielded a large influence. Now, smaller companies like Déclic, Hibiscus, Moradisc, Liso Musique, and JE Productions are competing against Henri Debs Productions and the Paris-based BMG/Ariola, Phonogram, Philips, and Sony. Not to be stopped, Henri Debs of Henri Debs Productions and Jean-Michel Mauriello of Studio Hibiscus indicate that they have developed a communication network with foreign publishers, distributors, and artistic agencies.

Influenced by the wider market that zouk has created, Rigobert Montpierre, a sound engineer at Henri Debs Productions, has sampled his own zouk sound and put it on a background track that dominates most of Debs's recordings. Also, a quick glance at the credits of any locally produced compact disc in Guadeloupe and Martinique will list the same musicians. Yet when a band gives a live concert, its sound can be slightly different from the compact disc because different musicians participate.

Compared to the 130 million compact discs sold annually in France and its overseas territories, twelve thousand titles are sold per year in Martinique (Auslander 1996, 198). Eighty-five of them are new releases, but only twenty will sell well. A very popular album usually generates a sale in Martinique of 4,000 to 6,000 copies, depending upon the degree of investment applied to its promotion. Obviously, the French Caribbean market is small, which explains why a sale of 10,000 copies of a compact disc is considered to be a major success (Léandy 1997, 40), especially when the mean figure for a CD is between 7,000 to 10,000 in the Caribbean market.

In Guadeloupe, Henri Debs of Henri Debs Production devotes ninety per-cent of his market to zouk. According to him a sale of 2,000 copies of a compact disc is mediocre; a sale of 5,000 would be considered successful. Ordinarily, it takes a musician, singer, or band a year to prepare a CD, and a well-received video is shown on local television for about nine months while others last only three. Debs adds that what pleases the local audience does not necessarily attract outsiders. His policy is to reject seventy percent of the songs presented to him and to remove a CD from his two stores' shelves within six months if it sells poorly. One of his competitors, Mauriello of Studio Hibiscus, reports that only twenty percent of the CDs produced by his company are profit-making.

A breakdown of the number of copies sold in Martinique provided by Evariste Cannenterre,[16] a record store manager, confirms Debs's comments. He notes that tourists buy Kassav', Malavoi, and other distinctive local mu-sic; the youth want raggamuffin, reggae, and new zouk groups; middle-age people purchase Mario Canonge and other biguine and jazz records. For the solo albums made by Kassav' singers, the earlier Saint Éloi *Misik cé lanmou* (1982) and *A la demande* (1984) still sell very well (now as CDs) along with Marthély's *Touloulou* (1984). Buyers judge these three albums to be more original and a move away from the recognizable Kassav' sound. In a matter of fact way, customers pay the costly price of 80 Francs ($16) for a cassette and 120 to 150 Francs ($24 to $30) for a compact disc. The costs are as high as they are because of production expenses and import tariffs.

Record companies respond to market demand and can themselves create such a demand. Strenuous efforts are made to influence the choice with the cultivation and promotion of a "star," for record companies understandably use the star's name and media-constructed personality to sell records. In 1990, under Eric Basset's direction in France to invest in world music, Déclic Productions opened its doors. In 1994, Basset decided to open branch offices in Guadeloupe and Martinique. In January 1995, Patrick Borès of Déclic Guadeloupe reported that Zouk Machine has been its most successful group.[17] The trio's *Zouk Machine: Back Ground Expérience 7* held the num-ber one slot for several months with a sale of 300,000 copies, which was followed by more than 750,000 copies of *Maldòn* (1989). Not wanting to rely solely upon Caribbean productions, which constitute seventy percent of the market (of which fifty percent is zouk), Déclic has ventured into the marketing of North African and a small number of French mainland re-cordings.

As previously mentioned, performers who wish to be full-time profes-sionals move to Paris. There are no state-run music conservatories on the islands, and the recognition given to musicians is derived from magazine and televised interviews. SACEM protects the entertainers' musical rights in France and its overseas territories.[18] In terms of royalties, RFO pays ten percent of the total; the radio stations 19.80 francs ($3.76) per song played; the television stations 135 francs ($27) per song played; the concerts give forty-four percent of box office sales; and night club owners hand over thirty-five percent of the gate to the musicians.[19] Those who receive royalty payments are the arrangers of musical scores, composers of lyrics, producers, distributors, and artists. Arrangers are paid between ten and fifteen percent of the singers' royalties. A high-profiled artist gets 50 centimes ($0.10) per CD sold; a lesser known artist only 3 or 4 centimes per CD after the first 1,000 or 3,000 compact discs are sold. Also, the average daily rental cost for a studio is 6,000 francs ($1,200) for a minimum of ten days with each studio musician being paid about 2,500 francs ($500) for his participation on a compact disc.

Usually, the costs of airplane tickets, hotels, and posters are covered by sponsors.[20] Based upon these cited figures, an enormous number of records must be sold in order for the musicians to survive. The figures also illustrate the need to go on tour. To protect their financial income, artistic diversity, and economic contribution to the French music industry, the Mouvement des artistes et musiciens antillo-guyanais (MaMag), presided by Béroard, was founded in 1998 (Gallon 1998, 24). Not happy with their deracinated status on the pan-global market, members of the organization want musicians to be aware of their rights when negotiating contracts and decry being classified in the roots or world music categories.

A Family Affair

Almost all the major French Caribbean musicians come from families where a member or two are either amateur or professional musicians or singers. For example, Paulo Rosine of Malavoi came from a family where his aunt played an instrument; his father the violin; and his brothers Fanfan and Jean a guitar and saxophone. Jean-Paul Soime's aunt was Léona Gabriel, the first diva of the biguine. Madame Mavounzy was a singer and her son Robert a saxophonist. In addition, Kali has performed with his son Ti Ken, brother Paul "Ives" Monnerville, uncle Max Ransay, and wife Hélène Marigny.

Personal contacts with African musicians have resulted in strong connections between makossa and zouk ever since Jean-Claude Naimro and Claude Vamur of Kassav' and Paulo Albin, a former member of Perfecta, alternated studio sessions and live concerts with Manu Dibango. Edith Lefel sang backup on "Missounwa," the 1989 hit and album of the same title by Monique Seka, the Ivorian queen of Afro-zouk. Other zouk musicians have played with and helped to promote Meiway, who is also an Ivorian singer. Pepe Kalle and Empire Bakuba of the former Zaire composed "Pon moun paka bougé" (Nobody is moving), a *soukous-zouk kouassa kouassa* dance tune in the mid-1980s. To prove its interest in the Zairean public, Kassav' pronounced the sentences "A man'e maboko" (Ladies clap your hands) and "Tout le monde maboko" (Everybody clap your hands) to the delight of the audience when it performed in the local stadium in Kinshasha. Kassav' vocalists spoke the slang called *Hindoubill*,[21] so popular in the urban Kinshasha where contact with Americans and American music occurred since the 1960s.

By paying close attention to the cultural and linguistic characteristics of the Zairean public, Kassav' saw its popularity soar, especially when its video of "Syé bwa" (Saw the wood)[22] on *Vini pou* (1987) was filmed in Kinshasha. An integral part of the entire musical production, the audience's feedback was needed for Kassav' and other bands and singers to make modifications. Such a popular music depended on oral transmission and iconography, not on literacy. In complicity with the mass media, this popular music involved allegiances of a regional, ethnic, or class nature. Not to be forgotten, musicians and singers negotiated public performance space by selling songs, engaging an audience, and perfecting stage presentations.

Usually, singers are smaller in appearance than they appear on stage. The height of the stage and the audience's imagination come into play. A spotlight shining on soloists in either a square or circle plays an integral part in the public performance space. Soloists standing in the center of the light come to life as they move and vocalize. And Alan Lomax insists that within any culture or subculture, "singing is a rather standardized kind of behavior. It must be so since a main function of song is to symbolize cultural identity, and to permit groups of performers to vocalize together and their listeners to share in a common experience" (Lomax 1976, 17).

This sharing of a common experience in Guadeloupean and Martinican popular music between audiences and performers certainly affects sociopolitical behavior through the bétonisation campaign and the slow but changing reconfiguration of male/female relationships. But family, as already noted by Malavoi, is the core and the means of support to enable the singers and musicians to push forward. Surely, having family or friends already in the local and tightly knit music business has not hindered aspiring musicians from entering the performance space of popular music. Across the trans-Atlantic and African diaspora, French Caribbean musicians and singers share performance space as they perform on each other's recordings.

Another familial relationship is the one among musicians, singers, and their agents, cultivated to pass on a variety of strategies for the promotion of recorded or filmed products with local and international radio and television stations and the press. The recorded product is always influenced by either local or Paris-based producers who are geared toward satisfying consumers' tastes. To be specific, live and recorded performances become the means by which musicians restore the integrity of their art and communicate effectively with their primary (Caribbean) audience through the seven awakening spaces of exile and childhood, gender, optimistic Creole, cultural politics, the deferential space for the drum, recontextualization, and the cultivation of public performance. Although most Martinicans and Guadeloupeans prioritize rhythms over lyrics, they automatically sing along, proving a coexistence. Thanks to popular lyrics, young women are seeking a "siwo." Whenever the French Caribbean public observes the debarkation of E.U. members on their shores, some of them exclaim "Voici les loups." Titles of former hits, these popular lyrics and others are proof that they constitute a family affair.

6 the recontextualization of urban music

The year 1995 was very active with songs ranging from le poète chanteur (poet-singer) Albéric Louison's zouk love "Raissa" to Daddy Pleen's raggamuffin (or ragga) "Touche pas à ta fille" (Don't touch your daughter) to Métal Sound's "Joue pas avec le Crack" (Don't play with crack). Rumors were circling that the once popular cadence band, La Perfecta, was going to be revived with most of its former band members (Paulo Albin, Marius Prian, Chris Dachir, and Jean-Paul Pognon). African American rap music had made its entrance into the French Caribbean by enthralling the teenagers and university students with its heavy bass, digital sampling, and rhythmical speech. Sitting in their parents' homes with personal computers, some of these students churned out their versions of raggamuffin (rap) in droves. However, the glaring difference between French Caribbean rap and that by African Americans was the former's lack of vulgarity.

On the other side of the spectrum were new bands like Kwak, Palaviré, Taxi-kréol, and Volt Face, which came on the scene with their mixture of Caribbean rhythms and African American soul and funk. Even Fal Frett reappeared with an album that featured Tony Chasseur singing a reprise of Alexandre Stellio's "Gran tomobil" (Big automobile). What struck me was the number of English words in some of the songs of many of the bands. Due to the impact of the media and the increased number of hours that they spend in front of the television watching American sitcoms and soap operas dubbed in French, French Caribbeans are developing a fascination with American pop icons and the desire to travel to the United States. And the practice of printing English and French translations or summaries of Creole lyrics on compact disc sleeves is slowly gaining ground.

~~~~~~~~~~~~~~

The singer Ralph Thamar has missed his calling. He should have been a social or intellectual historian. When Thamar talked about his songs, he automatically provided their historical backgrounds, recreated their milieu and time period, and gave colorful descriptions of the people associated with them. In minute detail, he described Morne Pichevin, a colorful slum of Fort-de-France that was torn down to construct the headquarters and an outdoor parking lot for the newspaper *France-Antilles*. Not wanting to interrupt the flow of Thamar's riveting account of the musicians of Morne Pichevin, I restrained myself from raising more questions. Through his words I could visualize the small lively bands of musicians and the shouted words of encouragement that the listeners rained down upon them.

~~~~~~~~~~~~~~

When the pianist Mario Canonge came by my hostess's residence, he was as exuberant in his speech as he is on the piano. Canonge jokingly spoke about how he sold his own recordings to Martinicans who thought that he ought to give them away. He told this story:

"Hey man, how about buying my CD?"

"What? It can't be worth much if you have to sell it. CDs are to be sold in a record store. Give it to me."

"Are you kidding? I've got to earn a living."

Not at all insulted, Canonge, who is based outside of Paris, chuckled during the recitation. Because he is so down-to-earth in his manner, Martinicans ignore his fame and treat him like a family member who should bring gifts.

~~~~~~~~~~~~~~

The hot band in Guadeloupe in January 1995 was Volt Face. Intrigued, I wanted to meet the band to find out about its international orientation. One day the brother of a friend with whom I was staying in Guadeloupe phoned to tell us that Volt Face was going to be featured on the local, televised variety show *Partitions*. He said that the band would be rehearsing that after-noon at the Zénith Club in Gosier, a suburb of Pointe-à-Pitre. His sister and I jumped into her car and took off for Gosier. The two of us decided to crash the rehearsal. When we got to the club, I glibly told the security guard that I was a journalist on assignment to cover the new popular Guadeloupean bands. The guard stepped aside, and we got in!

Volt Face was jamming and did not stop when they saw us two strangers. George Décimus, the band director and one of the former founders of Kassav', was dressed in Bermuda shorts and intent on playing the bass guitar. Jeff Joseph, a singer from Dominica, sang "Imajiné" (Imagine), "O Madona," and "If I Say Yes" with the Guadeloupean singers Dominique Panol and Dominique Coco. The Cameroonian Jean-Pierre Kingue, bare chested and with a blue and white bandanna wrapped around his head, was pounding away on the drums. There was, indeed, a high level of excitement in this room from an infectious music! When the band stopped for a break, I boldly approached Jeff Joseph and introduced myself. He was surprised I knew he had first recorded with an English-speaking Dominican band called the Gramacks.

As long as you remember what you have seen, nothing is gone. LESLIE SILKO (1977, 231)

All the Antilles, every island, is an effort of memory... DEREK WALCOTT (1992, 9)

In preparation for the acceptance of the 1992 Nobel Prize for literature, the St. Lucian writer Derek Walcott wrote a speech in which he spoke about the process of renaming and of finding new metaphors. He said: "The stripped man is driven back to that self-astonishing, elemental force, his mind. This is the basis of the Antillean experience, this shipwreck of fragments, these echoes, these shards of a huge tribal vocabulary, these partially remembered customs, and they are not decayed but strong. They survived the Middle Passage" (Walcott 1992, 11). In this context, contemporary musicians draw upon songs of the past that are made available through recordings, films, cassettes, and vinyl records. Like all innovative people, they create something new by expanding the boundaries of former hits with a slightly different twist. Moreover, they recognize affinities between their new compositions and the older recordings. Thus, the arena in which the musicians recreate anew is called "recontextualization."

This notion of recontextualization is not unique to French Caribbean music. It has been stated through the use of other terms. For instance, when Nelson George bemoaned the disappearance of African American rhythm and blues into a bland crossover type of music, he used the term *retronouveau* to define an embrace of the past to create "passionate, fresh expressions and institutions . . . to bring back some of the soul and subtlety its audience deserves" (George 1989, 186). In his study of memory and history linked to the act of imagination, the French historian Pierre Nora (1989, 19) coined the term *lieux de mémoire* (sites of memory)[1] to describe its capacity for metamorphosis and an endless recycling.

Walcott, George, and Nora all support turning to memory to make something new, something fresh and original. By discovering new uses of the old, musicians reopen issues of signification, and their middle-aged and older listeners respond satisfactorily to the conjuring up of memories that have been tucked away. These processes of rediscovery and reinvention recuperate what Walcott calls "the shipwreck of fragments, these echoes, these shards of a huge tribal vocabulary, these partially remembered customs . . . not decayed but strong" (Walcott 1992, 11). Hence, these newly composed songs (drawn readily from either gwo ka and bèlè rhythms or from the biguine, mazurka, and quadrille) imbue the present with a sense of continuity that does not fixate on the past. Thus, portions of the musicians' memories combined with past compositions are within the new music because the past is reconstituted in conjunction with the present.

Of course, there are always those (particularly the youth) who oppose this mix of the old with the new and who consider music like raggamuffin or hip-hop to be new forms. These younger opponents' arguments fluctuate around the possibility of nostalgic stagnation, the fear of stifled originality, and the belief that the Caribbean really has nothing to offer. Nevertheless, this chapter will prove the contrary. The argument in favor takes into consideration the place where memory, history, and imagination meet to reveal what has been suppressed in French histories of the French Caribbean. In this regard, Terry Dehay says: "Remembering is the process of reclaiming and protecting a past often suppressed by the dominant culture, and in this sense, as revisioning, it is essential in the process of gaining control over one's life."[2] Each musical revisioning contains a blend of many cultures (Indian, African, European, and Asian) while remaining uniquely Caribbean and reflecting social oppositions that exist on islands that are governed and controlled by France. Within this construct and this recontextualized space, musicians and songwriters are able to reflect upon a cross-culturalism to forge musical differences from one island to another.

Since the 1980s French Caribbean musicians including the Bernard brothers, Mario Canonge, and Taxikréol have been reclaiming their oral history to pay tribute to retired or deceased musicians who almost slipped into oblivion or were never fully appreciated or understood during the course of their active careers. Singers like Jocelyne Béroard, Edith Lefel, Tanya St. Val, and Ralph Thamar sing renditions of traditional tunes by such composers as Loulou Boislaville, Marius Cultier, and Kassav'. Some individuals such as Céline Flériag and the band Palaviré look squarely at the generation gap, while Jean Michel Rotin and Franck Balustre pay homage to their Latin and African American idols. Volt Face's contribution has been the inclusion of the cadence of Dominica into zouk, hip hop, and hard rock.

None of these musicians and singers fall into the trap of presenting a one-sided cultural assertion that excludes another. Instead, they utilize the recontextualized space to prove the multiple dimensional sides of Caribbean music through their choice of dances, singing styles, themes, and physical appearance. Without a doubt, these are multiple changes, but they are what makes the use of the recontextualized space so advantageous. As a result, this chapter discusses how some musicians and singers enter into a circular reinscription of the past to express ongoing social and artistic aspirations though a recontextualized space.

Marius Cultier: The Pivotal Figure

By the time Marius Cultier reached his twenty-second birthday, he had already directed the Office de Radiodiffusion Télévision Française (ORTF) Band in Guadeloupe and Martinique. Born in 1942 in Fort-de-France, Cultier grew up in a household where his father was an amateur musician who had purchased many instruments. By age eight, Cultier was able to play eight of them. Though at age fourteen he suffered the tragedy of losing both of his parents, his older sisters encouraged him to finish school. Heavily affected by his parents' deaths, he poured all of his energy into music.[3] In 1956, Cultier discovered African American jazz through a friend who received records directly from the United States. Not only did Cultier listen to jazz, especially Thelonius Monk, but also to salsa and the mambo. This caused him to practice until he created a blend of jazz and French Caribbean music, which was to earn him eventually a first prize as an amateur among professionals with his interpretation of Monk's 1954 "Round Midnight" at the International Piano Contest in Puerto Rico in 1963 (Cally 1996, 70).

In 1966, Cultier left Martinique with the intention of only spending a few days in the United States. He soon settled in Canada but also concentrated on establishing himself as a pianist in Canada, France, and the United States. Meanwhile, in Martinique, the beginning of the 1970s were considered to be a cultural desert. In an effort to revitalize the cultural scene, Aimé Césaire, with other local politicians from the Parti Progressiste Martiniquais (PPM), obtained funding from the French government to form OMDAC (Municipal Office of Cultural Action of the City of Fort-de-France), which was to become SERMAC (Municipal Service of Cultural Action). During this period Cultier kept returning to Martinique in search of musicians to play with him (one was the bassist Alex Bernard). In 1976, he spent a week in Paris at the Olympia and won the Prix de l'Académie de Jazz de Paris. Afterwards he was enticed to return to Martinique with the offer of running a project, organized by AREPMA (Association for the Research and Teaching of Antillean Musical Production), to integrate professional artists into Martinican society. Unfortunately, Cultier found the job to be beset with problems, and, out of total frustration, he remarked: "I want to leave this place. I have done nothing in this country. It's here in this country where I suffer the most. I have never understood the intellectual infra-structure of an Antillean, OK? Martinique? It is better to leave it to the whites."[4]

Cultier's dreams were to earn his living as a full time professional musician and to contribute to the cultural evolution of Martinique. He had returned home to create a private musical school and to be the founder of the Antilles Guyane Jazz Institute. But these two dreams were not to be realized. Gisèle, Cultier's embittered wife, took the initiative to approach the Guadeloupean producer Henri Debs for up-front money and a record deal for her husband. Debs's response was negative, so the Cultiers produced Marius's compositions themselves and opened up a music store in downtown Fort-de-France.

On 12 December 1982, at the Salle Gaveau in Paris, Cultier and the singer Jocelyne Béroard jointly won first prize for "Un concerto pour la fleur et l'oiseau" (A concerto for the flower and the bird) at the Chanson de la composition d'outre mer (Overseas song and composition contest) that was sponsored by SACEM, SPACEM, and RFO. At this same ceremony with the groups Crystal and Sunshine, Tony Chasseur sang a second Cultier song called "Si jodi ou ni an ti shagren" (If today you have a little sadness), a modern biguine with the opening style of a ballad with a lightweight theme. In 1983, Cultier represented Martinique at the Jazz Festival in Angoulême, France. He also played for visiting major jazz artists and singers in Fort-de-France at the Impératrice bar. However, these prizes and opportunities were still not enough because Cultier felt that he was not receiving his due in Martinique.

The journalist Lucienne Chénard commented that Cultier always gave the appearance of being a little mad (Chénard 1986b). Nonetheless, Cultier managed to open La Bohème, a small piano bar in Fort-de-France, where he sometimes cried while playing the piano. These crying spells were attributed to Cultier's heavy indulgence of alcohol. A lonely, sad, and sick man who was somewhat misguided, he wanted to be taken seriously as a musician rather than a troubadour. His last public appearances in December 1985 were to be at the Jazz and Popular Music Festival at CMAC and at La Défense in Paris with Alex Bernard, Jean Claude Montredon, and Alain Dracius. Later, on 23 December 1985, at the age of forty-three, Cultier died from complications of cirrhosis of the liver. His family prepared the ground floor of the home for his wake on Lamartine Street.[5]

Cultier's death, according to Mano Césaire, "brought a reevaluation of

French Caribbean music and a recognition of the professional musician. The musicians before Cultier's arrival were considered to be nothing but *amuseurs publiques* (public jesters), because musicians were not taken seriously."[6] Musicians were necessary to make people dance, laugh, and have fun. However, after Cultier's death, the Martinican public suddenly realized that musicians had a role to play in society, one of contributing to Martinican culture. Also, before this realization, only literature was considered to be what had been known as high culture.

Bearing this in mind, when Malavoi conceived its prize-winning 1992 *Matébis,*[7] Cultier's "Un concerto pour la fleur et l'oiseau" was selected to be performed by its original singer, Jocelyne Béroard. Earlier, for the January 1991 televised broadcast of Michel Traoré's documentary "Un homme, une passion" (A man, one passion), Béroard had sung the song with a feathery French chanteuse touch, accompanied by Rosine on the piano. For the occasion she dressed the part, appearing in a floor-length, flowered dress to create the illusion of being a flower. But Béroard returned to her trademark black when she recorded the song a second time for Malavoi's *Matébis* show at the Zénith. To reinforce the fact that she was acting out the role of a flower, Béroard sang in a voice lighter than normal, carefully enunciating each word in time with Rosine's piano playing, and lengthening the final syllable of each word in the final stanza.

The well-crafted "Un concerto pour la fleur et l'oiseau" obviously relates the sensual relationship between a bird and a flower:

Si Bon Djé té tounen mwen an flè
Man té ké mandéy shanjé-w an ti zouézo
Lé swé le maten té ké vini
Man té ké kontan wouè tout alantou mwen

~~~~~~~~~

(If God turns me into a flower,
I will ask him to change you into a small bird.
You will come out at night and in the morning.
How happy I will be to have you all around me.)[8]

The flower desires to create her own nestlike space of self-enclosure wherein she can keep the bird, opening up her petals to engulf him in her love. Embodying the fragile female who awaits the male bird, the flower is attached to a stem lodged in the earth. Thus, she is obliged to await the bird's return.

The bird is a free agent whereas the flower is anchored in a passive but hopeful expectation. Symbolic of flight and a wanderer, the bird only returns to mingle within the flower's petals when he thinks it is the right moment. Choosing the timing with care, the couple will discover magic mutually in their private wonderland.

Picked for her beauty and sweet aroma, the flower personifies sensual gratification. In the rose-tinted dawn she willingly opens her petals to be the chosen one. Through the inducement of dreams and a deeper level of introversion she hopes to entice the bird. If not, she will patiently await a new dawn for the bird's return because she believes that he belongs with her:

> Avan la rozé piti maten
> An boté man té ké wouvè pétal mwen
> An té ké si fiè ki'w shoizi mwen
> Ki man té ké ofè-w tout nèkta mwen

> (Before the first pink of dawn
> in beauty I will open my petals to you.
> I will surely be proud if you should choose me.
> I will offer you all of my nectar.)

The song lends itself to two interpretations. One is that it is a lyrical narration about a lovesick woman. Another is that Cultier figuratively hides the narrative's intent behind a description of a bird and flower to depict an ambiguous relationship between the Caribbean and France. In the latter version, the Caribbean, in the disguise of a flower, entices France with its natural beauty despite the financial burden of subsidizing its economy. Caught under the Caribbean spell with its perfumed flowers that masks Cultier's love-hate relationship with Martinique, France is caught in a spider-like web of intoxication against her better instincts.

In Cultier's Footsteps

Influenced by Cultier's technique of commingling American jazz and Caribbean rhythms, Mario Canonge, a fellow Fort-de-France native, studied music for free with Père Elie and then relocated to France in 1979 to study sound engineering at the Université de Paris at Vincennes. Soon thereafter, he left the university to study music at the Conservatoire de Musique de

Paris. During this time he became one of the co-founders of Ultramarine, with whom he played for four years (Thaly 1992, 21). During his stint with Ultramarine he won first prize at a piano festival held at La Défense in 1983, at which some of the participants were Marius Cultier, Alain Jean Marie, and Eddy Louiss. Two years later, to his sorrow, Canonge learned that Cultier had died.

Constantly seeking new musical experiences and challenges, Canonge accepted Jacob Desvarieux's invitation to participate in Kassav's 1988 and 1990 Grand Méchant Zouk shows. In between these time periods, Canonge also found time to coordinate another group, Sakiyo, whose members included Tony Chasseur, Michel Alibo, and Jean Paul Pognon. The group became known for such Canonge compositions as "Bisou sucré" (Sweet kiss) and "La Rochelle." When Paulo Rosine fell too ill with cancer to perform,[9] Canonge replaced him during Malavoi's live engagements in 1992 and helped to form the short-lived Akoustik Zouk with Thamar, the three Bernard brothers (Alex, Jacky, and Nicol), Dominique Bougrainville, Bib Monville, and Maurice Marie Louise.

When the 1990s arrived, the highly ambitious Canonge decided to compose, write, produce, and sell his own records. The first was the 1991 *Retour aux sources* (Return to the origins), an album with his friends' participation. The singer Ralph Thamar agreed to record the mazurka "Lésé palé" (Let them talk) and "Bèl kado" (Beautiful gift), songs with autobiographical references to Canonge's private life. A third song, "Lakensyèl souvenir" (Rainbow memory), was a dedication to Eugène Mona and Marius Cultier.

In 1994, almost ten years after Cultier's death, Canonge and Thamar collaborated on *Hommage à Marius Cultier*. Placing his hands on the keyboard, Canonge quickly composed the music for "Mayo" (Cultier's nickname). After hearing the tune Thamar was so inspired and full of memories of his five-year stint with Cultier that he picked up a pen, a piece of paper, and wrote the lyrics in thirty minutes.[10] "Mayo" opens with a jazzy piano solo by Canonge, and then Thamar joins in as he wistfully sings and captures Cultier's spirit:

Sa ou té mandé pou lan mizik
Sé pa té plis ki ti bren rèspé
Ou byen voyajé mé fòk ou trimé
Pou mennen péi nou a monté
Ki dan la jwa ki dan la penn
Ou kité plen bèl mizik pou nou
Si jòdi yo ka réspékté-y té o-o

Sé pas ou goumen tou lé jou
A prézan sé nou ki pou kontinué
Menm si-w ka mantché nou

〰〰〰〰〰

(What you wanted for our music
was nothing but some respect.
You traveled frequently.
You also had a hard time trying to push our
country ahead.
Whether it be in joy or in pain
you left us plenty of good music.
If today one respects it,
it's because you fought well every day.
Now, it is we who must continue
even if we miss you.)[11]

Wanting to describe how Cultier was able to influence so many upcoming musicians, Canonge also blended together a composite of the late pianist's hits for the jazz-inspired instrumental "M.C. 2 M.C." (Marius Cultier to Marius Cultier) and wrote the lyrics for "Gadé mas pasé" (Look at the procession of masks). The latter was something Cultier often said whenever people asked him how he was doing. According to Thamar, Cultier's responses were most likely "Mwen la" (Okay, I am here) or "Mwen ka gadé mas pasé" (I am only looking at the procession of masks).[12] That was to say, the masks of joy, happiness, and sadness were on the faces of the passers-by who paraded in front of him. Most fittingly, "Gadé mas pasé" and its video were frequently broadcast on Martinican television during Carnival 1995, when masks were worn.

Again, for his 1993 *Trait d'union* (Connecting link), Canonge reached back to the past to write "Non musieu" (No mister). The composition, sung by Béroard, recounts the tale of a vendor woman who sells dolls on the *savane* (park) in the center of Fort-de-France. An honest and hardworking woman, she rises at 4:00 in the morning to assemble her dolls. When she is approached and propositioned by a male client, her retort "Non musieu, mwen pa fanm fasil" (No mister, I am not a loose woman) is uttered with pride. She also tells the stranger about her "dous è agréable" (kind and agreeable) boyfriend while chasing him away with the words: "Alé déplacé kontinué vo shimin sorté lésé mwen / mwen sé an fanm kréyòl" (Go, move

away, continue on your way, get away, leave me / I am a Creole woman).[13]
Taken by surprise by this man's negative and aggressive behavior, she falls
upon her ethnic and gender identities to foil the man's attempt to reduce her
to a sexual commodity.

A similar circumstance takes place in Joby Valente's "Ay promnen musieu" (Get lost, mister) of the 1960s:[14]

> Lòt jou mwen alé dansé
> Mwen jwen on bour byen sapé
> I dit mwen: "Manm'zelle vous êtes très chic.
> Que faites-vous dans la vie?"
> Mwen ki an Antillaise
> Mandé mwen ki sa ka rivé
> Pouki musieu ta la
> Ka posé kèsyon kon sa.
> Mandé mwen ki sa ka pasé
> Pouki kon la

~~~~~~~~~~~

> (The other day I went dancing.
> I met a well-dressed man.
> He said to me: "Miss, you look good.
> What do you do?"
> I am an Antillean.
> I asked myself
> why did this intruder want to mettle
> in my business?)[15]

Although the venue is different (a public dance) from the one in "Non musieu," the young woman also recoils from the male stranger's unwelcomed
advances. The man openly declares his interest in her. He then specifies that
women who go out with him must have a car and a family subsidy. Annoyed
by the man's bold behavior, she thinks: "Conpè a ni an bèl toupé" (This jerk
has an inflated ego). Unlike Canonge's "Non musieu," the more outspoken
woman taunts the unwanted suitor with the final questions: "Adan ki léta
zòt yé la a / Zòt dépozé kò zòt barbo?" (What is wrong with you? Are you
now playing the pimp?)

Written about twenty years apart, Canonge's and Valente's songs are reminiscent of Léona Gabriel's earlier "A si paré" (see chapter 3). What links the

three songs are the sentences, "Mwen sé kréyòl" (I am a Creole), "Mwen sé an fanm kréyòl" (I am a Creole woman), and "Mwen ki an Antillaise" (I am an Antillean). All three carry the message: "I stand on my own; I am not to be fooled around with." However, the difference between the woman in Gabriel's "A si paré" and those of "Non musieu" and "Ay promnen musieu" resides in the fact that their financial circumstances differ. Whereas the woman of "A si paré" had been betrayed and financially abandoned by her lover, the women of "Non musieu" and "Ay promnen musieu" are gainfully employed and reject strange men's unwanted sexual advances.

The latter two songs thereby reflect the impact of the women's movement and societal expectations. Canonge's and Valente's songs introduce well-dressed professional women who are not to be mistaken for prostitutes. What concerns them is that some men do not make such a distinction. With their overblown, lusty egos, the men display a macho behavior that the women are supposed to find appealing in spite of their rudeness. In the case of "A si paré," the woman is either a mistress or a housewife who is determined to find another way to support herself and her child. Despite the differences in the three women's financial situations, the three songs construct women who take great pride in their identity as Creole Caribbean women. The themes of misplaced male arrogance and female pride function as metaphors for what is happening in contemporary French Caribbean societies. Canonge and Valente join Gabriel in advocating a change and demonstrate that not all women tolerate being mistreated sexually or financially.

Another approach to societal change is found in Canonge's "Si ou sa revé" (If you can dream) from the 1995 Arômes Caraïbes (Caribbean aromas). This time a stranger meets an old man on the road who calls himself a magician. While listening to the old man, the younger man daydreams about the power of the magician's wand. If the magician is telling him the truth, all of his dreams will be realized. No longer will countries around the world endure conflicts. Thanks to the magician's wand, the flick of his wrist can alter historical events. The wand uncovers the suppressed past to gain some manner of control over the present. Most importantly, the magician's wand also wipes out oppression and creates an idyllic society. Like a historian, Canonge confronts a stack of frayed memories to recontextualize other ones, turning personal experiences into those of the entire society.

The Flériag Version

Coming from a family of fifteen children, where her oldest brother and two of her sisters sing, Céline Flériag followed in their footsteps, singing in the chorus for several bands in the 1980s. Her musical preferences were the biguine and mazurka, and she performed for four years with Majumbé, three years with Malavoi, and sometimes for Guy Vadeleux, and Kali.[16] Concerned about what kind of future lay ahead for Caribbean people, Flériag, mother of a son, opened up her home in 1994 to offer medical care for a neighboring St. Lucian girl with a heart ailment. Her concern for children and humanity at large coincided with similar remarks made by the Puerto Rican writer Ana Lydia Vega: "Women's lives, to be sure, are always more collective because we're mothers, we take care of children, we tend to our parents when they're ill, we are neighbors. Men don't have this kind of life, one that is integrated with the community" (quoted in Hernandez and Springfield-Lopez 1994 , 818).

Without question, Flériag's belief in the Caribbean community at-large carries over into her popular 1994 "Rèv mwen" (My dream) from *Karamèl:*

Aa, si an jou man té pé
Mété le mond kon mwen sé voudré
É si dimen mwen té pé ni an shans
Pou réalizé sa
Lavi té ké diféran
Pa té ké ni lanmizè
Tout ti manmay
té ké trouvé an bagay
Pou manjé tou léjou

Non, lavi a tro rèd
É sé nou menm ki ka fè tou sa
Si pa té ki kannon
Nou pa té ké wouè ladjè piès koté
Tout moun anni oublyé ki sa ki solidarité
Ou sé di sé sinéma
Tèlman tout sa difisil a kwè

An shanté lapé pou lumanité
An shanté kay nou ka pòté lanmou
An shanté pou tou sa ki maléré
An shanté kay nou ka pòté lanmou
Le mond antyé

Pou fè tout moun konprann
Ke sa té ké pli bèl ke nou otan
Tout moun té ké fredoné an shanté
Plen pawòl lanmou
Woui, sé man sé voudré
Men fòk zòt dakè ban mwen lanmen
annou sanblé kò nou
Sé ansanm sèlman ke nou ké rivé
Y za ni tròp lanmizè pou nou rété indiféran

Annou éséyé sèlman
Alò, fò nou koumansé shanté
An shanté la pé pou lumanité
An shanté kay nou ka pòté lanmou
An shanté pou tou sa ki maléré
An shanté kay nou ka pòté lanmou

〰〰〰〰〰

(Oh, if only I could
create the world as I would like.
If tomorrow I could be lucky enough
to realize this.
Life would be different.
There would be no misery.
From all over the world
children would have something
to eat every day.

No, this life is made up of too many hardships.
We are responsible for it.
If no cannon existed,
nowhere would wars be waged.
We all forgot the meaning of solidarity.
Like a movie
it's so difficult to believe.
A peace song for humanity.
A song from home that brings love.
A song for the unhappy.
A song from home that brings love.

Yes, indeed, this lovely song would have spread
all over the world.
It would have made everybody understand
that this is far more beautiful than we are.
Everybody would have hummed a song
loaded with love.
The earth would have revolved on a
nice song from home.
Yes, this is my wish,
but I'll need your hand.
Let's get together.
It's only together that we could make it.
There is too much hardship for us to remain indifferent.

Let's give it a try.
Let's start singing
a peace song for humanity.
A song from home that brings love.
A song for the unhappy.
A song from home that brings love.)[17]

"Rèv mwen" is a call for people to stop the killings and wars that occur when the concepts of peace and solidarity are forgotten. Throughout the song Flériag establishes a connection with people who are constant complainers and therefore sings this song to disperse some love. In her own words, Flériag describes "Rèv mwen" as being a very simple song. "People sit in front of a television and constantly watch scenes depicting war, poverty, hopelessness, and hunger. There is another side to life than these images. People should not have to dream about the worst side of life."[18] Hence, the song selections from *Karamèl* bring attention to traditional values through the symbolism of a sweet candy of brown-colored caramel mixed with peanuts. They also confirm that Flériag is an optimistic *locale* (a traditionalist).

For Flériag, being a *locale* means, in part, that she prioritizes familial relationships, as does Jean-Paul Soime in "Kolédés" for Malavoi. For example, in "Mazouk-Rag" (Mazurka Ragga) Flériag presents the meeting of two generations. A grandfather teaches his granddaughter how to dance the mazurka of the 1950s and is, in turn, introduced to the raggamuffin steps of the 1980s by his granddaughter:

Papy montré mwen
Ki mannyè pou dansé
Anti mazouk pitché
San dé pyé-w man mélé
Mwen té ké enmen nou mélanjé pa nou
Pou nou santi kò nou byen
Papy balansé
Tout kò mwen za paré
Pour suivre la cadence
De la danse d'antan
Tchenbé lanmen mwen
Pou montré mwen
Kouman yo ka dansé an mazurka

Je te promets Papy
Si tu me fais danser
De te faire découvrir
Les secret du ragga
Tu sentira bien vite
Tes genou se muscler
Tes reins se débloquer
Ta jeunesse retrouvée

Papy ou ka wouè sa pa byen difisil
Pou ke wou épi mwen nou rivé avansé
An pa mazurka é an bon son ragga
Sé pazapa nou kè rivé
Sé byen an mazurka ke man ka dansé la
É ou byen kontan sa
Sa-w ka fè la-a
Mé sé ragga Papy
Ou wouè, sa pa si lèd ki sa
La nuit du mazurka fait danser le ragga
Et avec toi Papy, le courant est passé
Je te montre le ragga et toi la mazurka
Alors papy tu vois, toi et moi c'est complet
Manmay ès zòt wouè
Ki mannyè pou nou fè
Nou la jeunès antan
Partajé sa nou yé

An nou fè le pa
Papy byen kontan sa
Épi tout bagay kay alé
Ça, c'est le ragga-mazurka
C'est toi, c'est moi, c'est nous Papy
Je te montre le ragga et toi la mazurka
Ba men lanmen Papy
Sa ki tan mwen sé ta-w

~~~~~~~~~~~

(Grandpa, show me
how to dance
a nice mazurka.
Without your feet I am confused.
I would like us to dance together
in order for us to feel great.
Swing, Grandpa.
I am all ready
to pursue the rhythm
of the old time dance.
Hold my hand
and show me
how the mazurka is danced.

Grandpa, I promise you that
if you make me dance,
I'll make you discover
ragga's secrets.
It won't take you too long to feel
strength in your knees,
to have no blockage in your kidneys, and
to rediscover your youth.
Grandpa, you see, it's not that difficult
for you and I to move forward together.
One mazurka step and one ragga step.
It's only step-by-step that we could make it.
I am dancing the mazurka.
Don't you like it?
What are you doing?

This is the ragga, Grandpa.
You see, it's not crap.
The mazurka night makes ragga dance.
It clicked with you, Grandpa.
I show you the ragga, and you show me the mazurka.
Grandpa, do you see how you and I complement each other?

Did you guys understand
how we should proceed
so that those who were young once
share what we are?
Let's take the first step.
Grandpa loves it.
Everything will work out fine.
This is mazurka-rag.
It's you; it's I; it's we, Grandpa.
I teach you ragga; you teach me the mazurka.
Hold my hand, Grandpa.
What belongs to me also belongs to you.)[19]

This sharing of dance steps to the mazurka and ragga confirm that each generation has something to offer the other. It also reminds one of Nketia's essay on music and play during which he remarked, "approaching music making as a play activity can enhance the conviviality of a social occasion, facilitate the sharing of individual and group sentiments or the pure communication of both aesthetic or social values" (Nketia 1990, 29). Neither the grandfather nor granddaughter rejects the other's taste in music without listening to it. While teaching each other dance steps to their preferred music, the grandfather and granddaughter engage in a history lesson within recontextualization. The granddaughter's final statement, "What belongs to me also belong to you," encompasses personal growth and a sensitivity across generations.

The Flexible Bernard Brothers and Fal Frett

One of the most talented families on the contemporary Martinican musical arena is the Bernards. The grandfather, Armand, was a violinist, and his sons Gaëtan and Parfait continued the tradition: the former was another violinist and the latter, a keyboard player. Raised in a household where music totally surrounded them, it was only natural for Parfait's sons Alex, Jacky, and

Nicol to love playing instruments. Alex, the oldest and a bass player, is the only full-time musician among the brothers since he quit his job at the Hôpital de la Meynard. He studied with Edmond Michalon and, as a bass player, joined the Jeunesse Étudiante Catholique (Catholic student youth group), to which other aspiring musicians belonged, such as the pianist Paulo Rosine and the flutist Serge Lossen. In 1969, he joined the Merry Lads, which evolved into Malavoi, and he continues to play with the band today. Furthermore, between the two disbandments of Malavoi in the 1970s, Alex took the opportunity to go on tour in Canada with Marius Cultier.

The multiple instrumentalist Jacky, born four years after Alex, commenced playing the piano at age eleven. In 1970, he passed his baccalaureate and left to study law in Paris at the Faculty of Assas. While there he began to perform at Caribbean venues and worked in the recording studios. In 1975, he returned to Martinique where he played the piano and keyboard in piano bars, especially at the Inn of Monsieur Duban in the town of Rivière Salée.

Nicol, the youngest of the three, born in 1956, familiarized himself with several instruments, but at age fourteen, he seriously studied the bongos and other percussion with Colette Frantz and eventually with Henri Guédon. Since then Nicol has become known as an accomplished percussionist.[20] In 1969, Nicol participated in a jazz concert with his brothers at the Cercle Martiniquais. Afterward, he left to study in Paris, where he became a member of Guédon's newly composed Cosmos Zouk. At age nineteen in 1976, he returned to Martinique and agreed with his brothers, Jacky Alpha, and Bib Monville to create Fal Frett.

In 1976, Fanny Augiac proposed that Fal Frett should make its debut before the public at the Centre Martiniquais d'Action Culturelle (CMAC).[21] The band's first concert repertoire was taken from its first record *Fal Frett*, which was released by Jacky Nayaradou's 3A Productions. Afterward, Ralph Thamar and Robin Vautor joined the band, with Jacky Bernard functioning as the leader on the second album *In the Wake of the Sunshine*. Jacky was responsible for organizing the program so that the music in each set followed harmonic key changes. In this same role, Jacky coordinated Fal Frett's 1997 concert with three invited guests (Canonge, the percussionist Paco Charlery, and the saxophonist Luther François). One of the high points was a concerto for two pianos played by Canonge and Jacky.

In general, what makes Fal Frett stand out is the band's distinctive sound, which some call jazz fusion. This is in reference to the band's incorporation of traditional Martinican musical themes and an extension of them along more jazzy lines. Most often, Fal Frett's music is instrumental; people usually sit down and listen to it in a concert hall, a piano bar, or on a purchased recording at home. The music is characterized as having a discreet, cool sound with touches of Chick Corea, Herbie Hancock, Stanley Clarke, and Weather Report—all very appealing to jazz aficionados. Fal Frett also opts for what Michel Thimon calls "a more global concept opened to rhythms all across the world" (Thimon 1997b, 8). The independent Bernard Brothers, who have only found time to record six albums in twenty-one years, are too busy performing for the sheer delight of it to do studio work. To explain their strong reasons for being musicians, the Bernard brothers candidly state on their first album: "Music is a source of communication. With communication, we hope for peace. To find love and joy is to have peace. It is we who are Fal Frett."[22]

The Musical Cocktail Punch

In the 1980s, Franck Donatien, a guitarist and son of the musician Fernand Donatien (see chapter 4), called upon some of his friends to organize a musical band under the name "Taxikréol."[23] He, Suzy Trébeau, and others recorded one album that was half-heartedly received. As a result, Trébeau left to sing backup for Malavoi and to join another band called Kwak. Convinced that he could launch his own successful band, Donatien did not stop trying. The next time he convinced a different group of friends (Danièle René Corail and Janick Voyer as lead singers, Gilles Voyer on keyboard, Richard Marie Claire on bass, Max Télèphe on flute and saxophone and John Antoine on saxophone, George Gromat and Alain Ravaud on trumpets, Hervé Laval on drums, and Marc Séraline on percussion) to work with him, which led to the 1994 release of *Special Request* under the same name of Taxikréol. This time Donatien's formula of fusing zouk with jazzy biguine reminiscent of the 1940s and Haitian compas of the 1970s worked out favorably. The album enjoyed an enormous success, gathering two 1994 Prix SACEM-Martinique statues for "Special Request" and "Malgré tout" (In spite of everything).

Not afraid to confront political realities, Donatien's "Special Request" is a satire about what typically happens during an election year. In this case, a crafty politician named Lulu Badjol delivers a campaign speech full of empty statements that annoy his constituents. Beginning with an announcement distorted by a loud speaker, the public message is "Stop, dépéché / ouvè zyé pou gadé / Missié Badjol ké palé / I filé lang li sèt fwa dan bouch li" (Stop, hurry up / Open your eyes to look at Mister Badjol speak / He turns the language around seven times in his mouth).[24] True to form, Badjol makes false promises in French:

J'assassinerai le chomage (sé sa ou di).
J'éliminerai les impôts (sé sa ou di).
Je construirai des ponts, les rivières viendront en temps utile (sé sa
ou di).

〰〰〰〰〰〰

[I will assassinate unemployment. (That's what you say.)
I will eliminate taxes. (That's what you say.)
I will construct bridges; rivers will come later, if necessary. (That's what
you say.)]

After his speech a strange noise is heard accompanied by the rolling of
drums. Sound effects simulate a crowd scene with the echoing of undistin-
guishable sounds, followed by a saxophone solo for transitional phrasing.
The soloist Max Télèphe duplicates a politician's speaking voice; the crowd
replies in the fifth stanza that it cannot trust what the two-faced Badjol says
because he is so manipulative:

Pawòl ké tonbé
Missié Lulu déchainé
I ka driblé tout moun
Bèl pawòl ka fè siwawa dan goj-la
A byen gadé sé li ki té mantché pou nou byen

〰〰〰〰〰〰

(Running off at the mouth,
Lulu puts everybody in his pocket.
His speech overflows with beautiful promises.
If you say so, he is the one we needed
to make us feel good.)

"Special Request" is a denunciation of politicians like Lulu Badjol, who promote themselves and enrich themselves at the expense of others. Their motto
is survival through compliance with the French politics of *régionalisme*. The
arrogant Badjol makes false promises that casually bounce off his audiences
who tune them out. Using highly vernacular Creole rather than direct commentary, Donatien expresses his opinion of shady politicians via the persona
of Badjol. The constant repetition of the refrain, "Special Request, kout'

lang' ka fè déga pou an mandat" (Special request, the tongue shoots out words that are destroying everything all around, just for an election), implies that Badjol uses language in a slippery fashion, giving the song a litany-like character and effectively capturing the voters' dissatisfaction.

Playing different kinds of music that are disseminated throughout the Caribbean, Taxikréol proves that popular music is dynamic. For example, its name taxi kréol (Creole taxi) comes from Haiti, where brightly painted *tap-taps* (buses), converted into taxis with slogans and a sound system, are driven. Traveling in taxis around the islands exposes passengers to salsa, soca, zouk, reggae, the blues, and raggamuffin. Going along for the ride is Taxikréol with its varied albums: *Special Request, Siwo Fuel,* and *Empreintes Hommage à Fernand Donatien.* For example, Trinidadian "ole talk," a parody of a humorous calypso, serves as the base for Donatien and Max Télèphe's "Come Zis Afternoon" from *Siwo Fuel* (1995). Since the song is sexually oriented, René-Corail and Télèphe raise their voices at the end of each line to emphasize the last syllable of the suggestive lyrics that are overlaid with comical and provocative teasing. Acting the part of a man who derives pleasure from flirting with women, Télèphe says (among many things): "I want you to come zis afternoon / Pou nou pé palé anglé" (To teach us English); "Darling, I want you to come this afternoon"; and "Pou mwen fèw palé fransé!" (To let me make you speak French).[25] Immediately, listeners comprehend that these double entendres are a prelude to lovemaking lessons.

Next, there is Donatien's "Ebony Roots," an amalgamation of Jamaican reggae, Trinidadian soca, African American blues and rap, and Martinican zouk and bèlè that represents the band's venture into the diversity of the Caribbean and trans-Atlantic regions:

Sòti Memphis, Tennessee
Rivé Mon Dézes ni an bout
An sakré bout
Pa menm an fon syèl
Ou pé ké wouè zombi Elvis
Voyé lavwoua
Dan shanté Ti Emil . . . Ti Emil

Mé ni an koté an shimin
Eti tout moun tonbé dakò
Easy . . . San yo fòsé
Kay misiz Debra

Déyè vyé juke box la, in Louisiana
Ni bèl tanbou ka roulé
Tout lannuit . . . tout lannuit
Ebony roots, coming from Africa
Travèsé lanmè-ya
Pousé kon vyé zèb anmè
Toupatou, tout koté, touléjou
Sòti dépi Guyana, rivé Louisiana
Adan ti bar-la, déyè vye boutik la
Tou pré kwazé-ya
Sé la pou tann son ka désann
Nèg ka babyè
Dèyè vyé bab labsent yo-a
Tout vyé mennto, tout bwabwa
Ka dansé . . . ka grinyé

Sé menm moul la ki fè yo
Menm solèy la ki brilé
La po-yo, zépòl-yo
Sòti dépi Guyana, rivé Louisiana
É lè misyé Slim dégaré gitay-la
Pou y ba nou dé nòt Blues
Tout moun anlè
Kantapou Debra
Y ka mandé lé répondè
Ou sé konprann ou adan
An vyé pit . . . larégale
Ebony roots, coming from Africa
Menm ti mannyè bòdzé-a
Menm feeling la, menm swing la
Menm bay-la
Sòti dépi Guyana, rivé Louisiana

〜〜〜〜〜〜〜

(Coming from Memphis, Tennessee
to go to Morne des Esses is a ride.
Quite a ride.
Not even in the center of the sky
are you going to see Elvis' ghost.

Respond
to Ti Emile's song . . . Ti Emile.

There's a path, a road about which
everybody easily agrees.
Without making an effort
at Miz Debra's
behind the old juke box in Louisiana
a drum is divinely played.
All night long, all night long.
Ebony roots, coming from Africa.

Crossing the sea
bitter weeds grew
everywhere, all over the place, everyday.
Ebony Roots, coming from Africa.
Coming all the way from Guyana to Louisiana.
In the bar, behind the old country store
next to the crossroad,
the beat is divine.
The Black rascals speak loudly
behind their red eyes,
behind their crummy beards full of alcohol.
The obeah men! Everybody
dances and smiles.

They came out of the same mold.
The same sun burnt
their skin and their elbows.
Coming from Guyana to Louisiana.
When Mr. Slim takes out his guitar
to play the Blues,
everybody gets crazy.
As for Miz Debra,
she asks them to respond.
You feel like you are in

a "pit" in Régale.
Ebony Roots, coming from Africa.

The same happy-go-lucky attitude.
The same feeling, the same swing.
In one word, the same thing
coming from Guyana to Louisiana.)[26]

Donatien once remarked that Taxikréol's music is "accessible and returns to the concept of a Caribbean *métissage* (mixture), expressing humor which animates a group linked by the complicity that creates music" (Th. Dz 1995b, 40). This is very well expressed in "Ebony Roots" when it opens with "Yeah! Hey man, listen to me," spoken in a jazzy African American slang interspersed with rap, laughter, a saxophone solo, and a bèlè solo. The colloquial expression creates an informal tone to signify approval in a club atmosphere. Background voices and hand clapping are heard on the soundtrack along with shouts in French of "C'est bon" (That's good) and "Vas-y" (Go ahead) to encourage the musicians at play.

Representative of a transculturation with its merger of anglophone and francophone rhythms, "Ebony Roots" elicits a thrill at the prospect and wonder of something new as Taxikréol "travels" from Guyana to Louisiana. Crafted as if the song was composed ad hoc with its twists and turns, the continuation of the slave masquerade is recalled. A veiled warning is made about Elvis Presley's ghost hovering around the bèlè drummer, Ti Emile, who comes from Morne des Esses (known as the authentic village of bèlè). What is not spoken, but is understood, is the well-known story that Elvis had recontextualized African American music to launch his career while those from whom he copied never earned any credit or royalties. However, it does not matter, because the spirits and legacies of the African American blues singer Memphis Slim[27] and the Martinican bèlè drummer Ti Emile are intertwined through the Middle Passage and have reappeared through the same molding craftsmanship of Taxikréol's musicians.

Similar sound effects, resembling a tight Motown backup singing technique, are also heard on Kwak's albums. During his tenure with and direction of Kwak,[28] Philippe Joseph, who now performs with Kassav', insisted that the group should not depend upon an individual. Each member was responsible for writing at least one song per album. For Kwak's second album *A dé, vlopé!* (To hug each other) Joseph wrote the lyrics and music for "Pa grandi" (Don't grow up); those for "Pa mélé" (Don't gossip) were done by Suzy Trébeau (lyrics) and Anthony Lowenski (music). "Pa grandi" deals with a young boy's reluctance to grow up: "Mwen imajiné ki man pasé tout lavi / San janmin grandi et san janmin vielli" (I thought that I would spend life / not growing up and getting old).[29] Mistakenly, the ten-year-old boy thinks that playing hooky will make all his problems evaporate. Very stubbornly, he insists "An nou rété toujou piti / nou pli kontan / Sa sé plézi" (Let's remain a child / We are happier / That's the pleasure.)

The United Negro College Fund's motto, "A mind is a terrible thing to waste," comes to mind upon hearing "Pa grandi" and "Pa mélé." While a young boy wants to slow down the growing up process, Milo, the adult in "Pa mélé," conducts his life like a carefree boy:

Ladjè chomaj épi mizè
Ka roulé
Mé Milo sanfouté
I pa mélé
Sapé kon an prens

~~~~~~~~~~

(Wars, unemployment, and misery
are going on.
But Milo does not give a damn.
It does not bother him
to be smartly dressed like a prince.)[30]

Milo's attitude stems from the fact that he always relies upon his mother's support to get him out of his scrapes. However, his mother reaches her breaking point when she warns him that his life will change after her death:

An bon jou tou sa kéy shanjé
Milo réfléchi
Sa pa lavi
Mété dlo on divan-w

~~~~~~~~~~

(One day all of this is going to change.
Milo, think about it.

This is not life.
Grow up.

These two songs by Kwak parallel the political entanglement of the French Caribbean with France. The Indépendentistes argue that ties must be cut with France if the French Caribbean wants to move from the continuously dependent, childlike state reported in "Pa grandi." The Creole proverb "Mété dlo on divan-w" from "Pa mélé" literally translates into "Put water in your wine," but the implication is that Milo is to conduct himself like a responsible adult. In this second song about Caribbean manhood, a set of social manners emerges that falls short. Milo dresses well, but he depends on his mother. Milo attracts women, but he is not dependable. According to Milo's mother, he needs to confront his failings and engage in a self-critique necessary for personal growth. Not in agreement with Milo's behavior, the Kwak songwriters unequivocally want to see action-oriented Caribbean men who use tactics to empower themselves.

In support of Kwak's position is another band, Palaviré. Convinced that each generation learns from the other, the all-male Palaviré consists of two generations of musicians. Its name palaviré,[31] given to them by Ina Césaire, means "round trip." To explain further, Claude Césaire, the band's leader and pianist, comments on the generational link:

One has rarely seen this formation of two generations with totally different influences. For example, look at my father's generation whose influences were Latin and Cuban music. For my generation it is jazz and American, like the singers Al Jarreau and Michael Jackson. The originality of Palaviré is this confrontation of different models and styles, but they run together in a very genial manner.[32]

Claude Césaire, who also happens to be Mano Césaire's son and Ina Césaire's cousin, is well aware that Palaviré will probably be compared to Malavoi since his father Mano Césaire had been the latter group's founder. Regardless, Claude points out that Palaviré's music is more swinging and foot tapping than Malavoi's. Having released two albums, *Plézi* (Pleasure) and *Tête à Tête*, the band's aim is to make a more palatable music to reach a wider audience and to avoid being classified in one category. Simultaneously, Palaviré wants to situate its music within a recontextualized space where one's taste for music leads either to a former Malavoi compact disc or a current Kwak recording.

Until the founding of Palaviré, Claude played jazz based upon Martinican, Trinidadian, and Cuban rhythms either as a solo act or with a trio. Two of these rhythms—Cuban and Martinican—are heard on Palaviré's version of Ina and Mano Césaires' "La vi sé an bato" (Life is like a boat). The first version of "La vi sé an bato" appeared in an abbreviated form on Thamar's 1991 *Caraïbes*. Considered to be too long, the record producers cut some of its verses and changed the title to "Nostalji" (Nostalgia).[33] Later, Mano and Ina Césaire re-released the song under its original title for their version on Palaviré's *Tête à Tête* (1995).

This act of recontextualization recalls William E. B. DuBois's term "structural amnesia," since the original version of "La Vi sé an bato" is rescued from its shortened and hidden place on Thamar's album. In comparison, the Palaviré version is in a classical style and slower. When Thamar sings the line about drumming, one actually hears the gwo ka. On the Palaviré version, an exchange between the soloist and the backup singers occurs. Expressive of happiness and good fortune, Jean Claude Gertrude sings in a classical style about a boat that moves confidently through the water—a metaphor for Black people's lives, spent on a stormy and treacherous sea:

La vi sé an bato
Tèt an ba, pié an wo
Yo di la vi sé an konba
Pié an wo, tèt an ba . . .
Bato-a ka pran dlo
Tèt an ba, pié an wo
Yo di nou rivé isiya
Pié an wo, tèt an ba
Lan mè ja shayè nou
Dépi toujou jòdi jou, péyi-a, sé nou

La pli-a ka chanté lanmou
An tan, anlè, an jou
Délè ni an moman
La nostalji ka fè an ti détou isit
Ka véyé zafè-nou pou li
Sa déshaviré la vi . . .
San mwin ké touné dlo
Pié an ba, tèt an wo
I ka bat ba nou tout gwo ka
Pié an wo, tèt an ba. . . .
Zò mwin sé "filibo"

Tèt an ba, pié an wo
An tout bwa, pa ni piès la vwa
Pié an wo, tèt an ba . . .

∿∿∿∿∿∿∿

(Life is like a boat.
Head down, feet up.
People say that life is a battle.
Feet up, head down.
The boat goes on water.
Head down, feet up.
People say we arrived here.
Head down, feet up.
The sea already deported us.
Today, and always, the country is still ours.

The rain sings love.
One time, one hour, one day.
Sometimes, there is a moment where
nostalgia makes a small detour.
It keeps an eye on our affairs
that destabilizes life.
My blood turns into water.
Feet up, head down.
Play us a note on the gwo ka.
Feet up, head down.
My bones are porous.
Head down, feet up.
There's no path in the woods.
Feet up, head down.)[34]

To conjure up the boat's up and down movements, Palaviré accentuates the violins as they provide backup for the duet between Gertrude and Marcel Rodrigue. Fighting to remain afloat amidst the choppy waves, the song winds down with a violin crescendo and the striking of one piano note. Therefore, the boat is a passage through time and space as well as an unconscious need to recast one's life. As they rest within its womb-like shape, the boat's motions lull its inhabitants and break down their defenses while encouraging confession, conversation, and receptivity. A resurgence of Martinican history is translated through the symbolic crossing of the ocean and a liquid absence of tension toward peace.

Of course, the historical value of "La Vi sé an bato" cannot be overlooked, because the song is a revisioning of history. It becomes evident that there are two perspectives—one emphasizing the bleakness of daily life and the other documenting the determination to survive. In an attempt to reconstruct racial oppression within a recontextualized space, the songwriter, Ina Césaire, seeks to contain a self-directed rebellion and to turn it into a more constructive way of resistance. Using a multilayered Creole that prohibits an easy entry into the text, Césaire alternates the expressions "Pié an wo, tèt an ba" (Feet up, head down) and "Tèt an ba, pié an wo" (Head down, feet up)," to indicate that she is not interested in complacent Caribbean subjects. In other words, her subjects' heads might be bowed today, but they hope to be able to raise them tomorrow. To emphasize Césaire's stance, the collective background vocals onomatapoetically duplicate the forward and backward movements of a boat.

Contrary to the gloom depicted through such references as destabilization and no path in the woods, the Caribbean subjects gain a critical consciousness which enables them to understand their lives. What sustains them is their belief that "Dépi toujou jôdi jou, péyi a, sé nou" (Today, and always, the country is still ours)." Here the songwriter acknowledges Black kinship. Admittedly, her subjects' lives are marked by horror, but kinship and water (a symbol of life) are avenues by which to offer change, with Caribbean feet pointed in an upward angle while "la pli ka chanté lanmou" (the rain sings love).

Swimming the Currents

During his attempt to define the struggles of an African writer with his past, the Kenyan Ngugi wa Thiong'o wrote in *Homecoming* (1972) that the writer should be "swimming, struggling, defining himself, in the mainstream of his people's historical drama. At the same time, he must be able to stand aside and contemplate the currents. He must do both: simultaneously swim, struggle and also watch on the shore" (Thiong'o 1972, 39). To take Ngugi's thoughts a little further, neither African writers nor Caribbean musicians are restricted to one version of a written history. While on shore they hear many rhythms and file them away for a later day, only to rediscover them in either a newly recontextualized composition or a rendition with a slightly different flavor. In this way, they swim the currents and resuscitate a cross-cultural consciousness. In addition, and as a consequence, their method of writing and composing is backed both by well-known facts and by a recycling of memories and oral history.

Plans to swim in the currents are in the making for the Martinican Franck Balustre's forthcoming album, which will feature a tribute to the Santo Dominican merengue guitarist Juan Luis Guerra.[35] Singing sixteen to twenty-four measures of Guerra's "Ojala que llueva cafe" (Hear the raining of coffee) in Spanish, Balustre duplicates the merengue with a little zouk coloring. Although he does not understand all of the political nuances in "Ojala . . . ," Balustre strongly feels that he should salute Guerra.[36]

Interestingly enough, Wilfrido Vargas, another Santo Dominican meringue player, remaps his version of Kassav's 1984 "Zouk la sé sèl médiakaman nou ni" on his *Wilfrido 86 — La Medicina* (Wilfrido '86—The Medicine).[37] Releasing the song under the title "La Medicina" Vargas recasts the song with suggestive Spanish merengue love lyrics to make it more relevant to the Dominican situation. On the debate about the relationship between history and art, Balustre and Vargas use interventions by Guerra and Kassav' to counteract the imposition of a non-history. These exchanges between Santo Dominican and French Caribbean musicians demonstrate that they are swimming in the currents of recontextualization.

Instead of looking afar to Santo Domingo for inspiration, George Décimus, one of the first Guadeloupean founders of Kassav', invited Jeff Joseph, the former lead singer of the Gramacks from neighboring Dominica, to join his newly created band. The choice of the band's name of Volt Face is symbolic because it means an "about turn" away from the recognizable Kassav' zouk sound. With a heavy bass guitar sound accentuated by drums and a very fast tempo, Volt Face causes quite a splash on the Guadeloupean music scene with its mixture of hip hop, African rhythms, zouk, and reggae. Light on lyrics but with catchy eclectic danceable tunes, the band's "Zouké light," "Imajiné," and "O Madona" topped the record charts in 1994 and 1995. The vocalists (Kathryn Thélamon, Jeff Joseph, Dominique Coco, and Dominique Panol),[38] sing in Creole, but they slip in some English words to demonstrate their versatility.

Whereas Décimus looked toward Dominica for the former Gramacks singer Jeff Joseph, the young Jean Michel Rotin searched even further for inspiration. Singing in an unintelligible Creole, Rotin managed to soar in popularity in Guadeloupe because he crafted his image after that of an African American icon of his, Michael Jackson. He imitated Jackson's dancing style with the moon walk, twirls, jerky movements, and hand gestures. From 1994 to 1995, Rotin sported a conked hairstyle reminiscent of the 1960 Motown acts like the Temptations and the Miracles, and dressed in tight dark jeans with a floppy oversized shirt. A slightly built, dark skinned man, he did not resemble his idol, but, like Jackson, he sang in a light falsetto, catching the Guadeloupean teenagers' fancy. Since they had watched televised videos of Jackson, Rotin quickly won this young group's admiration. In the blink of an eye, the fans could pretend that they almost had a Jackson clone who was just as quick on his feet.

To be fair to Rotin, he sings funky zouk songs that bear no resemblance to Jackson's hits like "Billy Jean," "Thriller," or "Bad." With great glee, in 1994, Guadeloupean teenagers rushed to the record stores to purchase *Héros* (Rotin's first solo effort). When Rotin's video clips of "Héros" (Heroes) and "Cigarèt" (Cigarette) are viewed on television, the young fans imitate the singer's dance steps in their homes, on the school grounds, and at concerts. Undoubtedly, Rotin's dancing and the Jacob Desvarieux and Jean Claude Naimro backed music composed by L. Romain outweigh such nonsensical lyrics from "Cigarèt" as "Kon san a sigarèt / Pa di-w kè lavi kout é-w viv a dé mil a lè / Paské lé ou ké vyé ou kè vlé réparé" (Like cigarette ashes / Don't say that life is short and that you live at 2,000 kms an hour / Because when you're old you won't be able to do what you did when you were young).[39]

The big surprise is that Rotin completely changed his image for his 1997 second album *Solo*. He shifted to dressing like a bare-chested, hip-hop African American singer with the entire paraphernalia: oversized baggy jeans, baseball jacket, and sneakers combined with dark sunglasses, a bald head, and a large gold medallion around his neck. He explained this major change of appearance by saying that "I always find it monotonous to be doing the same thing" (Chenière 1997a, 38). In Rotin's case, he borrows from African American music to assert his own changes, a metaphorical ocean crossing that leads to a recontextualized self and music. The Caribbean is no different from any other region whose musicians celebrate an ongoing exchange of revitalizing tones and rhythms, and at the same time mix elements of déjà vu into something new and distinct. Also, to be realistic, nobody familiar with Caribbean music will confuse a Bob Marley reggae song with a Rotin number.

These innovative musicians' appropriation of traditional music with zouk, hip-hop and jazz is invigorating. Such a fusion responds to the differences in taste as well as reflects the social and historical specificities of French Caribbean music. For instance, Canonge has listened carefully to Wynton Marsalis's records in order to understand his concept of jazz. In a 1995 interview, he mentions that it "took him five years to realize that Marsalis was rehabilitating New Orleans jazz to make it reemerge."[40] Consequently, Canonge sees the connection between Marsalis's concept of jazz and his own method of blending African American jazz with French Caribbean music to be similar to the sampling found in hip-hop.

The pride in being a French Caribbean and the crafting of songs are linked in an emphasis on memory inside a recontextualized space. In this space, memory is used to trace the collective development of a people and its history. Through the acts of writing, playing, and singing songs, French Caribbean bands tap into, unearth, and synthesize scattered fragments of a collective, oral history to create new, hybrid forms of memory inside a recontextualized space. The return to biguine, mazurka, cadence, and compas is not a nostalgic stagnation but a restoration of cultural continuity of half-remembered lyrics and melodies to reflect the changing times.

In hindsight, Taxikréol's decision to write "Ebony Roots" and "Come Zis Afternoon" in mixed French-and English-based Creole is a stance to show its pride in the hybrid nature of Caribbean languages derived from slavery. The band exercises the freedom to blend Creole and various Caribbean musics by simultaneously drawing upon cultural memories not only of their forefathers but of Blacks across the African diaspora as redemptive features. However, according to the Guadeloupean producer and musician Freddie Marshall, this practice of blending three languages is not unique to Taxikréol because Guadeloupean bands like Les Vikings de Guadeloupe did likewise in the 1970s.[41]

Nowhere in these songs does one see a present that is unmarked by the past. Cognizant of the tension between the imagined and reality, the quoted songs reinforce what Manuel, the protagonist of Jacques Roumain's *Les gouverneurs de la rosée* (Masters of the dew) says: "I am planted in this soil. I am rooted in this earth," and "Life is a thread that doesn't break, that can't be lost" (Roumain 1944, 56, 114). Manuel devotes his life to finding water to save his Haitian village and to bringing a sacrificial end to the warring factions among the villagers. Unlike Manuel, the songwriters do not sacrifice their lives to attract fans. They recreate history by writing down their words and melodies in order not to forget what no longer exists. Thus, they tap into an oral history to construct a hybrid soil within the liberating confines of recontextualization.

7 a deferential space for the drum

The Ambivalence of a Cultural Voice

I am convinced that there is something very spiritual about the drums. The pounding rhythms seep into the soles of your feet and slide up your limbs until you begin to dance in unison with them. Well aware of the power of the drums during the years of slavery across the African diaspora and of the colonial laws that prohibited their playing, I was astounded to learn that ambivalence surrounding the drum still lingers in the French Caribbean. As a consequence of uprisings, constant strikes, and the founding of political parties advocating independence from France, the gwo ka and bèlè have become the instruments of communication.

When I went to keep my appointment with Sully-Cally, a Martinican percussionist, dancer, and writer, one of the issues we discussed was the state of drumming. While people love this music for Carnival, some of them still do not value it enough to see it as a commercial product. They continue to relegate drumming to specific activities like Carnival or political rallies. To give an example, in Fort-de-France in 1995, Sully-Cally managed a record store. He featured a bèlè drum prominently in the display window, and he carried an inventory of traditional and folk music. In his store, a customer could purchase compact discs by Sully-Cally, Djo Dézormo, Kali, Guy Konkèt, Malavoi, Marcé, Mona, and Vélo. The downside was that the majority of potential customers were more attracted to record stores like Nuggets, Librairie Antillaise, Hibiscus Records, and Rubicolor, where they could purchase zouk, raggamuffin, and foreign recordings. As a consequence, Sully-Cally had to close down his store and display the compact discs in the Office of Tourism across from the pier. Not a quitter, Sully-Cally has since published a book on Martinican and Guadeloupean musicians of jazz and traditional music. (He previously wrote an earlier one in 1990 on the bèlè and gwo ka.) In addition, he continues to promote the importance of the bèlè in the media and at a variety of festivals.

On the other hand, private schools that teach youngsters drumming are cropping up in Guadeloupe and Martinique. In fact, I took a gwo ka lesson from the maké drummer Pierre Narouman across the street from the Université des Antilles et de la Guyane in Pointe-à-Pitre. Narouman showed me where to place my hands on the drum and had me practice each of the seven gwo ka rhythms. The lesson prompted me to read the books and essays written about drumming by Isabelle Leymarie, Jacqueline Rosemain, Françoise and Alexandre Uri, and Sully-Cally.

Sully-Cally and Kafé, a Guadeloupean percussionist, patiently demonstrated the playing of bèlè and gwo ka rhythms and spoke to me about the history of the drums. They each described the process of making the bèlè and gwo ka. I also attended private parties where either the bèlè or gwo ka were played and accompanied by dancers and singers. To my joy, José Galas presented me with the July 1993 "6e Festival Gwoka" (Sixth gwoka festival) video-tape to watch at my leisure; the video featured my one-time teacher Pierre Nouraman and members of the Geoffroy family of Kan'nida. Several meetings in Paris and Fort-de-France with Henri Guédon, a Martinican percussionist, gave me another level of understanding about his workshops on Afro-Caribbean drumming, his paintings of musicians, and his own playing of percussion instruments for his jazz and Afro-Latin bands.

In December 1995, when I interviewed Freddie Marshall, a Guadeloupean promoter, he recalled how he helped to launch a Carnival band called Plastic Boys. It was a band that fused horn instruments with plastic containers—three-to-five gallon containers used to store salted fish. These plastic containers were recuperated and recycled as drums by the Plastic Boys. The band also incorporated the low sound of the St. Jean Carnival drum rhythms into its repertoire, serving as the base for the first formation of Kassav' by Pierre-Edouard Décimus at the end of the 1970s.

The practice of playing the ti bwa (bamboo sticks) upon plastic containers has continued with the founding in Martinique of another Carnival band called Plastic Système. Carnival is also the site where one hears the Guadeloupean Akiyo's Brazilian-sounding olodum drums. The sounds and the beating of the gwo ka and bèlè resonate throughout the towns of Martinique and Gaudeloupe during the annual February Carnival festivities. There is an euphoria in the air; the revelers instinctively know that the drumming is infectious. An instrument inter-twined with its populations' indigenous past, the drum duplicates the beating of its revelers' hearts and pulses as well as mine.

We need the drum every day.
When we work; when we breathe.
My friends, the drum is the nation's strength.
CHARLY LABINSKY, "Tambou dan tchè nou"[1]

People want to kill the drum.
If someone tells me the drum is a man,
then we have to look after it, preserve its life.
EUGÈNE MONA, "Tambou séryé"[2]

In Africa and its diaspora the drum has a complex history. It has always been an important cultural voice for Africans as seen in the writings of négritude poets and those of the Nigerian Chinua Achebe and the Guinean Camara Laye. Among the Igbo, as noted in Achebe's *Things Fall Apart* (1959), the drum was like "the pulsation of the heart. It throbbed in the air, in the sunshine, and even in the trees, and filled the village with excitement" (Achebe 1959, 44). Today, in the whole of West Africa, drums are used to herald the arrival of a well-known political figure, to open soccer and wrestling matches, and to enhance many important festive, ceremonial, and religious occasions.

Foreigners, especially European colonial authorities, had always treated the drum with a sense of apprehension and ambivalence. Captain T. K. Winterbottom, a British district officer based in colonial Nigeria in Achebe's *Arrow of God* (1964), was terrified of hearing the beating of drums for fear of losing control and giving priority to what he considered to be a primitive music by "savage" people. He even asked himself: "Could it be that the throbbing came from his own heat stricken brain?" (Achebe 1967, 36). In total cultural confusion, Captain Winterbottom's scientific assumption was that he must have been hallucinating. In a different way, the Frenchman Clarence in Laye's *Radiance of the King* (1971) thought the beating of the drum was a simple exercise, thereby reducing the drum's importance. Clarence learned later from an African beggar that the drum had been a cultural voice of the ancestors that linked generations after generations of drummers in Africa.[3]

When we move to the Americas, the allegiance to the drum is played out in "Pé tambou a" (Don't play the drum), a French Caribbean folktale, through a contest of wills between Kinsonn', a master Caribbean drummer, and a French Catholic priest (Georgel 1963, 140–46). In preparation for his wedding, Kinsonn' asks the parish priest how much it will cost to have the church bells rung for his marriage ceremony. When the priest quotes an exorbitant price, Kinsonn' decides to play the bèlè drum underneath the catalpa tree during a special Sunday ceremony. Not only does his drumming disturb the priest, but the entire congregation loses interest in the sermon and decides one-by-one to join Kinsonn' outside. To his discomfort, and against his better judgment, the priest follows his congregation outside and joins them in succumbing to the drum's spell. Kinsonn's drumming is capable of producing unexplainable and spontaneous body movements in all of the listeners. The moral of this folktale is that the bèlè subverts the Catholic priest's rules and religious teachings. It is this spiritual awakening, contrary to Catholicism, that induces so much fear in the colonial authorities and thereby creates a historical legacy.

The French Caribbean people have had an ambivalent relationship with the *tambou* (drum), which they have alternately embraced and thrust aside. Just as in the United States and other countries where people of the African diaspora were enslaved, in Martinique, Guadeloupe, and French Guyana the drum was outlawed by the sugarcane plantation owners, French government officials, and Catholic priests as soon as they learned the Africans were using the drums as a means of communication. In anger and pride, some Africans (the nèg' maroons) fled to the *mornes* (hills), planned insurrections, and continued to play the drums. To counteract the effect and power of the drums, the colonial French government officials led a campaign to construct a negative image of traditional African culture among the African slaves.

Even after the abolition of slavery, the Africans were powerless to prevent the colonial government from instigating a musical battleground along class lines. Within the developing urban centers of Saint-Pierre and Fort-de-France in Martinique and those of Basse Terre and Pointe-à-Pitre in Guadeloupe, the drum was replaced with the piano or another European instrument, resulting in a decline in drum playing in succeeding generations (Conrath 1989, 224). As expected, some segments of French Caribbean society, eager to emulate French values and preferences, associated the drum with poverty, backwardness, and the Creole language of the Black rural farming class, whereas the piano represented an upward social mobility, the French language, and an assimilated lifestyle that emulated the French. Yet the gwo ka (gwoka, groska, or ka) of Guadeloupe and the bèlè *(bel air)* drums of Martinique were still heard in the outlying rural areas. As a result, until recently, the piano and the drum symbolized a dichotomy of lifestyles and values.

In this regard, "Manzé Ida" (Miss Ida), an innovative song composed by Hervé Laval for Taxikréol's 1994 *Special Request,* speaks of the gender-based objections, societal restrictions, and the elevated status of the drum.

Ida viré au péi épi panié diplom li
Ki voisinaj, ki la fanmi, tout moun ka néyé dan champan'
I toujou fè moun plézi, san i gouté an ti doucè
Mi jodi i déclaré sé lan mizik i lé joué

~~~~~~~~~~~~

(Ida is back home.
She came back loaded down with diplomas.
The neighbors, the family, everybody
toasted the event with champagne.
She has always given pleasure without even thinking
about herself, but today she declares her desire
to be a musician.)

Ida's middle-class parents raise strong objections when she informs them of
her intention to be a professional drummer. Her father, who fought in the
last war, prefers the trumpet while her mother chooses the violin. When Ida
leaves home with a drum under her arm, no one stops her, but, in the refrain,
Taxikréol encourages Ida in her career choice.

Gadé manzel filé ti bwa a
Sé pa tanbou twa pédal
Sé la ki ni wotè
Aïe!
Manzé Ida
Gadé léta tanbou-w mété mwen
Roulé Manzé Ida

~~~~~~~~~~~~

(Look at how the young woman plays the ti bwa with dexterity.
Not the trap drum with three pedals.
The one that doesn't put [me] in a state
Ay!
Don't give it up.
Miss Ida,
keep the drum and put me in a state.
Roulé Miss Ida.)[4]

In keeping with the current times, the intervention of the mass media and external approval are accountable for the change of an ingrained social prejudice for Ida's parents. Upon seeing Ida perform to acclaim before an audience on television, they begin to value their daughter' playing. In addition, the parents' change of opinion reflects the Martinican percussionist Henri Guédon's belief that the contempt for the drum persists even though it might be buried under a superficial layer of politically correct approval:

In Martinique, the piano was considered an instrument of the bourgeoisie, a piece of furniture. I myself was disgusted with the piano because of this. Learning to play the piano was a social education, bourgeois, just like the violin. For a long time the drum was forbidden in this milieu. Then, later on, without any transition, there was an abrupt change of consciousness, and snobbery monopolized the drum. Now everybody wants to play the drum because one thinks it is as acceptable an instrument as the others, which still demonstrates a contempt for this instrument.[5]

Contrary to Guédon's belief in no transition, years of cultural activist movements, beginning in the 1970s, coincided with a public recognition and a promotion of the drum into a deferential space. The promotion of Martinican and Guadeloupean music became linked to the creation of separatist parties in Guadeloupe, among which were the Union Populaire pour la Libération de la Guadeloupe, the Union Générale des Travailleurs de la Guadeloupe (General Union of Workers of Guadeloupe), the Union des Paysans Pauvres de la Guadeloupe (Union of Poor Peasants of Guadeloupe), and the Mouvement Populaire pour la Guadeloupe Indépendante (Popular Movement for Independent Guadeloupe). In Martinique, there was already in existence Aimé Césaire's Parti Progressiste Martiniquais (PPM) and the newly created Mouvement Indépendant Martiniquais (MIM). The word *culture* began to appear in the party slogans, as did the term *le patrimoine* (patrimony). Most particularly, there was the 1972 creation of SERMAC (Municipal Services of Cultural Activities) by the PPM in the center of Fort-de-France, a place where artists congregate, discuss their work, and perform. Constant reference to the patrimoine implies that Martinican and Guadeloupean musicians are reassessing the positioning of the drum in a deferential space to restore pride for the instrument through their public statements, lyrics, and musical performances.

Bang Bang: The Drum in its Rightful Space

A cover made from a goatskin and a base made from a tree trunk cut to make a wooden barrel or rum keg are characteristic of the Caribbean drum. The goatskin is stretched over the body of a wooden barrel and tied by a stringing technique. Since man kills the goat and cuts down the tree to create the spiritual *tambou,* many percussionists view the process as a cycle of life, death, and rebirth. This organic relationship between the drum and the created world emphasizes Lloyd W. Brown's (1978, 150) conclusion that art is not separate from society and experience because art and the artist speak out on behalf of a community-perceived experience in which the drum is the voice of its creator. Consequently, the drum symbolizes history's cycles and represents the artistic imagination of singers and drummers.

The drum's basic ensemble in Martinican folk music consists of the bèlè and the ti bwa, the first for rhythm and the second for melody. Trap drums and congas are added to the composition of popular bands, along with a collection of other instruments. In Guadeloupe, three gwo ka drums are played with bare hands: the single-headed *boula* to provide the basic rhythm; the smaller, single-headed *marqueur* for solo playing; and the *tambou ba.*

The Martinican *tambou bèlè,* which originated from the ancient Fon of Dahomey (now called Benin), is totally different from and more complicated than the gwo ka. In fact, aspiring Martinican drummers find it easier to study how to play the gwo ka *figures* (rhythms) rather than the bèlè.[6] The difficulty is attributed to the eight complicated but somewhat overlapping bèlè figures. The *kanigwé's* and *bélia's* dance steps are similar to those of the quadrille; the *katel* relates the story of a duel; the *mavombé* is a dance of the work fields. The *ting bang* is characterized by backward and forward arm movements. *Kalenda,* a flirtatious dance, has two versions (urban and rural), and, as already discussed, the *ladja* is a fighting dance. The *grand bèlè* is the eighth and last figure with a variety of positions.[7]

The names of the seven gwo ka figures and dances are also the same: the *mendé* (Carnival dance); *woulé* or *roule* (waltz); *graj* (manioc work dance); *toumblak* (joyful love dance); *kaladja* (sad love dance); *kagenbel* (sugarcane work dance); and *léwoz* (incantatory dance).[8] Each figure has a distinctive beat and is usually played separately. A typical gwo ka dance begins with a circular formation in which each dancer pays respect to the drum by bowing with an extended right hand. The following commands are issued by the singer to the drummers:

Kaladja a Mimil o
Kongie, ka la ba, mwen
Tambouyé kongne ka la ba mwen

〰〰〰〰〰〰

(Oh Emile, play the kaladja.
Come beat the ka for me.
Drummers beat the ka for me.)

Guilbault notes that dances that accompany bèlè and gwo ka drumming "feature spectacular interactive playing, dancing, and singing, . . . characterized by a call-and-response form, close coordination between the dancers' steps and the rhythmic strokes of the drummer, and the obvious, intense involvement of the lead singer, who sings constantly at full volume with no vibrato, often exploiting the top of his or her voice range" (Guilbault et al. 1993, 18). Henceforth, the singer is prompted to make demands such as the ones by Napoléon Magloire in the léwoz entitled "En rivé" (I'm here) or by Cassius in the woulé-based "Pas bon moin coup" (Don't Hit Me), both from Vélo's original 1963 *Vélo gwoka*,[9] produced by Marcel Mavounzy for Emeraude, and released by Elsodun for a second time in 1994:

Frappé ka la pou mwen
Tambouyé frappé ka la pou mwen
Sonné ka la mwen
Chéri la vwa ba mwen
Ami lévé la vwa ba mwen

〰〰〰〰〰〰

(Beat the ka for me.
Drummer beat the ka for me.
Make the ka resonate for me.
You, darling, over there, sing for me.
Friends, join in with me.)[10]

Caribbean dances are integrated into specific social situations such as a rite of passage, a human life cycle, an affair of the heart, and the passage of seasons. Before dancers participate, they must know the dance movements that coincide with the eight bèlè and seven gwo ka rhythms. Active participation by everyone in attendance is the essential ingredient for a communal performance. Not segregated by age, gender, or class, the dancers gather together at nightfall. Sometimes, a woman will play the drum and be the lead singer, although traditional bèlè and gwo ka drumming is dominated by men.[11] Starting around 9:00 P.M. or later, the lead singer chants; the lead drummer beats one of the figures with the other drummers joining in while the dancers' feet move in unison with the music either within a *ronde* (circle) or standing side-by-side. Whenever the drummers make a break, the dancers come to an abrupt stop, listen for the lead drummer's next figure, and proceed to dance. When a dancer goes into a concentrated trance inside of the ronde to locate the hidden beat within the polyrhythms, the other dancers move outside of the ronde to avoid breaking the spiritual link.

Very effectively, drummers and singers help to bring a variety of emotions to the surface. They support the dancers and perpetuate a visible, African-based choreography through the continuity of music as a socio-cultural activity. Bèlè and gwo ka songs are characterized by a call-and-response form in which interchanges of lyrics, vocables, drumming, and dancing punctuate the performance. The singer's voice becomes incantatory, predicting the mood in conjunction with the drums. Careful and good drummers have to fight against being swept away by the vibration of the drum beneath their hands and on the heels of their feet, which are placed along the base of the drum. If they are fortunate to play with other drummers who appreciate the notion of musical togetherness and avoid overshadowing each other, the percussionists create an atmosphere that produces a very emotional audience.

Vélo: Drummer of the Streets

An illustration of the importance given to Vélo is found in one of the first Kassav' songs, "Love and Ka Dance" on Kassav's *Love and Ka Dance* (1979). The lyrics, "Wo-o Ti Vélo / Wo-o Ti Vélo / Nou vini kouté Vélo / Wo-o Ti Vélo" (Whoa Uncle Vélo / Whoa Uncle Vélo / We've come to hear Vélo / Whoa Uncle Vélo),[12] are quite simple, but the song includes all seven gwo ka rhythms. Vélo, still considered to be the best Guadeloupean gwo ka player, became a national hero after his death after having lived and slept in the streets (Uri and Uri 1991, 133). To apologize for having taken so long to venerate him, the Guadeloupean people as a whole chose Vélo as their first emblematic figure.

Three years after the 1928 cyclone that destroyed large portions of Guadeloupe, Vélo (né Marcel Lollia) was born in 1931 in Pointe-à-Pitre. Vélo was destined to make the drum his life's passport. At a very early age, his father initiated him into the gwo ka. During the 1950s Vélo developed his skill by participating in the annual Carnival celebrations. However, he did not respect the traditional gwo ka rules of *léwoz* by playing separate *figures* (rhythms). Instead, he preferred to mix the *toumblak* and *kaladja* rhythms (Uri and Uri 1991, 134). As a result, "the current generation," according to Franck Jacques, "sees him as the precursor of the different forms of modern *ka* which are springing up in Guadeloupe."[13] In the 1960s, Vélo joined Madame Adeline's folklore troupe, which performed for cruise ship passengers who applauded the magic and speed-blur of his hands.

Falling upon hard times in the interim, Vélo spent nearly fifteen years in prison. Upon his release he roamed the streets of Pointe-à-Pitre, where he could be heard playing the gwo ka at the Place de la Victoire in payment for a meal or a drink of *tafia* (rum mixed with a local plant). Overwhelmed by sadness and destitute, the homeless Vélo fell into a downward spiral of alcoholism and mental illness while insisting that he could live totally from his music. As he resisted efforts to help him, drumming remained his one link with reality. It seemed as if his arms flew around the drum, and his hands caressed the drum's skin while the sounds, issuing from the drum's belly, thundered and swirled around the audience.

Even though Vélo was not actively involved in politics, some Guadeloupean political parties used him, after his death, as a symbol of resistance, for he was seen as a revolutionary who never gave up on his own music or his country. Credited with having single-handedly perpetuated the gwo ka traditions through a period of the mid-twentieth century when the style had suffered a serious decline, Vélo was hailed as a "roots" hero by the thousands who attended his funeral that was fit for a king on 5 June 1984.

Henri Guédon: A Versatile Artist

Born on 22 May 1944 in Fort-de-France, Henri Guédon managed to organize La Contesta, his first musical group, by age twenty (Cally 1996, 103). He simply called upon his friends, Paulo Rosine (vibraphonist), Denis Dantin (drummer), Michel Pacquit (pianist), and Romul Pinel (conga player), to make a record on the Henri Debs label with the Guadeloupean pianist Alain Jean Marie. Their first big success was "Son tambou la" (The sound of the drum) on which one heard the sentence: "Ti Jojo ka joué tambou" (Uncle Jojo is playing the drum). This venture into the music world led to Guédon's 1965 participation in the first "Jazz Fusion" concert at the Chat qui Pêche club in Paris.

In spite of this early attempt in music, Guédon initially planned to study *Arts plastiques* (fine arts) in Paris. Although he did not know it at the time, his art studies were not to exclude his burgeoning interest in the drums. Multi-talented, Guédon had also been a former judo champion from 1963 until 1965. Thus, in response to numerous questions asked about his dual career, Guédon equated his interest in music to the calm he regained after a judo match: "My music is like judo, full of action but, at the end, only one movement. Further, the rhythm itself is likened to judo in the sense that it doesn't unwind wildly even if today's judo has become very aggressive."[14]

Called one of the greatest contemporary percussionists, Guédon was awarded a Maracas d'or in 1979, the first year of its creation, to acknowledge the cultural values of Black francophone people. Before Kassav's reign he launched the term *zouk* with the records *Cosmos zouk* in 1972 and *Zouk Expérience* in 1975. In 1980, Guédon was invited to Olympia to perform with the salsa players Johnny Rodriguez and Andy Gonzalez. In 1981, his creation for drums, *Tamboo pera* (Pera drum), at the Palais des Glaces gave him the idea to propose another concert composed of a quartet of percussion instruments. This concert gave him enough material for the three albums *Retour* (1981), *Afro-Blue* (1982), and *Afro-Temple* (1984). Also, in 1981, Guédon created the Institut de Percussions in the Éditions Leduc building in Montrouge, a Paris suburb, at which he taught students how to play the congas, bongos, and timbales.[15] The Institut was to be followed with the founding of the Monthey-Caraïbes project in Monthey, aimed at familiarizing children and adults with Caribbean rhythms.

Aggressive and ambitious, Guédon next decided to accept an invitation to compose for a classical orchestra. In 1983, Philippe Langlais, leader of the Orchestre d'Harmonie du Havre, called upon Guédon to experiment with a blending of classical and jazz music. Liking a challenge, Guédon composed *Opéra triangulaire,* which premiered at the Printemps de Bourges. On 16 March 1983, he received the Grand Prix International du Disque from the Académie Charles Cros for the musical creation of the *Légendes et contes des Antilles.* From 1984 to 1988, Guédon constantly toured in Europe, the United States, Africa, Canada, and the Caribbean. Despite his heavy tour schedule, he managed to compose an homage to Aimé Césaire at the Festival d'Avignon in 1988; *La Marseillaise en trois continents* for the city of Bagneux in 1992; and the *Nomadisme musical aux Caraïbes* for the city of Courbevoie in 1993.

In 1994, in collaboration with Lisette Malidor and Isabelle Gratiant, Guédon composed the musical *La Madone* (The madonna), based on the 1947 clerical swindle of Martinicans who gave money to see the Madonna.

In 1996, Guédon celebrated his twenty-fifth year in music in Martinique with planned and impromptu concerts, culminating in a filmed biographical RFO 1 television salute. A future project for Guédon with his new Latin Jazz Band will be the preparation of the album *Latin Be Bop* to pay homage to the African American trumpeter Dizzy Gillespie (Chenière 1996a, 33).

Guédon's appreciation for jazz and other diasporic music comes as no surprise, for he links his passion for the drum and other musical interests to their African historical past. His album *Retour* evokes the huge deportation of slaves in the horrendous triangular trade. The music evokes a dreamscape of black ships en route to the Americas, pushed backwards by the magic of the winds and the sea toward the African coastline. For example, "Isle de Gorée" (Gorée island), which is a mixture of the Cuban guaguanco dance-drumming style and the bèlè, conjures up painful memories connected with the transport of slaves to the Americas. Always an artist, Guédon creates compositions that equate colors with the unfolding of rhythms. Thus, the 1981 *Retour* confirms Guédon's conviction that Caribbean musicians ought to attach an equal importance to Afro-Caribbean drumming because it ais entrenched in their past and present. Guédon is also a writer of textbooks. His teaching manual *De l'onomatopée créole à la percussion* (Van de Velde, 1981) was written in collaboration with Mauricette Catillon. Guédon's other books, written only by him, are *Écoute les Antilles* (Armand Colin, 1984a), *Percussions* (Alphonse Leduc, 1984b), and *Guide pratique Rhythm's Section* (Alphonse Leduc, 1985).

Pitak: Contemporary Drumming

Dédé Saint Prix and his Avan Van band were the first to record *chouval bwa* (merry-go-round music) on *Avan Van tombe d'amour* (1984). *Chouval bwa*, whose literal meaning is "wooden horse," became associated with bands that performed alongside and sometimes in the middle of the carousels at patron saint festivals in Martinique. Its rhythm relies on a heavy emphasis on onomatopoeia (Scaramuzzo 1987, 20). Singers in such bands sound as if they are coming out of a loudspeaker. In chouval bwa, a lead accordion is accompanied by a string bass and by high- and low-pitched slaps on the drum. Nicknamed the *roi de chouval bwa* (chouval bwa king), Saint Prix, who has performed as a guest drummer with La Sélecta, E+, Malavoi, Mona, and Pakatak,[16] uses the lineup of accordion, bamboo flute, kazoo, string bass, electric bass guitar, and drums for the Avan Van band. His latest choice of instrument is the *lambi* (conch shell).

Composer, flutist, saxophonist, teacher, and percussionist, Saint Prix relocated from Martinique to France, where he found a teaching post in the twentieth arrondissement of Paris. His French colleagues were taken off guard when Saint Prix arrived at work with his press clippings and asked them to attend his concerts at such places as the Olympia. Although he became a full-time professional musician in 1988, Saint Prix continued to teach, but only part time, African Caribbean drumming for children in his workshop in Angoulême.

Constantly in demand, Saint Prix travels frequently to the Caribbean to conduct workshops and to perform. Wanting to share his love for the drums, Saint Prix created a mini-Carnival with his Djiba Association of student interns for various French festivals. With his own band composed of Franck Galin (bass), Mario Mass (keyboard and flute), Michel Reman (drums), Thierry Boukou (ti bwa and chorus), and Marie Céline Chroné (chorus), Saint Prix toured in the United States, Italy, Sweden, England, and the Caribbean. One of his most memorable concerts is the one he organized to commemorate the late Eugène Mona. Within a temporary deferential drum space at the Cité de la Musique in Paris on 15 and 16 June 1996, Saint Prix and his band shared their passion for African Caribbean drumming and Mona's music before a highly enthusiastic audience (Hersile-Héloise 1996, 46). Invited musicians who shared the stage were the flutist Max Cilla, the lyricist Roland Brival, the bèlè singer Ti Raoul Grivalliers of Martinique, the master gwo ka player Carnot, and the Akiyo percussion band of Guadeloupe.[17]

The open-minded and generous Saint Prix has also lent a helping hand to two zouk women artists. In 1992, reveling in the excitement of sheer playing, he collaborated with Joëlle Ursull to produce "Amazone" on *Black French* (see chapter 3). In 1995, Saint Prix also composed the duet "Balanséy Lala" (Swing Lala) with Tanya St. Val for *Chouval bwa sans frontières* to animate people with feeling for the drum. The duet proved to be a hit, and Saint Prix won the 1996 Prix SACEM for it in the category of traditional music.

Another Martinican chouval bwa enthusiast is Pierre Michel "Bago" Balthazar. A former hand drummer for Pakatak with Saint Prix, Bago is based in Paris, where he has leaned toward jazz and done backup drumming for many French Caribbean musicians. In 1992, Bago released his first solo album, *Wouspel,* but it was his second album, *Tambour battant,* in 1996 that received widespread praise for its intricate arrangements that explore chouval bwa, biguine vidé, jazz, and salsa. Heard on this dynamic album are invited singers such as Tony Chasseur and Marie Céline Chroné on the chouval bwa "Solososo," which was a minor hit for Carnival '96. Another cut, the song "Tambour battant" (Beating drum), sings praise of famous Martinican and Guadeloupean drummers: "Ou toujou ka di mwen sa sé bagay vyé nèg / Ti Emile, Ti Avoul, Eugène, Jojo sé sa yo tout ka jwé" (You're always hearing the voice of the old Black [ka] players / Ti Emile, Ti Ayoul, Eugène, Jojo, all of you play the ka.)[18]

Marcé, a pseudonym for Bernard Pago, is a third Martinican drummer who fosters the chouval bwa. After eighteen years of performing as a singer and drummer for the Groupe Folklorique Martiniquais, Marcé resigned to form his own Toumpak Band. Integrating bèlè and gwo ka rhythms into most of his compositions, Marcé experiments with different instrumental lineups with the drums, ti bwa (two wooden sticks played on the side of a drum or on a large bamboo stick), flute, and cha cha (a gourd filled with sand or beans).[19] His musical compositions are characterized by heavy drumming, which is a change from Saint Prix's lighter and repetitive style. In 1995, Marcé and his Toumpak Band accepted the trophy for Best Album at the Prix SACEM ceremonies for Marcé et Toumpak sé kon'w le.

During the late 1960s, the Guadeloupean Guy Konkèt, formerly Guy Conquête, promoted the gwo ka tradition as a symbol of Guadeloupean heritage and national independence. Jazz guitarist Gérard Lockel, who runs a small club out of his house in Baie Mahault, created a Creole radio program Casimir Letang from 1969 to 1970, on which he promoted local musical traditions (Jallier and Lossen 1985, 40). He later adapted gwo ka music to jazz and produced three albums with his own group, Gwo Ka Modèn. In 1981, Lockel began to train musicians in the gwo ka modèn (gwo ka method)[20] method for setting the phrasing and rhythms for other instruments.

Claude "Colo" Vamur of Kassav' comes from Sainte Anne, Guadeloupe. Fascinated by drum rhythms he heard at the Fête des Cuisinières and at Vélo's live performances, the young Vamur began an unofficial internship by playing the trap drums for semi-professional groups (the Vikings, Rapaces, and Maxel's) and occasionally for the singer Daniel Forestal and the saxophonist Robert Mavounzy.[21] His parents thought he was undergoing a passing fancy because well-raised children were not to entertain the notion of becoming musicians. Marching down the streets beating a drum, according to Vamur, "was a statement that you were a nèg' maroon (an ignorant Black bumpkin) or an uncultured Black."[22] In spite of his parents' disapproval and desire for him to become an electrical engineer, Vamur enrolled in a music school run by the drummers Kenny "Klook" Clarke and Dante Agostini to learn more about rhythm, pitch, and syncopation as soon as he completed the regulatory military service in France.[23]

While in Paris, Vamur met some members of the Ryco Jazz Band whom he had known in Guadeloupe. Their reunion resulted in his joining their band. This employment led him to an introduction to the Cameroonian saxophonist Manu Dibango during one of the Ryco Band's sessions. Impressed by what he had heard of Vamur's technique, Dibango invited Vamur to join his band the next day in a studio to record the soon-to-be famous "Soul Makossa." For the next four years (1972 to 1976) Vamur toured with Dibango while "Soul Makossa" was well-received around the world (Cally 1996, 272). Upon Vamur's return to Paris, Eddy Louiss, the Martinican jazz organist, invited the drummer to join his group. Pleased to be in demand, Vamur proceeded to divide his time, playing for both Louiss and Dibango. Finally, Louiss asked him to make a choice. This request escalated into a heated argument when Vamur chose Dibango's band. When Dibango's popularity and concert invitations began to wane, Vamur's exposure to jazz, biguine, and makossa paid off with engagements with different bands until the 1982 call came from Jacob Desvarieux to join the newly-created Kassav'.

As a member of Kassav', Vamur primarily plays zouk in the gwo ka Carnival *mendé* figure of 4/4. His two solo records, *Lévé mwen* (1987) and *Héritage pou ...* (1994), provide the proof that he is at ease playing gwo ka figures as well as zouk and African rhythms. Thus, the vitality of his crossover drumming technique comes from a complete understanding of the numerous sounds that it is possible to make. The instrumental "Natif" (Native) from *Héritage pou ...* is an example with its mixed wordless vocal singing that resembles African American gospel and Guadeloupean folk song.

This fusion of various African types of diasporic music on Vamur's albums is representative of what he calls "geographical skidding across the archipelago."[24] Vamur's skidding is directly derived from his careful observations of how drummers place their hands on drums to solicit specific notes, multiple downbeats, and rhythms. He especially watches how lead drummers move their fingers, sit in front of a drum, and begin the beat, rhythm, and timing for the supporting musicians in a band. Accordingly, Vamur carries forth this exploration of drum aesthetics, imitating the drummers he greatly admires. Vamur instinctively knows that having "the feeling" of great drumming is not sufficient. As a result, he continues to take lessons whenever he has free time. His dedication to technical improvement supports Duke Ellington's statement: "The basic concern should not be the instrument, but the taste and skill of the person who plays it" (Ellington 1973, 412). Vamur's hard work is worthwhile because he insists that it is the drummer who sets the rhythm and keeps pushing the music forward to make it more dynamic with a reliance upon multiple combinations and pauses.

Like Vamur, Sully-Cally desired to be a drummer when he was a child.

Born the oldest of five children in Gros Morne, Martinique, and raised by his grandmother, Cally is a trained dancer, drummer, actor, and comedian. By age twelve he was playing the bèlè. At such a young age he participated in dance competitions in Gros Morne and attended Saturday night balls without his grandmother's knowledge.[25] Cally's passion for the drum has been celebrated in his publications on the lives and works of over one hundred Martinican, Guadeloupean, and French Guyanese musicians. Cally's publications resulted from extensive research on the history of Caribbean music. With painstaking detail, Cally produced two important books based on music and its creators: *Musiques et danses Afro-Caraïbes* (1990) and *Le grand livre des musiciens créoles, Tome I* (1996). Having received the state diploma for the practice of traditional instruments in the fall of 1996, Cally can now teach at any music conservatory in Martinique or other French territories to initiate students into the wonders of the Martinican drum. The diploma has also paved the way for Cally to open his own school of music, if he should decide to do so.

Well aware of the drum's ambivalent past, Cally has spoken in a private interview about the cultural rupture in Martinique between 1940 and 1970, marked by the drum's marginalization. Ironically, the fact that the bèlè was for thirty years confined to the rural northern part of Martinique inadvertently contributed to its survival.[26] If the drum had not been nurtured in this part of Martinique, the bèlè songs and figures would have disappeared, overwhelmed by the urban biguine and mazurka. Hence, Guadeloupean and Martinican music, as noted by Guilbault, "became an arena for political confrontation. The traditional drums, the gwo ka in Guadeloupe and the ka [bèlè] in Martinique, which had been abandoned for a few decades, were suddenly back in force, held up and played as a symbol of national identities" (Guilbault et al. 1993, 32).

Cally's drumming technique is in response to something inside him. Each stroke heard on his solo *Paroles de tambours* (1992) is a pulse in itself. The *damié*,[27] the battle dance from the northern part of Martinique, is Cally's preferred figure because of its quickness and raw power. Strongly believing that the drum is a mystical instrument, Cally states: "A mystery surrounds it. It lets off something magical. It is a heritage that remains with us from the past" (Michel 1996, 35). His hope is to capture the drum's mystery by opening a museum which will contain every Caribbean drummer's recordings. Since each drummer has a style of playing that is dependent on his mood and the weather, Cally wants to create a deferential drum space through a museum that will enable visitors to experience the magic and the uniqueness of Caribbean drumming.

Another Guadeloupean fascinated by the gwo ka is Sergius Geoffroy, who came from Sainte Anne, Guadeloupe of the Grands Fonds, a region of hills and valleys. From age fourteen, Geoffroy began to sing publicly and became known as one of the best gwo ka singers at funeral wakes (AV 1996, 12). Death rituals are strictly adhered to as friends and family gather around the deceased to recite prayers, to play *pilé kako, zizpan, chamda,* and *sové vayan* games, and to sing funeral hymns. All of these funeral rituals are an integral part of the Sainte Anne area, and the heritage was transmitted to Geoffroy by his parents. In 1980, because of Geoffroy's active involvement in traditional music, he persuaded his brothers Francky (a.k.a. Zagalo), Hilaire, and René; his sisters Viviane, Brigitte, and Christiane; and several neighbors to join him to form the group Kan'nida, a term referring to a labor song from the Grands Fonds region.[28] By 1996, Kan'nida had recorded eight albums, of which *Vis an nou* (Our vices) was one. The group has also performed the seven gwo ka figures for its show *La véyé o swa la* (The wake is tonight) for fifteen years.

Tikatan: The Drum as a Lyrical Theme

The *ladja (l'agia, laghia* or *ladia)* battle dance, unlike the damié, heralds from the south of Martinique. Popularized by Mona (see chapter 4), the ladja is composed of four elements: the singer soloist, the dancers, the drum, and the ti bwa. The improvisation of the singer soloist and the drummers adds a rich texture to the song. The soloist's voice is nasalized and drawling.

Heavily influenced by Ernest "Vava" Dovin, considered to be one of the best bèlè bass drummers in Martinique, Mona was very pleased when Dovin joined his band. After much discussion with Dovin, the percussion instruments selected for Mona's band were the *tambou di base* (bass drum), *batterie* (trap drum), *tambou bèlè,* and *toumba.* Mona also brought back the bamboo flute and the *tambou dibas* (small drum). Very compatible, Mona and Dovin spent several years performing together and developed a very close friendship. As a consequence, Mona was inconsolable when he learned of Dovin's death. To ease his pain, Mona composed "Tambou séryé" (Serious drum) as a testimony to his love for the drummer and their mutual respect for the drum:

Mi mwen lè Monayis
Tanbou fòk zot tout pran mwen
Mi mwen lè Monayis

Mona di fòk zòt tout pran mwen
Wi, fòk zòt tout pran mwen

Sé manmay-la paré pou tchwoué tanbou-a
Tchwoué tanbou-a
Sé gran nonm-la di mwouen tanbou-a
Sé an moun
Fodra nou tchenbè-y
Fodra nou swanyé-y
Mwen ka mandé la vi ba tanbou-a
É man lé ba-y lavi-ya
Mano di mwen an nou ba-y lavi
Papa di mwen an nou ba-y lavi
Rastòk di mwen an nou bay lavi
An nou lavi, an nou bay lavi
An nou bay lavi
Gran nonm lévé, gran nonm palé
Man lé sav poutchi nou pa ka tann

Mwen tanbou, ou asiz anlè mwen
Man santi shalè dèryé-w
Shalè dé zyé-w
Lodè san laswè-w
Sé lodè lansan pou mwen
Dé lanmen-w épi talon-w ka shèshé
A sav sa man té yé pou papa-w
Pou manman-w
Gran manman-w, gran papa-w
Tout jénérasyson tchè rasin nèg

E ben woui
Sé mwen ki ba yo la fòs
Pas man ni pouwoua
Ba sa ki lé
Fòs épi kouraj
Fòs pou yo rèd san manjé
Fòs pou yo fouyé
An lanplasman kay anti moman
Lè yo tann woua mwen

Man fè yo kominiké épi lafòs dan o
Energie, vibration, lumière

Man lévé an nonm ki té ja mè dé fwa
Man fè lèspri rantré an kòy
Jwoué mwen, lwoué mwen
Man sé an mèt
Wi, mèt nèg ki nèg pou bon
Gran nonm lévé, gran nonm palé
Man lé sav poutchi nou pa ka tann

Tounnè! Pa mandé mwen lò
Pa mandé mwen lajan
Pa mandé mwen djaman
Men shèshé mannyè pou ban mwen
Plis plas pou man ba-w plis sans
Pou-w konprann sians tanbou-a
Sé tchè-w man ka pézé a laksyon
Sé andidan boyo-w man ka travèsé
Shak jou
Lè ou bon kon sensèr

Lè man pézé-w ou bon kon sensèr
Man ka ba-w lavi épi lèspri
Man ka fè-w krazé lannwit gan jou
An plen midi
Tiré shimiz-ou, météé-w an lotcho mon fi
Roulé asi mwen, dèt limyè pou vini
Pa otchipé-w di ti-bwa-a
An nou jowoué ba moun-an ki fè
Lavi-a an sèt miliar lanné-a
Fran nonm lévé, gran nonm palé an lè
Sav poutchi nou ka tann

Ti-gason le mistèr sé mwen
Météé mwen an koté pou man santi mwen byen
Kouvé mwen, shofé mwen
Réspekté mwen
Pa pésé ou benyen kò-w
Lè nou kay jwenn pou nou palé

Men lavé tchè-w
Lavé lidé-w, lavé-lang-ou
Lavé lèspri-w épi vini
Pa vini épi dout, pa vini ataton
Vini franshman
Man ké fè di-w an enstruman
Pas an nèg épi an tanbou sé janmen dé san twa
Man ka pézé, miziré, konté
Man ka ba man lé
Pouvoir, Connaissance, Intelligence
Mwen Tanbou, man déklaré
Woui, Mona sé an tanbou osi
Gran nonm lévé gran nonm palé
Man lé sav poutchi nou pa ka tann

Si nonm ou kouché
Ou pou lévé épi ti-bren pli anba tanbou-a
Ou pou vini léjè men fò
Lèd men puisan
Ou pou kriyé Aaaa
Ou pou santi-w étranj men pa fou
Ou pou santi-w vizité
Men pa agrésé
Ou pou santi-w solid
Lè ti bolonm tanbou-a rivé anlè-w
Sé fòs, sé fòs frè-ya
Sé fòs, sé manifèstasyon, sé fòs
Mèsi bondiyé, mèsi bondjyé

〰〰〰〰〰

(Here I am the Monayist.
Drums! You all have to take me.
Here I am the Monayist.
Mona said you all have to take me.
Yes, you all have to take me.

They are all ready to kill the drum,
to kill the drum.
The old folks told me that the Drum

is actually a person,
and that we'll have to keep him alive.
We'll have to care for him.
I am asking for life for the Drum.
I want to breathe life into the Drum.
Mona told me to give life to him [the drum].
My father told me to give life to him [the drum].
Rastok told me to give life to him [the drum].
To give life to him, to give life to him,
to give life to him.
The old men stood up and talked:
"I'd like to know why the devil we do not listen."

Mona (speaking in the voice of the drum):
I, Drum, you are seated on me.
I feel the warmth of your behind.
The warmth of your eyes and
the smell of the blood of your sweat
are like incense to me.
Both of your hands and
your heels are seeking to know
what I once was for your father,
for your grandmother, for your grandfather,
and for Black people's ancestors.

Yes, indeed!
I gave them strength
because I have the power
to give it to whomever wants it.
Strength and courage.
Strength so that they can be valiant without food.
Strength so that they dig
the foundation of a house in a jiffy.
Upon hearing my voice
I made them relate to the Almighty Strength.
Energy, vibration, light.
Twice I raised from the dead a man who was dead.
I returned his soul to his body.
Play for me; worship me.
I am the Master of Black people.

They have to be good.
Old men stood up and talked.
I'd like to know why the devil we do not listen.

Damn it! Do not ask me for gold.
Do not ask me for money.
Do not ask me for diamonds.
Make sure you give me
more room so that I can give you more power
to understand the science of the drum.
I evaluate your heart according to your deeds.
Every day I go through your innermost being.

When you are good and sincere
after my evaluation,
I bestow both life and intelligence upon you.
At noon I make you overcome the night.
My dear, take off your fine clothes and wear rags.
Come on! Beat me. More light is still to come.
Don't mind the ti bwa.
Let's play in honor of He who made
life in seven billion years.
Old men stood up and talked.
I want to know why the devil we do not listen.

Son! I am the Mystery.
Put me somewhere where I can feel well.
Cover me. Warm me up.
Respect me.
You need not wash
to come to see me.
Clean your heart,
your spirit, your tongue,
and your soul.
Come without doubts. Come straight.
Frankly come.
I'll turn you into an instrument
because a Black man with a drum becomes one.
I measure, weigh, and count.
Upon my will I give:

"Power, Knowledge, and Intelligence."
Therefore, I, the Drum, declare that
Mona is also a drum.
Old men stood up and talked.
I want to know why the devil we do not listen.

If you, my friend, are bent over,
you'll surely get back up metamorphosed.
Thanks to the drum.
You'll surely get lighter but stronger.
You'll surely be ugly but powerful.
You'll surely shout "Aaaa."
You'll surely feel strange but not insane.
You'll surely feel the spirit in you.
However, you will not feel aggressive.
You'll surely feel stronger.
My friend, when the drum is within you,
it is nothing but strength.
Nothing but strength and divine manifestation.
Thank you, Lord. Thank you, Lord.)[29]

Structured to describe the power of the drum and its spiritual continuity, "Tambou séryé" opens with the chant that Mona is the drum. Speaking in the voice of the drum in the guise of an elderly wise man, Mona relates how the drum's strength flows directly into him, the drummer, when he places his heel upon its skin. The wise elders who understood the drum's traditional power are celebrated. The young drummers' skillful playing in Mona's band is attributed to the ancestors who guide them and give them confidence.

This transfer of the drum's power between generations reminds one of a yearly event in Benin, the West African nation that Sully-Cally claims is the origin for the bèlè. Once a year there is a Sato funeral ritual that pays homage to the dead in order for the deceased to be integrated and absorbed into the spiritual world.[30] Children, who compose the Sato band, participate in this passage from the visible into the invisible worlds. Orphans of the deceased, they circle around the Sato drums, which come in pairs of the ornate male and plain female, and jump up to hit the center of them with curved sticks. While the child orphans play the Sato, old women, covered in mud and wearing raffia necklaces, play the role of the widows. To prevent the deceased from tormenting those who are still in the land of living, the women go to the sacred source of *yatonou* to purify themselves. Their washing of the mud off of their bodies to the accompaniment of the Sato symbolizes the removal of any curses that the deceased might have left behind.

The volume and the instrumentation of the Sato lend an urgency to the annual funeral ritual. The same can be said about the volume and instrumentation of "Tambou séryé," which shifts from a slow, Congolese-based rhythm to a faster, Brazilian beat, thereby creating a mounting tension and lending an urgency to the narration. Transitions are distinguished by a full stop with the inclusion of African chanting. The tune is celebrating an affirmation of an individual act of possession. An active and willing subject, Mona, in the role of the drum/speaker, advises his listeners to prepare themselves for a ritual cleansing.

By beckoning his listeners to join him in this spiritual journey, Mona rightfully reclaims the drum from its ambivalent and regional spaces to situate it directly in the center of a deferential space as the main instrument in his band. Chronicling the political debates about the drum, Mona declares that in order for the drum to live, it must take on a life of its own and ask man to glorify him. As soon as the drum's spirit flows into Mona's body, the singer proclaims that he, Mona, is the drum. From an African-based religious perspective, the deceased are not dead. Therefore, Dovin's spirit rises up in "Tambou séryé" and passes through Mona while he performs.

Echoes of Mona's concerns about the drum in "Tambou séryé" are also found in Kafé's "Opérasyon ka" (Operation ka), on his 1992 *Gwoka Métamowfozys Mòd* (The gwo ka mode of metamorphosis), wherein it is stated: "Tanbou ka chanté / Tann van ja vanté / Mwen tanbou mwen lavi sé pou toultan" (The drum is singing / Hear the wind already blowing / I, the drum and life, am forever here).[31] Using the bass, polymetric sounds, and the mendé figure to call attention to the drum's powers, Edouard Ignol Hélène,[32] known professionally as Kafé, sends out waves of feeling with an oral chanting to plead how Guadeloupean life is anchored to the gwo ka as its primal source.[33] A seeker of the truth, Kafé reveals a love, an anger, and an urgency in his lyrics: all representative of his output.

For *Gwoka Métamowfozys Mòd*, Kafé uses a different gwo ka rhythm for each song. Relying on supporting drummers to add other phrases and accents, Kafé's drumming on "Opérasyon ka" inspires action and harmony. The line "Fò nou pasé gouté lavi" (We have to taste life) from the first refrain tied into the chorus's important utterance, "Atann si lontan pou yo pòté misik / Annou on tan bon tan mové" (Counting on them for a long time to bring the music / Let's do so in good and bad times), are historically based lyrics that question people's values and substantiate what Kafé calls *santiman ka* (*ka* feeling).

Acting in support of Mona and Kafé's belief in the drum's power is Lébèloka, a Martinican percussion band entirely composed of women.[34] Consisting of nine drummers, Lébèloka is the second Martinican band of any kind to consist of only women. The idea for Lébèloka was the result of a brainstorm that took root when the percussionist Willy Léger was an active performer for a 1991 cultural arts festival in Fort-de-France. Since its conception, Lébèloka's first single compact disc with "Dans ka" (Inside the ka) on side A and "Poutchi sa" (Why that) on side B has a following. Surprisingly, "Poutchi sa," a remake of a Léger song, is the one that was listed on the Sun FM hit list of May 1997. Initially a novelty for the Martinican public, the all-woman band is gradually gaining acceptance. Suzie Singa, one of Lébèloka's members, discusses the future of the drum: "I believe the drum is in the process of making a comeback. We hope to give people the desire to play and to train on this instrument."[35]

Called the first instrument of communication, the drum has its own language and cultural voice that affect human beings when they hear certain rhythms. Since the rise of the discussion of patrimony and of new political parties in Martinique and Guadeloupe, many people have taken an interest in drumming. In the face of assimilation, a fight for economic independence, and metropolitan sovereignty, musicians like Mona, Saint Prix, Cally, and Guédon delved into the history of French Caribbean drums. In so doing, they revitalized the drum to sustain a rich indigenous music through either their recordings, live performances, or organized workshops.

"The drum," said Kali, "is our inspiration. All generations sing about it" (Bouvier 1993, 44). Curiously, Kali's search for "authentic root music" duplicated that of Mona. Although a generation apart, Mona and Kali reappropriated the drum as well as the bamboo flute and banjo, proving via these instruments that they were, indeed, integral parts of the national consciousness. After all, the primacy of the drum on both islands in Carnival is a testimony to its longevity and importance within the internal fabric of Martinican and Guadeloupean cultures.

Resistance to the drum in Guadeloupe and Martinique is on a decline at the end of the twentieth century. Linked with politics and a Creole identity, French Caribbean percussionists are experimenting with the drum in urban concert settings. By making a concerted effort to reestablish the drum in a deferential space, certain percussionists have taken a political stance by foregrounding a folk music that used to be restricted inside a rural community to reach wider connections in the urban areas. As discussed above, the French Caribbean deferential space for the drum performs two simultaneous functions: it invigorates a spiritual link to the African past and serves as an advocate for socio-political rights and a freedom of expression.

epilogue

La musique antillaise, ça ne s'explique pas. C'est un feeling. FRANCK
TENAILLE (1979, 73)

This study highlights a variety of Martinican and Guadeloupean
popular songs and musical trends between 1970 and 1996 that exist within the imaginary confines of "awakening" spaces. The ad-
jective "awakening" does not imply that French Caribbean popular
music is in a process of development, for its music has been in existence for over a hundred years. The deliberate choice of "awakening" pertains to the piggyback effect of domains wherein the journey into one of them naturally leads into others within a circuitous
route of seven identifiable spaces.

The initial interest in "awakening" spaces also stems from the
teaching of contemporary English- and French-language Caribbean
literature, and a decision to approach each space from a different
perspective. However, the formulation of these thoughts about such
spaces in music is partially attributable to the writings of Victor
Turner and J. H. Kwabena Nketia: the first, an anthropologist; the
second, an ethnomusicologist. The two are from different ethnic
backgrounds and areas of speciality, but their thoughts about music
and the community are similar. Turner's discussion looks at the
ways in which "a group or community seeks to portray, understand, and then act on itself" (Turner 1977, 33). He reports that
public reflexivity takes the form of performance, encompassing
codes, structural status, law and order, and an in-between state of

liminality. For his part, Nketia's (1974) study of Akan culture in Ghana through music shifts from the tradition to the event. He posits that Akan music is essential to life because it is integrated into the social, economic, political, and cultural framework of a Ghanaian community.

This connection between the community and musical performance can be illustrated by looking at Malavoi, who began to record at the beginning of the 1970s. A number of the band's songs had been concerned with childhood and exile, thereby creating a safe space tied into the spatial landscape of Martinique. Since the founders of Malavoi had been teenagers who were still attending high school, a natural inclination was for them to write lyrics about the familiar. Thus, to be gripped by nostalgia in the 1970s—or in the present—was to see childhood converted into memory within a place of inventiveness. The smell of rain from "Apré la pli," the culinary process of grilling *dyôkôs* in "Kolédés," and the adult narration of a specific geographic space in "Exil" constituted a nourishing reality. Unfortunately, the object of their nostalgia—Martinique as a pastoral landscape populated by plants, animals, birds, and human beings—has largely disappeared (especially in the Fort-de-France area). Richard Price (1998, x–xi), who visited Martinique for the first time in June 1962 before the founding of Malavoi, mentions that the landscape had then been marked by dirt roads, hardly any cars or telephones, and large green spaces that slanted down to the sea. Today, some of these green spaces are dotted with malls, cement buildings, and highways choked with cars. Nevertheless, the Martinican landscape, as it existed before the changes, still lives on in the songwriters' memories, music, and lyrics. Landscape spaces do not disappear completely, because people inherit and inhabit them.

In contradistinction to Malavoi's nostalgic songs are the angagé ones penned by Eugène Mona, Pôglo, Kali, and Djo Dézormo. The four songwriters look at how the sunny, sea-swept Martinican landscape has been riddled with violence: the bétonisation project, the student demonstrations, the influx of drugs, and the constant strikes. While selective Malavoi songs about childhood and exile insist on an understanding of the past, the four singers speak to the necessity of transcending the past to confront the present within a resistant space of cultural politics. They are aware of the control that the French have in shaping them. In fact, their songs point out how the dominant French society controls Martinique and its people without ever placing a hand on the people. The question is, how does one resist? In Jean Crusol's (1986, 188) assessment of the economy of Martinique (which also pertains to Guadeloupe), economic development must address three critical factors: colonialism, an inherited plantation economy, and the contemporary world.

Crusol believes that government officials have to find a way to reduce a dependence on public transfers that amount to about eighty percent a year from France.

Unable to reconcile themselves to a dependent status, some songwriters construct a Creole detour around the ideological blocks erected by the French. Consequently, their music and lyrics become metaphors for defining a fluid reality and a reshaping of their multiple identities as a Caribbean people. In spite of their different stances and the creation of a safe space of childhood and exile and another of cultural politics, the Malavoi songwriters and the four angagé singers agree upon their love for their island and people. Joining them is the zouk band Kassav', with its creation of an optimistic Creole space. Kassav's telling of stories through Creole lyrics uncovers hidden histories about slavery, exile, racial prejudice, and the joys and sorrows that mark love relationships. Although the trend across the two islands has been the recording of Creole lyrics, I have paid particular attention to Kassav', because it was the first French Caribbean band to win numerous French gold records and to tour around the world before audiences of 15,000 people or more. They and their fellow musicians draw on the power of Creole words to recover the mastery of their lives while establishing national and transnational reputations. Given this application of language as tool of emancipation, Kassav' and other zouk bands also open a venue for women to have a more active voice in the music industry.

Women have participated alongside men in constructing Guadeloupean and Martinican music. To illustrate this, I have related the stories of Léona Gabriel, a biguine singer and songwriter of the 1920s through the 1960s, and six zouk singers. I have called attention to their lyrical texts about a more autonomous state of being. Like women across the world, French Caribbean women suffer from the Cinderella complex; they hope that one day their princes will come and ride off with them into the sunset. When the princes neither materialize nor fail to fit into their fanciful illusion, disappointment sets in, and the struggle to face reality begins. Thus, the six zouk women songwriters, who do not represent the entire region or women who compose lyrics on other topics, examine their options and decide to become independent *amazònes* rather than submissive *doudous*.

A natural course of events is to find a performance space and to plan concerts which will attract and hold audiences inside and outside of the Caribbean. A major French festival where French Caribbean musicians showcase their talent is the Printemps de Bourges. This five-day festival is held in April and divided into two sections. The first is devoted to well-known musicians; the second to the promotion of newly discovered singers and musicians. Twenty-five national radio stations, eleven international stations, and one hundred and fifty overseas departments' related stations are directly involved in identifying talent in France, Africa, and the Caribbean. The eighty or more concerts per year are held in ten different halls with a total audience of about 80,000 (Léandy 1997, 40).

In the French Caribbean, there is the biannual summer FESTAG in Gaudeloupe, organized by Freddie Marshall. More summer festivals featuring instruments such as the guitar and clarinet exist in Martinique. In addition, the zouk singer Eric Virgal organizes annual Carnival song contests in February and the Festival de la chanson féminine in August. The government owned Centre Culturel des Arts in Pointe-à-Pitre and the Atrium (which just opened in 1998) in Fort-de-France also host concerts all year long. Such festivals provide the structural frame in which musicians and singers expand their repertoires, introduce other techniques, and stretch the boundaries in experimentation.

Since the French Caribbean region is not cut off from the world, its musicians and songwriters are exposed to music across the African diaspora and other regions through the media, recordings, and travel. For Gage Averill, this borrowing of other music to create one's own is not unique to Martinicans and Guadeloupeans. For instance, he notes that the Haitian band Zèklè blended compas with funk and American jazz-rock in the tradition of Wayne Shorter's Weather Report and used the bass as a more prominent instrument and integrated dual synthesizers (Averill 1997, 123). Also, in the late 1970s, when Bob Marley and other Jamaicans were creating reggae, they turned to and appropriated American rhythm and blues. Therefore, like their precursors across the Caribbean region and elsewhere, entertainers like Mario Canonge, Fal Frett, Céline Flériag, Taxikréol, and Volt Face recontextualize traditional melodies. Jacques Attali considers this cultural intermingling to be representative of a new social discourse in which recontextualization allows for "the creation of one's own code" and the choice "to interlink with another code" (Attali 1985, 132).

Whatever the case, one instrument that has never disappeared is the drum. In connection with the oral tradition, percussion instruments are the backbone of French Caribbean culture. For example, Mona's voice on "Tambou séryé" and that of the drum are repositories of the ancestors. Man and instrument fuse and become an extension of each other, paying homage to the ancestors. Mona, the man, promotes an exchange, a merger, with the drum through a call-and-response interaction. To explain, the opening prelude to "Tambou séryé" establishes that Mona is a *marqueur de parole* (storyteller). During the course of the lengthy song he recites a *ladja de parole,* the story of a traditional dance whose aim is to simulate a fight. When Mona introduces the song with the announcement, "Mi mwen lè Monayis / Tanbou fòk zòt tou pran mwen (Here I am the Monayist / Drums! You all have to take me), someone in the audience terminates Mona's sentence by saying "International" to which Mona replies, "Ouais, international." The drum's magical essence draws the audience into its folds when Mona dramatically raises and lowers his voice to emphasize the words: "réspecté, connaissance, and intelligence." Mona's storytelling approach in "Tambou séryé" and interaction with the audience definitely enforce Nketia's position that music shifts from the tradition to the event. Consequently, Mona and other percussionists (Cally, Guédon, Kafé, Saint Prix, and Vélo) connect and reconnect percussion to the social fabric of their communities. Moreover, the writing about the deferential space for the drum also duplicates the oral storytelling mode, dotted with biographical digressions about individual percussionists and the interrelationship between gwo ka and bèlè rhythms with dance.

Abena Busia once remarked that "words are a changing and living force . . . [they] can create and destroy, alienate and sustain" (Busia 1990, 290). Obviously, songwriters are fascinated by words—how they sound to their ears, feel in their mouth, and fit with their music. For instance, let us look at the compact disc cover and four of the songs on Patrick Saint Éloi's *Zoukamine* (1994). A frontal close-up picture of Saint Éloi shares space with a second one of him as a child. The smaller picture is strategically located above Saint Éloi's left shoulder, offering an optimistic double gaze toward tomorrow. Two generations are transmitted, juxtaposing the experienced Afro-Parisian adult (then thirty-five) in the larger frame with that of him as a curious, innocent Guadeloupean child. Attractively packaged in shades of blue, the photograph within a photograph invites one to open the compact disc case and journey into songs which discuss, among others, the selection of one's friends ("Ki moune"), the hopeful renewal of a broken May-December relationship ("Ki jan ké fè"), the digestion of a zouk vitamin ("Zoukamine"), and the sadness of observing a teenage prostitute ("Flè de nuit"). After listening to the songs and closing the cover, a second look at the photographs now gives us an insight into Saint Éloi's character as a performer and songwriter and a glimpse into Guadeloupean society. Moreover, each of the pictures makes certain demands, for the past cannot be disavowed. The man recalls the child he was; the child foresees the adult he is to become. In addition, the music and lyrics cause some French Caribbeans to develop a more critical consciousness during their search for a way out of a world that is closing in on them. This particular space might have been defined by Turner as liminal, but it is the one Saint Éloi occupies and claims as his own.

The symbolism of the compact disc's dual photographs of childhood and adulthood (the past and present) with an outward gaze toward the future reinforces what has been articulated in the seven chapters about French Caribbean popular lyrics and music. Lyrics, music, and performance embody spatial and temporal connotations, require a collaborative effort of mutual support, and are international in sound. Traveling and performing in distant and local places to spread around the seeds of one's music and lyrical messages are natural requirements for the understanding of the Self. "A village," states Nketia, "that has no organized music or neglects community singing, drumming, or dancing is said to be dead" (Nketia 1974, 20). Thus, the French Caribbean musical village is alive and not separate from its communal and popular cultural contexts.

notes

Acknowledgments

1. Some original lyrics have been copied from those published in books or on the jacket covers of albums, cassettes, and compact discs.

Introduction

1. Interview, Emmanuel "Mano" Césaire, 1995.

2. See Anselin 1979, 103. Valéry Giscard D'Estaing, Minister of Finance, and Louis Jacquinot officially signed for the creation of BUMIDOM on 26 April 1963 under the Michel Debré government. Aimé Césaire labeled it "a one-way substitution for genocide without a return ticket."

3. The unemployment rate for French Caribbeans in France was 12 percent in 1975. In 1995, 45,000 Martinicans were unemployed and 25,000 received family subsidized payments. On the two islands the unemployment figure remains around 30 percent for a primarily youthful workforce.

4. The two islands' economies are based on sugarcane, bananas, tourism, and light industry. Sugar production has declined, while most of the sugarcane is now used for the production of rum. Tourism has become more important than agricultural exports as a source of foreign exchange. Meat, grain, and vegetable products are imported from France, contributing to the chronic trade deficit that requires large annual transfers of aid from France.

5. The Haute Autorité was replaced by the CNCL, which consisted of thirteen members appointed for nine years and had a monopoly on radio.

6. See Cook 1993 and Palmer and Sobers 1992, for more details about the reconstruction of the radio and television broadcasting stations and nine-member independent bodies. The dates differ for the cited laws in the two publications.

7. Ibid., 228–31.

8. Kassav' dedicated its 1995 *Difé* album to Obringer.

9. See Uri and Uri 1991, 140. Gilles Sala, a Guadeloupean composer of about
250 songs, was the pioneer of radio broadcasts on the ex-ORTF to promote French
Caribbean music. On Radio Guadeloupe he hosted *Chants et rythmes de l'Union
française* (Songs and Rhythms from the French Union), a thirty-minute show featuring poems, songs, and Creole dance music with the group Karukéra. The show was
distributed by Paris Inter.

10. Other former afternoon television shows on RFO 1 in Martinique that featured musicians were *Clairière* and *Actu-Quot.* The former used to be hosted by Gérard César, who was replaced by Léa Galva; the latter by Alain Rodaix.

Chapter One

1. See Bouvier 1994a, 50. Malavoi is a very generous band that has promoted
many artists such as Marijosé Alie, Ralph Thamar, Pipo Gertrude, Céline Flériag,
Suzy Trébeau, Mario Canonge, and the Haitian Beethova Obas.

2. Fanny Augiac, the then director of CMAC, helped to organize Malavoi's tour
to Columbia, South America.

3. See Ouanély 1996, 44. As a follow-up, Malavoi played "Ababa" on a December 1996 RFO 1 special show, *Le plus grand zouk du monde,* hosted by Léa Galva
and Laurent Boyer at the Palais Omnisport in Bercy outside of Paris, before an audience of 16,000 fans. "La Filo" is the first song on the album bearing its name.

4. Malavoi, "La Case à Lucie," *La Filo,* G. Debs 1024; Reissued on *La Case à
Lucie,* Blue Silver 8221 and *Jou ouvè,* Blue Silver 034–2.

5. Interview, Ina Césaire. 1995.

6. Malavoi, "Sport national," *La Case à Lucie.*

7. Malavoi, "Apré la pli," *La Case à Lucie;* reissued on *Jou ouvé.*

8. Interview, Ina Césaire.

9. Interview, Ina Césaire.

10. Malavoi, "Jou ouvé," *Jou ouvè.*

11. Rosine was awarded the 1988 Prix SACEM-Martinique as composer for
"Jou ouvè."

12. The *ti baum* is a small to medium-sized tree of the Euphorbiaceae family,
used for fuel and posts. Twigs and branches from the *ti baum* were intertwined to
make the walls of slave huts, plastered over with either a lime or clay mixture. Sometimes a medical tea is made from the bark.

13. Interview, Ralph Thamar. 1995.

14. Ralph Thamar, "Exil," *Exil,* G. Debs 1504. In 1992, Thamar also recorded
"Exil" for *Matébis,* Déclic 10541–2, and *Matébis en concert,* Déclic 470–2, 1993.

"Exil" is the first song Mano asked his cousin Ina to write for a Malavoi production. Its original version was cut by the recording company without consulting the songwriter. In 1988, Ina, as author, and Thamar, as interpreter, won a Prix SACEM-Martinique for the song.

15. Interview, Marijosé Alie. 1995. Alie gave some historical information about "Caressé moins." Her intention was to write the song for Ralph Thamar, who thought the title was too feminine. His suggestion was for her or another woman to sing it. Alie agreed and metaphorically called "Caressé moins" the tree that was hiding in the forest.

16. Malavoi, "Caressé moins," *Zouël*, G. Debs 014/15; reissued on *Légende (Best of Malavoi)*, Déclic 304389, and *Matébis*.

17. Malavoi, "Mwen menm bout," *An Maniman*, Déclic 302268.

18. Malavoi, "Kolédés," *An Maniman*.

19. Interview, Jean-Paul Soime.

20. Shawna Moore-Madlangbayan did the English translations of the Creole songs for Malavoi's *Shé Shè*. Her name is listed among the credits on the CD cover.

21. Guilbault et al. 1993, 39. Also see Chénard 1982, when Rosine had made the same remarks.

22. Malavoi, "Malavoi," *Zouël*; reissued on *Malavoi au Zénith*, Mélodie/Blue Silver 2402.

23. Malavoi, "Mizik Matinik," *Shè Shé*, Déclic 8418432.

24. Malavoi, "Gens moin," *La Case à Lucie*.

Chapter Two

1. "Jean-Pierre Jardel," *Antilla*, 22–28 février 1990, 36.

2. The study of Creole as a language enjoys acceptance. The Université des Antilles et de la Guyane offers a Diplôme Universitaire de Langues et Cultures Créoles (DULCC) with classes taught in and on Creole. The language is heard on the radio and television and is sometimes used for local journals. Creole dictionaries are published, and Richard Crestor's *Annou palé kréyòl* (Let's Speak Creole), a Guadeloupean Creole language program on audiotape, exists. In 1993, Patrick Chamoiseau of Martinique won the Prix Goncourt for his novel *Texaco* (in which he blended French and Creole).

3. See Burton 1993, 19. The debate surrounding the problem of orthography for Creole has yet to be resolved. Acrolect Creole reflects the morphological and lexical infiltration of the French language; basilectal Creole is based on phonetic principles to create a distance from the French language with neologisms.

4. Interview, Patrick Saint Éloi. 1995.

5. Cited in Eyre 1994, 15. There are two types of cassava: one is nonpoisonous, giving tapioca, and the other "bitter cassava" is poisonous. To rid the root of its poison, it is grated and crushed. The grated cassava is then packed into a strainer to

drain off the poison, dried to make flour, and then used to make cassava bread or a sweet version of coconut sugar cake.

6. Pierre-Edouard Décimus left Kassav' in 1989 to form the group Kwid; George Décimus moved back to Guadeloupe, left Kassav', and founded Volt-Face. The 1998 group roster consisted of Jean-Philippe Marthély and Jocelyne Béroard (Martinique, vocals); Patrick Saint Éloi (Guadeloupe, vocals); Jean-Claude Naimro (Martinique, keyboard, arranger, and vocals); Jacob Desvarieux, (Guadeloupe, guitar, arranger, and vocals); Philippe Joseph (Martinique, second keyboard); Patrick Saint-Elie (Martinique, percussion); Claude Vamur (Guadeloupe, trapset drums); Freddy Houssepian (France, trumpet); Hamid Belhocine (Algeria, trombone); Claude Thirfays (France, saxophone); Guy N'Sangue (Senegal, bass); Natalie Yorke (Trinidad, chorus); and Karla Gonzales (Trinidad, chorus). On the 1995 *Difé* cover new members are listed, and some of the previous members are not mentioned.

7. For the term *matador,* see chapter 3, n. 7.

8. Kassav', "An-ba-chen'n la," *An-ba-chen'n la,* G. Debs 027. Text appears in Conrath 1987, 162–63.

9. Interview, Patrick Saint Éloi.

10. For the eighth album *Banzawa* (1983), the producer Georges Debs hired the French sound engineer Didier Lozaic and rented the first digital recording studio in Paris to establish the timbre of the snare drum. The Lozaic formula worked, for 40,000 copies of the album were sold.

11. Kassav', "Wonderful," *Kassav #3,* 3A 205.

12. Text appears in Conrath 1987, 135–36.

13. Interview, Jean-Claude Naimro. 1995.

14. Ibid.

15. Kassav', "Mwen alé," *Tekit izi,* Sony 472873.

16. Kassav', "Mwen viré," *Tekit izi.*

17. Patrick Saint Éloi, "West Indies," *Mizik-cé lan mou,* Moradisc 2M 2009.

18. Jean-Philippe Marthély's "Bel kréati" held third place for several weeks on the chart, causing the sale of 30,000 copies of the album.

19. Jean-Philippe Marthély, "Bel kréati," *Touloulou,* G. Debs 023.

20. Jean-Philippe Marthély and Patrick Saint Éloi, "Sé-pa-djen-djen," *Ou pa ka sav,* G. Debs 034.

21. Text appears in Conrath 1987, 171. In 1985, "Sé-pa-djen-djen" ranked number three on the charts. Marthély was voted the number-one singer by le palmarès de Canal Tropical in Paris.

22. Patrick Saint Éloi's "Ki jan ké fè" was number two on "Le Top Sun" charts in Martinique for the month of July 1994.

23. Patrick Saint Éloi, "Ki jan ké fè," *Zoukamine,* Sonodisc 7283.

24. Interview, Patrick Saint Éloi.

25. Patrick Saint Éloi, "Pa douté," *Bizouk,* Sonodisc 7247.

26. Saint Éloi was the guest on the RFO 1 Guadeloupean television variety show "Partition."

27. Patrick Saint Éloi, "Silans," *Difé,* Columbia 4806972. 45.

28. Kassav', "Ou chanjé," *Tekit izi.*

29. Interview, Jean-Claude Naimro.

30. Jocelyne Béroard, "An lè," *Milans,* CBS 468723.

31. Kassav', "Solèy," *Lagué moin,* CEL 6791; reissued on *Vini pou,* CBS 460619.

32. Interview, Jocelyne Béroard. 1995.

33. Patrick Saint Éloi, "Zoukamine," *Zoukamine.*

34. Interview, Patrick Saint Éloi.

35. Liner notes by Patrick Saint Éloi for *Zoukamine.*

36. Kassav', "Jijman hatif," *Difé.*

37. Kassav', "Difé, soupapé," *Difé.*

38. Bergman 1985, 21–22. Another episode occurred when Kassav' performed in Libreville, Gabon before an almost empty stadium due to poor advertisement. Not only was the band not paid, but their passports were confiscated until they paid their hotel bills and concert fees! Shady African freelance promoters tried to capitalize on Kassav's fame. Billy Bergman recalls that some promoters booked a sports stadium and put up large posters of the Kassav' musicians all over Abidjan in the Ivory Coast. These promoters convinced George Tai Benson, a well-known television personality, to give them free publicity and sold all the tickets. The most important but missing link was that the promoters never signed a contract with Kassav' and fled before the onslaught of the duped customers' anger.

39. "La Guadeloupe a fait un triomphe à Kassav'," *Antilla,* 17–28 mars 1986, 6–7. At the Anse Bertrand stadium 30,000 people arrived two hours ahead of time. When the concert began, 50,000 people were in attendance. In the 1990 census Guadeloupe's population was listed as 330,000. Thus, 50,000 people represented over 15 percent of the population that attended Kassav's free concert.

40. See Benoit 1990, 34. Michel d'Alexis of Les Aiglons of Guadeloupe held the record for the most sales of his cadence single "Cuisse-la" (The Thigh) until Kassav's "Zouk-la sé sèl médikaman nou ni," which stayed on the charts as number one for six months.

41. George Décimus and Jacob Desvarieux, "Zouk-la sé sèl médikaman nou ni," *Yélélé,* G. Debs 002.

42. Furthermore, Kassav's response to the debate lies in its dedication written on the *Yélélé* cover: "à ceux des nôtres qui ont grandi de l'autre côté de la mer, pour qu'ils n'oublient pas leurs racines" (to those who have grown up across the sea so that they do not forget their roots).

43. Its 17–27 November 1988 North American tour also included one-night performances in Washington, D.C., Los Angeles, Miami, Boston, and Montréal. While in New York the Haitian band, Tabou Combo, and Kassav' performed together, and their concert was billed as a *bataille des géants* (battle of the giants).

44. See Gardinier 1989, 39. Kassav' signed with CBS to continue to grow creatively and to capture the American audience.

45. Interview, Eric Andrieu. 1995.

46. Henri Debs Productions, Moradisc, Cellini, and Déclic-Guadeloupe are the producers in Guadeloupe. In Martinique, there are Studio Hibiscus, Déclic-Martinique, Rubikolor, GD Productions, and JE Productions. Studios are available for recording an album, but the actual pressing, distribution, and marketing are controlled by French record companies based in Paris. To earn a profit, Henri Debs Productions only presses enough records to satisfy the French Caribbean market for three months to a year. Kassav' recorded twelve albums between the period of 1980 and 1987 with Georges Debs Productions without a signed contract.

Chapter Three

1. Cited in Jacquey and Hugon 1984, 22. This was an interview with Maryse Condé during which she discussed her ambivalent feelings about Africa and the notion of an Antillean identity. The original French was "Etre femme et antillaise, c'est un destin difficile à déchiffrer."

2. Alexandre Stellio, born Fructueux Alexandre, was a well-known Martinican clarinet player (based in Paris) and one of the founding fathers of the classical biguine. His most popular reign was during the early 1920s until the late 1930s. The biguine (to begin) consists of two refrains with two couplets. It was very popular between 1910 and 1960, featuring an interplay between the clarinet and the trombone. Born on French Caribbean plantations and representative of the bourgeoisie, its melody is European, but its rhythm is African.

3. Gabriel's first marriage was to the French composer of Russian origin, Léo Daniderff, from whom she divorced shortly thereafter. She was soon married a second time to Soime, a professional Martinican military doctor and hospital administrator. Gabriel accompanied her husband to West Africa, where they lived for a couple of years while he fulfilled his military obligations.

4. Surena 1998, 35–66. Andrée Belmat spent hours with me discussing the traditional biguine songs and the terms *pacotille, léchèl poul,* and *doudou.*

5. Another version of "Jennés bò kanal" appears in Gabriel 1966, 67.

6. Another version of "Léchèl poul" appears in Gabriel 1966, 107.

7. A *matador* was a beautiful woman who wore a special costume and lots of gold jewelry. Her arrogant way of behaving and seductive walk pointed to her social position as a kept woman who rarely married. Subject of several biguines, the Guadeloupean Raphaël Zachille's prize-winning "Bèl matadô" (Beautiful Matador) is duplicated in its entirety in Benoit 1990.

8. See Burton 1993, 81. The stereotype of the smiling sexually available Black or mulatto doudou goes back to the eighteenth century and received its classic formation in "Adieu foulards, adieu madras" (Adié foula! Adié madras, in Creole) believed to have been written by the governor of Guadeloupe, M. Bouillé de Lisle, in 1769.

9. Another version of "A si paré" appears in Gabriel 1966, 23. Edith Lefel sang a remix of the song for her *Rendez-vous,* Déclic/Rubicolor 8413792.

10. Another version of "Linfidèl ou lanmou Lily" appears in Gabriel 1966, 139.

11. Interview, Jocelyne Béroard. Her first composition, "Mové jou," was written while she was a passenger in a taxi on her way to see Jacob Desvarieux. When she arrived, she showed the lyrics to Desvarieux and Jean-Claude Naimro. Right away, the three of them began to work on the music to accompany the song. Upon its completion and recording she was especially anxious about her mother's response. To her surprise, her mother not only liked it, but asked why wasn't the song more forceful in its message.

12. Kassav', "Mové jou," *An-ba-chen'n la*. Text appears in Conrath 1987, 159–60.

13. Interview, Léa Galva. 1995.

14. Kwak, "Kontinué," *A la kwakaans*, Hibiscus 191216.

15. Interview, Léa Galva, 1995.

16. Kwak, "Mennen mwen," *A dé, vlopé*, Hibiscus 94003-2.

17. Kwak, "Mennen mwen." This song stayed on "Le Top Sun" charts for over three months during the summer of 1994.

18. In 1993, Galva was awarded the Prix SACEM-Martinique for "Kontinué," which had been on "Le Top Sun" charts in the winter.

19. Liner notes for *Comme dans un film*.

20. Joëlle Ursull, "Joujou," *Comme dans un film*, Col 473923-2.

21. See Melki 1989 and Chénard 1994, 14–15. It was Tanya St. Val who asked to join the trio, but Ursull was actually replaced by Jane Fostin.

22. De Montelov 1989. Ursull did *Miyel* (CBS 462433) with the Kassav' guitarist Jacob Desvarieux.

23. Eurovision is the European recording industry's annual awards ceremony for the best records throughout Europe for the year. Ursull's jointly wrote "White and Black Blues" with the French singer Serge Gainsbourg for *Black French*. The song placed second in the competition, and the album turned gold.

24. Edith Lefel sings "Somnifère" on Ronald Rubinel, *Jeux de dames*, Déclic 09703-4.

25. Edith Lefel, "Marie," *Mèci*, Sonodisc 63303.

26. In Dance 1992, 175. During the course of Dance's interview with the Jamaican writers Velma Pollard and Pamela Mordecai, the topic shifted to love. Pollard spoke about the disillusionment that can creep into a relationship.

27. Trébeau grew up adoring music. She has two brothers and a brother-in-law who are musicians.

28. Kwak, "San mandé," *A dé, vlopé*.

29. Kwak, "Zone intérdite," *A dé, vlopé*.

30. Interview, Suzy Trébeau, 1995.

31. Tanya St. Val, "Fanm mous," *Mi*, Philips 526548.

32. Interview, Tanya St. Val, 1995.

33. Interview, Tanya St. Val.

34. This quote and those that follow are from Tanya St. Val, "Lanmou kréyòl," *Zouk A Gogo*, Debs 7HDD 2460.

35. "Tanya Saint Val et les lauréats du Viéme festival jazz à la Martinique," *France-Antilles Magazine,* 5–11 February 1994, 51.

36. See Schwarz-Bart 1989b, 116–27. Béroard had many interests beside singing. From age six she imitated the French singer Edith Piaf. While a teenager she was a swimming champion in Martinique. Her father, a dentist, and her mother, a secondary English teacher, advised her to take piano lessons. Visits to see her maternal grandmother drew Béroard's attention to the records of Léona Gabriel, Mme Mavounzy, and Manuela Pioche. These listening sessions with her grandmother sparked her interest in a singing career that was delayed when she initially studied pharmacy at the Université de Caëns. After her recovery from a car accident, she abandoned pharmacy to move to Paris, where she studied at the École des Beaux Arts, painted, and sold some of her watercolor paintings. Finally, living in the French headquarters of music in Paris, Béroard was able to pursue her dream of a singing career.

37. Jean-Philippe Marthély and Patrick Saint Éloi, "Pa bisouin palé," *Ou pa ka sav.* The correct Creole spelling of "bisouin" is "bizwen."

38. The Philadelphia International Records team, Kenny Gamble and Leon Huff, actually wrote the lyrics and music for "Turn Off the Lights" and "Close the Door."

39. Interview, Jocelyne Béroard.

40. Kassav', "Ké sa lévé," *Difé.*

41. Kassav', "Ké sa lévé." The song ranked number one in December 1995, winning Béroard the 1995 Prix SACEM-Martinique for author of the year and a gold record for *Difé.*

42. Jocelyne Béroard, "Siwo," *Siwo,* G. Debs 036.

43. Interview, Jocelyne Béroard.

44. See Fitte-Duval 1982, 12–13. The festival took place on 5 May 1992 at the Hotel PLM Batelière in Schoelcher, featuring Orphelia of Dominica, Lewis Méliano of Guadeloupe, Jocelyne Béroard of Martinique, and Cédia Sylviane of French Guyana.

45. Interview, Suzy Trébeau.

46. Interview, Jocelyne Béroard.

47. Lola Martin is a Martinican woman singer who sang biguine songs until her marriage in the 1950s. She has since moved to the United States. Jenny Alpha, also from Martinique, used to sing in Paris nightclubs, but she decided to invest her energy into being an actress and comedienne. Manuela Pioche and Madame Mavounzy were both Guadeloupean singers who sang biguine and folk songs with the local orchestras. There is even an active Manuela Pioche Association for Women in Pointe-à-Pitre. Moune de Rivel, in her late seventies, is still active as a performer in France, where she resides.

48. Hersile-Héloise 1995a, 41. Gérard César of RFO 1 jokingly called Léa Galva a "touche à tout" (a dabbler in everything). This joke prompted the name of Galva's new television show *Touchatou,* which premiered in November 1995.

49. Thimon 1996, 46–47. Galva was contacted by Ronald Rubinel about mak-

ing an album. In March 1996, they began to work on it with help from Taxikréol, who composed four of the seven songs.

50. Jallier and Lossen 1985, 64. Inspired by the proverb, Maryse Condé published a short story entitled "La châtaigne et le fruit à pain," translated as "The Breadfruit and the Breadnut" by Richard Philcox. The story appeared in Adine Sagalyn, ed. *Voies de pères, voix de filles: Quinze femmes écrivains parlent de leurs pères* (Paris: Maren Sell, 1988).

51. Kassav', "Fanm chatenn," *Difé.*

52. Joëlle Ursull, "Amazòne," *Black French,* CBS 466854–4.

53. Ibid.

Chapter Four

1. See Averill 1997 to learn about politics and popular music in Haiti.

2. This song reminds one of Léon Damas's négritude poem "Hoquet" (Hiccup) from *Pigments* (Paris: Gallimard, 1937), which dramatizes the assimilated values of the mother when she admonishes her son's desire to play the banjo instead of the violin.

3. Another version of "Nèg ni mové mannyè" appears in Jallier and Lossen 1985, 55.

4. Arnold 1981, viii. Arnold describes the Schoelcher monument, located in a prominent place in downtown Fort-de-France. Schoelcher's outstretching paternal hand proclaims that freedom comes from France, whose generosity alone assures the prosperity and liberty of her children overseas.

5. See Burton 1992, 64. I am especially indebted to Burton's essays on political and cultural developments in Martinique, which are listed in the bibliography.

6. Taxikréol, *Empreintes hommage à Fernand Donatien,* Rubicolor 85151.

7. Another version of "Les Faux mulâtres" appears in Pierre-Charles 1975, 171–72.

8. The deceased singer, composer and musician from Martinique is frequently spoken of as a warrior. Tears glitter in women's and men's eyes and their voices choke with emotion when they talk about Mona as a man, performer, and singer.

9. Eugène Mona, "Tan pis pour moi," *An Goulouss cé lan mo,* 3A 051; reissued on *Eugène Mona, Vol. 1 (1975–1978),* Hibiscus 88050–4.

10. Eugène Mona et son groupe du Marigot, "Bois brillé," *Boi brilé,* HPR 52; reissued on *Témoignage Live,* Hibiscus 88024.

11. Eugène Mona, "Bois brillé." A slightly different version appears in Mandibèlè 1992, 84.

12. Delsham 1991, 7. Delsham recalled the first time he heard "Boi brilé": "I knew Eugène Mona on the earphones; I no longer know in which year. My transitor radio resonated from a voice mixed with tenderness, power, revolt and also violence while singing 'Bwa brilé.'"

13. Cally 1990, 59–72. *Agia,* or *ladja,* is a Bantu word from the Congo. Ladja,

whose leg movements are similar to the Brazilian capoeria's high leg sweep and hip-spinning ballet performance, is a warrior dance performed to the accompaniment of bèlè music.

14. Eugène Mona, "Agoulou cé lan mò," *An Goulouss cé lan mò;* reissued on *Témoignage Live.*

15. Ernest "Vava" Dovin, Mona's best drummer and called the greatest bèlè drummer of Martinique, was from Quartier Pérou of Sainte-Marie; he constructed Mona's house in Dominante in Marigot. He and Mona pondered the meaning of mysticism, religion, and the good and the bad on a daily basis under the mango tree.

16. Interview, Félix Fleury. 1995. Born in Marigot, Fleury met Mona at age twenty. The two men became closer than brothers, and Fleury joined Mona's band as the manager. At five in the evening on Fridays Mona arrived at Fleury's bar/restaurant *Le Ghetto,* the hangout for local musicians.

17. *Blan manjé* or *blanc-manger au coco* is a coconut milk dessert with a gelatin base mixed with almond essence, a pinch of salt, and condensed milk.

18. The ragga singer, Princess Lover, bravely sang "Face a Face" on the March 25, 1995 RFO 1 telecast of the Prix de SACEM 1994 award show. Previously, Céline Flériag sang it with the Chorale Emeraude de Sainte-Marie in April 1992 with Ti Ken (Kali's teenage son) on percussion.

19. Eugène Mona, "Face a Face," *Blanc mangé,* Hibiscus 88037-2.

20. Eugène Mona, "Lizo," *Blanc mangé.*

21. Eugène Mona, "Maître Chacha," *Témoignage Live.*

22. Personal conversation, Maryvonne Charlery, 7 February 1995.

23. Interview, Félix Fleury.

24. Ibid.

25. Mandibèlè 1992e, 21–23. Mona's sister said that her brother had been called "De Gaulle" because he was born during the period of the general's glory and their grandparents gave him this nickname. His sister stated, "He'll never be De Gaulle because his pseudonym is encased in a spiritual and divine life. Those who do not enter the *traversée de désert* are not God's chosen. They must pass by this path of realization. Christ fell several times to return to glory. My brother returned to glory. I suppose that he is fine wherever he is (the great Martinican musician that I know)."

26. There are two spellings for this title which is frequently the case for acro-lectal Creole—*Pa molli* for the album and "Pa moli" for the song.

27. Interview, Pôglo. 1995.

28. Pôglo, "Pa moli," *Pa molli,* Rail 60–283

29. Pôglo, "Lèspwa," *Pa molli.*

30. Pôglo, "Sasévwé," *Pa molli.*

31. Interview, Pôglo.

32. See Clark 1989, 599–605. Kali studied at the Institut Martiniquais d'Études d'Edouard Glissant (IME), where he learned English and met his life-long friend and manager, Eric Andrieu. While in attendance Kali was exposed to Glissant's ideas on

folk culture as a route to popular theater and as a means of identifying the cultural *opacité* (opaqueness) of Martinicans.

33. Marie-France Brière, director of variety shows for the public channel, chose Kali to represent France at the 1992 Eurovision after he won the 1991 Francovision. Kali was very surprised because he thought that his Rasta dreadlocks would have been an impediment.

34. Kali, "Monté larivyè," *Racines 2*, Hibiscus [no catalogue number]; reissued on *Racines 1 et 2*, Hibiscus 88020.

35. Kali is already a winner of other awards: the 1989 Hurard Coppet Maracas d'or; the 1990 Prix-SACEM Martinique for the best album; and the first prize for the first Francovision competition in 1991. The competition was organized by Antenne 2 at the Adolphe-Adams Theatre in Longjumeau.

36. Interview, Eric Andrieu, 1995. The present Déclic-Martinique producer and the former manager of Kali, Andrieu explained that Kona Lota means "Love Dream."

37. Kali, "Pran patché-w," *Lésé la tè tounen*, Déclic 191344-2.

38. Kali, "Blan enmen Nèg," *Lésé la tè tounen*.

39. True to his word, in the summer of 1995, Kali released *Débranche* (Unplugged), containing former 6th Continent hits and some new titles such as "Tifi Congo" (Little Congo) and "Débranché," all played on acoustic instruments. Kali's move to Paris resulted in some changes in the formation of his band. First, the keyboard player, Vasco Noverraz, left. Second, Kali's brother Pim, who played drums, was replaced by Kali's teenage son, Ti Ken. Third, Kali's sister, Sabrina Ransay, joined the chorus with his wife, Hélène Marigny, who has performed for all of his live performances. These changes, however, have not affected Kali's ongoing songwriting collaboration with Rémy Bellenchombre, the ex-6th Continent director.

40. "Allez Kali, alé la Fwans." *TV Magazine*, 2–8 mai 1992, p. 8.

41. Confiant 1988, 20. Confiant compares this scheme to the former South African apartheid bantustans. *Bétonisation*, a threat of cultural genocide and environmental destruction, refers to the spread of concrete supermarkets, housing developments, and secondary residencies. The mayor of Le Marin supports the construction of 150 holiday villas, which requires the draining of the mangrove swamps. The draining would kill the animal and plant life that it has been sustaining.

42. Kali, "Ile à vendre," *Ile à vendre*, Hibiscus 51204-2; reissued on *Lésé la tè tounen*.

43. Djo Dézormo, "Voici les loups," *Voici les loups*, Hibiscus 88031. Text appears in Pulvar 1990a, 12.

44. Dézormo won the 1990 Prix SACEM Martinique for "Voici les loups" under the category "succès de l'année" (success of the year).

45. Personal telephone conversation, Djo Dézormo, November 1994.

46. Djo Dézormo, "Moyeloup," *Krttk*, DL 12005.

47. From the early to mid-1980s, fifty bomb explosions or attempts had been organized by the Caribbean Revolutionary Army (ARC). In October 1983, following

the U.S. invasion of Grenada, the ARC took responsibility for the bombing of the United States consulate in Fort-de-France (which has since closed down and moved to Barbados). Other sites in Martinique were a television relay station and the Court of Appeals in December 1983 and a *gendarmerie* (armed police barracks) in April 1984.

48. Dézormo won first prize in the 1975 Fort-de-France vidé Carnival contest for "Blé pal, blé fonsé." The song can be found on *Djo Dézormo 25 lanné chanson (1973–1998)*, JEP 98001/3. 1998.

49. See Reno 1995, 42. From 1986 to 1992, the number of supporting votes for the Indépendantiste movement tripled, passing from 7.9 percent to 23.4 percent, and bringing an end to Césaire's 1981 moratorium on the question of the island.

50. The stunning paradox is that Alfred Jeanne-Marie, mayor of Rivière Pilote (the stronghold of the Indépendantiste MIM) for twenty-eight years, president of MIM for twenty years, and a retired school teacher, put in his candidacy for the June 1998 elections for a seat in the French National Assembly and won with 64 percent of the vote. Jeanne's conduct is baffling, for, as one of the founding members of MIM, he repeatedly stated that he could never go begging for money before French government officials. One wonders if Jeanne is dealing with the position that some marginalized people take: If I am accepted into the mainstream, perhaps my credibility will rise among my people. In support of this position is the fact that he got the majority vote. The writer Raphaël Confiant, one of Jeanne's supporters, explained his action and that of other Martinicans as follows: "It is a symbol of a sick department in France."

51. In Martinique, the békés control 60 percent of the local economy and own most of the land. "Dûr, dûr, d'être béké" (So hard to be a béké) was one of the popular songs for Carnival 1999. The song recounts the eight-week dockers' strike in 1998 that crippled the exportation of bananas. Because the Fort-de-France port was blocked, tons of bananas rotted on the boats, a loss of revenue for the béké banana plantation owners.

52. Djo Dézormo, "Sé le 22 mé," [No catalogue number].

Chapter Five

1. The violinist Soime said that people do not buy recordings for their compact discs' covers.

2. Interview, Lewis Méliano. 1997.

3. Cited in Alexandre, 1982, 8. See also Anselin 1982.

4. The Fête des Cuisinières is held every August in Pointe-à-Pitre. The women march in the streets, carrying food on a tray.

5. Mme. Mavounzy, "An ké ba-w sa," *A la recherche du temps des biguines*, Cellini [No catalogue number].

6. Zouk Machine, "Zouk Machine," *Zouk Machine: Back Ground Expérience 7*, Debs 2431; reissued on *Le Best of Zouk Machine*, BMG 74321296422.

7. Zouk Machine, "Zouk Machine." Text appears in Guilbault et al. 1993, 160–61.

8. Interview, Yves Honoré. 1995.

9. Zouk Machine, "Maldòn," *Maldòn*, Déclic 260244; reissued on *Le Best of Zouk Machine.*

10. Personal conversation, Lowell Fiet, 29 May 1997.

11. Personal conversation, Michelle Hammond and Anicet Mundundu, 15 December 1996.

12. Patrick Saint Éloi, "Ki jan ké fè," *Zoukamine.*

13. In 1902, the Mt. Pelée volcano erupted in Saint-Pierre, Martinique, claiming 30,000 victims. There was only one survivor, a prisoner who was protected by the thick walls of his cell. Before the eruption Saint-Pierre had been the capital city and the center of biguine music.

14. See Davis and Troupe 1989, 272. Miles Davis's comments about band formation could have been in reference to Malavoi. He said, "The quality of the musicians is what makes a band great. If you have talented, quality musicians who are willing to work hard, play hard, and do it together, then you can make a great band."

15. Malavoi, *Titin bèl,* Video, RFO Martinique, 1994.

16. Interview, Evariste Cannenterre. 1995. Cannenterre was the manager of the Librairie Antillaise record shop at the Rond Point shopping center in Schoelcher, a northern suburb of Fort-de-France. He mentioned that cassettes, compact discs, and videotapes are very expensive due to taxes, transportation costs, and import duties. The reason is that these items are not made locally, but in France.

17. Interview, Patrick Borès. 1995.

18. See Chenière 1998, 44–45. SACEM is the acronym for Society of Authors, Composers, and Editors of Music. The organization's headquarters is in Paris, with branches in Guadeloupe and Martinique. Christian Boutant created the Prix SACEM pour la Martinique in 1988. He reported in 1998 that eight hundred entertainers were registered with SACEM. He thinks that music ought to emancipate the population and be an object of political reflection.

19. Sonia Laventure, *Magazine Eco Info,* RFO Martinique 1, 28 June 1996. This information was reported on a television show.

20. Air France used to sponsor Kassav' and Malavoi, but the airline never featured the music of either band on its flights. The conclusion is that the sponsorship was monetary in terms of transportation and videotaping, but full support was not forthcoming for millions of passengers would have been exposed to the bands' music.

21. Personal conversation, Anicet Mundundu, 15 December 1996. The Zairean slang *Hindoubill* is a mixture of English, French, Lingala, and Kikongo. The youth begin a sentence in Lingala and switch to *Hindoubill.* There is a Lingala text of "Siwo" to reflect Zairean male/female relationships, but it does not follow the original version. Also, a Zairean composed a song that parallels the lyrics of James Brown's "Sex Machine" and Zouk Machine's "*Zouk* Machine."

22. In 1988, "Syé bwa" earned Kassav' its fourth gold record for the year. The other three gold records were for "Rété," "Siwo," and "Bizness."

Chapter Six

1. Nora 1989, 19.

2. Dehay 1994, 43–44.

3. Portions of this June 1979 RFO Guadeloupe radio interview with Cultier were replayed on the 23 December 1985 RFO Martinique special tribute to Marius Cultier on the day of his death.

4. "Marius Cultier, on aurait dû foutre un monument à ce con-lâ," *Foucouyan'*, 1983.

5. Today, a street is named after Cultier in the Terres-Sainville section of Fort-de-France, where he spent his youth.

6. Interview, Emmanuel "Mano" Césaire. 1995.

7. The idea for *Matébis* occurred at a rehearsal to gather together old friends, including Eugène Mona, who died before the recording. Malavoi won the 1992 Prix de SACEM-Martinique Album for the Year for *Matébis;* Eric Andrieu of Déclic-Martinique reported in May 1995 that 75,000 copies had been sold.

8. Malavoi, "Un concerto pour la fleur et l'oiseau," *Matébis*, Déclic 10541-2.

9. Interview, José Privat. 1995. Privat also began to replace his neighbor Paulo Rosine in 1989. He is now Rosine's permanent replacement.

10. Interview, Ralph Thamar. With a sense of wonderment, Thamar talked about this episode because it was so rare for him to write a song during such a short period of time.

11. Ralph Thamar and Mario Canonge, "Mayo," *Hommage à Marius Cultier,* Déclic 09702-2.

12. Interview, Ralph Thamar.

13. Mario Canonge et le groupe Kann, "Non musieu," *Trait d'union*, Kann/Mélodie 09635.

14. Joby Valente, pseudonym for Marguerite Dersion, was a radio announcer for Tropic FM in Paris. She played the guitar, composed socially conscious songs, and sang for various orchestras in Paris during the 1950s through 1970s.

15. Another version of "Ay promnen musieu" appears in Pierre-Charles 1975, 115–19.

16. Interview, Céline Flériag. 1995.

17. Céline Flériag, "Rèv mwen," *Karamèl*, Déclic 50336-2. The well-made video and recording of "Rèv mwen" with the teamwork of Mano Césaire's music and Flériag's voice could not help but be a success. Flériag's first solo effort won her the 1994 Prix SACEM Martinique as best female interpreter.

18. Interview, Céline Flériag.

19. Céline Flériag, "Mazouk-Rag," *Karamèl*.

20. Cally 1996, 24–36. In 1982, Nicol Bernard joined Malavoi after the release of *Roro marott*. He still teaches percussion at SERMAC and has been a member of the West Indies Jazz Band since 1987. Jacky also plays with the West Indies Jazz Band at numerous festivals in the Caribbean. Among the many short-lived bands with which Alex performed were the Universitaires and Contestaires with Rosine, Jacky Alpha, and the Pastel brothers, followed by the Brazilian Salon Gonzalves' Mars Club.

21. The Centre Martiniquais d'Action Culturelle is funded by the local government to hold concerts.

22. Liner notes on Fal Frett, *Fal Frett*, 3A [No catalogue number]. N. d. Also, a personal conversation, Marie-Nelly and Jean-Albert Privat, 1995. The Privats said that *fal frett* refers to the action of being overcome, gripped, or stunned by something.

23. Thimon 1994c, 32. *Caribbean Flash* was the name of Taxikréol's first compact disc with the two popular songs "Jojo" and "Confidences."

24. Taxikréol, "Special Request," *Special Request*, Teka 001–2.

25. Taxikréol, "Come Zis Afternoon," *Siwo Fuel*, Teka 695–01.

26. Taxikréol, "Ebony Roots," *Siwo Fuel*.

27. An African American blues pianist with lots of recordings, Memphis Slim, the former Peter Chatman, moved from Tennessee to Illinois and France, where he died from kidney failure in 1988. His 1940 "Beer Drinking Woman" and 1948 "Everyday I Have the Blues" were his claim to fame. Very active, Memphis Slim was well known in the Parisian circle of African, Caribbean, and French musicians. Hence, the linking of his name to the bèlè drummer-singer Emmanuel "Ti Emile" Casérus was not done in an arbitrary fashion by Taxikréol.

28. *Kwak* in Guyanese Creole means cassava. The band initially consisted of Christian Louiset, José Marie-Rose, Alain Dracius, Anthony Lowenski, Suzy Trébeau, Jean-Luc Guanel, Léa Galva, and Philippe Joseph.

29. Kwak, "Pa grandi, " *A dé, vlopé*.

30. Kwak, "Pa mélé," *A dé, vlopé*.

31. On "Cool Links" through Netscape a more detailed definition of *palaviré* is given. In a figurative sense, *palaviré* in Creole means "roundtrip" which is a necessary and permanent trip between the past and the present, youth and maturity, and a happy modernity reconciled with creativity, humor, and seriousness. The term was deliberately chosen so that people would pay attention to the multiple sounds of French Caribbean music to please their souls and bodies.

32. Interview, Claude Césaire. 1995. The initial line-up of musicians for Palaviré consisted of Mano Césaire, Lino Aléman, and Christian de Négri on violins; Patrick Saint Elie on percussions; Claude Banys on bass; José Zebina on drums; Claude Césaire on piano; Alwin Lowenski on tenor and soprano saxophone; Jean Claude Getrude and Rodrigue Marcel on vocals.

33. Interview, Emmanuel and Ina Césaire. 1995.

34. Palaviré, "La Vi sé an bato," *Tête à Tête,* Hibiscus 95003-2.

35. See Austerlitz (1997). Juan Luis Guerra began the 1990s as the hottest property in the international Latin market.

36. Interview, Franck Balustre. 1996.

37. Sincere thanks to George Lipsitz for sending me a copy of Vargas' *La Medicina* and making me aware of its existence. Vargas' work in the 1980s was characterized by a creative hip fusion of traditional merengue with other Caribbean rhythms such as zouk.

38. Chenière 1997c, 45. Songs are located on *Volt Face Live,* CNR Music 300-3702. In 1996, Dominique Coco and Dominique Panol quit the band.

39. Jean-Michel Rotin, "Cigarèt," *Héros,* Korosol 7284.

40. Interview, Mario Canonge.

41. Interview, Freddie Marshall. 1995.

Chapter Seven

1. See Kali, *Roots,* Hibiscus 51204-2. Charles "Charly" Labinsky, a percussionist who played for Eugène Mona and currently plays for Kali's band, wrote the lyrics for "Tambou dan tchè nou" (The drum resonates in our heart).

2. Eugène Mona, "Tambou séryé," *Témoignage Live;* reissued on *Eugène Mona, Vol. 1 (1975–1978).*

3. Laye 1971, 36–37. The actual quotation is: "The drummers are drawn from a noble caste and their employment is hereditary."

4. Taxikréol, "Manzé Ida," *Special Request.*

5. Interview, Henri Guédon. 1995.

6. Interview, Sully Cally.

7. Cally 1990, 75–81. The bèlè is also divided along regional lines: *bèlè du nord* from the Sainte-Marie-Marigot area and the *bèlè du sud* from the Lamentin, Diamant, and Rivière-Pilote area.

8. Ibid., 69.

9. See Thimon 1997a, 24–25. Studio Hibiscus has a special Prestige Collection of Caribbean Music that releases hard-to-find vinyl records on compact discs. One of these releases is the unedited *Vélo gwo ka,* which contains eleven songs that were originally recorded in Le Moule and Gosier, Guadeloupe, with the singers Napoléon Magloire, Cassius, and Anzala.

10. Vélo, "Pas bon moin coup," *Vélo gwoka,* Elsodun CC 2-714.

11. There are a few women bèlè singers. One was the late Epsilane Ste.-Ruse, who sang bèlè du sud. Another is Simeline Rangon, who makes up her own lyrics to standard bèlè rhythms.

12. Kassav', "Love and Ka Dance," *Love and Ka Dance,* 3A [No catalogue number.] 1979.

13. Franck Jacques's liner notes on *Vélo gwoka,* Elsodun CC2-714.

14. "Guédon, le judojazzman," *L'Équipe,* 22 August 1979.

15. See Paty 1982. Having a good ear for special effects, Guédon has removed toys, decanters, flasks, batteries, and Tibetan utensils from their stereotyped uses to incorporate them into his repertoire for his *Quartet de percussions*. Guédon said, "I utilize instruments in their universality, a little like the language of true spindle-tree similar to the art of Picasso and Moretti." To commemorate the fiftieth anniversary of the French overseas departments (DOM), the mainland French post offices held a contest to select the best design for a special stamp. Guédon won the contest for his submission; the stamp was issued in Martinique on 16 November 1996.

16. Thimon 1995c, 49. Pakatak, founded by Saint-Prix, included four women dancers.

17. Akiyo leads a procession every year for Carnival. The band consistently sings socially oriented songs, such as "Tanbou" (Drum) and "Pyèj" (Trap) on *Dékatman* (1995) and "Black Boat People" on *Mouvman* (1993). Sometimes, the band's technique is likened to the Carnival oludum drumming heard in Bahia of Brazil.

18. Bago, "Tambour battant," *Tambour battant*, Déclic 50434.

19. Cally 1996, 159. Marcé is known for mixing gwo ka and bèlè figures (especially for the *kalenda* figure) for his concerts.

20. Van Lévé, based in Basse-Terre, is another group of percussionists who incorporate gwo ka modèn and promote Guadeloupean culture.

21. Interview, Claude "Colo" Vamur. 1995.

22. Ibid.

23. See Hennessey 1990, 206–208. From 1967 to 1972, the master drummer Clarke ran the Kenny Clarke Drum School with Dante Agostini and the Premier Drum Company at the Selmar premises in Paris. Clarke also taught at the École de Jazz du Conservatoire Municipal de Saint-Germain-En-Laye. He placed an emphasis on rhythm, syncopation, and the role of the drummer as an accompanist.

24. Interview, Claude Vamur.

25. Interview, Sully Cally. 1995.

26. Ibid.

27. See Leymarie 1996, 59–60, for discussion of the *damié*.

28. Franck Cotellon's liner notes on Kan'nida's *Vis an nou*, Indigo 1996.

29. Eugène Mona, "Tambou séryé," *Eugène Mona Vol. 1*.

30. The Sato drums are on display in the ethnographic Adande museum in Porto Novo, Benin, West Africa.

31. Kafé, "Opérasyon ka," *Gwoka Métamowfozys Mòd*, Debs 1335-2.

32. Interview, Kafé. 1995. Also a trumpet player, Kafé was encouraged by Vélo to play the drums. To substantiate Vélo's belief in him, Kafé hand-carved three gwo ka drums, which stand in the center of his living room.

33. In addition, Kafé uses the gwo ka for healing therapy for the sick at the CHRU Hospital in Pointe-à-Pitre, which has created another kind of deferential drum space.

34. Hersile-Héloise 1995b, 24. Lébèloka is composed of Dominique Mehala, Marie-Catherine Vanitou, Manuella Berenice, Nicole Koné, Maryse Polyte, Renée-

Lyse Tesor, and Suzie Singa. Its members play the djembé, ti bwa, ka médium basse, and the doum doum basse.

35. See Chenière 1997d, 46. Willy Léger taught most of these women drummers at SERMAC. Tambour système, composed of these students, was the first all-woman group of drummers. To learn more, see Hersile-Héloise 1995, 24.

bibliography

Anon. 1979. "Guédon, le judojazzman," *L'Équipe,* 22 August.

Anon. 1983. "Marius Cultier: on aurait dû foutre un monument à ce con–là." *Fouyayan'.*

Anon. 1986a. "Un groupe en or! Un médicament en or," *Tropic Magazine,* March.

Anon. 1986b. "La Guadeloupe a fait un triomphe à Kassav'." *Antilla,* 17–28 March, 6–7.

Anon. 1990. "Jean-Pierre Jardel." *Antilla,* 22–28 February, 36–37.

Anon. 1993a. "Allez Kali, alé la Fwans! TV *Magazine,* 2–8 May, 8.

Anon. 1993b. "Le soleil a rendez-vous avec Kassav' au Zénith." *Magdom,* July-August, 23.

Anon. 1993c. "Mario Canonge: Il est important pour nous de conserver ce rythme et cet état d'être." *Antilla,* 10–16 December, 29.

Anon. 1994. "Tanya Saint-Val et les lauréats du VIème festival jazz à la Martinique." *France-Antilles Magazine,* 5–11 February, 51.

Anon. 1995. "Tanya St. Val: Un nouvel album." *Créola,* March-April, 6–7.

Anon. 1995. "Jocelyne Béroard: la dame de coeur de Kassav'." *Créola,* 16 August–15 September, 5, 7.

Achebe, Chinua. 1959. *Things Fall Apart.* Greenwich, Conn.: Fawcett.

———. 1964. *Arrow of God.* London: William Heinemann; rpt. New York: John Day Company, 1967.

Adorno, Theodor. 1990. "The Curves of the Needle." Translated by Thomas Y. Levin. *October* 55: 48–55.

Alcide, Kerwin. 1994."Tanya et Johnny: le duo insolite." *France-Antilles Magazine,* 19–25 November, 53–54.

Alexandre, Camille. 1982. "Lewis Méliano: une chanteuse pas comme les autres." *Télé 7 Jours,* 31 May–6 June, 8–9.

Ampigny, Marie-Line. 1987. "Kassav': L'année de tous les succès." *France-Antilles,* 17 May.

————. 1992. "Le père de Kassav' se raconte." *France-Antilles Magazine,* 11–17 December, 60–61.

————. 1993."Dans l'intimité d'une étoile, Edith Lefel." *Magdom,* December [1992]–January, 22–26.

Anselin, Alain. 1979. *L'Émigration antillaise en France: Du bantoustan au ghetto.* Paris: Éditions Anthropos.

————. 1995. "West Indians in France." In Richard Burton and Fred Reno, eds. *French and West Indian.* Charlottesville: University Press of Virginia.

Anselin, Danielle. 1982. "Festival de la chanson féminine en Martinique." *Mizik,* 25.

Arnold, A. James. 1981. *Modernism and Negritude: The Poetry and Poetics of Aimé Césaire.* Cambridge: Harvard University Press.

————. 1994. "The Erotics of Colonialism in Contemporary French West Indian Literary Criticism." *New West Indian Guide* 68, nos. 1–2: 5–22.

Auslander, Phili 1996. "Performance and the Anxiety of Simulation." In Elin Diamond, ed., *Performance and Cultural Politics.* New York: Routledge.

Austerlitz, Paul. 1997. *Merengue: Dominican Music and Dominican Identity.* Philadelphia: Temple University Press.

AV. 1996. "Vis an nou d'après Kan'nida," *France-Antilles Magazine,* 21–27 December, 32.

Averill, Gage. 1997. *A Day for the Hunter, A Day for the Prey: Music and Power in Haiti.* Chicago: University of Chicago Press.

Azoulay, Elaine. 1988. "Le punch antillais." *Télérama,* May.

Bébel-Gisler, Dany. 1985. *Léonora: l'histoire enfouie de la Guadeloupe.* Paris: Seghers; *Leonora: The Buried Story of Guadeloupe.* Translated by Andrea Leskes. Charlottesville: University Press of Virginia, 1994.

————. 1989. *Le défi guadeloupéen: devenir ce que nous sommes.* Paris: Éditions Caribéennes.

Benoit, Edouard. 1990. *Musique populaire de la Guadeloupe de la biguine au zouk 1940–1980.* Pointe-à-Pitre: AGETL.

Bergman, Billy. 1985. *Good Times Kings: Emerging Africa Pop.* New York: Quill.

Bernabé, Jean. 1986. "Chroniques d'une fin de vacances, Pt. I: Zouk et zouk." *Antilla,* 24 September–1 October, 15–16.

Bernabé, Jean, Patrick Chamoiseau, and Raphaël Confiant. 1989. *Éloge de la créolité.* Paris: Gallimard.

Berton, Yves. 1992. "Kali, le rasta français de l'Eurovision." *Le Parisien,* 9 May.

Bhabha, Homi K. 1994. *The Location of Culture.* New York and London: Routledge.

Bouvier, Fred. 1993. "Kali: j'aime être difficile," *France-Antilles Magazine*, 29 January–4 February, 44–45.

———. 1994a. "Christian de Négri raconte Malavoi." *France-Antilles Magazine*, 12–18 November, 48–52.

———. 1994b. "Pipo Gertrude: il a fallu se battre." *France-Antilles Magazine*, 12–18 November, 53.

Brown, Lloyd W. 1978. *West Indian Poetry*. Boston: Twayne.

Burton, Richard. 1992. "Towards 1992: Political-Cultural Assimilation and Opposition in Contemporary Martinique." *French Cultural Studies* 3:61–86.

———. 1993. "Maman-France Doudou: Family Images in French West Indian Colonial Discourse." *Diacritics* 23, no. 3: 69–90.

Burton, Richard, and Fred Reno, eds. 1995. *French and West Indian: Martinique, Guadeloupe, and French Guiana*. Charlottesville: University Press of Virginia.

Busia, Abena A. 1990. "The Gift of Metaphor: Symbolic Strategies and the Triumph of Survival in Simone Schwarz–Bart's *The Bridge of Beyond*." In Carole Boyce Davies and Elaine Savory Fido, eds., *Out of the Kumbla: Caribbean Women and Literature*. Totowa: Africa World Press.

Cally, Sully. 1990. *Musiques et danses Afro-Caraïbes*. Paris: Lézin.

———. 1996. *Le grand livre des musiciens créoles*. Vol. 1. Paris: Dominique Rabussier.

Cartey, Wilfred. 1991. *Whispers from the Caribbean*. Los Angeles: Center for African American Studies, University of California.

Case, Frederick Ivor. 1989. "Edouard Glissant and the Poetics of Cultural Marginalization." *World Literature Today* 63, no. 4: 593–98.

Césaire, Aimé. 1991. "Discours du moratoire." *Le Naif*, June, 13–15.

Chamoiseau, Patrick. 1986. *Chroniques des sept misères*. Paris: Gallimard.

———. 1988. *Solibo magnifique*. Paris: Gallimard.

———. 1992. "Mona comme Solibo." *Karibel Magazine*, July-August, 60–62.

———. 1993. "Une journée créole en pays dominé." *Antilla*, 5–11 November, 3–5.

Chénard, Lucienne. 1982. "Malavoi: leurs violons n'iront plus aux bals." *Télé 7 Jours*, 21 June.

———. 1986a. "Jocelyne Béroard la belle et les bêtes," *Télé 7 Jours*, 1–7 March.

———. 1986b. "Ne pleure plus, Marius, c'est fini." *Télé 7 Jours*, 4–10 January.

———. 1993. "Hommage à Paulo Rosine." *TV Magazine*, 13–19 February, 19.

———. 1994a. "Joëlle Ursull: passions plurielles." *TV Magazine*, 11–17 June, 14–15.

———. 1994b. "Patrick Saint Eloi, le plein de zoukamine." *TV Magazine*, 18–24 June, 16–17.

Chenière, Eddy. 1996a. "Guédon, le nomade artistique." *France-Antilles Magazine*, 8–14 June.

———. 1996b. "Tanya Saint–Val, la pierre précieuse." *France-Antilles Magazine*, 7–13 September, 46–48.

———. 1997a. "Jean-Michel Rotin: le retour réussi de héros." *France-Antilles Magazine,* 11–17 January, 8–9.

———. 1997b. "Marthéloi: La nouvelle combinaison." *France-Antilles Magazine,* 25–31 January, 46–47.

———. 1997c. "Volt Face, la musique électrik." *France-Antilles Magazine,* 19–26 April, 45.

———. 1997d. "Lébèloka: Fanm tanbou." *France-Antilles Magazine,* 10–16 May, 47.

———. 1998. "Rencontre avec Christian Boutant." *France-Antilles Magazine,* 16–22 May, 44–45.

Citron, Marcia. 1993. *Gender and the Musical Canon.* Cambridge: Cambridge University Press.

Clark, Beatrice Stith. 1989. "IME Revisited: Lectures by Edouard Glissant on Socio-Cultural Realities in the Francophone Antilles." *World Literature Today* 63, no. 4: 599–605.

Cohen, Arnault. 1999. "La musique antillaise s'essouffle." *France-Antilles Magazine,* 17–18 April, 4.

Collins, Patricia Hill. 1990. *Black Feminist Thought.* Boston: Unwin Hyman.

Conan, Eric. 1999. "Martinique: Ce département dont le patron est indépendaniste." *L'Express,* 4–10 March, 86–91.

Condé, Maryse. 1979. *La Parole des femmes.* Paris: L'Harmattan.

Confiant, Raphael. 1985. *Le Nègre et l'Amiral.* Paris: Grasset.

———. 1998a. "Pa voté: échec et mat?" *Antilla,* 28 April, 17–18.

———. 1988b. "Le Mangrove de Belfond massacrée." *Antilla,* 10 April, 20.

Conrath, Philippe. 1986. "Jocelyne Béroard." *Libération,* 30 April–1 May.

———. 1987. *Kassav'.* Paris: Seghers.

———. 1989. "Mizik Antiyé." *Antilles,* October, 223–25.

Cook, Malcolm, ed. 1993. *French Culture Since 1945.* New York and London: Longman.

Coridun, Victor. 1990. *Carnaval de Saint-Pierre.* 2d edition. Fort-de-France: Auguste Flaun.

Crusol, Jean. 1986. "An Economic Policy for Martinique." In Paul Sutton, ed., *Dual Legacies in the Contemporary Caribbean: Continuing Aspects of British and French Dominion.* New York: Frank Cass.

Dance, Daryl. 1992. "Conversation with Pam Mordecai and Velma Pollard." In Daryl Dance, ed., *New World Adams.* Leeds: Peepal Tree Press.

Daniel, Dalila. 1989. "Pôglo." *Télé 7 Jours,* 25–31 March, 14–15, 58.

Dash, Michael. 1975. *Jacques Stéphen Alexis.* Toronto: Black Images.

Davis, Miles, with Quincy Troupe. 1989. *Miles: The Autobiography.* New York: Simon and Schuster.

Davies, Carole Boyce, and Elaine Savory Fido, eds. 1990. *Out of the Kumbla: Caribbean Women and Literature.* Totowa: Africa World Press.

Davies, Carole Boyce. 1994. *Black Women: Writing and Identity.* New York: Routledge.

de Certeau, Michel. 1988. *The Practice of Everyday Life*. Translated by Steven Rendall. Berkeley: University of California Press.

de Montelov, Michael. 1989. "Joëlle Ursull et Chanëel." *Télé Star,* 5 June.

Dehay, Terry. 1994. "Narrating Memory." In Amritjit Singh, Joseph T. Skerrett and Robert E. Hagan, eds., *Narrating Memory: Memory, Narrative and Identity*. Boston: Northeastern University Press.

Delsham, Tony. 1991. "Mona seulement après la mort." *Antilla,* 27 September–3 October, 7.

Dibango, Manu. 1994. *Three Kilos of Coffee*. Chicago: University of Chicago Press.

Dorsinville, Max. 1976. "Senghor or the Song of Exile." In Rowland Smith, ed., *Exile and Tradition: Studies in African and Caribbean Literature*. London: Longman and Dalhousie University.

Ellington, Edward Kennedy. 1973. *Music Is My Mistress*. New York: Da Capo/ Doubleday.

Ernst, Max. 1993. "Le soleil a un rendez-vous avec Kassav' au Zénith." *Magdom,* July-August, 23.

Erwan, Jacques. 1987. "Malavoi à la conquête du monde." *Paroles et Musique,* April, 18–21.

Evans, Graeme. 1991. *Africa O-Ye!* London: Guiness Publishing.

Eyre, Banning. 1994. "Kassav's Medicine Magic Multinational." *Rhythm Music Magazine* 3, no. 6:14–17, 52.

Fanon, Frantz. 1952. *Peau noire, masques blancs*. Paris: Éditions de Seuil; *Black Skin, White Masks*. Translated by Charles Lan Markmann. New York: Grove Press, 1967.

Fitte-Duval, Annie. 1982. "Festival de la chanson féminine caribéenne." *Le Naif,* 11–18 May, 12–13.

Forbes, Jill. 1995. "Popular Culture and Cultural Politics." In Jill Forbes and Michael Kelly, eds., *French Cultural Studies: An Introduction*. Oxford: Oxford University Press.

Frith, Simon. 1989. "Why Do Songs Have Words?" *Contemporary Review* 5:77–96.

———. 1996. *Performing Rites*. Cambridge: Harvard University Press.

Gabriel-Soime, Léona. 1966. *Ça! C'est Martinique*. Paris: Presses de l'imprimerie la productrice.

Gallon, G. 1998. "MaMag: Les musiciens antillais défendent le patrimoine." *France-Antilles Magazine,* 16–22 May, 24–25.

Gardinier, Alain. 1988. "Kassav': CBS nous permet de gagner de l'argent." *Rock N'Folk,* May, 39.

George, Nelson. 1989. *The Death of Rhythm and Blues*. New York: E. P. Dutton.

Georgel, Thérèse, ed. 1963. *Contes et légendes des Antilles*. Paris: Fernand Nathan.

Glissant, Edouard. 1989. *Caribbean Discourse*. Translated by J. Michael Dash. Charlottesville: University Press of Virginia.

Guédon, Henri. 1984a. *Écoute les Antilles*. Paris: Armand Colin.

———. 1984b. *Percussions*. Paris: Alphonse Leduc.

———. 1985. *Guide pratique Rhythm's Section*. Paris: Alphonse Leduc.

Guédon, Henri, and Mauricette Catillon. 1981. *De l'onomatopée à la percussion*. Paris: Van de Velde.

Guilbault, Jocelyne et al. 1993. *Zouk: World Music in the West Indies*. Chicago: University of Chicago Press.

Hennessey, Mike. 1990. *Klook: The Story of Kenny Clarke*. Pittsburgh: University of Pittsburgh Press.

Hernandez, Elizabeth, and Consuela Springfield-Lopez. 1994. "Women and Writing in Puerto Rico: Interview with Ana Lydia Vega." *Callaloo* 17, no. 3:816–25.

Hersile-Héloise, Eric. 1993. "Jean-Paul Soime, la musique d'une âme revoltée." *France-Antilles Magazine*, 31 July–6 August, 53–55.

———. 1995a. "Touchatou: une émission sur mesures." *France-Antilles Magazine*, 2–6 December, 40–41.

———. 1995b. "Willy Léger continuera-t-il à se battre seul?" *France-Antilles Magazine*, 14–20 October, 24–25.

———. 1996. "Il est devenu artiste pédagogique." *France-Antilles Magazine*, 27 January–2 February, 46–47.

———. 1997. "Les frères Bernard: bien ancrés dans la qualité." *France-Antilles Magazine*, 5–11 April, 33–35.

Hewitt, Leah. 1995. "La Créolité 'Haitian Style.'" In Maryse Condé and Madeleine Cottenot-Hage, eds., *Penser la créolité*. Paris: Éditions Karthala.

Hintjens, Helen M. 1992. "France's Love Children? The French Overseas Departments." In Helen M. Hintjens and Malyn Newitt, eds., *The Political Economy of Small Tropical Islands*. Exeter: University of Exeter Press.

———. 1995. "Constitutional and Political Change in the French Caribbean." In Richard Burton and Fred Reno, eds., *French and West Indian*. Charlottesville: University Press of Virginia.

Hodge, Merle. 1990. "Challenges of the Struggle for Sovereignty: Changing the World versus Writing Stories." In Selwyn Cudjoe, ed., *Caribbean Women Writers*. Wellesley: Calaloux.

hooks, bell. 1990. *Yearning: Race, Gender and Cultural Politics*. Boston: South End Press.

———. 1994. *Outlaw Culture: Resisting Representations*. New York and London: Routledge.

Hountondji, Paulin. 1983. "Reason and Tradition." In O. Oruka and D. A. Masolo, eds., *Philosophy and Cultures*. Nairobi: Bookwise Limited.

Hurley, E. Anthony. 1997. "Loving Words: New Lyricism in French Caribbean Poetry." *World Literature Today* 71, no. 7:55–60.

Jacquey, Marie-Clothilde, and Monique Hugon. 1984. "L'Afrique, un continent difficile: entretien avec Maryse Condé." *Notre Librairie* 75:21–25.

Jallier, Maurice, and Yollen Lossen. 1985. *Musiques aux Antilles: Misik bô kay*. Paris: Éditions Caribéennes.

Kenyatta, Jomo. 1938. *Facing Mount Kenya*. London: Secker & Warburg.

Keser, Bernard. 1992. "Malavoi: Matébis une échapée a douze à travers d'inédites traces." *Antilla*, 31 July–6 August, 31–32.

Kpatindé, Francis. 1989. "Jocelyne Béroard: La voix d'or du zouk." *Jeune Afrique Magazine*, January, 32–33.

Lamming, George. 1960. *The Pleasures of Exile*. London: Joseph; rpt. Ann Arbor: University of Michigan Press, 1992.

Laurencine, Ronald. 1985. "Kassav': Zouk Machine? Interview avec Pierre-Edouard Décimus et Ronald Laurencine." *Antilla*, 28 July–4 August, 15–20.

Laye, Camara. 1971. *Radiance of the King*. New York: Vintage.

Leclerc, Franck. 1985. "Jocelyne Béroard de A à Z." *France-Antilles Magazine*, 29 July–4 August, 40–42.

Léandy, Luc. 1997. "Ruff Nèg: souvenirs du Printemps de Bourges." *France-Antilles Magazine*, 3–9 May, 40–41.

Lewis, Barbara. 1995. "No Silence: An Interview with Maryse Condé." *Callaloo* 18, no. 3:543–50.

Leymarie, Isabelle. 1996. *Musiques Caraïbes*. Paris: Cité de la Musique/Actes Sud.

Lipsitz, George. 1990. *Time Passages: Collective Memory and Popular Culture*. Minneapolis: University of Minnesota Press.

———. 1994. *Dangerous Crossroads: Popular Music, Post-Modernism and the Poetics of Place*. New York: Verso.

Lomax, Alan. 1976. *Cantometrics: A Method in Musical Anthropology*. Berkeley: University of California Extension Media Center.

McClary, Susan. 1991. *Feminine Endings: Music and Gender and Sexuality*. Minneapolis: University of Minnesota Press.

M. A. 1995. "L'événement Kassav'." *France Antilles*, 22 November, 8.

Mandibèlè. 1990. "Voici le loup: analyse d'une chanson-symbole." *Antilla*, 9–16 March, 11–13.

———. 1992a. "Interview Max Cilla." *Karibel Magazine*, July-August 26–28.

———. 1992b. "Marilène Mauriello." *Karibel Magazine*, July-August, 36–38.

———. 1992c. "Avec Martine Dovin: de bons amis, il n'en existe plus." *Karibel Magazine*, July-August, 17–18.

———. 1992d. "Rencontre avec l'autre pilier du groupe Mona ou la part de vérité de PLM." *Karibel Magazine*, July-August, 12–13.

———. 1992e. "La soeur d'"Eugène Mona." *Karibel Magazine*, July-August, 21–23.

Manuel, Peter. 1997. *The Caribbean Currents*. Philadelphia: Temple University Press.

Martin, Denis C. 1987. "Malavoi: le punch de la Martinique." *Jazz Magazine*, March.

Maximin, Daniel. 1981. *L'Insolé soleil*. Paris: Éditions du Seuil.

May, Lyne. 1995. "Kali: plus d'une corde a son cou" *Carib'n*, July-August, 8–11.

Melki, Guy. 1989. "Tropicalement vôtres." *Paroles et musique*, 18 May.

Ménil, René. 1987. "L'hommage de René Ménil à Paulo Rosine." *Antilla*, 19 February, 27.

Michel, William. 1996. "Sully Cally: l'hom' tambou." *France-Antilles Magazine,*
    12–18 October, 35–37.

Mondésir, Edmond. 1992. "Mona légendaire." *Karibel Magazine,* July-August,
    42–50.

Morrison, Toni. 1987. "The Site of Memory." In William Zinsser, ed., *Inventing the
    Truth: The Art and Craft of Memoir.* New York: Houghton-Mifflin.

Muenier, Jean-Pierre, and Brigitte Léardée. 1989. *La Biguine de l''oncle Ben.'* Paris:
    Éditions Caribéennes.

Nayaradou, Jacky. 1992. "Dans la lignée des grands." *Karibel Magazine,* July-
    August, 39–41.

Ndebele, Njabulo. 1996. "A Home for Intimacy." *Mail & Guardian,* 26 April–2
    May, 28–29.

Nketia, J. A. Kwabena. 1974. *Music of Africa.* New York: W. W. Norton.

———. 1990. "The Play Concept in African Music." Unpublished Paper. Laura Bol-
    ton Series.

Nora, Pierre. 1989. "Between Memory and History: *Les lieux de mémoire.*" Trans-
    lated by Mark Roudebush. *Representations* 26:27–24.

O'Conner, Lorraine. 1993. "Docteur Zouk." *Caribbean Beat,* Winter, 8–10; 13–14;
    16.

O'Franc, Kathie. 1994. "Le printemps créole de Zouk Machine." *France-Antilles
    Magazine,* 7–13 May, 21.

Ouanély, Joël. 1996. "Ce soir sur RFO: le plus grand zouk." *TV Magazine,* 21–27
    December.

Palmer, Michael, and Claude Sorbers. 1992. "France." *The Media in Western
    Europe.* London: The Euromedia Group/Sage Publications.

Pareles, Jon. 1988. "Zouk, a Distinctive, Infectious Dance Music." *The New York
    Times,* 20 May.

Paty, Jean-Marc. 1982. "Henri Guédon: percussions de tous les pays." *Nouvelles lit-
    téraires,* 28 January–4 February.

———. 1987. "Malavoi à cordes et cuivres." *Le Matin,* 5 April.

Père Elie and Antoine Maxme. 1992. "Mona." *Karibel Magazine,* July-August,
    29–34.

Pfaff, Françoise. 1993. *Entretiens avec Maryse Condé.* Paris: Éditions Karthala.

Pied, Henri, and Patrick Chamoiseau. 1988. "Le Risque d'une séduction." *Antilla,*
    28 April, 14–16.

Pierre-Charles, Livie. 1975. *Femmes et chansons.* Paris: Soulanges.

Pineau, Gisèle. 1995. "Écrire en tant que noire." In Maryse Condé and Madeleine
    Cottenot-Hage, eds., *Penser la créolité.* Paris: Éditions Karthala.

Plougastel, Yvann. 1986. "Le swing des îles: le zouk détrône la biguine." *L'Événe-
    ment du jeudi,* 7 May.

Polomat, Véronique. 1996. "Lewis Méliano ressuscitée." *Sept Magazine,* 5 Decem-
    ber, 25.

Pratt, Ray. 1990. "Women's Voices, Images, and Silences in Popular Music." In

Diana Raymond, ed., *Sexual Politics and Popular Culture*. Bowling Green: Bowling Green University Popular Press.

Price, Richard. 1998. *The Convict and the Colonel*. Boston: Beacon Press.

Pulvar, Jean-Marc. 1990a. "Djo Désormo: mode d'emploi d'un succès." *Antilla*, 15–21 March, 11–14.

———. 1990b. "Jocelyne Béroard canaille, pas dévergondée." *Antilla*, 11–17 May, 36–41.

Quarmenil, Frédéric. 1996. "La fausse note de Malavoi." *France-Antilles*, 23 November.

Reins, Sacha. 1988. "Jocelyne Béroard la diva du zouk." *Elle*, 9 May.

Renault, Jean-Michel. 1993. *Bonjour la Martinique*. Lyons: Les Créations du Pélican.

Reno, Fred. 1995. "Politics and Society in Martinique." In Richard Burton and Fred Reno, eds., *French and West Indian*. Charlottesville: University Press of Virginia.

Rigby, Brian. 1991. *Popular Culture in Modern France*. London: Routledge.

Ritz, David. 1985. *Divided Soul: The Life of Marvin Gaye*. New York: McGraw Hill.

Rivel, Moune de. 1982. "La flûte magique d'Eugène Mona." *Bingo*, August.

Rosaldo, Renato. 1985. "Imperialist Nostalgia." *Representations* 26:107–22.

Rosemain, Jacqueline. 1986. *La Musique dans la société antillaise (1635–1982)*. Paris: L'Harmattan.

———. 1993. *Jazz et biguine: les musiques noirs du nouveau monde*. Paris: L'Harmattan.

Rosenblum, Trudi Miller. 1995. "Island's Africa Fête Eyes More Dates, New Markets." *Billboard*, 14 January, 1, 65.

Rouget, Gilbert. 1985. *Music and Trance: A Theory of the Relations between Music and Possession*. Chicago: University of Chicago Press.

Roumain, Jacques. 1944. *Les Gouverneurs de la rosée*. Paris: Éditeurs Français Réunis; *Masters of the Dew*. Translated by Langston Hughes and Mercer Cook. New York: Collier, 1972.

Ruprecht, Alvina. 1990a. "Radio Tanbou: Function of the Popular Media in Guadeloupe." In John Lent, ed., *Caribbean Popular Culture*. Bowling Green: Bowling Green University Popular Press.

———. 1990b. "Mass Media in Guadeloupe." In Stuart H. Surlin and Walter G. Soderland, eds., *Mass Media and the Caribbean*. New York: Gordon and Breach.

Sartre, Jean-Paul. 1969. "Orphée noire." In Léopold Senghor, ed., *Anthologie de la nouvelle poésie nègre et malgache de langue française*. Paris: Presses Universitaires de France.

Scaramuzzo, Gene. 1987. "The Magic Music of the French Antilles Part 3: The Roots." *Reggae & African Beat* 6, no. 1:20–23.

———. 1994. "Is America Finally Ready for Kassav'?" *The Beat* 13, no. 6:50–53.

Schwarz-Bart, Simone. 1972. *Pluie et vent sur Télumée Miracle*. Paris: Éditions du Seuil.

———. 1989a. "Ina Césaire: Un conte de vie et de mort aux Antilles." In Simone and André Schwarz-Bart, eds., *Hommage à la femme noire*. Ludion, Belgium: Éditions Consulaires.

———. 1989b. "Jocelyne Béroard, une star qui ne se prend pas pour une étoile." In Simone and André Schwarz-Bart, eds., *Hommage à la femme noire*. Ludion, Belgium: Éditions Consulaires.

Shukman, Henry. 1992. *Travels with My Trombone: A Caribbean Journey*. New York: Crown Publishers.

Sieger, Jacqueline. 1981. "Interview avec Aimé Césaire." *Afrique*, 5 October, 64–67.

Silko, Leslie. 1977. *Ceremony*. New York: Viking Press.

Smith, C. C. 1988. "Report from Martinique: île entre deux mondes (Island Between Two Worlds)." *Reggae & African Beat* 7, no. 1:22–25.

Snyder, Emile. 1976. "Aimé Césaire: The Reclaiming of the Land." In Rowland Smith, ed., *Exile and Tradition: Studies in African and Caribbean Literature*. London: Longman and Dalhousie University Press.

Surena, Eliane. 1988. "L'Image de la femme à travers la chanson antan lontan." In Frédérique Aumis et al., eds., *Femme livre d'or de la femme créole*. Pointe-à-Pitre: Raphy Diffusion.

Tenaille, Frank. 1979. "Antilles/Paris." *Le Monde de la Musique* 11:72–73.

Th. Dz. 1995a. "Les atouts de Kassav." *France-Antilles Magazine*, 8–14 July, 41–43.

———. 1995b. "Siwo fuel ça . . . carbure pour taxi." *France-Antilles Magazine*, 12–18 August, 40–42.

Thaly, François. 1992. "Mario Canonge à la musique au coeur." *Karibel Magazine*, 11 February, 21–22.

Thimon, Michel. 1989. "Kali au Grand Carbet." *France-Antilles*, 22 December, 20.

———. 1994a. "Le Kwak nouveau pour les vacances." *France-Antilles Magazine*, 9–15 April, 16–17.

———. 1994b. "Le nouveau Kwak." *France-Antilles Magazine*, 23–29 July, 64.

———. 1994c. "Taxikréol, toujours plus haut." *France-Antilles Magazine*, 13–19 August, 32–33.

———. 1994d."Tanya Saint-Val." *France-Antilles Magazine*, 25–31 December, 33–34.

———. 1995a."Les Prix SACEM 95: nos meilleurs artistes." *France-Antilles Magazine*, 23–29 March, 46–48.

———. 1995b."Palaviré le deuxième." *France-Antilles Magazine*, 2–8 July, 40–42.

———. 1995c."Dédé Saint-Prix, l'ambassadeur." *France-Antilles Magazine*, 16–22 September, 48–49.

———. 1996. "Léa, la féline." *France-Antilles Magazine*, 27 July–1 August, 46–47.

———. 1997a. "Hommage aux grands maîtres du folklore guadeloupéen." *France-Antilles Magazine*, 1–7 February, 24–25.

———. 1997b. "Fal Frett pour le plaisir des oreilles." *France-Antilles*, 12 April, 8.

———. 1998a. "Francisco, une légende vivante." *France-Antilles Magazine*, 10–16 January, 46–47.

———. 1998b. "Djo Dézormo, sans cravate." *France-Antilles Magazine,* 21–27 February, 43.

Thiong'o, Ngugi wa. 1972. *Homecoming.* London: Heinemann.

Traoré, Mamadou. 1986. "Jocelyne Béroard la voix d'or des Antilles." *Aminor,* 1 July.

Turner, Victor. 1977. "Frame, Flow and Reflection: Ritual and Drama as Public Liminality." In Michel Benamou and Charles Caramello, eds., *Performance in Postmodern Culture.* Madison: Coda Press.

Uri, Françoise, and Alexandre Uri. 1991. *Musique et musiciens de la Guadeloupe.* Paris: Con Brio.

Walcott, Derek. 1974. "The Caribbean: Culture or Mimicry?" *Journal of Interamerican Studies and World Affairs* 16, no. 1:3–14.

———. 1992. *The Antilles: Fragments of Epic Memory.* The Nobel Lecture. New York: Farrar, Straus and Giroux.

Warner, Keith Q. 1982. *Kaiso! The Trinidad Calypso.* Washington, D.C.: Three Continents Press.

Warner-Vieyra, Myriam. 1982. *Juletane.* Paris: Présence Africaine.

Wilson, Elizabeth. 1990. "Le Voyage et l'espace clos—Island and Journey as Metaphor: Aspects of Woman's Experience in the Works of Francophone Caribbean Women Novelists." In Carole Boyce Davies and Elaine Savory Fido, eds., *Out of the Kumbla: Caribbean Women and Literature.* Totowa: Africa World Press.

Zimra, Clarisse. 1990. "Righting the Calabash: Writing History in the French Francophone Narrative." In Carole Boyce Davies and Elaine Fido, eds., *Out of the Kumbla: Caribbean Women and Literature.* Totowa: Africa World Press.

Zobel, Joseph. 1950. *La rue cases-nègres.* Paris: Présence Africaine.

discography

Akiyo. 1993. *Mouvman*. Déclic CD 066-2.

———. 1995. *Dékatman*. Déclic Tape 50491-4.

Marijosé Alie. 1988. *Gaoulé*. Barclay LP 841 026-1.

Bago. 1992. *Wouspel*. Rythmo CD 838552

———. 1996. *Tambour battant*. Déclic CD 50484.

Béroard, Jocelyne. 1985. *Siwo*. G. Debs LP 036.

———. 1991. *Milans*. CBS CD 468723.

Cally, Sully. N. d. *Paroles de tambours-Damyé*. Sully Cally Productions SRC Tape 92.

Canonge, Mario. 1991. *Retour aux sources*. Natal CD 150960.

———. 1995. *Arômes Caraïbes*. Kann Tape 08756.

Canonge, Mario, et le groupe Kann'. 1993. *Trait d'union*. Kann/Mélodie CD 08635.

Canonge, Mario, and Ralph Thamar. 1994. *Hommage à Marius Cultier*. Déclic CD 09702-2.

Caso Viking Guadeloupe. 1978. *Caso Viking Guadeloupe Exploration*. 3A LP 172.

Décimus, George, and Jacob Desvarieux. 1983. *Goree*. G. Debs LP 035.

———. 1984. *Yélélé*. G. Debs LP 002.

Desvarieux, Jacob. 1983. *Banzawa*. G. Debs LP 016.

Dézormo, Djo. 1977. *Sé le 22 mé*. No catalogue number.

———. 1990. *Voici les loups*. Hibiscus CD 88031.

———. 1994. *Kritik*. DL Tape 12005.

Fal Frett. N. d. *Fal Frett*. 3A [No catalogue number].

———. N. d. *In the Wake of the Sunshine*. 3A 167.

Flériag, Céline. 1994. *Karamèl*. Déclic CD 50336-2.

Galva, Léa. 1996. *Galvinisée*. Déclic CD 50549-2.

Guédon, Henri. 1982. *Afro-blue*. Harmonica Mundi LP LDX 74780.

———. 1996. *Rétrospective*. Frémeaux & Associés CD FA 048.

Kafé. 1988. *Gwoka Métamowfozys Mòd*. Debs LP 1335-2.

Kali. 1989. *Racines 1 et 2*. Hibiscus CD 88020.

———. 1990. *Racines 2*. Hibiscus [No Catalogue number].

———. 1991. *Ile à vendre*. Hibiscus 92013-2.

———. 1992. *Roots*. Hibiscus CD 51204-2.

———. 1993. *Lésé la tè tounen*. Déclic CD 191344-2.

———. 1995. *Débranché*. Déclic CD 8405442.

Kassav'. 1979. *Love and Ka Dance*. 3A LP [No catalogue number].

———. 1980. *Kassav' #3*. 3A LP 205.

———. 1980. *Lagué moin*. CEL LP 6791.

———. 1982. *Eva*. 3A LP 210.

———. 1985. *An-ba-chen'n la*. G. Debs LP 027.

———. 1987. *Vini pou*. CBS CD 460619.

———. 1989. *Majestik zouk*. CBS Tape 511.

———. 1992. *Tekit izi*. Sony CD 472873.

———. 1993. *Kassav' Live au Zénith sé nou menm'*. Tristar CD WK 57777.

———. 1995. *Difé*. Columbia CD 480697-2.

Kwak. 1992. *A la kwakaans*. Hibiscus CD 191216-2.

———. 1994. *A dé, vlopé*. Hibiscus CD 94003-2.

———. 1995. *Lé ga mèci*. Hibiscus CD 95005-2.

Lébèloka. 1996. *Dans' ka*. Rythmo-Disc CD Single W. L. 02-1.

Lefel, Edith. 1988. *La Klé*. G. Debs LP 043.

———. 1992. *Mèci*. Sonodisc Tape MC 63303.

———. 1996. *Rendez-vous*. Déclic/Rubicolor CD 8413792.

Malavoi. 1982. *Roro marott*. 3A LP 214.

———. 1983. *Zouel*. G.Debs LP 014/15.

———. 1986. *La Filo*. G. Debs LP 1024.

———. 1987. *La Case à Lucie*. Blue Silver LP 8221.

———. 1987. *Malavoi, au Zénith*. Blue Silver LP 2402.

———. 1988. *Légende (Best of Malavoi)*. Déclic CD 304389.

———. 1988. *Jou ouvé*. Blue Silver CD 034-2.

———. 1992. *Matébis*. Déclic CD 10541-2.

———. 1993. *Matébis en concert*. Déclic CD 4702-2.

———. 1994. *An Maniman*. Déclic CD 302268.

———. 1996. *Shé Shè*. Déclic CD 8418432.

Marthély, Jean-Philippe. 1984. *Touloulou*. G. Debs LP 023.

———. 1993. *Si sé taw*. Sonodisc CD 66767.

Marthély, Jean-Philippe, and Patrick Saint Éloi. 1985. *Ou pa ka sav*. G. Debs LP 034.

Mavounzy, Madame. N. d. *A la recherche du temps des biguines*. Cellini LP. [No catalogue number].

Mélanio, Lewis. N. d. *Lewis Méliano et les Skah Shah d'Haïti et #1 Plus.* Musique des Antilles L. P. 4678.

Mona, Eugène, et son groupe du Marigot. 1970. *Bois brilé.* HPR LP 52 Parade.

———. N. d. *An Goulouss cé lan mo.* 3A LP 051.

———. 1989. *Témoignage Live.* Hibiscus CD 88024.

———. 1991. *Eugène Mona Vol. 1 (1975-1978).* Hibiscus Tape 88050-4.

———. 1991. *Eugène Mona Vol. 2.* Hibiscus CD 191212.

———. 1991. *Blanc mangé.* Hibiscus CD 88037-2.

Naimro, Jean-Claude. 1985. *En balatè.* G. Debs LP 026.

Palaviré. 1994. *Plézi.* Hibiscus CD 94002-2.

———. 1995. *Tête à Tête.* Hibiscus CD 95003-2.

Pendergrass, Teddy. 1978. *Life Is a Song Worth Singing.* Philadelphia International LP 35095.

———. 1979. *Teddy.* Philadelphia International LP 36003.

Pôglo. 1989. *Pa molli.* Rail Production 3LP 60 283.

Rotin, Jean-Michel. 1994. *Héros.* Korosol CD 7284.

Rubinel, Ronald. 1995. *Jeux de dames.* Déclic CD 09703-4.

Saint Éloi, Patrick. 1982. *Misik-cé lan mou.* Moradisc CD 2M 009.

———. 1990. *A la demande.* GDC CD 1020.

———. 1992. *Bizouk.* Sonodisc CD 7247.

———. 1994. *Zoukamine.* Sonodisc CD 7283.

Saint-Prix, Dédé. 1984. *Avan Van tombe d'amour.* G. Debs LP 1301.

———. 1995. *Chouval bwa sans frontières.* Déclic Tape 50487-4.

St. Val, Tanya. 1989. *Zouk A Gogo.* Debs Tape 7HDD 2460.

———. 1991. *Soul Zouk.* Philips CD 510774-2.

———. 1994. *Mi.* Philips CD 526548.

6th Continent. 1995. *L'intégrale de 6ᵗʰ Continent.* Déclic CD 50485-2.

Taxikréol. 1994. *Special Request.* Teka CD 001-2.

———. 1995. *Siwo Fuel.* Teka CD 695-01.

———. 1997. *Empreintes Hommage à Fernand Donatien.* Rubicolor CD 85151.

Thamar, Ralph. 1987. *Exil.* G. Debs LP 1504.

———. 1991. *Caraïbes.* Déclic Tape 05.

Ursull, Joëlle. 1988. *Miyel.* CBS CD 462433.

———. 1990. *Black French.* CBS Tape 466854-4.

———. 1993. *Comme dans un film.* Col Tape 473923-2.

Vamur, Claude. 1987. *Lévé mwen.* Mélodie CD 1804.

———. 1994. *Héritage pou . . .* Déclic CD 50367-2.

Vélo. 1994. *Vélo gwoka.* Esoldun CD CC2-714.

Volt Face. 1995. *Volt Face Live.* CNR Music CD 300-3702.

Zouk Machine. 1986. *Zouk Machine: Back Ground Expérience 7.* Debs LP 2431.

———. 1989. *Maldòn.* Déclic CD 260244.

———. 1994. *Clin d'oeil.* BMG CD 74321164582.

———. 1995. *Le Best of Zouk Machine.* BMG CD 74321296422.

interviews

Alie, Marijosé; 10 May 1995, Diamant.

Andrieu, Eric; 5 April 1995, Fort-de-France.

Balustre, Franck; 20 December 1996, Gosier.

Béroard, Jocelyne; 24–25 May 1995, Paris.

Borès, Patrick; 30 January 1995, Pointe-à-Pitre.

Boutant, Christian; 8 February 1995, Fort-de-France.

Cally, Sully; 8 May 1995, Fort-de-France.

Cannenterre, Evariste; 30 April 1995, Schoelcher.

Canonge, Mario; 3 March 1995, Schoelcher.

Césaire, Claude; 2 April 1995, Robert.

Césaire, Emmanuel; 2 April 1995, Robert.

Césaire, Ina and Emmanuel; 26 April 1995, Fort-de-France.

Debs, Henri; 26 January 1995, Pointe-à-Pitre.

Flériag, Céline; 2 May 1995, Fort-de-France.

Fleury, Félix; 28 April 1995, Marigot.

Fontaine, Wilfred; 22 April 1995, Lamentin.

Galva, Léa; 10 March 1995; Schoelcher.

Guédon, Henri; 30 April 1995, Fort-de-France.

Honoré, Yves; 14 December 1995., Pointe-à-Pitre.

Kafe; 14 December 1995, Pointe-à-Pitre.

Marshall, Freddie; 11 December 1995, Pointe-à-Pitre.

Méliano, Lewis; 13 April 1997, Pointe-à-Pitre.

Naimro, Jean-Claude; 24 May 1995, Paris.

Pôglo; 4 May 1995, Dillon.

Privat, Jose; 25 April 1995, Didier.

Saint Eloi, Patrick; 24 May 1995, Paris.

St. Val, Tanya; 5 May 1995, Fort-de-France.

Soime, Jean-Paul; 3 and 10 March 1995, Schoelcher.

Thamar, Ralph; 5 March 1995, Schoelcher.

Trébeau, Suzy; 3 March 1995, Schoelcher.

Vamur, Claude; 13 December 1995, Pointe-à-Pitre.

index

"Ababa," 17, 240n.3
Achebe, Chinua, 208
Africa Fête, 65
Africa numéro (Gabon), 1, 6
Agence Nationale pour l'Insertion et la Promotion des Travailleurs de l'Outre-Mer (ANT), 3
Agostini, Dante, 219
"Agoulou sé lan mo," 119–21, 248n.14
Akiyo, 218, 207, 255n.17
Akoustik Zouk, 146, 181
"Albé," 12, 16
Albicy, Jean Marc, 16
Albin, Jean-Paul ("Paulo"), 170, 173. See also La Perfecta
Albin, Michel, 181
Alexis, Jacques Stéphen, 14
Alger, Jean-Luc, 84
Alie, Marijosé: on "Caressé moins," 27–28, 241n.15; as lead singer and songwriter for Malavoi, 27; nostalgia for Martinique, 12, 27–31, 137–38, 148, 241n.16; schooling in music, 168
Alpha, Jacky, 88, 191
Alpha, Jenny, 101
"Amazòne," 103–4
Ampigny, Marie-Line, 68
"An-ba-chen'n la," 45–48, 242n.8

Andrieu, Eric, 66, 108, 244n.45. See also Déclic Martinique
angagé (songs), xi, 8, 108, 234
"An ké ba-w sa," 153, 250n.5
"An lè," 57
"An mouvman," 38, 158
ANT. See Agence Nationale pour l'Insertion et la Promotion des Travailleurs de l'Outre-Mer
Antilles Télèvision (ATV), 7
"Apré la pli," 19, 21–22, 234, 240n.7 (chap. 1)
AREPMA. See Association for the Research and Teaching of Antillean Musical Productions
Armstrong, Louis, 118
Arnold, A. James, 247n.4
Arrow of God (Achebe), 208
"A si paré," 76–77, 82, 183–84, 244n.9
Association for the Research and Teaching of Antillean Productions (AREPMA), 177
Association pour la Sauvergarde du Patrimoine Martiniquais (ASSAUPA-MAR), 136
Attali, Jacques, 236
ATV (Antilles Télèvision), 7
Augiac, Fanny, 191, 240n.2
Auslander, Philip, 167

Avan Van, 217. *See also* Saint Prix, Dédé

Averill, Gage, 236, 247n.1

"Ay promnen musieu," 183–84, 252n.15

Bago. *See* Balthazar, Pierre Michel

"Balanséy Lala," 21

bals, 2, 154

Balthazar, Pierre Michel (pseud. Bago), 218–19, 255n.18

Balustre, Franck, 147, 202, 254n.36

"Banzawa," 48, 242n.10

Basset, Eric, 169. *See also* Déclic Productions (Paris)

"Bay chabon," 159

Bébel-Gisler, Dany, 40, 111

békés, 2, 66, 109, 144, 250n.51

bèlè (bel air), 1–2, 9, 197, 212, 254nn. 7, 11

bélia, 212

"Bèl kado," 181

"Bèl kréati," 51, 242n.19

Bellenchombre, Rémy, 131–32, 134, 136

Benoit, Edouard, xi

Bernabé, Jean, 40–42, 64

Bernard, Alex, 171, 191

Bernard, Armand (grandfather), 190

Bernard, Gaëten (uncle), 190

Bernard, Jacky (brother), 191

Bernard, Nicol (brother), 167, 191

Bernard, Parfait (father), 190

Béroard, Jocelyne, 19, 38, 60, 78–79, 246n.36; on the creation of an intimate space, 98; dispute with Jacob Desvarieux, 101; and fans, 71; hopeful nature of her songs, 58, 92–101, 246n.39; and MaMag, 170; and Marius Cultier, 78–80; "Mové jou," 78–79, 245n.12; on the name Kassav', 43; "Pa bisouin palé," 93–98, 246n.41; *Siméon*, 50; "Siwo," 90, 246n.43; song texts characterized, 163, 245.11

bétonisation, 136, 144, 171, 249n.41

biguine, 1–2, 8, 17, 176, 221

"Bisou sucré," 181

Black Star Liner, 127

Blanc mangé, 122, 248n.17

blancs-pays, definition of, 2

"Blan enmen Nèg," 134–35, 249n.38

"Blé pal blé fonsé," 142, 250n.48

Blood, Sweat, and Tears, 43

BMG-Ariola, 155, 168

"Bois brillé," 116–18, 247n.10; and the color black, 247n.12; and the poor farmer, 247n.11

Boislaville, Loulou, 133

Borès, Patrick, xii, 169, 251n.17. *See also* Déclic Guadeloupe

Bougrainville, Dominique, 181

boula, 212

Brival, Roland, 59, 218

Brown, Lloyd W., 212

Brown, Stuart, 108

Bumidom (Bureau pour le Développement de Migration des départements d'outremer), 3, 239n.2

Burton, Richard D. E., 113, 241n.3, 247n.5

Busia, Abena, 237

Ça! C'est Martinique (Gabriel), 69

Cahier d'un retour au pays natal (Césaire), 22

Cally, Sully, 206–7; on the *damié*, 221; on the state of drumming, 206, 221

Cannenterre, Evariste, 169

Canonge, Mario, 174, 176, 180–84; concert in memory of Marius Cultier, 146; and Fal Frett, 191; participates in Grand Méchant Zouk shows, 181; at La Défense, 181; physical image of, 152; and Sakiyo, 181; and Ultramarine, 181; on Wynton Marsalis, 204–5

"Caressé moins," 12, 27–28, 137–38, 148, 241n.16

Caribbean Feminist Song Festival, 100, 236, 246n.44

Carnival, 66, 108, 137–38, 148, 206

Carnot, 218

"Carrément News," 132

Cartey, Wilfred, 4

Casérus, Emmanuel ("Ti Emile"), 120, 197

Cassius, 213

CBS (now Sony), 132, 243n.44

Centre Martiniquais d'Action Culturelle

(CMAC), 17; appearances by Mario Canonge and Ralph Thamar, 146; director,
Fanny Augiac, 240n.2; as venue for Marius Cultier's last appearances, 178; as
venue for Fal Frett's debut, 191, 253n.21
Certeau, Michel de, 23
Césaire, Aimé: founder of the PPM, 112; at
funeral of Paulo Rosine, 25; mayor of
Fort-de-France, 112–13; and 1981 moratorium, 113, 250n.49; and négritude,
13–14; poetry, 22–23; search for le mot,
72
Césaire, Claude (great-nephew), 12, 199,
253n.32
Césaire, Emmanuel ("Mano") (nephew), 12;
on Afro-Cuban-Latino sound, 2; collaboration with cousin, 19–22, 200, 240n.4;
founder of Malavoi, 16; on influence of
Marius Cultier, 178–79; and Marti-
nique, 23–25, 146; schooling in music,
168; on syncopation, 163
Césaire, Ina (daughter): affection for Marti-
nique, 23–24, 31; collaboration with
cousin, 19–22, 200, 202, 240n.4; ethno-
logical studies, 22–23; feels like a for-
eigner in France, 22; memories of Morne
Rouge, 20–21
Césaire, Suzanne (wife), 14, 22
César, Gérard, 7, 246n.48
Chamoiseau, Patrick, 41–42, 109, 112, 119
Charlery, Maryvonne, 108, 125, 248n.22
Charlery, Paco, 191
Chasseur, Tony, 80, 173, 178, 218
Chénard, Lucienne, 163, 178
chouval bwa, definition of, 217
Christophe, Jocelyn, 154. See also Tympan
Productions
Chroné, Marie-Céline, 218
Chronique des sept misères (Chamoiseau),
112
"Ciagrèt," 204, 254n.39
Cilla, Max, 115–16, 121
Claire, Richard Marie, 192
Clarke, Kenny ("Klook"), 192, 219,
255n.23
"Close the Door," 97

CMAC. See Centre Martiniquais d'Action
Culturelle
CNCL. See Commission Nationale de la
Communication et des Libertés
Coco, Dominique, 203, 254n.38
Coco Loco (club), 133
Colin, Jean-Pierre, 5
Collins, Patricia Hill, 15
"Colozou," 7
"Come Zis Afternoon," 194, 205, 253n.25
Commission Nationale de la Communica-
tion et des Libertés (CNCL), 6
compas, Haitian, 2, 17, 44
Condé, Maryse, 13, 71, 73–74, 102,
247n.50
Confiant, Raphaël, 41–42, 112
Conquête, Guy (pseud. Guy Konkèt), 207
Conrath, Philippe, 5
Conseil Supérieur de l'Audiovisuelle (CSA), 6
Constance, Julien, 16
Coppet, Hurard, 74
Coridun, Victor, 110
Corps musical, 123
Cosmos Zouk, 191
Creole, 39–40; and cultural identity, 72–73;
GEREC, xi, 40, 241n.2; heritage, 19;
Kassav's creole songs, 41; language, 39,
149; linguistic boundaries of, 41, 162;
orthography, 40, 241n.3
Crusol, Jean, 234–35
CSA. See Conseil Supérieur de l'Audio-
visuelle
Cultier, Gisèle, 178
Cultier, Marius, 177–80; and AREPMA,
177–78; concert in his honor, 146,
252n.5; death of, 178; his parents'
deaths, 177; last public appearances,
178; and the ORTF band, 177; and
Ralph Thamar, 25; unhappiness of,
178

Dachir, Chris, 173
Damas, Léon Gontran, 13, 247n.2
damié, 221, 255n.27
Daniel, Dalila, 147
"Dans ka," 230

Dantin, Denis, 215
Davies, Carole Boyce, 13
Debs, George, 168
Debs, Henri, xii, 168–69, 178, 215
Décimus, George: early training in music,
    168; first success, 48; among founders of
    Kassav', 40; joins Volt Face, 203
Décimus, Pierre-Edouard: and Kassav', 40–
    41, 43, 207; new rendition of "Solèy,"
    57–58; and St. Jean Carnival, 207; "Won-
    derful," 48–49, 242n.11, 242n.12;
    "Zouk-la sé sèl médiakamn nou ni," 48
Déclic Guadeloupe, 169. See also Borès,
    Patrick
Déclic Martinique, 66, 109. See also An-
    drieu, Eric
Déclic Productions (Paris), 169. See also Bas-
    set, Eric
"Défans ka vini fòl," 110
"De Gaulle." See Nilècame, Venus Eugène
De Gaulle, Charles (General), 112
Dégras, Sylvain, 158. See also Tec Pro Scène
Dehay, Terry, 176, 252n.2
De l'onomatopée créole à la percussion
    (Guédon), 217
de Montaguère, Annick Collineau, 152
de Négri, Christian, 16, 164, 168
Dépestre, René, 14
de Rivel, Moune. See Jean-Louis, Cécile
Dersion, Marguerite (pseud. Joby Valente),
    183–84, 252n.14
Desvarieux, Jacob, 37–38, 59, 63, 64, 132;
    clashes with Jocelyne Béroard, 101;
    among founders of Kassav', 40; Grand
    Méchant Zouk, 67; on popularity of
    zouk, 42; raspy delivery, 163
Dézormo, Djo. See Gros-Désormeaux,
    Joseph
Dibango, Manu, 163, 171, 220
"Difé, soupapé," 38, 60–63
Dimanche gras, 137
Dissonance, 41
"Doméyis," 65
DOMS (Overseas Departments), 1, 4
Donatien, Fernand, 113, 192
Donatien, Franck: leader of Taxikréol, 192;
    as composer, 192–97

Dorsinville, Max, 22
doudou, defined, 74, 244n.8
doudouisme, 75, 102
"Doudou Menard," 119
"Dous," 92–93
Dovin, Ernest ("Vava"): bèlè bass drummer,
    222; close friend of Mona, 114, 120–21,
    248n.15; song in his memory, 222–28
Dracius, Alain, 178
Du Bois, W. E. B., 200
Dumas, Alexandre, 141

Earth, Wind, and Fire, 43
"Ebony Roots," 194–97, 205, 253n.26
Ecoute les Antilles (Guédon), 217
"En lè mon la," 12, 16
"En rivé," 213
E+, 217. See also Saint Prix, Dédé
Espace créole (journal), 40, 241n.2
Ethnikolor, 84
European Union (E.U.), 42, 109, 140
Eurovision, 83, 133, 245n.23
"Exil," 19, 22, 25–27, 31, 234, 240n.14
Expérience 7: and Déclic Guadeloupe, 169;
    and Freddie Marshall, 153; and Tanya
    St. Val, 91; and Zouk Machine, 153–58

"Face a Face," 122–23, 248n.19
Fal Frett, 190–92; CMAC debut of, 191;
    jazz fusion of, 173, 191; and 3A Produc-
    tions, 191, 236, 253n.22
"Fanm chatenn," 102–3, 247n.51
"Fanm mou," 89–90, 245n.31
Fanon, Frantz, 19
FESPACO (Pan-African Film Festival), 154
Festival de la chanson féminine, 100, 236,
    246n.44
Fête de la musique, 65
Fête des cuisinières, 153, 219, 250n.4
Fiet, Lowell, 158, 251n.10
"Filé zètwal," 44
"Flè de nuit," 237
Flériag, Céline, 184–90, 236, 252nn. 16,
    18
Fleury, Félix, 106, 107, 125–26, 248n.16
Flyy, 7
"Fonds Larion," 146

Fontaine, Wilfred, 65

Forestal, Daniel, 219

Fort-de-France: Atrium, 236; Cathedral, and funeral of Pauolo Rosine, 24–25; Ciné Théâtre, 17; *France-Antilles* (newspaper), 174; Impératrice bar, 178; Lycée Schoelcher, 14, 16; Aimé Césaire as mayor of, 112–13; Morne Pichevin, 174; Terres-Sainville, 16. *See also* CMAC; Grand Carbet; SERMAC

Fostin, Jane, 151, 155–57

France: Bumidom, 3; *négropolitains,* 4, 148; radio stations, 6–7; recording studios, 168; rising unemployment rate, 239n.3; Studio Zorrino, 38

France-Antilles (Fort-de-France newspaper), 174

François, Luther, 191

Frantz, Colette, 13, 16, 191

Frith, Simon, 148

Fructueux, Alexandre (pseud. Alexandre Stellio), 74, 132–33, 244n.2

Gabriel, Léona (pseud. Mlle Estrella), 71–78, 244n.3; "A si paré" compared to songs by Canonge and Valente, 183–84; belief in romance, 104–5; biguine songs, 75–78, 235; and Creole, 72; and Radio Martinique, 74; role model for Jocelyne Béroard, 100; Jean-Paul Soime's aunt, 170; and Alexandre Stellio, 74; use of the term *matador,* 103

"Gadé mas passé," 146, 182

Galva, Léa: belief in love, 104; brief marriage, 80–82, 245n.18; and dance, 70, 80; and *doudouisme,* 102; on Joëlle Ursull's show, 80; and Kwak, 70, 78, 102; solo album, 246n.49; and television, 7, 102

Gaoulé (album), 131

Gaoulé (band), 131

General Isho, 127

Gengoul, Dominique, 84

"Gens moins," 35, 241n.24

Geoffroy, Sergius, 222. *See also* Kan'nida

George, Nelson, 175

George Debs Productions, 17, 48, 66

GEREC. *See* Groupe d'Etudes et de Recherches de la Créolophonie

Gertrude, Jean-Claude, 146–47, 200–201

Gertrude, Jean-Marie ("Pipo"), 146–47, 152

Gillespie, Dizzy, 217

Glissant, Edouard: and concept of *antillanité,* 14; and antiphrasis, 72; on artist as a spokesperson, 44

Gramacks, 175, 203. *See also* Joseph, Jeff

grand bal, 17

grand bèlè, 212

Grand Carbet (concert hall), 70, 106, 127, 132, 147, 149

Grand Méchant Zouk, 67, 181

Granel, Lucie, 69

"Gran tomobil," 173

Grivalliers, Ti Raoul, 218

Gromat, George, 192

Gros-Désormeaux, Joseph (pseud. Djo Dézormo): Carnival songs, 138–44; and date of 1848 emancipation, 143; meager royalty check, 141; and MIM, 138, 140; and RLDM, 143; and the violent phase of Martinican history, 142; wins Prix SACEM, 249n.44

Groupe d'Etudes et de Recherches de la Créolophonie (GEREC), ix, 40

Guadeloupe: bombings, 142, 249n.47; Centre culturel des arts, 150, 236; economy of, 239n.4; and E.U., 109; as overseas department of France, 1, 39; and mainland France, 144; 1928 cyclone, 214; outward migrations to France, 3, 15; population of, 4; and World War II, 112

Guanel, Jean-Luc, 80

Guédon, Henri, 215–17, 237; on ambivalence toward drumming, 211, 254n.5; awarded Grand Prix Internationale du Disque, 216; coins the term *zouk,* 216; founder of the Institut de Percussions, 216, 255n.15; and La Contesta, 215; and Nicol Bernard, 191; publications of, 217; and the sport of judo, 216, 254n.14; workshops on the drum, 207

Guerra, Juan Luis, 203, 254n.35

Guide pratique Rhythm's Section (Guédon), 217

Guilbault, Jocelyne, 52, 67, 241n.21
gwo ka (gros ka and ka), 1–2; dances, 214;
   rhythms, 214; shift to urban venues, 9;
   songs, 152, 213, 222, 229
gwo ka modèn, 219, 255n.20
Gwo ka Modèn (band), 219. See also
   Lockel, Gérard

Hancock, Herbie, 192
Haute Autorité de la Communication Audio-
   visuelle (HA), 5–6, 239n.5
Hélène, Edouard Ignol (pseud. Kafé), 207,
   229–30, 237, 255n.33
Henri Debs Productions, 154, 168–69,
   244n.46; studio, 91
"Héros," 204
Hewitt, Leah, 136
"Hey, Rasta," 134
Hibiscus Records, 206
Hilaire Hartoc (band), 131
Hill, Axell, 102
Hindoubill, 171, 251n.21
"Histoire d'amour," 70
Hodge, Merle, 39, 73
Homecoming (Thiong'o), 202
Honoré, Yves, 83, 153, 155, 157. See also
   Expérience 7; Zouk Machine
hooks, bell, 1, 14–15, 88
Houllier, Guy, 83, 153, 155, 157. See also
   Expérience 7; Zouk Machine
Hountondji, Paulin, 135
Hurley, Anthony, 152

"Iche Manman," 84
"If I Say Yes," 174
"Ile à vendre," 108, 136, 144, 249n.42
"Imajiné," 174
"I Miss You," 70

Jabert, Constance, 16
Jackson, Michael, 152, 203
Jacques, Franck, 215, 254n.13
Jacquet, Guy, 43
Jardel, Jean-Pierre, 39, 241n.1
JE Productions, 168, 244n.46

Jean-Louis, Cécile (pseud. Moune de Rivel),
   101, 115
Jean-Marie, Alain, 181, 215
Jean-Marie, José, 131
Jeanne, Max, 41
"Jennès bô kanal," 75, 244n.5
"Je suis en paix avec le monde," 101
"Jijman hatif," 59–60, 243n.36
J. M. Harmony, 80
John-Lewis, Méliano (pseud. Lewis Méli-
   ano): artistic philosophy, 151, 250n.3;
   battle against prejudice, 150–51; false ru-
   mors about, 150, 250n.2; mentioned,
   100
Joseph, Jeff, 174–75, 203. See also Gramaks
Joseph, Philippe, 60, 80, 197
"Joue pas avec le Crack," 173
"Joujou," 82–83, 86, 245n.20
"Jou ouvè," 24–25, 240n.10 (chap. 1)
Juletane (Warner-Vieyra), 73
Jurad, Simon, 88

Kafé. See Hélène, Edouard Ignol
kagenbel, 212
kaladja, 212, 215
kalenda, 212
Kali. See Monnerville, Jean-Marc
kanigwé, 212
Kan'nida, 207, 222, 255n.28
kassav, described, 43, 241n.5
Kassav', 158–63, 243n.38; concert at Anse
   Bertrand stadium, 63, 243n.39; CBS-
   Sony contract, 65; and disc jockeys, 66;
   first gold record, 64, 243n.40; first
   North American tour, 243n.43; as lack-
   ing a distinct political ideology, 64,
   243n.42; live performances of, 67,
   158–60; projected image of, 152; records
   pirated, 63; sold-out concerts, 65; solo albums, 169; songs of hope, 58, 243n.32;
   sponsored by Air France, 251n.20; struggles with local and multinational record
   companies, 43; superstar status of,
   63–64; and the Zairean public, 171
katel, 212
Kenyatta, Jomo, 109

"Ké sa lévé," 98–99, 246n.41
"Ki jan ké fè," 52, 159–62, 237, 242n.23
"Ki moune," 237
King, Martin Luther, Jr., 118
Kingue, Jean-Pierre, 174–75
"Ki non a manmanw," 41
"Kolédés," 12, 29–31, 187, 234, 241n.18
Konda Lota Festival, 134, 249n.36
Konkèt, Guy. See Conquête, Guy
"Kontinué," 80–82, 88, 245n.14
Kool and the Gang, 43
"Korosol," 49
Kuti, Fela Ransome, 132
kwak, definition of, 253n.28
Kwak: and African American rhythms, 173;
   Creole roots and identity of, 41; first al-
   bum, 197–99; Léa Galva's departure, 70

Labinsky, Charly, 132, 208, 254n.1
"La Case à Lucie," 17–19, 240n.4
"La Consommation," 113
La Contesta, 215
ladja (also l'agia, laghia or ladia: dance),
   119, 126, 212, 222, 247n.13
"Lakay Adan," 119
"Lakensyèl souvenir," 181
"La Marseillaise en trois continents," 216
lambi (instrument), 217
Lamming, George, 36
Lang, Jack, 5
Langdon-Winner, 148
Langlais, Philippe, 216
"Lanmou kréyòl," 90, 245n.34
La Perfecta, 2, 170, 173
"La Rochelle," 181
La Rue cases-nègres (Zobel), 34
La Sélecta, 217
Laval, Hervé, 192, 209
La Viny, Gérard, 110–11
"La Vi sé an bato," 200–202, 254n.34
Laye, Camara, 208, 254n.3
Le Ghetto (restaurant), 106
Le Grand livre des musiciens créoles (Cally),
   221
Le Nègre et l'Amiral (Confiant), 112
le patrimoine (term), 211

Le Rêve Antillais, 67
Lébèloka, 230, 255n.34
léchèl poul, definition of, 74–75, 244n.4
"Léchèl poul" (song), 75–76, 244n.6
Lefel, Edith: as backup singer, 19, 84, 171;
   commitment to women's causes, 83–86,
   104; RCI Trophée for "SOS mémé," 84;
   and Ronald Rubinel, 84; as soloist, 73;
   and taboo subjects, 78
Léger, Willy, 230, 256n.35
Leiris, Michel, 22
Léonora: l'histoire enfouie de la Guadeloupe
   (Bébel-Gisler), 111
"Lésé palé," 181
"Les Faux mulâtres," 113, 247n.7
Les Gentlemen, 25. See also Thamar, Ralph
Les Gouverneurs de la rosée (Roumain),
   205
"Lèspwa," 107, 128–30, 248n.29
léwoz, 212, 215
Leymarie, Isabelle, 207
"Linfidèl ou lanmou Lily," 77–78, 245n.10
Lipsitz, George, 72–73
Lise, Claude, 123–24
Liso Musique, 168
L'Isolé soleil (Maximin), 13
"Lizo," 123–24, 248n.20
Lockel, Gérard, 219. See also gwo ka modèn
Lollia, Marcel (pseud. Vélo), 214–15; and
   the death of, 215; and Kassav', 214;
   mixed rhythms, 215; as "roots" hero of
   Guadeloupe, 215
Lomax, Alan, 171
Longlade, Lucky, 125
Lossen, Serge, 16, 191
Louis, Roland, 92
Louise, Maurice Marie, 181
Louison, Albéric, 173
Louiss, Eddy, 181, 220
"Love and Ka Dance," 214, 254n.12
Lowenski, Anthony, 198
"Lucifé, Belzébithe, Macmahon," 153
Lugiery, Eric (pseud. Pôglo), 126–37, 144;
   and birds, 131, 248n.31; at the Grand
   Carbet, 127; home of, 107; lyrics of,
   128–31; and Pawòl 7, 127; pseudonym,

Lugiery, Eric (*continued*)
128; and Rastafarianism, 126–27; the
two spellings of "Pa moli," 248n.26
Lundi gras, 137

Madame Adeline's folklore troupe, 215
Mlle Estrella. *See* Gabriel, Léona
Magloire, Napoléon, 213
"Maître Chacha," 124, 248n.21
Majumbé, 185
malavoi, definition of, 7–8, 13, 32–33
Malavoi (orchestra), 163–67, 251n.14; audiences, 164; compact discs, 206; cultural affirmation of, 36; generosity, 240n.1; individuality, 164; and the *Matébis* show, 179; as the Merry Lads, 16, 19; projected image of, 152; and songs about exile, 234, 241n.22; sponsored by Air France, 251n.20; three stages of growth of, 16–17; the venues, 164; and the violins, 163–67, 169, 171
"Malavoi" (song), 33–34
"Maldòn," 155–57, 251n.9
"Malgré tout," 192
MaMag. *See* Mouvement artistes et musiciens antillo-guyanais
Manikou (club), 146
Maniri, Suzy, 80
"Manzé Ida," 209–11, 254n.4
Marcé. *See* Pago, Bernard
Mardi gras, 137–38, 148
Marfata, 131
"Marie," 84–86, 245n.25
Marie-Claire, Maurice, 181
Marigny, Hélène, 170
Marley, Bob, 121, 126, 135–36, 236
marqueur, 212
Marsalis, Wynton, 204–5
Marshall, Freddie: on the blending of languages, 205; as a concert organizer, 44, 147; and Expérience 7, 153; on the Plastic Boys, 207; producer of Kassav', 39, 43
Marthély, Jean-Philippe ("Pipo"): collective voice of, 98; interpretation of "Fanm chatenn," 102–3; inventive Creole lyrics of, 41; "Pa bisouin palé," 98; playback at

Queen's, 147; racial tolerance of, 59–60; the rich tenor voice of, 163; the romantic lyrics of, 51–52, 162, 242n.21; vocal style, 162–63
Marthély, Sonia, 38
Martin, Lola, 101, 246n.47
Martinique: economy of, 143–44, 239n.4; eruption of Mount Pélée, 110; impact of World War II on, 112; migrations to France, 15; as overseas department of France, 1, 39; population of, 4; and Rastafarianism, 108, 120, 126–27; sugarcane factories, 144
matador (or *matadò*), definition of, 44, 75, 103, 242n.7, 244n.7
Matébis (compact disc), 179, 252n.7
Mauriello, Jean-Michel, 122, 141–42, 168
Mauriello, Marilène, 122
mavombé, 212
Mavounzy, Lise (Madame Mavounzy), 153, 170
Mavounzy, Marcel, 213
Mavounzy, Robert, 170, 219
Maximin, Daniel, 14
"Mayo," 181–82, 252n.11
"Mazouk-Rag," 187–90, 252n.19
mazurka, 2, 17, 176, 221
McClary, Susan, 151
"M.C. 2 M.C.," 182
Média tropical, 6, 240n.8 (introduction). *See* Obringer, Gilles
Meiway, 171
Méliano, Lewis. *See* John-Lewis, Méliano
mendé, 39, 212, 229
Ménil, René, 164
"Mennen mwen," 82, 245n.16
Mercredi des Cendres, 138
Merry Lads, 16, 191. *See also* Malavoi
Métal Sound, 173
Michalon, Edmond, 191
Michalon, Pierre-Louis, 120, 126
Miles, Della, 53
MIM. *See* Mouvement Indépendantiste Martiniquais
Mitterrand, François, 113
"Mizik Mat'nik," 34–35, 241n.23
Mofwaz (journal), 40

Mona, Eugène. *See* Nilècame, Venus Eugène

Mondésir, Edmond, 115

Monk, Thelonius, 177

Monnerville, Ivon, 131

Monnerville, Jean-Marc (pseud. Kali): 126–37, 249n.39; awards, 133, 249n.35; and the banjo, 132; called "the banjo man," 135; and *bétonisation,* 136–37; and CBS, 132; on the drum, 230, 249n.40; and Eurovision, 133; and Gaoulé, 131; manager, 108; on migration, 134–35; plays *chouval bwa,* 132; pseudonym, 113; and 6th Continent, 131–32; schooling, 131, 248n.32

Monnerville, Paul Ives ("Pim"), 131, 170

Montanez, David, 131

"Montangn é vèr," 110

Montpierre, Rigobert, 168

Montredon, Jean-Claude, 178

Monville, Bib, 181, 191

Moore Madlangbayan, Shawna, 12, 35, 241n.20

Moradisc, 168, 244n.46

Morrison, Toni, 87

Mouvement artistes et musiciens antilloguyanais (MaMag), 170

Mouvement Indépendantiste Martiniquais (MIM), 138, 142–43, 211, 250n.50

"Mové jou," 44, 69, 78–79, 86, 88, 245n.12

"Moyeloup 2809F90," 108, 141–42, 249n.46

Municipal Office of Cultural Action of the City of Fort-de-France (OMDAC), 177

Municipal Service of Cultural Action (SERMAC), 80, 177, 211

Musiques et danses Afro-Caraïbes (Cally), 221

"Mwen alé," 50, 242n.15

"Mwen malad'aw," 37, 44

"Mwen menm bout," 28–29, 241n.17

"Mwen viré," 50, 242n.16

Naimro, Jean-Claude: and Roland Brival, 59; duet with Béroad, 92; first solo album, 38; and Gaoulé, 131–32; on *korosol,* 48–49; mistrust in "Ou chanjé," 54–57, 243n.28; the music of, 204; personal

contacts with African musicians, 170; relationship with audience, 158–59; and traditional music, 65; and zouk love songs, 162

Nayaradou, Jacob ("Jacky"), 43, 116, 191. *See also* 3A Productions

Nayaradou, Jolème, 113

Ndebele, Njabulo, 34

nèg maroon, definition of, 219, 255n.22

"Nèg ni mové mannyè," 110–11, 247n.3

"Nègresse," 150–51

négritude, definition of, 13, 144, 208

négropolitains (or *zoreils noirs*), 4, 148

Néret, Nicole (pseud. Princess Lover), 248n.18

Nilècame, Venus Eugène (pseud. Eugène Mona), 113–26; bare feet of, 113–14; death of, 106, 122, 126; and the *flajolé,* 115; labeled "crazy," 115; as a *marqueur de parole,* 236; outcries against, 124–25; and Père Elie, 121, 125; as a *porteparole,* 119; pride in being a Black man, 116–18; pseudonym, 114; and Studio Hibiscus, 122; and 3A Productions, 116; and the *traversée de desert,* 121–22

Nketia, J. H. Kwabena, 190, 233–34, 238

"Non musieu," 182–84

Nora, Pierre, 175

"Nostalji," 199, 253n.33. *See also* Césaire, Emmanuel; Césaire, Ina; Thamar, Ralph; "La Vi sé an bato"

Nouraman, Pierre, 207

Noverazz, Vasco, 131, 133

Obringer, Gilles, 6, 240n.8 (introduction). *See also* Média tropical

Obydol, Christiane, 151, 153, 155–57

Office de Radiodiffusion-Télèvision Française (ORTF), 5, 177

"Ojala que llueva café," 203

"O Madona," 174, 203

OMDAC. *See* Municipal Office of Cultural Action of the City of Fort-de-France

"Opérasyon ka," 229, 255n.31

ORTF (Office de Radiodiffusion-Télèvision Française), 5, 177

"Oublye ma vi," 80

"Ou chanjé," 38, 54–57, 243n.28
"Ou pa ka sav," 41
Overseas Departments (DOMS), 1, 4

"Pa bisouin palé" (expression), 105
"Pa bisouin palé" (song), 66, 69, 93–98,
    246n.37
pacotille, definition of, 74–75, 105, 244n.4
Pacquit, Marie-Claude, 106
Pacquit, Michel, 215
"Pa douté," 53, 242n.25
Pago, Bernard (pseud. Marcé), 206, 219,
    255n.19
"Pa grandi," 197–99, 253n.29
Pakatak, 132, 217, 255n.16
palaviré, definition of, 199, 253n.31
Palaviré: and the Césaire cousins, 199–202;
    as the meeting of two generations, 199,
    253n.32; palatable music, 199
Palcy, Euzhan, 49–50. See also *Siméon*
"Pa mélé," 198–99, 253n.30
"Pa moli," 128, 248n.28
Pan-African Film Festival (FESPACO), 154
Panol, Dominique, 203, 254n.38
Parti Progressite Martiniquais (PPM), 112–
    13, 144, 177, 211
"Partitions," 7, 174
"Pas bon moin coup," 213, 254n.10
Patiron, Joseph, 131
"Pa touché lou-a," 124–25
Paty, Jean-Marc, 163–64
Pawòl, 127–28
Peau noire, masques blancs (Fanon), 19
"Pèd filaou," 38, 59
Pélée, Mount, 110, 251n.13
Pendergrass, Teddy, 97
Pepe Kalle and Empire Bakuba, 171
Percussions (Guédon), 217
Père Elie, 121–22, 125, 180
Perry, Lee ("Scratch"), 92
Phonogram, 92, 168
Picord, Maritz, 153
Pineau, Gisèle, 28
Pinel, Romul, 215
Pioche, Manuela, 101
Plastic Boys, 207
Plastic Système, 148, 207

Pleen, Daddy, 173
Pluie et vent sur Télumée Miracle (Schwarz-
    Bart), 34
Pôglo. *See* Lugiery, Eric
Pognon, Jean-Paul, 173, 181
Pointe-à-Pitre: Centre Culturel des Arts, 39,
    150, 236; Déclic Productions, 169; FES-
    TAG, 236; Henri Debs Studio, 91; Liso
    Musique, 168; Place de la Victoire, 215;
    Radyo Tanbou, 6
political parties (Guadeloupe): Mouvement
    Populaire pour la Guadeloupe Indé-
    pendante, 211; Union Générale des Tra-
    vailleurs de la Guadeloupe, 211; Union
    des Paysans Pauvres de la Guadeloupe,
    211; Union Populaire pour la Libération
    de la Guadeloupe, 211
political parties (Martinique): Mouvement
    Indépendante Martiniquais (MIM), 138,
    142–43, 211, 250n.50; Parti Progressiste
    Martiniquais (PPM), 112–13, 144, 177,
    211
Pollard, Velma, 85, 245n.26
Porry, Philippe, 164
"Poutchi sa," 230
PPM. *See* Parti Progressite Martiniquais
"Pran patché-w," 134, 249n.37
Presley, Elvis, 197
Prian, Marius, 173
Price, Richard, 234
Prince Fumance, 127
Princess Lover. *See* Néret, Nicole
Printemps de Bourges, 216, 235
Privat, José, 12, 252n.9
Prix SACEM (Martinique), 67, 102, 133.
    See also Boutant, Christian
Pulvar, Marc, 16
punchs en musique, 2

"Raché tchè," 65
Radiance of the King (Laye), 208
radio stations (France): Média Tropicale, 6;
    RFI, 6–7; RFO, 6, 240n.10 (introduc-
    tion); Radio Nova, 6
radio stations (Guadeloupe): RFO Guade-
    loupe, 53, 150; Radio NJR, 6; Radyo
    Tanbou, 6

radio stations (Martinique): Radio Balisier, 6; Radio Banlieu Relax, 127; Radio Campus 96.7 FM, 6; RLDM (Radio Lévé Doubout Martinique), 143; Radio Martinique, 74; Radio Sun FM, 6; RFO Martinique, 36

raggamuffin, definition of, 35

"Raissa," 173

Ransay, Liliane, 131

Ransay, Max, 131

Rapaces, 219

Ras Dou, 127

Rastafarians, 108, 120, 126–37

Ravaud, Alain, 192

RCI (Radio Caraïbes Internationale), 6

Redding, Otis, 118

"Reggae Dom-Tom," 132

Rémion, Marcel, 16

Renciot, Eddy, 6. *See also* radio stations (Martinique), Radio Campus 96.7 FM

René Corail, Danièle, 192, 194

retronouveau, 175. *See also* George, Nelson

"Rèv mwen," 185–87, 252n.17

Rodrigue, Marcel, 201

Romain, L., 204

Rosaldo, Renato, 31

Rosemain, Jacqueline, 207

Rosier, Pier of Gazoline, 132

Rosine, Paul ("Paulo"): on cultural identity, 32; death of, 36; funeral of, 24–25; illness of, 181; member of the Jeunesse Étudiante Catholique, 191; musical career of, 164–65; as pianist and arranger for Malavoi, 16–17; Prix SACEM, 240n.11; and the relaunching of Malavoi, 17; replacements, 12, 181

Rotin, Jean-Michel, 152, 203–4

"Roulé la bodé," 153

Roumain, Jacques, 205

Roussier, Dominique, 70

Rubinel, Ronald, 84, 206

"Rupture," 84

Ryco Jazz, 219

SACEM. *See* Syndicat des Auteurs, Compositeurs, et Editeurs de Musique

Saint Éloi, Patrick: as *chanteur de charme,*

50; on the cover of *Zoukamine,* 237; and Creole linguistic boundaries, 162; earlier albums, 169; "Ki jan ké fè," 159–62, 251n.12; and male power, 52; on choice of metaphors, 53; and the Middle Passage, 37–38, 45–47; and Della Miles, 53; on music as a therapy, 59; vocal style and timbre, 159; "Zoukamine," 58–59

Saint-Hilaire, Archange, 74

St. Jean Carnival (rhythm), 207

Saint-Pierre (town), 110, 131, 209

Saint Prix, André ("Dédé"), 16, 152; and Avan Lévé, 217; and *chouval bwa,* 237; and the Djiba Association, 218; as a guest drummer for various bands, 217; percussion workshops, 218

St. Val, Tanya: as backup singer, 91; collaboration with Willy E. Salzédo, 70; concert at the Grand Carbet, 147; on "Fanm mou," 90; interest in the blues and jazz, 91–91; singing style of, 90; studio of, 91; and taboo subjects, 78; the Tino St. Val band, 91

Sakiyo, 181. *See also* Canonge, Mario

Sala, Gilles, 240n.9 (introduction)

Salvador, Henri, 101

Salzédo, Willy E., 70

Samedi gras, 137

"San mandé," 86–88, 245n.28

santiman ka, 230

"Sasévwé," 130–31, 248n.30

Sato drums, 228–29, 255n.30

Scaramuzzo, Gene, 44, 65–66

Schoelcher, Victor, 110, 143, 247n.4

Schwarz-Bart, Simone, 34, 147

"Sé dam bonjou," 7

Seka, Monique, 171

"Sé le 22 mé," 143, 250n.52

Senghor, Léopold Sédar, 13

"Sé pa djen djen," 51–52, 242n.20

Séraline, Marc, 192

Séraline, Yves-Marie, 36

SERMAC. *See* Municipal Service of Cultural Action

Shades of Black, 65

Shè Shé (compact disc), 31–32

Shorter, Wayne, 236

Shukman, Henry, 163
"Si cé oui," 53
"Si jodi ou ni an ti shagren," 178
"Silans," 53–54, 243n.27
Silko, Leslie, 175
Siméon (film), 49–50
Singa, Suzie, 230
"Si ou sa revé," 184
"Siwo" (song), 66, 69, 99–100, 246n.42
siwo (term), 99, 192
6th Continent, 127, 131–32
Slim, Memphis, 197, 253n.27
Snyder, Emile, 23
Soime, Jean-Paul: on compact discs, 250n.1;
    familial relationships, 187; food imagery
    in "Kolédés," 28–29; home of, 11–12;
    and Malavoi, 16; on Malavoi's music,
    163; and the Merry Lads, 16; nephew of
    Léona Gabriel, 170; representation of
    Guinea in "Mizik Mat'nik," 34; school-
    ing in music, 168
Soleil cou coupé (Césaire), 22
"Solèy," 57–58, 243n.31
Solibo magnifique (Chamoiseau), 119
"Somnifère (Paroles des femmes)," 83–84,
    86, 245n.24
"Sové Jesus Christ," 121
"Special Request," 192–94, 253n.24
"Sport national," 19–21, 240n.6 (chap. 1)
Stellio, Alexandre. *See* Fructueux, Alexandre
Studio Davout, 19
Studio Hibiscus, 88, 122, 141, 168,
    244n.46, 254n.9
Studio Zorrino, 38
Sturm, Jean-Pierre, 150
Surena, Elena, 69
"Syé bwa," 37, 171, 252n.22
Syndicat des Auteurs, Compositeurs, et
    Editeurs de Musique (SACEM), 170,
    251n.18

Tabou Combo, 65
tambou bèlè, 222
tambou dibas, 222
tambou di base, 222
"Tambou séryé," 119, 222–29, 236, 254n.2,
    255n.29

"Tambour battant," 218
tanbou, 209, 212
"Tan pis pour moi," 114, 247n.9
Taxikréol (band): first compact disc,
    253n.23; origin of name, 194; the politi-
    cal realities of certain songs, 192–94;
    Trindadian ole talk, 194; two formations
    of the band, 192; use of Creole lan-
    guages, 205
Tec Pro Scène, 158
Télèphe, Max, 192–93
"Téléphonez la femme au galop," 153
Tenaille, Franck, 233
Thamar, Ralph: Akoustik Zouk, 181; career
    of, 25; and "La Case à Lucie," 19; and
    the Césaire cousins, 25–27; on the Cre-
    ole language, 149; first solo album, 200;
    writes lyrics for "Mayo," 181, 252n.10;
    on the musicians of Morne Pichevin,
    174; public image of, 152; and a solo ca-
    reer, 412n.13; and a soloist for Malavoi,
    25; and the traditional tunes of, 176
Thélamon, Kathryn, 203
thés dansants, 2
Thimon, Michel, 146, 192
Things Fall Apart (Achebe), 205
Thiong'o, Ngugi wa, 202
Third World, 126, 128
3A Productions. *See* Nayaradou, Jacky
Three Musketeers, The (Dumas), 141
ti baum, 24, 240n.12
"Ti bouchon," 119
ti bwa, 212, 222
Ti Ken, 170
ting bang, 212
Tino St. Val's band, 91
"Titin bèl" (song), 165–67
"Titin bèl" (video), 167, 251n.15
Touchatou, 7, 246n.48
"Touche pas à ta fille," 173
Touloulou (album), 51, 169
toumba, 212, 222
toumblak, 215
Toumpak, 219. *See also* Pago, Bernard
Traoré, Michel, 36, 179
traversée de désert, 121–22
Trébeau, Suzy, 11; admiration for Béroard,

70, 100; as a backup singer for various bands, 88; the first Taxikréol, 88, 192; a member of Kwak, 80; siblings, 245n.27; the songs of, 86–88, 198
Tristar, 65
"Trop filo," 59
Turner, Victor, 233, 237
"Turn Off the Lights," 97
Tympan Productions, 154

Ultramarine, 181. See also Canonge, Mario
"Un concerto pour la fleur et l'oiseau," 178–80, 252n.8
"Un homme, une passion," 179. See also Traoré, Michel
Uri, Alexandre, 207
Uri, François, 207
Ursull, Joëlle: on the betrayal of friendship, 82–83; on the cover of Black French, 104; and Eurovision, 83; in the Miss France competition, 83; as a soloist, 83, 103–4, 153; three albums of, 83, 245n.22; Zouk Machine, 80, 83, 245n.21

Vadeleux, Guy, 88, 185
Valente, Joby. See Dersion, Marguerite
Vamur, Claude ("Colo"): the compact discs of, 39; drummer for Kassav', 219; former drummer for Manu Dibango and Eddy Louiss, 220; on the fusion of African diasporic music, 220, 255n.24; playing of the mendé, 220; schooling in music, 219
Varasse, Prince Aziz, 127
Vargas, Wilfrido, 203, 254n.37
Vautor, Robert, 191
Vega, Ana Lydia, 185
Vélo. See Lollia, Marcel
Versol, José, 88
Vété-Congolo-Hanétha, 106
vidés, definition of, 137

Vikings de Guadeloupe, Les, 43
VIP (Véritables Icones Publiques), 158
Virgal, Eric, 88, 236
"Viva Malavoi," 36. See also Séraline, Yves-Marie; Traoré, Michel
"Voici les loups," 139–44, 172, 249n.43
Volt Face, 174–76, 203, 254n.38
volt face, definition of, 203
Voyer, Gilles, 192
Voyer, Janick, 192

Wabaps, 25. See also Thamar, Ralph
Walcott, Derek, 31, 175–76
Warner-Vieyra, Myriam, 73
Weather Report, 192, 236
"West Indies," 50–51, 242n.17
Wilson, Elizabeth, 86
"Wonderful," 48–49, 242n.11, 242n.12
woulé (or roulé), 212

Zénith (club), 174
Zénith (concert hall), 5, 65, 154–55, 158, 179
Zimra, Clarisse, 77
Zion Train, 127
Zobel, Joseph, 34
Zone Franche Association, 5
"Zone intérdite," 86, 88, 245n.29
Zorobabel, Dominique, 151; 153, 155–57
zouk, definition of, 44
Zoukamine (compact disc), 237
"Zoukamine" (song), 58–59, 237, 243n.33
Zoukamine (TV show), 7
"Zouké Light," 203
"Zouk-la sé sèl médiakaman nou ni," 8, 48, 59, 64, 68, 243n.41
"Zouk Machine" (song), 154, 250n.6
Zouk Machine (trio): concert at the Zénith, 153; contract with BMG-Ariola, 155; and Expérience 7, 7, 153; first gold record of, 154; photograph of, 151; sexy zouk songs of, 155–58, 251n.7; Tympan Productions, 153; Joëlle Ursull, 83